"CONTROL FREAK"

(the spirit of divination)

Janet Carter, Esq.

Host of:

The Advocate Radio Program

ADVOCATE
PUBLISHING

ADVOCATE PUBLISHING

3000 W. Mac Arthur Blvd.
Suite #209
Santa Ana, CA 92704

Soft cover edition first published August 2011, edited and reprinted June 2012.
ISBN: 978-0-9855239-0-9

ABOUT JANET CARTER:

After obtaining a Master's Degree in Counseling Psychology, Janet became a "born again" Christian. She then attended Law School and went on to become Legal Counsel to many churches, non-profit ministries and Christian clientele.

After gaining years of litigation experience, Janet moved out of the courtroom and into the conference room. Based on 1 Corinthians 6:1-6, Janet began serving as a Christian Mediator and/or Settlement Negotiator. Janet's unique combination of gifts, skills and talents has facilitated the resolution of a wide variety of disputes in accordance with both the Word of God and the laws of the land.

Janet is also the host of THE ADVOCATE RADIO PROGRAM: a "live" call-in radio program providing both legal and personal problem-solving advice with a Biblical perspective. Janet's own life experiences, those shared with her clients, as well as the numerous radio inquiries she has addressed, have given her a rich background upon which to base her legal and Biblical advice.

"CONTROL FREAK"

(the spirit of divination)

"I know the plans I have for you,"
announces the Lord. "I want you
to enjoy success. I do not plan to
harm you. I will give you hope for
the years to come"
(Jer 29:11, NIRV).

ADVOCATE
PUBLISHING

TABLE OF CONTENTS

Table of Contents

"CONTROL FREAK"

Table of Contents

Table of Contents

"CONTROL FREAK"

Table of Contents

Table of Contents

"CONTROL FREAK"

Table of Contents

Table of Contents

"CONTROL FREAK"

Table of Contents

Table of Contents

"CONTROL FREAK"

Opening Argument:

Perhaps you picked up this book because of its title: "CONTROL FREAK". You may either think of yourself as a "Control Freak" or you may think of someone else in your life as a "Control Freak". Maybe still, a friend or family member recommended this book implying that you were either one, or the other-- or worst of all, both.

"CONTROL FREAK" has been written for the "Christian Community" which I define as: those born again believers who claim Jesus Christ as both their Lord and their Savior. More specifically, it has been written for "mature" believers who already have a solid working knowledge of the Word of God (Heb 5:14); who are living and walking by faith, not by sight; who have submitted their lives and their wills to the Lordship of Jesus Christ; and who, to the best of their ability, continue to live for Christ without compromise, no longer seeking to fulfill their own agendas.

Opening Argument

"CONTROL FREAK" is not another "pop" Christianity book that you can read through in a day; but rather, it is a "text" book for serious followers of Christ. At its core, is the realization that in order for you to fulfill God's plan for your life, it is mandatory that you learn how to eradicate the "spirit of divination" (synonymous with "the spirit of control"), which is currently alive and well, working its evil purposes in your own "mature" ... "Christian" life-- as we speak.

Now, this is *really* *not* a good thing, as you will soon find out. In fact, it evidences that there is a very serious flaw in your character. That's right-- a "chink in your armor" that must be shored up so that you can fulfill your God-given destiny during your lifetime.

You will learn exactly how the "spirit of divination" takes over and controls our "Christian" lives, homes, churches, ministries, workplace, and certainly society at large. Indeed, the spirit of control is currently at work in one form or another and to one degree or another, in every single solitary relationship we have. This fact is evidenced by your attempts to control people and/or circumstances; as well as the attempts by other people (with whom you have interpersonal relationships), to do the same.

Opening Argument

Unless you are cognizant of the teaching contained in this text and have taken the prescribed action to eliminate the spirit of control from your own life, its devious work will continue. Once you understand the origins of the spirit of divination, not only will you be intent upon eliminating the *control* that other "Control Freaks" have in and over your life; but you too will eliminate any of your own personal "Control Freak" tendencies, as a matter of course.

Once the light of interrogation goes on, revelation will emerge; the yoke will be broken, the strongman will be bound, gagged and removed. Your "quality of life" as a result of functioning solely under His direction, will ascend to new unimaginable heights and as a result, the primary goal of this text will be achieved:

Once freed from the control of others and living exclusively unto the Lord and not to man, at long last, members of our Christian Community can finally step into their rightful positions of purpose. Those individually tailored plans that the Lord foreordained for their lives can then be revealed, understood, and carried out-- without interference. Once we all get into position and fulfill our assignments, the world is destined to become a better place for everyone.

Opening Argument

After reading, understanding, and implementing the concepts in this text, you will be changed for the better-- *forever*.

I give thanks for this text to all the people who love me, <u>and</u> to all those that still hate me; to those who brought me up, <u>and</u> to those that let me down; to those who held me, <u>and</u> to those that dumped me; to those who gave to me, <u>and</u> to those that tried to extort from me; to those who stood by me in my time of trouble, <u>and</u> to those that cut and ran; to those men of God who taught and encouraged me, <u>and</u> to those men that *think* they're of God, but don't even know Him; to those who just checked in on me yesterday, <u>and</u> to those that haven't even thought of me for years; to those who acknowledged the gifts given to me, <u>and</u> to those that mocked and condemned me.

Whether it was you who played a role that enriched my life with blessings, or attempted to unmercifully torment me, because of my relationship with the King, *everything* has worked out in *my* favor!

Whenever you need Him, the Lord will *always* step up to the plate and hit a homerun in your life!

"CONTROL FREAK"

Opening Argument

Being About The Father's Business:

Keep about your work. Do not flinch because the lion roars, do not stop the devil's dogs, do not fool away your time chasing the devil's rabbits. Do your work. Let liars lie, let sectarians quarrel, let the devil do his worst, but see to it that nothing hinders you from fulfilling the work God has given you.

He has not commanded you to get rich. He has never bidden you to defend your character. He has not set you at work to contradict falsehood (about yourself) which Satan and his servants may start to peddle. If you do those things, you will do nothing else; you will be at work for yourself and not for the Lord.

Keep at your work. Let your aim be as steady as a star. You may be assaulted, slandered, wounded, and rejected, you may be abused; but see to it with steadfast determination, with unfaltering zeal, that you pursue the great purpose of your life and object of your

Opening Argument

being until at last you can say, "I have finished the work which You have given me to do." (John 17:4b)

[Author Unknown, shared by Gayle Grenier.]

"CONTROL FREAK"

CHAPTER 1: Going for the Jugular

I don't know if it was the gory movies from my past, but I had always thought that *"Going for the jugular"* meant that once the jugular vein (which runs down the neck) was slit, because the heart was located nearby and was still pumping, that the loss of blood spurting and spewing out all over the place was what caused the wounded person's instant demise.

However, when I researched it, I found out that when someone *"goes for the jugular"* and succeeds, the other person dies from causes *other than* loss of blood:

"In the sport of fencing, one of the most lethal moves is when the jugular vein is punctured. This is because the jugular vein returns blood from the brain, face, and neck to the heart. An opening in the jugular vein, when it communicates with the external environment, may allow

Going for the Jugular

small bubbles of air to be entrained into the vessel. As the air enters, a bloody froth can be produced, which, when drawn into the heart, may render the pumping action inoperative (valve lock). An air embolism due to a cut jugular vein may cause a victim, after one or two gasps, to collapse immediately."[1]

True enough then, "the jugular" is a blood vessel that when ruptured, can promptly eliminate life! The directive: *"Go for the jugular"* is an idiom used to refer to an all-out attack, or strike to the most vital part of the body.[2] The idea of *going for the jugular* has been taken from the killing action of the lion.[3] It has always referred to a swift, deliberate and calculated defeat of the enemy opponent, implemented without mercy.

For the purposes of our text, your Lion is from the Tribe of Judah (Rev 5:5) and the "jugular" is that chief underlying evil motive of the enemy which is so secretive, you may not even know of its existence. Our objective is to tear back the skin covering the enemy's jugular, expose its internal

---

[1] *The Dubious Quick Kill, Sword Wounds and the Circulatory System,* Maestro Frank Lurz (www.classicfencing.com)
[2] Colloquial; late 1800's, *Your Dictionary.com*
[3] Babylon.com

"CONTROL FREAK"

Going for the Jugular

workings and then mercilessly and permanently, eliminate it out of your life!

The "jugular" is the spirit of divination. It is the means by which the enemy uses others to control you and your life.

While we have all seen how the spirit of control works in some of the most obvious situations, such as a person who lives in bondage to sex, drugs, or alcohol and how that person's life is thus rendered useless for the Kingdom of God; the primary focus of this text however, will be unveiling and revealing how that same controlling spirit is at work in much more subtle ways in your own life, ways that you likely do not even realize.

This text will uncover, reveal and render powerless the *subtle means* by which the spirit of divination seeks to control your heart, mind and actions through the personal interactions you have with people in your life. Once you begin to see how "the game" is played and get used to how it "feels" when that controlling spirit is trying to govern your conduct, the blinders will be taken off and you will then be prepared to eliminate it from your life completely.

Going for the Jugular

This text will provide you the tools to do so. So get ready! As a *good* *soldier* at the end of this text (but <u>not</u> before finishing), you will be called upon to take action.

Realize that your adversary doesn't want you to be educated about the spirit of divination/control. He'd much rather have you live out the rest of your days, under its influence, all the while mistakenly *thinking* you are living out God's plan for your life.

Devil ... the jig is up!

But before I jump too far ahead of myself, please allow me the opportunity to lay some foundation. Foundation, foundation, foundation; a solid foundation is not only essential to any good legal argument, but it's also central to the "paradigm shift" training that you are about to undergo.

Indeed, it is the foremost key to your success.

"CONTROL FREAK"

CHAPTER 2: What is the spirit of divination?

━━━━━━━━━━━━━━━━━━━━━━━━━━━━━━━

We all know the story about King Saul and how his disobedience caused him to be dethroned. The prophet Samuel explained that, *"… rebellion is as the sin of **witchcraft** and stubbornness is as iniquity and idolatry. Because thou hast rejected the word of the LORD, He hath also rejected thee from being king"* (1 Sam 15:23, KJV).

The term "witchcraft" [4] is also translated "divination" in other passages of scripture such as: Numbers 22:7, 23:23; Deuteronomy 18:10; 2 Kings 17:17; Jeremiah 14:14; Ezekiel 13:6 and 13:23 (many of which will be addressed later in this text).

---

[4] Strong's Concordance #7081, transliterated "Qecem".

What is the spirit of divination?

At its core, "witchcraft" or "divination" is not only the force behind blatant disobedience to the Lord such as in the case of King Saul; but it also functions in much more subtle ways in an attempt to undermine the workings of the Holy Spirit in the life of a Christian.

The word "divination" is defined, in part, as: "man's attempts to know and **control the world and the future, apart from the true God.**" [5] The practices to which the label: "witchcraft" have historically been applied, are those which **influence another person's mind, body, or property against his or her will.**" [6]

"Witchcraft" is used to *control* people and the circumstances in their lives, against their own will. In much the same way, "divination" is used to *control* a person's conduct, circumstances and ultimate destiny, apart from God, or against God's will. Hence, the practice of "witchcraft" and the practice of "divination" both share the common thread of unwitting "control" exercised over the life of an individual.

---

[5] Vine's Expository Dictionary of Old and New Testament Words, Copyright © 2001, Thomas Nelson, Inc., Nashville, Tennessee. All rights reserved.
[6] Wikipedia: defining "Witchcraft"- Alleged Practices section.

"CONTROL FREAK"

What is the spirit of divination?

Therefore, throughout this text "the spirit of divination" and "the spirit of control" are used as synonymous terms. They describe that aspect of "control" which not only goes against a person's own will, but more importantly, goes against the will of God for that person's life.

When working effectually, "the spirit of divination" rules over a person's very existence: their heart, mind, thoughts, feelings, and actions; their property and possessions; indeed all of the circumstances in their life, including their ultimate destiny.

WOW! Selah.

How does this all "go down"?

Well, we know that once you become a "Christian", you all of a sudden have an *adversary* who is intent upon finding ways to chew you up and spit you out (1 Peter 5:8). Prior to that, you and he were getting along just fine ... *weren't you?*

I do not believe Satan is personally after many of us. Remember, he's not omnipresent, he's not omnipotent, he's not omniscient … in sum, he's not *all-o-that!* In fact, when the apostle Paul was dealing with the "thorn in his flesh" only a "messenger" of Satan was sent "to buffet" him (2 Cor 12:7, KJV). Satan didn't even bother to show himself.

This however, is unlike when Jesus was tempted in the wilderness (Luke 4 & Matt 4); that's when Satan was required to come in with his "A-Game" and yet, he still lost. So, instead of using the terms "Satan" or "the devil" throughout this text, the terms "enemy" or "opponent" will be used, while leaving Scripture references unedited.

In addition to Satan, we recall that there were also quite a few fallen angels, who got tossed out of heaven at the same time (Rev 12:4). We know that those minions are working, rank and file; out to do his dirty work here on earth, trying to trip up as many people, especially well meaning Christians, as often as they possibly can.

Since the Bible teaches us that we *do not war after the flesh* (2 Cor 10:3, KJV), and that we *wrestle not against flesh and blood* (Eph 6:12, KJV), we often naïvely think those passages are primarily referring to those fallen angels, and perhaps sometimes, to really *wicked* people; but certainly *never* to "Christians".

Enter in, "the spirit of divination"…

Now, let's re-think your previous position.

The spirit of control is primarily manifest (or at work) in our own interpersonal human relationships. The enemy intentionally brings trouble into interpersonal relationships because quite frankly, it's such fertile ground. It literally provides a continuous source of issues and circumstances conducive to causing a Christian to stumble, sin, and backslide and sometimes for years on end.

Think about it-- nearly every single day we all have virtually unending opportunities to be offended, hurt, angered, embittered, taken advantage of, ripped off, defrauded, lied to, cheated, mocked, gossiped about, abused and mistreated by someone ... *somehow* ... many of whom are usually calling themselves ... *"Christian"*.

Who in your life can make you the angriest? Who can make you feel the most emotionally distraught? Hurt?

What is the spirit of divination?

Rejected? Hateful? Bitter? This *control* over your very being usually comes through something a person did, is doing, or continues to do, which negatively affects and effects your life.

It doesn't necessarily have to be someone you love that sends you into a tizzy, either. It can be the coach of your son's team for refusing to put him in the game. It can be the grocery store clerk for carelessly squashing your bread. It can be your mother-in-law forever dictating how you should raise the children. It can be someone who cuts you off on the road and almost causes a fatal injury to you and your family.

The enemy finds great amusement when the spirit of divination is able to pit one well-meaning Christian against another in various situations. He then sits back and watches them roll stumbling blocks of offense at one another; back and forth, back and forth, back and forth, all the while knowing that *a house divided against itself cannot stand* (Matt 12:25, KJV).

This is what most Christians miss: The fact that the spirit of divination is at work in our own interpersonal relationships,

What is the spirit of divination?

seeking to undermine and oppose the work of the Holy Spirit. The spirit of divination is working to supersede the Holy Spirit's leading and guiding of your life and the lives of others. The spirit of divination uses you to try to control other people in your life and/or the spirit of divination is used by other people in your life, to try to control you; all to the exclusion of the leading and guiding of the Holy Spirit.

Due to the number of interpersonal relationships we all have, the opportunities for this defiant, controlling influence in our lives, is infinite. In fact, even when some toxic relationships are long over, other new relationships, with the same detrimental patterns of behavior, are just beginning. As long as you live on this earth, you will continue to encounter the spirit of divination in the context of your own interpersonal relationships, as it literally seeks to "run your life".

Why does it matter?

The answer should be obvious.

The more you allow another person (other than Jesus Christ Himself), to provide input, directives, demands, suggestions or their desires (which are all meant to influence or control your life and your decisions, your plans, your goals, your dreams, your efforts); the less likely you will be able to hear, let alone carry out the Lord's directives, assignments and plans for your life.

Now, that *was* the intention in the first place when you got saved, was it not?

The primary purpose of the spirit of control/divination is to use the people in your life as unsuspected and unsuspecting tools to supersede, thwart and undermine God's leading and guiding in your life; and instead, cause your life to be blindly led around by the spirit of control.

If you can be taken far enough off track you <u>will not</u> fulfill the assignments and plans that He has ordained for your life, because <u>you cannot</u>. If you remain captive, residing "in the box" you've been controlled into by others, the Spirit of God cannot possibly lead you to and through those special assignments He predestined for only your life to fulfill.

So directive number one, starting from this point forward— you must stop going to other people for advice about the

What is the spirit of divination?

Lord's will, assignments and plan for your life; and instead, start going to Him exclusively.

Since you claim a relationship with Him, then use it!

You may say, "Well it's biblical to go to others, because in a *'multitude of counselors there is safety'* right"? (Prv 11:14, 15:22, 24:6, KJV).

Well, let's re-think that application.

So you go around and ask as many people as you can find to listen what their counsel is, or what you should do about any given situation, right? But what if they all have *different* counsel on the *same* issue?

Then, what do you do?

That cannot possibly be the proper application of that Scripture! Running around here and there, seeking counsel from a multitude of different people and trying to apply it altogether (even when it differs); all the while looking and acting as if you've had no personal communication with *The Plan Maker* Himself?

What is the spirit of divination?

No. Rather, in a multitude of counselors (when they are all giving the *same or similar counsel* on a situation), *there is safety*. Certainly not when they are all in disagreement.

More importantly, what role, if any, does the Lord's still small voice play in all this running around you're doing?

"I bless the LORD who gives me counsel; in the night also my heart instructs me" (Ps 16:7, ESV).

Yet, "Christians" are making all these huge major life decisions about starting a church, starting a business, choosing a career, moving to another state, getting an education in a certain field, buying a home, marrying, divorcing, having a baby, starting a ministry, moving to Uganda ... by asking the people in their lives if *they think* it is the right thing to do or not.

I continue to marvel when I see "Christians" go from person to person, pastor to pastor, leader to leader, Christian to Christian, asking them these kinds of critical, life altering, destiny related questions; and all the while, making very little mention of what or how God spoke, directed, or showed them what to do about any of these things.

What is the spirit of divination?

Oh sure, they say they, *"Prayed about it"...* I mean gosh, they're *Christians* they have to say that! The real inquiry is what *did He say* in response to your prayer? Did He say, "Yes?" or "No?" or "Wait?" Or, have you heard no response yet from Him at all? The latter is still a good answer.

On the other hand, it's scandalous for me to imagine how many Christians <u>have</u> heard directly from the Throne of God and as a result, they *knew* what they were supposed to do with their life for the Kingdom's sake but then went and talked to somebody about it, who via the spirit of control, ended up *talking them out of it!*

Look, if you heard His voice, the inquiry and discussion would, or at least *should have been, <u>over</u>.* If God said it, you do it; who cares what everyone else's opinion is about it?

If you're really interested in having God lead and guide your life, you need to go to Him first about everything; looking and expecting to get your answer directly from Him, no matter how long it takes. Put other people aside and put a demand on the communication level of your relationship

What is the spirit of divination?

with God. He will come through with "His will" on every issue, in His timing.[7]

This presupposes, however, that you have a vital, ongoing, intimate relationship with Him, where you hear and know His voice; and that you're in His Word and learning His ways. If this does not describe you, then that's why you run to others for counsel. You have yet to cultivate a consistent, clear line of communication with Him for yourself.

If you are locked into the bad habit of calling your girlfriend, your neighbor, your "godly" friend, your pastor, your husband or wife, your mother, or even your mother-in-law, each and every time you need to make a decision, it's now time to make a drastic change in your behavior. None of those people, no matter how wonderful they are, have *"The Plan"* for *your* life.

Think about it this way: God's got "The Plan"... so why are you running around to everybody else asking what you should do about these things going on in your life? This makes absolutely no sense whatsoever!

---

[7] Reminder: I'm speaking to mature Christians.

What is the spirit of divination?

It reminds me of a lesson I was taught when I was very young, like eight years old, by my mother. When you're in a predicament where you're having trouble with a clerk in a store, or with a customer service representative who is incapable of providing a good resolution to your problem, or otherwise, "situationally challenged" shall we say? My mom always taught me to just take your request, situation, or problem straight to the top and "Ask for the Manager!"

So, why are *you* bothering with His subordinates?

"Whether you turn to the right or to the left, your ears will hear a voice behind you saying, "This is the way; walk in it" (Is 30:21).

When we have doubts or are facing difficulties, when others suggest courses of action that are conflicting, when caution dictates one approach but faith another, we should be still. We should quiet each intruding person, calm ourselves in the sacred stillness of God's presence, study His Word for guidance, and with true devotion focus our attention on Him ... having an

What is the spirit of divination?

eagerness to know only what God our Lord will determine for us.

Soon He will reveal by His secret counsel a distinct and unmistakable sense of His direction ... Are you uncertain about which direction you should go? Take your question to God ... where the lights and the darkness of this world cannot interfere and where the opinions of others cannot reach you. You must also have the courage to wait in silent expectation, even when everyone around you is insisting on an immediate decision or action. If you will do these things, the will of God will become clear to you ... All this will be your unsurpassed gift. It will be a heavenly experience, a precious eternal privilege, and the rich reward for the long hours of waiting.[8]

If you're brave enough to ask yourself, "*Why* must I always insist upon conferring with flesh and blood?" (ref. Gal 1:16, KJV), the honest answer (if you'll allow me to provide it), is

---

[8] *Streams in the Dessert*, June 20th excerpts, by L.B. Cowman, Copyright © 1966. Used by permission of Zondervan Publishing House. All rights reserved.

"CONTROL FREAK"

What is the spirit of divination?

relatively easy: (1) You're afraid of being criticized by the people in your life who will find out about your decision; and/or (2) you want to be supported by the people in your life for what you ultimately decide to do; and/or (3) you don't trust the reliability of your own line of communication with the Lord.

If you can't hear from God, or can't discern His voice, or don't know His Word well enough to tell what's of Him and what isn't, then do something about it. No matter what type of guidance, counsel, or answers you're looking for, the Lord Himself or the Word of God has already given you the answer, either directly; or He has given you precepts that will cause you to arrive at the right answer; or, He will reveal the answer in a special "Rhema Word" type of situation. He's also given you the Holy Spirit to lead, guide and confirm that answer to you.

No third party conference calls are ever necessary. Yet, at this point, it very well may be that you've been listening to so many other voices, that the Lord can't get a Word in edgewise.

What is the spirit of divination?

Still, there are other times when the real problem is that Christians just don't want to be "doers" of the Word (James 1:21, KJV). So they seek counsel from others to confirm their own desired course of disobedience, which is always in furtherance of their own agendas.

Yeah, sure, you can always get someone on board with *your plan,* especially with that irresistible "rose colored glasses" presentation of yours. But realize that just because you have the lawyering skills handy to get some "godly" person to agree with you, that doesn't mean the Lord agrees with either one of you.

Personally, I want to get to the destiny that the Lord has for me just as fast as I possibly can. I want to spend whatever years I have left fulfilling His assignments, purpose and plan for my life. I want that "abundant" life promised by the Lord in John 10:10 both, while I'm *on my way* to and through the fulfillment of His assignments and *once I reach* my destiny. Otherwise, what was the point of my existence here on earth in the first place?

If fulfilling my destiny in life is experienced as just one long, miserable journey, then that means I never gained entrance into the "Promised Land" or that "quality of life" that He had for me, where His *"yoke was easy and His burden was light"* (Matt 11:30, KJV).

Now, I don't know about you, but I do not want to waste any more of my life on some "flesh detour" that goes on for years because someone provided or confirmed to me, misguided "counsel". And, I certainly don't want any more "Christians" unsuspectingly working on behalf of the spirit of divination/control (which is straight from the pit of hell), to be used to influence my decisions; to delay, thwart, or undermine my progress; or to make my life any more difficult along the path to achieving that end.

There is a very grave risk that if you continue to allow your life to be influenced by the spirit of divination, you may never get to, let alone fulfill, the destiny God has planned for your life; and in the meantime, your "quality of life" will remain substandard.

If the *very thought* of that bothers you, keep reading.

What is the spirit of divination?

"CONTROL FREAK"

CHAPTER 3: The Devices and Wiles of the Enemy

"Lest Satan should get an advantage of us: for we are not ignorant of his <u>devices</u>" (2 Cor 2:11, KJV).

"Put on the whole armour of God, that ye may be able to stand against the <u>wiles</u> of the devil" (Eph 6:11, KJV).

When it comes to warfare with the enemy, the Bible states that we are up against two primary things: The enemy's "devices" and the enemy's "wiles".

In a nutshell, the term "devices" used in 2 Corinthians 2:11, refers to an **evil purpose**.[9]

---

[9] Strong's Concordance #3540, transliterated "Noema".

The Devices and the Wiles of the Enemy

The term "wiles" used in Ephesians 6:11, is the Greek word–*Methodeia,* which denotes **craft, deceit, a way, a cunning device.**[10]

In sum, Satan has an evil purpose (or device), as well as different ways, or methods (or wiles), in which to carry out that evil purpose. The distinction between "devices" and "wiles" becomes apparent in the context of an example using the oft-committed sin of adultery:

The enemy would like nothing more than to tempt a married Christian man to commit adultery. Then, after the fall with the other woman, cause him to stay in that backslidden condition for years (this is the evil purpose, or "device").

The enemy can however, choose from a wide variety of "wiles" to accomplish that evil purpose: the secretary at work, a woman at the gym, his wife's best girlfriend, the next-door neighbor, etc.

The most obvious evil purpose of the enemy, is to use the various wiles that are available to him, to cause a person to

---

[10] Strong's Concordance #3180, transliterated "Methodeia".

The Devices and the Wiles of the Enemy

either: never get saved; or if they do get saved, live a life in bondage to sin and remain in a backslidden condition for the rest of their life; or, otherwise live out their "Christian" life totally apathetic to the things of God. In none of these cases, will anything meaningful ever be accomplished for the Kingdom of God through their lives. This is, or should be rudimentary information that even a "new believer" already knows.

However, since we are "going for the jugular", we are not going to spend much time reviewing concepts such as the sins of the flesh (Galatians 5:19-21) and bondage to sins like, adultery, pornography, drug and/or alcohol addiction. These are all blatantly obvious works of the spirit of control.

What is worth mentioning, however, is if you're practicing any one of those sins, "The devil did not", I repeat, "did not" – "make you do it." The Bible says that, *"every man is tempted, when he is drawn away of his **own lust**, and enticed"* (Ja 1:14, KJV). Left unchecked, your James 1 lust opens the way for the conception of sin. If that sin is not dealt with swiftly, it begins to control your life and then at some point you simply cannot (of your own accord), stop practicing that sin.

The Devices and the Wiles of the Enemy

Proverbs 29:18 says, *"Where there is no vision, the people perish..."* (KJV). The word "vision" means: vision, oracle, prophecy, or *divine communication.*[11] The word, "perish" means: to *cast off restraint;* or show lack of restraint.[12]

In this context, without divine communication regarding your purpose and destiny in life, you do whatever you feel like doing and that includes continuing to practice that "pet sin" of yours. This is simply because you can't think of anything else better to do with yourself ... *except* sin of course.

Without having a vision for what the Lord wants you to do with your life; and without having that divine communication with Him necessary to carry out that vision, you cast off restraint; and as a result, you just sin, sin, sin and keep on sinning.

For those who lack divine communication with Him as to the vision or purpose for their lives what they do is: spend all their time *trying to control* what not to do (i.e. sin) ... *for*

---

[11] Strong's Concordance #2377, transliterated "Chazown".
[12] Strong's Concordance #6544, transliterated "Para`".

The Devices and the Wiles of the Enemy

God, instead of focusing their efforts on what <u>to do,</u> for the Kingdom of God.

They then get caught in the quagmire of trying to control their sin; which, due to their lack of vision or purpose they haven't got the power or restraint to control anyway and they therefore, forever live in defeat.

There is a remedy for practicing sin: Get in communication with God and seek Him diligently to figure out your God-given purpose in life; get a vision on how to accomplish and achieve that purpose; start writing it down; start acting it out; and in faith, start moving in that direction until you're at the point of *running* with the vision (Hab 2:2, KJV).

You then *won't even have time* to sin anymore! You'll be having the time of your life with the Lord because His plan for your life is *edgy--* Yes, it's a Cliff Hanger!

Don't think for a minute that the God whom, *without faith it is impossible to please* (Heb 11:6, KJV) has some boring, everyday, ordinary, yawner-type thing for you to do for the Kingdom.

The Devices and the Wiles of the Enemy

HA! Wrong answer.

He will tell you to do the craziest things <u>and</u> at the worst times possible. When His directives place a high demand on your faith, that's how you *really* know it is God Almighty at work in your midst!

So start today, now! Get up, out of your sin pit. Start acting on His directives, even if in the beginning, you're just taking baby steps. God can't guide you unless you're moving.

Eventually, you'll find yourself so busy seeking God, moving out and trying all these crazy faith-type things that your "pet sins" will automatically begin to dissipate. They'll begin dropping off like flies and eventually disappear from your life entirely. You won't even have time to *think* about your "pet sins" anymore, let alone continue practicing them. You'll have much better things to do with your time and energy. I just double-dog-dare you to try it.

This *should* go without saying, but you do realize, that if you don't get rid of those "pet sins" controlling your behavior, you'll never live out the plans and purposes the

The Devices and the Wiles of the Enemy

Lord has for your life, *right?* In which case, that would be a crime, would it not?

It's the crime of never completely experiencing or living out the life you've been given by your Creator to its highest and fullest potential. Worse, it's a crime that you knowingly, willingly and voluntarily are perpetuating *against yourself* and it could continue *throughout your entire lifetime!*

If you will allow me to assume that after this discussion you are now ready to clear out the "pet sins" and the other riff-raff in your life, then we can move on to address another crime that is currently being perpetrated against you as well.

Yet, unlike the one you've been perpetuating against yourself, this crime is <u>not</u> knowingly, willingly and voluntarily being committed in your life. In fact, the instigator responsible for the commission of this crime is so *slick,* you don't even know how or when this crime is taking place in your own life.

Interested?

Good.

Then let's next take a look into the "elements" of that hidden crime that's going on in your life right now shall we?

CHAPTER 4: Elements of the Crime

Time now, for our first Law School lesson in "Criminal Law" and a very brief primer on the general "elements" of a crime. "Elements" are the various points of proof presented by the prosecution to a jury, which are necessary to obtain a criminal conviction. The number of "elements" required to acquire a jury conviction varies dependent upon the crime committed. Some crimes have more "elements" than others.

If the prosecutor cannot prove each and every "element" standing alone, then he/she cannot prove the crime *beyond a reasonable doubt* as required by law. Therefore, if just one "element" fails, the defendant must be found "not guilty".

Without getting into the specific elements of any particular crime, we will be looking at three generic points that are always addressed by the prosecution during their presentation of the evidence in a criminal trial:

Elements of the Crime

1. MOTIVE
2. MEANS; and
3. OPPORTUNITY

MOTIVE: is the underlying reason, drive, push, or force behind *why* the crime was committed.

There are numerous "motives" but if we wanted to talk about a homicide, here are a few of the biggies: Jealousy-- over a spouse having an affair; Greed-- trying to get a greater share of the inheritance by eliminating another heir; and Vengeance-- "You killed my brother, so I'm going to do the same to you."

Interestingly enough, "motive" however, is never an "element" of proof required in a court of law. Nonetheless, it is always presented in a criminal trial so that the jury can understand *why* a person would commit the crime. Knowing the *why* behind the criminal activity helps to facilitate a conviction and get the criminal off the streets.

MEANS: is the *method* by which, or *how,* the crime was committed. There are numerous "means" available for the commission of a homicide. A <u>gun,</u> <u>knife</u>, or <u>asphyxiation</u>, are always functional for any murder plot.

<u>OPPORTUNITY:</u> relates to the *when* and *where* the alleged defendant had the "opportunity" or ability to commit the crime. This is where the concept of having an "alibi" comes in to play.

Let's say I was accused of murdering my husband for philandering in strip clubs in downtown Chicago (assuming there are some). If I can prove I was in England when the crime was committed in Chicago, I'd have an alibi.

My defense "dream team" would argue that I couldn't have possibly been the person who committed the crime at the strip club in Chicago, because at 12 midnight on December 31st, I was in England at a New Year's Eve party with the Duchess of York. Therefore, a jury would have to find me "not guilty" since I had no "opportunity" to commit the crime because, arguably, only One person can be in two places at the same time.[13]

---

[13] Namely, you know Who.

Now, applying these same principles and going back to our sin of adultery:

MOTIVE: What is the enemy's "motive"? Note: we are <u>not talking about *your* motive</u>, which you should have already caught, is your James 1 "lust". The *obvious* answer to this inquiry is, that the enemy's motive is to get you to backslide and remain in a state of practicing sin and never make it to heaven.

However, I submit to you that the enemy also has another "motive" that via the spirit of control, is not so obvious or apparent when working in your life.

MEANS: The enemy's *obvious* "means" or "wiles" used to create the temptation to sin have already been covered: (A) the co-worker at the office; (B) the person at the gym; (C) the next-door neighbor; or, for some of our most truly unfaithful, (D) all of the above.

However, I submit to you that the enemy also uses other "means" that via the spirit of control, are not so obvious or apparent when working in your life.

Elements of the Crime

<u>OPPORTUNITY:</u> The enemy's *when* and *where* the sin is committed is twofold. It could be at any*time* of day (when); and in any place, from the office, to the apartment, to Motel 6, (where). Dependent upon the facts, both *when* and *where* are usually very easily determined.

However, I submit to you that the enemy also uses other "opportunities" that via the spirit of control, are not so obvious or apparent when working in your life.

The enemy's "motive" "means" and "opportunity" are easy to determine in our adultery example. Yeah, yeah, yeah … *boring* … yawn! Way too *obvious.*

Ok, so now let's move on to talking about you. When it comes to the "motive" for the spirit of divination to work in your life, we can liken "motive" to "devices" or the evil purpose of the enemy (as referenced in 2 Corinthians 2:11), which relates to the force or drive behind *why* the spirit of divination seeks to do its work in your life.

When it comes to the "means" for the spirit of divination to work in your life, we can liken the "means" to the vast array of "wiles" of the enemy (as referenced in Ephesians 6:11,

Methodeia), which provide an assortment of ways in which spirit of divination influences your life.

When it comes to the "opportunity" for the spirit of divination to work in your life, we reference back to all of your interpersonal relationships; multiplied by the number of interactions taking place in those relationships on a daily, weekly, monthly, or yearly basis. Just do the math. As you can well imagine, the enemy's potential success ratio via these "opportunities" multiplies exponentially.

However, when applying these principles to how the spirit of divination works in our own lives, if we're not careful we can be easily swayed into simplistic thinking and ignorantly believe there is nothing more to the work of the enemy but, *the obvious.*

What we don't want to forget throughout this analogy is that the enemy is described in the Bible as being subtle, crafty, cunning and sly (Gen 3:1)[14] which is the antithesis, or opposite of-- "obvious".

---

[14] Strong's Concordance #6175, transliterated "'aruwm".

Elements of the Crime

So what's so sly or cunning about a backslider? Nothing. He or she is backslidden, so whoop-de-doo. There are certainly lots of backslidden Christians running around these days, so I'm not impressed.

Given the character of the enemy, we'd be fools if we didn't think and imagine beyond the *obvious*. We must, therefore, delve deeper into our analogy and not automatically jump to the conclusion that we've arrived at the answer for our own lives, just because we are capable of seeing the *obvious.*

In fact, let's make sure we're not being deceived by some *obvious* spoon-fed answer <u>straight from the enemy</u>. One that causes us to think that we've already got all of the information we need and thus, one that allows the enemy's hidden, clandestine work, to continue as such.

When we consider the character of the enemy and the two fronts we fight against: (1) his "devices", evil purpose or "motive"; and (2) his "wiles", or "means"-- the "opportunities" the enemy utilizes in an attempt to achieve his desired end, to a great extent, have just got to be more subtle than causing another Christian to backslide for all to see.

Come on, it just couldn't be that obvious!

Starting with "motive" I am proposing to you that the evil purpose of the enemy is even more noteworthy than any one time sin event; or even the practice of your "pet sins"; or even causing you to fall away from the Lord in a backslidden condition for years (though the enemy certainly likes it when that happens, too).

But, since Jesus died on the cross for all of our sins, past, present and future, even when we sin, we can still be restored. *"A just man falleth seven times, and riseth up again"* (Prv 24:17, KJV); and God will forgive you *if you confess your sin* (1 Jn 1:9, KJV). So there's just got to be something more to the enemy's "motive" than that.

I also believe the enemy's "motive" is far greater than just trying to get your one single solitary life to end up in hell. The enemy's motive cannot possibly hinge upon just seeing another "one" *bite the dust,* chalking-up of one more single solitary soul into eternal damnation.

Elements of the Crime

Nah, that's way too straightforward!

Come on THINK!

Realize, there's much more ground for the enemy to gain by the use of ongoing, covert, clandestine operations. What we must understand is that when we're combating with our adversary, the *spirit of control* is working in both obvious sin areas (as in the adultery example); as well as the *not so obvious* situations going on in our lives too, especially those that are not necessarily "sin" related per se.

The intent of this text is to *uncover* the "jugular" or those workings of the "spirit of control" that are <u>not</u> so obvious to the untrained Christian, because they are still hiding under layers and layers of skin.

So just imagine with me for a minute if you would ... wouldn't it be extremely subtle, crafty, cunning and sly-- if the enemy could throw you off track with God's plan for your life, yet all the while you *thought* you were doing just fine with the Lord, walking the straight and narrow?

What if you never even realized you had been derailed from His itinerary because *technically* you were not "practicing sin"?

WOW! Now wouldn't *that* be crafty?

What I am proposing to you is that the enemy has an ultimate evil purpose (motive), that is <u>not so obvious</u>; for which he uses several wiles (means) that are <u>not so obvious</u>; including the spirit of divination working in and through your interpersonal relationships in ways (opportunities) that are <u>not so obvious</u>, either.

The sum of which directly control you and your life and will ultimately control your destiny if you don't do something about it. In fact, by the time it's all said and done (unbeknownst to you), your actions end up being governed by the "spirit of divination" instead of the Spirit of God.

Now, Selah!

If I can prove this to be true in your life, you'd be forced to admit that it's an outright crime-- would you not?

Elements of the Crime

It's like one of those pickpockets they show on TV who is so smooth when executing their crime, that the victim doesn't even realize when it's happening. It's not until much later, when the victim goes to buy something, that he/she finally discovers their wallet is missing. Yet, by that time, all of the money has already been spent and it's too late to recover any of it.

That's exactly how the spirit of divination works in your life.

So don't wait until it is too late in life to figure out that you really haven't done much of *anything* for Christ, but tons of *everything* for all of the "Control Freaks" that you know. Do something about it *now* and recover whatever is left of your life for the Kingdom's sake.

In order to put a stop to the spirit of control ripping you off like that-- *anymore* ... that is, it's now time for us to go deeper and start pulling back that first, top layer of skin which is still covering the jugular: namely, "motive".

So what do you think the enemy's secret, undisclosed "motive" really is?

Have you ever played the game Clue?

Need a hint?   Well, here we go.

CHAPTER 5: THE MOTIVE-
The Christ v. The Anti-Christ

We have already established that the *obvious* goal or "motive" of the enemy is to influence a person's life to either never get saved; or, once they become a Christian, cause them to backslide and remain in bondage for their lifetime; or, become so apathetic to the things of God that they merely "exist" until they die. No one, in any of these cases will ever reach that high upward calling in Christ Jesus (Phil 3:14). Their lives will be spent "struggling" in their sinful state, never achieving much of anything for the Kingdom.

The Bible says, *If you faint in the day of adversity your strength is small* (Prv 24:10, KJV). So if you go down like that, you were an easy mark. Agreed?

We also know that for every thing of God, Satan tries to come up with a counterfeit or an "anti" (against God), or an "anti-to Christ" to present to us as a temptation to embrace and engage, instead of the real thing. This Biblical principle is demonstrated throughout scripture many of which we will cover in this text. But for starters, we have Christ, and we have the antichrist (1 John 2:18, 22; 4:3; 2 Jn 1:7); we have the Holy Trinity: Father, Son and the Holy Ghost; and we have the devil, beast and the false prophet (Rev 20:10).

We have the example of Jesus when tempted in the wilderness by the devil with the points of: the lust of the flesh, lust of the eyes, and the pride of life. In each case Jesus was presented with a counterfeit option (or temptation), to embrace or choose from instead of the genuine plan that the Father had for His life.

First, the devil presented the temptation of counterfeit provision by proposing that Jesus change the stone into bread during a time of fasting (the lust of the flesh). Second, the enemy proposed a counterfeit plan by offering Him the kingdoms of the world on the easy "fast track" plan. All Jesus had to do was to worship the devil and then He could forego fulfilling that painful sacrificial plan, already in place for Him to gain the kingdoms of the world (lust of the eyes). Third, the enemy proposed the temptation of counterfeit protection when he suggested that Jesus jump off the pinnacle. This would have been a misuse of the Father's hand of protection, in order to "show off" (or in demonstration of the pride of life).

For nearly everything the Lord establishes, the enemy seeks to establish a counterfeit for us to take, use, embrace or engage in, as a substitute for the real or genuine thing that the Lord wants us to have.

Additionally, for whatever the Lord *wants from us*, we can be sure that the enemy will propose a counterfeit option in order to thwart the Lord's receipt of the same.

Given this principle, the biggest hint I can give you as to the enemy's true "motive" is to review with you what the Lord has always *wanted from us*, His children. It will then become perfectly clear what the enemy, who is anti- to Christ, wants to try and intercept for himself instead.

A.   What Does the Lord Want from You?

From the very beginning, God has made it perfectly clear time and time again what He wants from us. Starting in the

THE MOTIVE- The Christ v. The Anti-Christ

Old Testament and confirmed later on again in the New Testament:

Hear, O Israel: The LORD our God is one LORD; And thou shalt love the LORD thy God with all thine <u>heart</u>, and with all thy <u>soul</u>, and with all thy <u>might</u>" (Deut 6:4-5, KJV).

Thou shalt love the Lord thy God with all thy <u>heart</u>, and with all thy <u>soul</u>, and with all thy <u>strength</u>, and with all thy <u>mind</u> (Lu 10:27 & Mk 12:30, KJV).

Oh, ok ... is that *all* He wants?

Ha!

Do you know what this means, practically speaking, when the Lord says He wants all of your "heart" "soul" "strength" "might" and "mind"?

Hold on tight ... cause here we go:

Your "heart" is: the center and seat of spiritual life, the soul or mind; the fountain and seat of the **thoughts, passions, desires, appetites, affections, purposes,**

endeavors of the understanding, the faculty and seat of the intelligence of the will and character of the soul so far as it is affected and stirred in a bad way or good; the soul as the seat of the sensibilities, affections, emotions, desires, appetites, passions.[15]

The Lord wants all that goes on in your "heart" given to Him, knowingly, willingly and voluntarily.

Your "soul" is: the (human) soul insofar as it is constituted; that by the right use of the aids offered it by God it can attain its highest end and secure eternal blessedness; the soul regarded as a moral being designed for everlasting life.[16]

Not only does God want you to have everlasting life with Him (which is always fine with us), but we also see that this definition includes our use of God's aids to attain *the highest end for our souls.* This definition encompasses not only holy and righteous living; but also more importantly, carrying out His purposes for our lives here on earth *prior to* reaching our eternal security in the afterlife.

---

[15] Strong's Concordance #2588, transliterated "Kardia".
[16] Strong's Concordance #5590, transliterated "Psuche".

Again, the Lord wants all that goes on with regard to your "soul" given to Him, knowingly, willingly and voluntarily.

Your "mind" includes: that faculty of understanding, feeling, desiring, the understanding mind, i.e. spirit, **way of thinking and feeling thoughts,** either good or bad.[17]

God wants to influence how you think about a thing, about a person, about a situation, about your life, about Him. This concept is confirmed in other parts of scripture:

"Therefore, prepare your minds for action; be self-controlled; set your hope fully on the grace to be given you when Jesus Christ is revealed" (1 Pe 1:13, NIV); and

*"The weapons I fight with are not the weapons the world uses. In fact, it is just the opposite. My weapons have the power of God to destroy the camps of the enemy. I destroy every claim and every reason that keeps people from knowing God. **I keep every thought under control in order to make it obey Christ**"* (2 Cor 10:4-5, NIRV).

---

[17] Strong's Concordance #1271, transliterated "Dianoia".

THE MOTIVE- The Christ v. The Anti-Christ

The Lord wants all that goes on in your "mind" to be given to Him, knowingly, willingly and voluntarily.

Your "strength" or "might" includes: **your abilities, force, strength and might.**[18]

In other words, He wants all of the physical capabilities that you have available to carry out His directives, plan and purpose for your life. He wants your strength submitted to Him, knowingly, willingly and voluntarily.

Without question, we must all agree this is quite an all-consuming definition of "you" is it not? Can you think of anything that "you" have, or about "you" that is missing from these components? Of course not.

The combination of your heart, mind, soul and strength encompasses *absolutely everything* you've been given to work with by your Creator, in its entirety. Now that you're saved the Lord wants it all back! *Knowingly, willingly* and *voluntarily* given over to Him, in submission and obedience to His will, so that He can use your life for something far

---

[18] Strong's Concordance #2479, transliterated "Ischus".

greater than those petty little things that you're striving about today.

This all-consuming "you" principal is confirmed in Romans 12:1-2 where it says, *"And so, dear brothers and sisters, I plead with you to give your bodies to God. Let them be a living and holy sacrifice -- the kind He will accept. When you think of what He has done for you, is this too much to ask? Don't copy the behavior and customs of this world, but let God transform you into a new person by changing the way you think. Then you will know what God wants you to do, and you will know how good and pleasing and perfect His will really is"* (NLT).[19]

In the parable of the pounds found in Luke 19 (similar to the parable of the talents found in Matthew 25), Jesus explained that after giving a pound each to his servants, before leaving, the nobleman said, *"Occupy until I come"*. The word, "occupy" means to "carry on business".[20]

---

[19] Throughout the remainder of this text the word "you" when used in quotation marks, is meant to refer to this all-encompassing definition of you-- your heart, soul, mind and strength/might.

[20] Strong's Concordance #4231, transliterated "Pragmateuomai".

THE MOTIVE- The Christ v. The Anti-Christ

When the nobleman returned he rewarded those who brought increase and he scolded those who did not. We can easily deduce that the Lord expects us to be good stewards by bringing increase and progression with the gifts and talents He has placed inside of us. In order to carry out and complete our assignments as He directs, this requires the exertion of effort on our parts. This is all a part of our individualized, Romans 12:1, *reasonable service*.

Realize that the enemy is fully aware that the combination of the power of the Holy Spirit, working in unison with your surrendered life (as encompassed by these definitions of "you"), would no doubt result in the slaying of one giant right after another, ad infinitum! It would mean the enemy's sure and swift defeat.

Are you with me?

Now, think for a moment ... it should become perfectly clear that the underlying evil "motive" of the enemy is to war against your ability to ever give all of "you" to the Lord, for His useful service in the first place.

B.   <u>What Does the Enemy Want from You?</u>

Having closely examined what the terms heart, soul, mind and strength encompass, not only helps clarify what the Lords wants from us; but it also helps us to see the flip side of what the anti-to Christ, or spirit of divination/control seeks to conquer in His stead.

The enemy, that force working anti-to Christ, wants the exact same thing! Yet, instead of gaining it knowingly, willingly and voluntarily like the Lord, the enemy has to take it by trickery and deceit. Only fools would want to submit themselves voluntarily to the enemy.

So for every facet of "you" that the Lord intended to be given to Him voluntarily to fulfill Kingdom assignments; the enemy's "motive" is to capture, control, and cause "you" to function as a person who is, anti-to Christ, instead. Best of all, if he can get you to do so *without knowing* you are, its all the better for fulfilling his evil purpose.

The anti-to Christ for your "heart" is idolatry. We are people prone to and easily given over to, "idolatry". Our hearts function somewhat like the second law of thermodynamics: left to itself, your heart will naturally gravitate towards idolatry rather than the worship of God.

That's pretty much how the heart of man operates. The enemy wants your whorish heart falling into one idolatrous situation after another, so that you'll remain in constant bondage to a person, place, or thing.

The anti-to Christ for your "soul" is not only hell after you die, but that you would also experience as much hell here on earth that the enemy can possibly squeeze into your lifetime.

Ultimately, yes, the enemy wants you to be thrown into the pit of hell so that he can torment and rule over you throughout eternity. Additionally, however, *during your lifetime* here on earth, he certainly does not want you pursuing, let alone achieving, that predetermined destiny and plan that God has for your life. That would have a positive effect on far too many people for benefit of the Kingdom. So he does his best to make your life miserable. That way, you won't have anything left to give to others in service to Him.

THE MOTIVE- The Christ v. The Anti-Christ

The anti-to Christ for your "mind" is to be consumed with the words and deeds of all of the controlling people in your life. The enemy wants you to be a "slop brain", allowing yourself to think about anything and everything that the spirit of control directs. His desire is to consume your thoughts with the spirit of fear, discouragement, bitterness, hatred, hurt, resentment, discontentment and worry. The enemy wants to invade and rule over all of your thought processes, so that the fruit of your thoughts would be murmuring and complaining; planning ways to offend others; contention and conflict. The enemy wants you to become one of those *miserable* "Christians" that no one can stand to even be around, let alone be of any *reasonable* service to the Kingdom of God.

The anti-to Christ for your "strength" is that you would become physically tapped out from all the efforts you've expended trying to appease all the controlling people in your life. Then when it came to doing anything for the Kingdom, you'd be *too tired,* too busy, too lazy, too depressed, too emotionally distraught, too worried, too fat, too poor, too sick, too _____ *whatever* (you fill in the blank), to do anything productive.

THE MOTIVE- The Christ v. The Anti-Christ

In that condition, you won't have the physical strength to carry out His assignments or will. Again, the Lord requires work, hard work-- heavy lifting over long periods of time (endurance). His plan is not going to be dropped in your lap without any plowing, sowing and laboring in the fields. Whoever told you otherwise, told you a lie!

Now, how's that for a hint?

The enemy's "motive" or evil purpose, or 2 Corinthians 2:11 "device", is to gain control over every single solitary aspect of "you" and your life by consuming your heart, mind, soul, body and strength to the fullest extent possible with all of his "Control Freak" nonsense.

The enemy's "motive" is to achieve that same type of "total control" over "you" *unwittingly and unwillingly*, that God desires for us to give to Him *knowingly*, *willingly,* and *voluntarily.*

So as "Christians" already destined for heaven, the enemy's "motive" doesn't have anything to do whatsoever with sending you to hell. But, it has everything to do with making certain that your life here on earth is not lived out according to the foreordained plans and purposes of your Creator.

So there you have it, the first layer of skin has been torn back! That is the evil "motive" of the enemy. It's subtle, it's sneaky, yes ... but it's not rocket science.

The far more devious inquiry relates to the next layer of skin still covering the jugular: the enemy's "means". In order for his "means" to be most effective and protracted, the spirit of divination both, obscures its efforts and conceals its successes.

Here's how.

CHAPTER 6: THE MEANS-
People Controlling Other People

Before we move on to discussing the enemy's "means" in great detail, let's first draw a bright line of distinction between "the Spirit of God" and "the spirit of divination" as it relates to the issue of "control" over your life.

As you well know, we were all created with the power of choice, the freedom to choose; or, to put it another way, the freedom not to be controlled. That's how God wanted it and so that's how He created us.

Due to this fact, we immediately realize that God wanted the very opposite of "control" for our lives by creating us with that unique power, or capacity of "choice" that we all possess as human beings. If the spirit of divination/control had been of God, He would have done the exact opposite.

After all, if anyone had the capability to "control" us, it would have been God Almighty Himself and Him alone.

In fact, this intention of God was unmistakably demonstrated in His giving Adam the "power of choice" to sin in the garden. If the spirit of control had been of God, there would have been no such "power of choice" given to man in the first place. The Lord *could have* created us like a bunch of robots so that He *could have* "controlled" us throughout eternity. Yet, notably, He *intentionally* did not.

This reality is not to be misconstrued, however, with the phrase so often used by Christians when they say, "God is in control." Yes, "God is in control" over every circumstance and situation that takes place here on earth; nothing takes Him by surprise. He is the Sovereign Creator and Ruler of the Universe. He does whatever He wants, however He wants, and whenever He wants. As a child of God, He has a hedge about you and He keeps His finger on the thermometer of your life. He has assured you "a way to escape" from any temptation that you face (1 Cor 10:13, KJV). He has a significant plan for your life and He expects you to live it out, knowingly, willingly, and voluntarily.

THE MEANS- People Controlling Other People

It is also true, however, that in wielding His Sovereignty, the Lord has a wonderful way of orchestrating circumstances to convince His servants to do His will; such as in the story of Jonah. Yet, had Jonah not changed his perspective during his three-day layover, the Lord would have simply cast him aside as "reprobate" (Jer 6:30, KJV) and used someone else to preach to the city of Nineveh.

In short, God is "in" control, but He is not a God "of" control.

The Lord wants our love and obedience to be given freely and voluntarily to Him, not because we were forced into it. Not because we were operating under His "control" like some "Stepford Wife" or "Stepford Husband."[21]

The Lord chose to draw us voluntarily unto Himself, by His great love and mercy. *"The LORD hath appeared of old unto me, saying, 'Yea, I have loved thee with an everlasting love: therefore with lovingkindness have I drawn thee'"* (Jer 31:3, KJV).

---

[21] I keep wondering, where's the movie on the husbands?

Therefore, we easily arrive at the conclusion that the Lord's very nature has nothing to do with "control" but rather, with love since *"God is love"* (1 Jn 4:8, KJV). He intended that we voluntarily enter into a relationship with Him by our attraction to His loving nature, not by being forced. For the *"goodness of God leads you to repentance"* (Ro 2:4, NKJV). *"Wherever the Spirit of the Lord is, He gives freedom"* (2 Cor 3:17, NLT).

The Lord *"stands at the door and knocks"* (Rev 3:20, KJV). You, by contrast, don't ever even have to open the door. He created you with a "free will" to either slam it shut, or open it up all the way and invite Him in. It's all on you.

We therefore easily conclude that the Lord has *never* sought to *control* "you" ... ever. So pray tell, who do you think *is* all about *controlling* "you" and your life?

Yep! And, "yes"... there's another one. The spirit of divination is yet another anti-to Christ. You can be certain, there actually is a "spiritual battle" going on today, and it's for "control" over "you" and your life.

THE MEANS- People Controlling Other People

Consider this possibility: Have you ever thought about how some people may actually be of more use to the enemy by *calling* themselves "Christian" and by living and moving in the "Christian" environment and in "Christian" circles, than they ever would be as backslidden wanna-be's who have no such access or influence?

If the enemy can *use "Christians"* in whom the spirit of control/divination influences the conduct of *other "Christians"* as his "means" to achieve his "motive" or end; then those "in-house" works of the enemy will almost always go wholly undetected.[22]

I believe that there are actually three "classes" or types of totally naïve and deceived "Christians" functioning "in-house" on behalf of the spirit of divination today.

The first naïve and deceived class are those Christians who are used by the spirit of divination *to control* the behavior of other Christians. They influence the decision making processes of genuine children of God and are used to thwart and derail them from ever reaching, let alone fulfilling their foreordained God-given assignments and

---

[22] "In-house" meaning, within the church: the Body of Christ.

destiny. All the while they themselves remain clueless to the fact that they are causing others to adhere to their misleading, spirit of divination-driven directives. This class is deceived because they actually think that they're helping you, me, and the rest of the world, with their counsel and advice.

The second naïve and deceived class are those Christians whose behaviors are *being controlled* by the first-class. Their voluntary assent in allowing others to direct, dictate and determine their decisions and actions, undermines, delays, and/or derails them from reaching and fulfilling their foreordained God-given assignments and destiny. All the while they themselves remain clueless to the fact that they are adhering to and complying with, misleading spirit of divination-driven directives. This class is deceived because they actually think that by doing what other people expect, direct, or demand of them (unless sinful of course), that it's the "right" thing to do.

I call the third naïve and deceived class of Christians, "bi-controlling". They are those with whom the spirit of divination functions in combination: both "controlling" others, as well as allowing themselves to be "controlled" *by* others. All the while they themselves remain clueless to the fact that they are both: influencing others to adhere to misleading spirit of divination driven directives; <u>and</u> at other times, in other relationships, they are allowing themselves to do the same. Dependent upon whether being *controlling* or being *controlled* during any given interaction, this class is also deceived on the same two accounts previously mentioned above.

Since none of these "mature" "Christians" are technically "practicing sin" they mistakenly think "it's all good" with the Lord, when in reality, the enemy is playing them all like chumps. None of them realize that through this mechanism or "means" of *control*, the spirit of divination has effectively suppressed or discounted the Lord's directives in and for their lives <u>and/or</u> in and for the lives of the people they're being used to control.

Did you get that?

"Christians" exercising the spirit of control over other "Christians". No, I'm not talking about demon possession; i'll clear that up in detail later. And no, I'm not talking about "sin" either. I'm not talking about a Christian telling another

Christian to stop practicing a sin. That's not being controlling, that's just admonishing holy and righteous living.

The secretive "motive" of the enemy is to consume "you" to the extent that "you" are unable to hear or carry out those directives necessary for you to fulfill the Lord's calling and purpose for your life. His "means" to achieve that end, is to use the spirit of control working in and through both your "Christian" and non-Christian interpersonal relationships. Of those two types, the more clandestine "means" take place in your "Christian" relationships. This is where controlling "Christians" mislead, misguide and misdirect your decisions and behavior apart from, or anti-to, the Spirit of God.

So now that the battle lines have been drawn, whose side are you on?

Are you in that first-class of *controlling* Christians? Do you seek to get people to do *what* you want them to do, *when* you want them to do it? Do you fuss, fight and manipulate whenever they resist?

THE MEANS- People Controlling Other People

Think about it and admit it! When you realize the spirit of control is not of God *at all*, and worse, that it's actually anti-to Christ … it's really kinda scary when you think about it; because *everyone* at one time or another has sought to control others to do "their will" in any given situation.

Not only is the spirit of control the opposite of God and everything He stands for, but again, when that controlling spirit gains access to your heart, mind, soul and strength, it is actually working against, or counter to, or anti-to, the leading of God's Spirit in your life. It's one thing to just not be getting anywhere with God yourself; but since we are either *for Him or against Him* (Matt 12:30, KJV), it's quite another thing to call yourself a "Christian" and actually be working against God.

If you're not a first-class *controlling* Christian, are you then a second-class *controlled* Christian?

That can be a pretty scary inquiry as well. If you have allowed your heart, soul, mind and strength to be taken from God's guidance and given over to others to guide, then not only will you become ineffective for the Kingdom of God, but more importantly, your life could actually be used to *detrimentally* effect the lives of other Christians and the Kingdom as well. If it seems as if you've been spending more time catering to the whims, demands and ultimatums of the *controlling* people in your life, to the point where the Spirit of God is no longer the One leading you, well then look-- it's working!

Additionally, with this second-class of *controlled* Christians, there is an even more cunning factor of the enemy at play. Most of the time, *controlled* Christians explain or "Christianize" their conduct of being controlled by others, by calling it: "humility" or "submission" or "honoring others" or "loving" or creating an atmosphere of "unity", when it's really nothing more than plain … "chicken". Or, put more civilly, it's really nothing more than a "chink in their armor" that needs to be shored up.

So for all you admitted second-class *controlled* Christians, get ready for some work on that armor of yours.

Then again, if we were all to be totally honest with ourselves, the truth is that we've all been *bi-controlling* at one time or another. With some people you're *controlling*, with others you're *controlled*.

THE MEANS- People Controlling Other People

I trust by this point that you are beginning to gain an appreciation for the craftiness of the enemy. Instead of being blatantly *obvious* about the workings of the spirit of divination, the enemy would much rather "control" your life on the "D-L".

He knows if you don't know it's going on ... you won't be able to do anything about it. If the spirit of divination is allowed to continue this course, you will never make it to fulfilling your God-given destiny. If the spirit of divination has anything to say about it, the plans the Lord has for your life to serve, touch, encourage, correct, bless and strengthen others (who also have their own Kingdom assignments to fulfill), will never be accomplished.

In short, if you don't make it to and through your own God-given assignments in life, many others may never make it to and through theirs either. This is all due to the fact that you weren't there to fulfill your own distinctive role. Sure, God can always use someone else, but because we are all so uniquely and individually created, it just wouldn't be the same ... *besides,* He wants to use you!

THE MEANS- People Controlling Other People

The Lord wants "you" to be freed up from the workings of the spirit of divination/control so that you become so closely in tune with His voice, that you will never again miss one Word, or divine directive emanating from His Throne. He wants "you" so in-step with His Spirit that you cannot possibly overlook your course. Then, once you get on it, you can start living out your God-ordained assignments, destiny and purpose here on earth.

So the obvious question now becomes are you ready to give up your attempts at *controlling* anyone else in your life *ever again*? Are you also ready to stop allowing others to exercise *control* over you? Are you ready to move to the Lord's side of this bright line and allow only the Holy Spirit to lead, guide, rule and reign in your life?

You don't need to know "how" in order to answer these questions in the affirmative. All you need to be is *willing* and let me deal with the "how" later on in the text.

Having unveiled the more conniving "means" aspect of the crime, I suspect the light bulb has just started to come on in your mind. That's good! It's another layer of skin being pulled back from the top of the jugular, so don't you dare turn off the switch!

Consider your enlightenment to be somewhat akin to the "lamp of interrogation". You know, the kind of glaring lamp they shined on the criminals in those old black and white movies. Expect this light to become brighter and brighter, as I continue to lay the foundation of this text.

My intention is to have your life backed so far into a corner within the next few chapters, that you'd be desperately looking for a way out.

Next up, the last element of the crime: "opportunity".

"CONTROL FREAK"

CHAPTER 7: THE OPPORTUNITY- Who Do You Love?

Now that the enemy's "motive" and "means" have been established let's move on to expounding upon exactly *when* and *where* the enemy presents us with the "opportunity" to bring about his underlying evil purpose. As touched upon previously, since the devil doesn't personally even have you as a blip on his radar, the way "opportunity" works is within our own interpersonal relationships; especially those we have with people we love.

The people in your life with whom you carry on interpersonal relationships are great in number and wide in variety. You have Christian friends, pastors, church leaders, respected ministers; you have heathen friends, co-workers, bosses; you have your spouse and/or ex-spouse; you have old romantic relationships, you have new or current romantic relationships; you have mothers and fathers, sisters and brothers, step-parents, half-brothers and sisters; you have neighbors, people you meet on the street … you get where I'm going.

Your relationships and interactions with other people play a very significant role as it relates to the "opportunity" for the spirit of divination to *control* "you".

What you do in various circumstances that require decisive action to be made or taken in and about your own life, usually revolves around one or more of your interpersonal relationships. Just one of these interactions, depending on the person and their degree of influence in your life, may cause you to do exactly what *that* person directs you to do, without your even checking-in with God first.

Most times it may seem like the "right" thing to do, but in reality, many times you were just led off the Lord's desired path and are now headed in the wrong direction because you took counsel from this other person. Whether it be due to that person's own sin lifestyle, their ignorance, or their manipulative intention; people come into our lives with the spirit of divination to try to influence us by directives, counsel, guilt trips, condemnation, hurt, offense, demands, love, affection, pleas, anger, abuse, pain, or by whatever "means" or *methodeia* are readily available to them to use to control "you".

The spirit of divination/control first influences them and then they in turn are used to influence, or *control* you. As a result they get you to do what the spirit of divination/control wants you to do; which remember, is the opposite of what God wants you to do. When multiplied by the number of interpersonal relationships you may have in a lifetime, there are literally unlimited "opportunities" for the enemy to lead you off track, each and every day of your life.

Now realize, when I say "interpersonal relationships" it does not necessarily mean they must be ongoing, reoccurring interactions either. You could have a one-time interaction with a person you have never even met before, but because of something they said or did, in which the spirit of control was at work, it can change the course of your life forever.

Understand a few important points about this concept of "opportunity":

THE OPPORTUNITY- Who Do You Love?

First, these people usually have no idea that they are being influenced by the spirit of divination to try to get you to act or respond on its behalf. Many of them will even argue that what they're advising you to do about your problem or situation is really sound "godly" advice and that it's for "your own good".

Second, many of them are *real* "Christians". They can even be church leaders, pastors and/or teachers, advising you or telling you to do something in response to a pressure or decision that needs to be made in your life. Yet, many times, this is but reasoned advice based on *their own understanding* (Prv 3:5); and the Lord Himself is actually not on board with their counsel to you at all.

Third, just because someone is trying to influence you, or even outright trying to control you via the spirit of divination, that's not to say that they're demon possessed, unsaved, or in any way, not *real* "Christians".

Fourth and again, I am not talking about sin issues. I'm not talking about someone advising you on whether to sin or not. That's too easy; that's too obvious. We're going much

80   "CONTROL FREAK"

deeper into the subtleties of the enemy, than the *obvious* practice of sin remember?

What we're talking about is the counter-influence of the people in your life (many of whom you love), who are being used to undermine the play-by-play decisions you make to fulfill the purpose and plan God has preordained for your life. Basically, we're talking about the most important thing going on in your life right now!

The Bible speaks of us as the "sheep of His pasture" (Ps 100:3, KJV). As sheep, we are already programmed to being led. That's why it is so important to make sure the Holy Spirit is the only One ... doing the leading.

The last thing you need is for some well meaning Christian friend, loved one, or godly leader to start setting goals for your life: directing you where you should go, what career path you should pursue, what kind of ministry you should start, who you should marry, what church you should go to, as well as any other decisions you should make about arriving at God's plan and destiny for your life, when quite frankly, they haven't a clue!

THE OPPORTUNITY- Who Do You Love?

News Flash: They're not God!

There is a faulty belief system out there that *real* "Christians" would never be used by the enemy to hurt you, harm you or negatively influence you and that they certainly would never be used to try and take you out of the will of God for your life.

Ha!

Just hang out a little longer within the Christian community and you'll see how utterly twisted that kind of thinking really is.

The reality is that born-again, Holy Spirit filled, Bible believing, genuine Christians, via the spirit of divination, can be used to "lead and guide" your life and cause you to miss the Holy Spirit's "leading and guiding" of your life; which, by the way, is His job exclusively (John 16:13). As a result, their influence can and will cause you to act outside of God's will for your life.

What makes a real Christian's influence even more alluring and useful to the enemy is that usually we are operating "off guard" when dealing with other Christians. So we more readily take or carry out their advice, recommendations and input, without ever checking-in with the Lord for ourselves.

I mean, after all, since they're "born again" the Holy Spirit indwells them too, right? That would mean that the Spirit of God leads them too, right? It should therefore be "safe" for me to listen to whatever they say and believe that it's straight from the Throne of God then too, *right?*

Wrong!

Et Voila! There we have it! The "opportunity" for the enemy to use his most subtle *wile*, the one that is least detected and least corrected. It's when *real* Christians (especially those beloved, or in leadership), while influenced by the spirit of control/divination, provide advice, directives, demands, requests, or guidance for the decisions, actions and/or circumstances that you face in your own life.

Most often, they are people you love, admire and respect enough to go to for advice in the first place. They don't even realize that what they've advised or said, or what they've suggested or directed you to do, was *meant* to control you. So don't bother confronting them, they'll fully deny it until the cows come home.

I recently got a call from a lady in distress because she had sublet a beautiful room from a man who initially represented that he was the "owner" of the property. She was living as roommates with other males, years younger than she was, but males nonetheless. She ended up getting ripped off for a tidy sum by "that man" whom she later found out, did not really own the home at all. After finally speaking directly to the real owner she realized that her roommate ("that man"), was being evicted for *his* failure to pay rent.

While she was asking me about her legal rights (which were few and far between), I mentioned to her that she may want to consider it as a "lesson learned", that God didn't want her living with other "men" even if they were years younger.

In response, she said she had sought "godly" counsel from other "godly" women in the church and that they all said it was "ok" to do. She therefore did not "receive" what I believed was the Lord's perspective on the situation. Instead, and in spite of being totally ripped off, she still believed she had done the right thing by initially moving into that kind of a male/female unmarried living environment.

Input and advice from *real* Christians can and is, being used by the enemy to control your behavior apart from God and causing you to get ripped off too. Perhaps not always with money like the lady that called me, but you can get ripped off in efforts expended, days of toiling, and years wasted; all the while doing things someone else, other than God, wanted you to do. What a crime!

Since it is not my intention to make you feel hopeless about your newly enlightened perspective, you should realize that the spirit of divination has also influenced the lives of several renowned Biblical characters as well.

Is starting as far back as the Garden of Eden early enough for you?

"CONTROL FREAK"

CHAPTER 8: Back to the Garden

▬▬▬▬▬▬▬▬▬▬▬▬▬▬▬▬▬▬▬▬▬▬▬▬▬▬▬▬▬▬▬▬▬▬▬▬

The Garden of Eden is where we first see the spirit of divination at work. Yep, you got it. Its influence came on the scene via the serpent's temptation of Eve to eat the forbidden fruit. It was successful in *controlling* Eve's behavior by deception ... battin' a thousand at that point.

In turn, the spirit of divination influenced Eve to offer or share the fruit with Adam. Adam gave in to Eve's offer and therefore, Eve was successful at *controlling* Adam's behavior. Needless to say, it's been downhill for mankind ever since.

There are several hypotheses over Adam's role in the fall of mankind and *why* (when present during Eve's interaction with the serpent), he allowed his wife to fall into this blatant act of disobedience. I am intentionally not going to spend any time discussing, let alone debating any of these theories.

What is wholly undisputed is the fact that Eve offered the fruit to Adam and he ate it-- period (Gen 3:6).

Further, theologians can only hypothesize as to *why* Adam himself sinned. The "why" isn't mentioned in the Bible. The only thing mentioned is the fact that he did. The best they can universally come up with is that Adam was born with the "freedom of choice" and so when it came to Eve's offer of the fruit, he simply made the *wrong choice.*

For our purposes the "why" that caused or influenced Adam to take the forbidden fruit from Eve and eat, is a very important issue to explore. We all know that the woman was "deceived" (1 Tim 2:14, KJV), but what was up with Adam?

In an attempt to answer the question of "why" Adam allowed Eve to influence him to the point of blatantly sinning against the Lord, we move into Law School lesson number two: "Trial Practice".

Back to the Garden

In a court of law, when there is no affirmative evidence of "motive" -- or *why* the crime was committed (as we have in this case with Adam), attorneys oftentimes seek to disprove every other plausible cause or reason *why* that they can think of for the jury. Afterwards, during closing arguments, the attorney will then point out that the reason they have adopted for their side of the case, is now the only feasible explanation remaining. This is done in order that any "reasonably minded" juror would also agree that *their* proffered cause as to *why* the crime was committed is the only remaining viable reason from which a juror should choose.

When one takes on the task of analyzing the *why* behind Adam's sin, since the Bible does not specify, we can all put on the hat of a Trial Attorney and in like manner, begin to eliminate the possibilities that factually, are simply not plausible. After concluding this analysis, we can then hold fast to those possibilities that are reasonable, rational, or that remain as viable *potential* causes explaining *why* Adam sinned. Then later, we can make use of that information to further enlighten our understanding of human nature.

With this roadmap in mind, there are certain possibilities that we can readily eliminate:

First, when exploring the question of *why* Adam sinned, I don't know about you, but the answer: "Because he had free choice" is far too simplistic for me. Look, we all have sin natures, but we don't always "bite" at sin when it's presented, now do we? (Pun, intended.)

Second, let's not be distracted by the sin of eating the forbidden fruit itself, so much either. The Bible (some argue intentionally) does not indicate what *type* of fruit it was on that tree. Most art renderings show it as an apple, but there really is no scriptural basis for that depiction. Nonetheless, for argument's sake, let's just say it was *an apple.*

The next expected inquiry from the religious community would then be, *"Well, what kind of apple was it?"* Was it a Red Delicious, a Golden Delicious, a Granny Smith, a Gala, a Pink Lady, or a Fuji apple?

I think we ask these kinds of questions in order to see if we can agree or identify with Adam's sin choice. In other words, "Yes Adam, *I understand why* you did it! I would have sinned with that sweet gala apple any day of the week, just like you did." Or, to the contrary, "Adam, you're such a fool! Why on earth did you bother to eat that sour granny smith apple? *Really*, Adam, was it all worth it?"

Focusing on the *type of fruit*, or the sin enticement itself, is not going to tell us *why* Adam sinned. He had several other types of apples (or fruit) to choose to eat from; it surely wasn't because he wanted to eat *that one particular* silly little gala apple.

Third, Adam did not commit a "need-based sin". Adam was not going through a famine, nor was he hungry and had nothing else to eat. It wasn't because he felt deprived or deserving. He was given permission to eat the fruit from every tree in the garden, except that one (Gen 2:16).

Fourth, it wasn't because this was Adam's first opportunity to sin or eat that particular forbidden fruit. Adam had previous opportunities to eat the forbidden fruit before Eve ever came on the scene, but notably, he never did.

Fifth, it wasn't because Adam had all these tremendous stressors or pressures in life that caused him to just go on "tilt" and sin. The lifestyle Adam lived up to the point of his sin, was simply divine! Hanging out in the presence of God daily. He was provided the opportunity to use his brainpower and imagination to name all the animals that ever lived on the face of the earth. And, without question, Adam was *the most important human being* on the face of the earth (being the only one, you know). So there wasn't even any *competition* for Adam in any area. Adam didn't have *anyone* or *anything* to be pressured or stressed about!

One thing is for sure (prior to Eve coming on the scene), there were no other humans on the face of the earth to antagonize, hurt and/or frustrate him and because all of his needs were met and because there was no one else's lifestyle to compare his with and thus become discontented, the stressors and pressures of life certainly were not *why* Adam sinned.

Sixth, Adam did not eat the fruit because he was just plain ignorant and had no idea that God commanded him not to do so. The Lord's directive was made very clear to Adam

"CONTROL FREAK"

from the get-go (Gen 2:16-17). Moreover, after the sin took place, Adam showed signs of trying to hide his sin.

These types of "evidences of guilt" are always used at trial to show that the criminal defendant *knew his conduct was wrong* or against the law. It's called the "mens rea".

"Mens rea" is a Latin term meaning, the "guilty mind". In criminal law it is viewed as one of the necessary elements of a crime. As a general rule, people who have acted in the absence of mental fault, or mens rea, are not prosecuted criminally.[23]

Adam's "mens rea" is seen in several actions he took after the fall. First, was his attempt to hide his sin with leaves to cover his nakedness. Then, there was his attempt to hide himself from an omnipresent God. Then, once placed on the witness stand, Adam attempted to use what we call the "empty chair defense" by pointing the finger at Eve, saying, "*it was the woman...*" (and when that didn't work), Adam even tried pointing to the Judge Himself, "*... that You gave me*" (Gen 3:7-12, KJV). These are all evidences of Adam's knowledge of his own guilt, or "mens rea".

---

[23] Wikipedia

Therefore, through process of elimination, the only remaining plausible raison d'être present in the Garden to explain *why* Adam sinned ... was Eve herself.

Had Adam ever sinned before Eve was present? No. Otherwise, we certainly would have heard about it in Scripture.

Prior to Eve coming on the scene, Adam enjoyed unadulterated dependency on his relationship with God. Prior to Eve coming on the scene, the fruit to which the fall was attributed had always been present and available for Adam to eat. Prior to Eve coming on the scene, Adam and God were getting along just fine, hanging out, naming animals and the like. In fact, it wasn't until Adam and Eve started hanging out *alone naked* together … that anything went amiss.

Hence we must conclude, and it is really undisputable, that Adam's sin-- the first sin of all mankind-- had a direct connection to his relationship with Eve. Specifically, her presence in his life, her presence in the Garden, and her offer to him to take of the forbidden fruit.

Back to the Garden

What would have happened if Adam had been mad, or in a quarrel with Eve, or had been harboring unforgiveness towards her? Well, he may not have been so compliant in taking her offer.

What would have happened *if* Adam had refused Eve's offer to eat the fruit? Instead of this interaction being the first ever-recorded incident of "sin" in the Bible, it would have been memorialized as the first ever-recorded "domestic dispute". (Since it's only the third chapter in Genesis, I suppose they were still on "honeymoon" and hadn't had their first fight yet.)

Therefore, any rational "reasonably" minded juror would be forced to conclude that the reason for Adam's sin, or *why Adam sinned, had something to do with his relationship to and with Eve.*

No rational "reasonable" person could take the position that the *why* behind Adam's sin, *had nothing to do with Eve.* After all, she's the one who undisputedly gave him the fruit!

Think of it this way: If Eve had never been created, would Adam have ever sinned? A closer look at the scriptures related to origins of this relationship between the loving couple provides us with further insight in answer to this question.

We know that God determined it was "not good" for Adam to be without Eve and so she was specially created by God to complete Adam (Gen 2:18, KJV). We also know how happy Adam was when he first laid eyes on her: *"This is now bone of my bones, flesh of my flesh"* (Gen 2:23, KJV). I don't suppose it gets any closer or more intimate than that.

So it's easy to surmise that Adam's "love at first sight" response to Eve created an immediate intimacy and dependency for her reciprocal love, approval, affection and acceptance. Whereas before, Adam's only relationship was with the Lord and He, by default, was the only person Adam was or ever had been, concerned about getting along with and/or pleasing.[24]

---

[24] Somehow, I imagine when it was just Adam and the Lord, that Adam just *knew* how much God loved him. After all, Adam was clearly the center of attention.

"CONTROL FREAK"

Back to the Garden

With just those few scriptural references we can conclude the following: according to the Creator of the Universe, Adam had a need for Eve; after she was created, Adam had an intense desire for Eve (which is no surprise given his need); and as a result, in order to pursue that "need" and fulfill that "desire" Adam did whatever he thought was necessary to safeguard his relationship with Eve.

Once Eve had been created, Adam then, all of a sudden faced a second "relational motivation", one that had not been present before someone "comparable" to Adam had been created. Namely, Adam's desire to be loved and accepted by Eve.

Thus the potential for conflicting affections or loyalties arose upon Eve's creation and her presentation to Adam as his wife. Arguably, without Eve ever having been created, Adam would have walked with the voice of the LORD in the cool of the day, sinless, throughout eternity (Gen 3:8, KJV), and none of us would even be here to discuss it.

We know that there is no temptation to sin, unless there are options to choose from, either right or wrong. Now, I won't call it an *affair* ... but as you know, Eve had been carrying on a rather brief interpersonal relationship with the serpent before taking of the fruit and then offering it to Adam.

Since we have already covered the origins of the spirit of divination, it is very easy to conclude that "it" influenced Eve to: look, take and eat of the fruit herself. Then, as the spirit of control continued its agenda, "it" next employed, or used Eve, to offer the fruit to Adam.[25]

The very act of Eve's offer of the fruit to Adam, created a pressure inside of Adam to take and eat the fruit; or otherwise, risk displeasing his wife and possibly losing her love and affection. While at the same time, Adam no doubt also knew ("mens rea"), that if he chose this course of action, his decision was going to be displeasing and disobedient to God.

The *why* behind Adam's sin had nothing to do with any of those other factors that we've already addressed and readily eliminated. Rather, it had everything to do with his relationship with Eve and Adam's choice between the only

---

[25] "It" or "it" (seen in quotation marks) when used throughout the remainder of this text shall refer to the spirit of divination/control.

two relationships he had at that time, which one would he value over the other?

Would his relationship with God be valued over his relationship with Eve, or vice versa?

You already know the answer.

Before the creation of Eve, there had been no motivation for Adam to sin because he never had to choose between conflicting interests with regard to his interpersonal relationships: God's directive not to eat the fruit <u>vs.</u> Eve's offer to eat the fruit.

However, once Eve came on the scene, for the very first time ever, Adam was confronted head-on with the "opportunity" to either disobey the commandment of God; or risk the loss of harmonious domestic relations with his new wife.

In short, Adam sinned in order to please his wife, to be accepted by her, and in order to maintain her love and approval. Adam's underlying motive, or *why* he disobeyed

God, came from his desire to please man (or woman in this instance), over pleasing God.

Not only was it Adam's need and desire for Eve's love and acceptance that set the stage for sin to enter into the world; but more importantly, the universal cause, or the *"why"* underlying Adam's sin (which was to please his wife more than pleasing God); entered in as well.

Now, don't you dare get mad at Adam-- we do the same thing all the time! I repeat: *"more importantly, the universal cause or the "why" underlying Adam's sin (which was to please his wife more than pleasing God); entered in as well."*

This is the universal cause that underlies each and every sin committed thereafter in the history of man: **All sin is motivated by a desire to "please man" (in this first case, woman), or others, or yourself, <u>more than God</u>.**

Period.

And, therein lies the crux of the problem for all of us.

CHAPTER 9:
The Chink in Your Armor

We all have at least one inherent weakness in common with one another. It's what I refer to as the "chink in your armor" (the CIYA, for short). To have a "chink in your armor" means that you have a weakness that, in the event of an attack, the enemy can slither up into, get up under, gain access through and strike! If the chink is not "shored up" or sealed up, you my friend ... are *going down.*

You can liken the "chink in your armor" (CIYA) to a quarter that has two sides to it: "heads" and "tails". The quarter, though two sided, spends in only one amount (.25 cents); likewise, the CIYA, though two sided, leads only one way ... *down*.

Like the quarter, both sides of the CIYA look very similar. In fact, they're almost indistinguishable, except for their slightly differing depictions. The "heads" side of the CIYA is the character flaw of being a "man pleaser". The "tails" side of the CIYA is the character flaw of "fearing man". Both of these sides are rooted in the same aim; they spend or play out almost identically; but when on display, they just look a tad bit different from one another.

Being a "man pleaser" (or "heads") comes from our innate desire to be accepted, admired, noticed, valued, loved and respected by others. "Fearing man" (or "tails") is a force that causes our behavior to conform to the demands desires and dictates of other people based in our "fear" of losing their acceptance, admiration, respect, love and affection, if we don't.

The "heads" side of the coin, being a "man pleaser" is innate (you're born with it); while the "tails" side of the coin, the "fear of man" is a learned behavior that you can change. Anything "learned" can be "unlearned".

You can see, no doubt, how they both feed into and off of one another, don't you? Put very simply, you're born with the desire for love and approval, so you do whatever the person you want love and approval *from,* wants you to do

The Chink in Your Armor

... and that, out of your fear of losing their love and approval, if you *don't.* This is the two-fold weakness in your character, "the chink in your armor" (the CIYA).

So, allow me to now put this all together for you: First, take both the "heads" and the "tails" sides of the CIYA; and then, add in the number of circumstances going on in your life right now, those things *that you want to happen* and/or those things *that you do not want to happen.* Those things that pressure you into making a decision or taking an action; that cause you to continually feel uneasy or uncomfortable, unless and until you decide or act upon them.

Next, add in the influence of all the *controlling* people in your life. Those who counsel you, advise you, demand from you (whether directly or indirectly), those who outright just tell you what to do and/or how to respond to any given circumstance; and, then add in those people you love, respect and admire, all those "near and dear" relationships that you're afraid of losing.

Include two more ingredients to the mix-- the enemy's "motive" to control "you" and his "means" (wiles) of using the people in your life to do so. Now, blend all of these ingredients up with the numerous "opportunities" made available in and through your unlimited personal interactions with others, and then …

BAM! Shaaaaazaaaaam!

We have effectively combined all of the necessary ingredients for a nuclear bomb to go off in your life!

Indeed, these combined factors are possibly *the* most powerful authoritative influence currently leading and guiding the decisions you make for your life each and every day. Any one of them standing alone, in and of itself, is strong enough to govern your behavior. So just imagine the enormity of their influence when combined and working in unison to effect the outcome of your daily decision-making processes.

You've got *dynamite* … and there will be an explosion.

No, it won't necessarily sound or look like an explosion, but the joining together of all of these factors is sure to provide fertile ground for the spirit of control to govern and dictate nearly every decision and action you make in your life.

If I lost you here, the problem with all of this is that the Holy Spirit is supposed to be the One leading and guiding your life. He's the One who is supposed to be giving you wisdom on how to make decisions and giving you direction on what actions to take in response to the pressures and trials of life. This is especially true if you ever expect to live out God's plan and purpose for your life.

Just take a brief look into the lives of a modern-day *loving* couple and I promise, this will all come together for you in an instant.

WARNING! It's time to put your sunglasses on.

Say there is a husband who is a very gifted craftsman. He loves working with wood, especially creating top end made-to-order, designer furniture. The husband so loves this kind of work, that he would do it for the rest of his life, even if he never got paid a dime! The Lord directs the husband to quit his current job and go full-time into the designer furniture making business.

The Chink in Your Armor

Now, we're not going to quibble over *how* he heard from God, whether through reading His Word, or the hearing/teaching of His Word, through prayer, through His still small voice and/or through other circumstantial confirmation. Let's just give it to the husband that he *really* heard from God and this *really* is God's directive for his life.

So he runs home to see his wife-- he's just so excited! He can't wait to tell her what God *finally* said. I mean, this has been the desire of his heart for years and he had simply been waiting for God to give him the "green light".

So, once he receives the directive from above, the husband runs home, rushes through the door and says, "Honey! Honey! God told me to quit my job and start the business I've always wanted to start for the last 20 years! *Oh Lord!* Finally! I'm so excited!"

The wife, in response ... (a fake smile slowing lifting on her face), automatically goes into interrogation mode by saying:

"What?"

"He what?"

The Chink in Your Armor

What did He say?"

"*How* did He tell you?"

"*What scripture* were you reading?"

"*How do you know* that was *really* God?"

"What on earth are you talking about, *quit your job?"*

After the husband answers all of these questions with his exhilarating story of Divine communication, the wife responds: "I'm *not sure* you can apply that scripture to this situation, *dear.*" "You *know* you've been mistaken about these kinds of things *before.*"

Needless to say, with each passing inquiry and comment delivered by the wife, the excitement that the husband once had, has slowly dwindled down to nothing.

The wife, her "flesh" now noticeably stirred up, starts to get "practical" and talk about the economics of the whole situation, by saying things like: "You know, we don't have *any* money saved in the bank." "How will we be able to pay for the children's tuition?" "What will we do about our health insurance?" "Bobby needs braces." "This really doesn't seem like the *right time* to try something like this, *dear*."

Despite the wind being taken out of husband's sail, the wife at this point has actually behaved herself in a pretty "godly" and circumspect manner (as reflected by her choice of words). Look, there are other wives out there who would have instantly said: *"Boy*, you are trippin' today! You are *not* quitting your job! No way! Not in this lifetime!"

But now, what is the husband to do? Remember, he just received a directive from Almighty God Himself to quit his job.

First of all, we already know that because his wife did not immediately jump on board in support of the directive God gave to the husband, his balloon has already been burst; and just like with Adam's wife Eve, her continued love, affection and support have now become "at issue".

Second, the wife's comments and questioning of her husband about whether it was *really* God speaking to him or not; and how economically, they're not going to make it if he does this; and by her reminding him that he has been mistaken about what "God said" in the past, has sent the husband into a tail spin of self-doubt.

He is now doubting his relationship with God; doubting that he really heard from God; doubting that it *is* the right time to do this kind of thing; doubting that God is really leading him; doubting that he will be successful; and worrying about this move being detrimental to himself and his family instead of it being a "blessing from above" as he first believed.

As to the faith he previously had working in his life to actually walk out of his long-term job and start a new business?

Ha!

That's now, long gone.

Do you see it? The spirit of control being used in and through his wife to bring all these doubts and hopefully cause the husband <u>not</u> to obey the directive of God; and instead, just "play it safe" for the rest of his life in his "secure" long-term job.[26]

So the husband is now faced with having to engage in all this "stronghold thinking" (to be discussed in detail later); as he battles within himself in order to make the ultimate decision: "Do I obey what God said? Or, do I play it financially 'safe', keep harmony in the home, affections in the bedroom and my children in private school?"

Sure enough as a Christian couple, the husband has the right to lead the family and the wife should submit and support this decision. But the reality is that very few husbands, men-of-God-kind-of husbands, will take this kind of dramatic step of faith without their wife being on board. In fact, most Christian marriage seminars teach couples *not* to take actions like this, unless and until, they are both in agreement.

All of a sudden, in the face of this *controlling* opposition, instead of feeling good and excited like he did at first, it

---

[26] The "security" of which, is really nothing but a fallacy.

now feels extremely risky to do what God wants him to do. After this brief conversation with his wife, the husband is now experiencing an enormous demand on his faith.

Not only does he need faith for the initial move of quitting his job and starting up the new business; but now, since he's got additional resistance from the wife (via the spirit of divination), he also needs even more faith to proceed than he would have otherwise, had she been in agreement.

Moreover, that negative *controlling* spirit will eventually emanate throughout the whole entire family, using each and every family member to try and undermine every step that the husband tries to take in obedience to the Lord's directive.

This husband has been a loyal and hard worker for over twenty years and this was but a portion of the plan that God had to use his life in this trade. It was the Lord's intention to bless and provide for the family, far and beyond what husband's meager little long-term job had been providing.

Yet, the spirit of control/divination won out and as to the opportunity? Well … the husband missed it! His wife's desires, directives, and doubts, controlled his ultimate decision. The husband never got to the place where God wanted to bless and prosper him, running his own business, doing what he loved to do the most.

Note also: this wife, who is an otherwise godly woman, has absolutely no clue that the spirit of divination has been working through her to keep her husband off course with God's plan for his life. She was just being *reasonable* and *rational* with the points she contributed to this "discussion", all of which were purportedly "in the best interests" of the entire family.

Yet, as a result of this negative response of the wife, the husband disregarded all that God had shown and directed him to do. What's worse is that the husband may then go on to use Scripture about "loving" his wife and maintaining "unity" in the home, in support of his decision to *abort the Lord's directive in its entirety.*

Wow! How deceptive is that? Subtle, crafty, clandestine, covert ... hmmm, remind you of anyone, or better yet, anything?

The Chink in Your Armor

Yes, I'm describing the serpent. And yes, the lights are growing brighter. We've just pulled back a bit more of that third layer of skin covering the jugular: "opportunity".

This is just one common day example of how the spirit of divination works within the confines of just one husband/wife relationship (or "opportunity"). "It" literally put a stop to the plan of God. The same forces were at work in the Garden with Adam and Eve. When you think about it, the commonalities are striking.

Now, think about how many relationships you have and imagine all the possible ways in which each person who speaks into your life has influenced you to do things anti-to Christ, or against what God really wanted you to do.

Why did you allow this to happen? *Why* did you allow their statements, opinions, or demands to "re-direct" your path instead of doing what God was telling you to do?

It's the CIYA!

So now that you have the general idea, let's delve deeper into each side of the CIYA. Your continued education will lead to further revelation of "its" application; and later, will help you to achieve "its" total and complete annihilation from your life.

CHAPTER 10: "HEADS"
You're a Man Pleaser

From the time we come forth out of our mother's womb until the time we die, we as humans, forever seek to belong, to be accepted, admired, noticed, valued, loved, and respected.

This desire is innate. Psychologists who study human behavior have echoed this sentiment from the very beginning of the "science" of psychology. From Freud's mama, to Maslow's hierarchy ... I'm not even going to bother with any citations on this concept, just go pull out a Psychology 101 textbook and read it for yourself-- or better yet, take a look at yourself.

Now, I'm not here to teach a lesson in psychology; besides, if you haven't already acknowledged the existence of these traits in your own psyche, then you're living a life of gross self-deception. If that's the case, you might as well drop this text right now because it's not going to help you.

To be accepted, admired, noticed, valued and loved is first seen in a young child's cry of: "Mommy! Daddy! Look! Look!" From going up their bunk bed ladder, to later in life, climbing the corporate ladder (where employees seek to be acknowledged and promoted for their contributions to the company), everybody wants to be noticed, loved, appreciated and admired.

Furthermore, starting in our first relationships with our parents or our earliest caregivers, we all learned that if we did what they wanted us to do, we obtained and maintained their approval, love, and affection. If we didn't? We got the belt!

As you grew up and matured, the same concepts applied, but the situations also matured and differed. Take a look at some everyday examples of people doing things in order to please others:

It's a mother-in-law who, whenever on the scene of "opportunity", you essentially allow to run your life. While determined to obtain or maintain her acceptance, everything you do is dictated by her input. Even after your latest interaction is long over, you just can't get her voice out of your head! As you continue to replay the communications you had during her most recent visit, your thoughts, heart and emotions are consumed for days, or months thereafter.

It's the boss who signs your paycheck, who tells you to do something in the workplace like lie, or "misrepresent" the facts, or do something else you know is in contradiction to the Word of God. If you don't comply, you'll risk losing your job and as a result, that *control* factor causes you to compromise.

It's a husband that you know is no longer in love with you, but who you keep striving and striving to please. You allow him to *control* you, from the clothes you wear, to your nail polish color, to the way you clean the house, to what you say and how you act in front of others. You've become a *controlled* robot, all in an attempt to re-gain his love, approval and affection.

It's a group or organization that you or your children belong to, where you want to be well thought of and held in high esteem. So you allow your behavior to be *controlled* by the expectations, comments, and requests of the other group members. As a result, you may always take on the responsibility of buying the coffee, bringing the snacks, buying the uniforms, taking the group out for pizza after the game, or whatever it may be. Even though you really cannot afford to spend that kind of time or money, you keep on doing these things just so they will all continue to praise and think highly of you.

It's the leadership at your church who place demands of service on your life, while at the same time saying things like, "Your *the only one* who really knows how to do this." "I know I can always count on you." "You're such a blessing!" As a result, your once pure–hearted service to the Lord becomes tainted with a type of *bondage to the next compliment*, as you continue to pursue pleasing those in authority, instead of pleasing God.

Everyone on the face of the earth wants to be liked, loved, honored, respected, complimented, well thought of, well spoken of, and dare I say ... *adored,* while living in harmony with the people they come in contact with everyday. Yes, that's the "ideal", but as you also know, it's obviously *not* the "reality".

While on its face, this drive or desire does not *appear* as if anything is necessarily *wrong* with it; after all, God wants us to live at *peace* (Ro 12:18) and in *unity* with others (Eph 4:3), *right?*

Right. <u>But</u> only, "*as far be it with you…*"(Ro 12:18, KJV); or "*if it is possible…*" (NKJV); or "*as far as it is possible …*" (BBE); or "*as much as it is possible…*" (GWT).

So there is a limitation to the concept. It is absolutely "<u>not</u> possible" to *always* live in unity and harmony with others who are being used by the spirit of divination to thwart God's plan for your life. We are not to compromise doing what God or His Word says, or what the Holy Spirit directs us to do, just to get along with, be accepted by, respected by, loved by, and/or to maintain peace with, other people.

"Think not that I am come in to send peace on earth: I came not to send peace, but a sword. For I am come to set a man at variance against his father, and the daughter

against her mother, and the daughter in law against her mother in law. And a man's foes shall be they of his own household" (Matt 10:35-36, KJV).

Therefore, the "heads" side of the CIYA, which is that drive or desire we all have by nature, to be "people pleasers" or "man pleasers", can actually function in opposition to the leading of the Holy Spirit. To some degree or another this "heads" desire causes all of us to make decisions based on our relationships with other people, to the exclusion of our relationship with God. It's exactly what Adam did when he chose to value his relationship with Eve, over his relationship with God.

Furthermore, the level of this drive/desire varies dependent upon *who* it is you are in a relationship with. If it's someone you love, like a spouse, parent, child, or sibling, you may have a greater drive/desire to choose "heads", than if it's someone you've come across for the first time in line at the grocery store, where the desire would be much less.

Here are a few translations of Paul's writing on the "heads" side of the CIYA for you to consider:

"HEADS" You're a Man Pleaser

"For do I now persuade men, or God? Or, do I seek to please men? For if I yet pleased men, I should not be the servant of Christ" (Gal 1:10, KJV).

"Do you think I am trying to make people accept me? No, God is the One I am trying to please. Am I trying to please people? If I still wanted to please people, I would not be a servant of Christ" (Gal 1:10, NCV).

"Obviously, I'm not trying to be a people pleaser! No, I am trying to please God. If I were still trying to please people, I would not be Christ's servant" (Gal 1:10, NLT).

"Now does that sound as if I were trying to win human approval? No! I want God's approval! Or, that I'm trying to cater to people? If I were still doing that, I would not be a servant of the Messiah" (Gal 1:10, CJB).

"Does this sound as if I am trying to win human approval? No indeed! What I want is God's approval! Am I trying to be popular with people? If I were still trying to do so, I would not be a servant of Christ" (Gal 1:10, GNT).

"HEADS" You're a Man Pleaser

"For is it man's favour or God's that I aspire to? Or am I seeking to please men? If I were still a man-pleaser, I should not be Christ's bondservant" (Gal 1:10, WNT).

The word "persuade" in the Greek means, in part: *to make friends of, to win one's favor, gain one's good will, or to seek to win one, strive to please one; to tranquillize ... or be persuaded of a thing concerning a person; to listen to, obey, yield to, comply with; to trust, have confidence, be confident.*[27]

The word "please" in the Greek means, in part: *to strive to please, to accommodate one's self to the opinions desires and interests of others.*[28]

WOW! There it is, every aspect of the "heads" side of the CIYA. *What's more* ... in the Greek!

As noted above, this desire to "please man" first presented itself in the Garden and has continued throughout the history of man. This desire to *"win one's favor, gain one's good will, and strive to please"* causes us to, *"to listen to,*

---

[27] Strong's Concordance #3982, transliterated "Peitho".
[28] Strong's Concordance #700, transliterated "Aresko".

obey, yield to and comply with" <u>man's</u> directives, demands, requests, or wishes for our lives; and sometimes, even when they are in direct contradiction to the Lord's.

The "heads" side of the CIYA is therefore a very powerful driving force that we all must contend with. Indeed, the power of the "heads" side of the CIYA can actually change a person's life for eternity. Take a look at a couple of Biblical examples:

"Heads" was the force behind Pilate turning Jesus over to be crucified, even after admittedly, failing to find Him guilty of anything deserving of death: *"Pilate answered and said to them again, "What then do you want me to do with Him whom you call the King of the Jews?" So they cried out again, "Crucify Him!" Then Pilate said to them, "Why, what evil has He done?" But they cried out all the more, "Crucify Him!" So Pilate,* **wanting to gratify the crowd,** *released Barabbas to them; and he delivered Jesus, after he had scourged Him, to be crucified"* (Mark 15:12-15, KJV).[29]

---

[29] We know that Jesus' crucifixion was God's plan for His life and that no man took Jesus' life, but rather, He willingly laid it down (Jn 10:18). The point being made, is that *the reason* behind Pilate's decision to turn Jesus over to be crucified, was based on his desire to "gratify the crowd" or be a "man pleaser".

"HEADS" You're a Man Pleaser

In John 12:42-43, we see that even though many of the chief rulers believed on Jesus, they were afraid to confess that belief to others because, "**they loved the praise of men** more than the praise of God" (KJV).

In this passage the chief rulers *believed* on Jesus, but never *confessed* or readily admitted that belief. In Romans 10:9 it says: *If thou shalt **confess** with thy mouth the Lord Jesus, and shalt believe in thine heart that God hath raised him from the dead, thou shalt be saved* (KJV).

No confession? No salvation. "Pleasing man" or seeking to be accepted or well thought of by man, is a force so strong that it can actually *control* a person's ultimate destiny and that, for eternity. Now that should be pretty scary for some people!

There are those who may say, "If God created us to be 'man pleasers' then what's wrong with it? Why do you call it a weakness? If God created us that way, wasn't it for our own good?"

Yes, it is wonderful to experience being loved and connected interpersonally with other people. Good interpersonal relationships are actually what make the world go round. However, if "pleasing man" becomes your first priority and your foremost desire or motivation in life, you can easily be *taken advantage of* by others operating via the spirit of divination, to do things outside of the will of God.

This innate need must therefore be monitored and brought into subjection just like anything else of "the flesh" so that it is not exploited and taken advantage of by the enemy.

Take another look at 2 Corinthians 2:11, where it says: *"lest Satan should **take advantage of us***; *for we are not ignorant of his devices"* (NKJV).

Lest Satan should *take advantage* ... take advantage ... *Take Advantage* ... TAKE ADVANTAGE ... *of us*.

In the Greek, to "take advantage" means: *"to seek to get more" "to get an advantage of" "to take advantage of" "to make gain of" or "to outwit"*.[30]

---

[30] Strong's Concordance #4122, transliterated as "Pleonekteo".

"HEADS" You're a Man Pleaser

When someone takes advantage of another, they usually intentionally play on a particular weakness of that other person. Due to that weakness, the manipulator then gets more out of them, more easily, than they would have otherwise, had there been no weakness in operation.

We cannot allow a God-given trait-- wanting to be loved, admired, valued and connected with other human beings to be exploited or *taken advantage of* by the enemy. This would allow him to fallaciously satisfy that innate "heads" desire with nothing but <u>counterfeit</u> offers, options and opportunities.

At the end of the day, whenever there is a conflict with God's desired behavior and man's desired behavior for your life, and you choose to "please man" over God, this is undeniable substantiation that you have a very serious chink in the "heads" side of your armor (CIYA).

So choose "heads"? You lose.

CHAPTER 11: "TAILS"
Your Fear of Man

■■■■■■■■■■■■■■■■■■■■■■■■■■■■■■■■■■■■■■■

Looking at the "tails" side of the CIYA coin, we next address your "fear of man". Unlike the "heads" side, the "fear of man" is something that is not innate; rather, it is a "learned" behavior. You should first know up front that anything that has been "learned" can also be "unlearned". So prepare yourself for some serious training, soldier.

Inherently at work on the "tails" side of the CIYA is yet another spirit, one that needs little introduction. It's *the spirit of fear* indelibly engraved in our lives through learning and experience. The "tails" side of the CIYA is considered a character weakness for a Christian because "fear" and "cowardice" are the opposite of "faith" and "courage".

The "fear of man" is somewhat akin to the concept of "peer pressure" which is mentioned mostly in relation to adolescent behavior. It's what psychology *says* causes them to try drugs and sex, to commit crime, and carry on other sinful behaviors. Yet, if the truth were told, "peer pressure" is alive and well today, operating in our adult population disguising itself as the "fear of man". Strike that! Alive and well working in our adult, *"mature" "Christian"* population today, *camouflaging* itself as the "fear of man".

It's true! We adults are just too embarrassed to admit it, or too unlearned to see it. This is why I am intent on ripping the skin off and exposing "the jugular" for the kill.

The *spirit of control* and the *spirit of fear* are like first cousins. When they get together they have lots of fun tearin' it up! Harmonizing and working in unison, they will win the battle over your decision-making processes nearly every single time. Whenever the spirit of control seeks to govern your conduct in a man-dictated direction, the spirit of fear via the *fear of man* cheerfully jumps in to help close the deal.

One perfect example of this concept is at court hearings, especially family law trials and more specifically, the one I just got out of today. I had been mentoring the attorney for the wife's side of a case and I came to court to try to help settle at least some issues with opposing counsel before trial began. During this time of settlement negotiations, the attorney for the husband made several varying "threat of loss at trial" scenarios during our discussions. These were nothing more than reasonable sounding "fear tactics" meant to try to strong-arm the wife into agreeing with the husband's settlement terms. The husband's attorney spent the entire time threatening *in an attempt to control* the wife, threatening to control, *threatening to control.*

Let me tell you, once you get a hold of what you're reading right now, "Control Freaks" will become so easily identifiable, instead of ever being threatened again, you'll just laugh at "it". It'll be hard not to.

Another example, if you think back for a minute, was our designer-furniture making husband. As you recall, most of the wife's negative comments were based on her fears.

When the spirit of control latches onto our fears, it can eventually rule, reign and govern each and every one of our decisions, as well as our related actions. That is, if we don't consciously do something about it.

"TAILS" Your Fear of Man

There are several Biblical examples of people modifying their behavior (or being *controlled*) as a result of these two CIYA kissin' cousins working in conjunction with one another. We're first going to take a look at the lives of a couple of well known kings; and then work our way through the religious leaders, the commoner, other very notable men and women of God and within a few chapters, we'll eventually be getting to you.

Let's get started with King Herod. Though he liked John the Baptist, he imprisoned him for his *brother's wife Herodias' sake* (with whom, by the way, he was having an adulterous affair; Matt 14:3). John had pointed out this sin to the king, and the mistress was apparently concerned that if she didn't get rid of John, his negative perspective would place her ongoing "fling" at risk.

So at first we see King Herod taking action to imprison John the Baptist for no legitimate reason, other than in an attempt to keep his mistress blissful, and there you have it! The CIYA "heads" side of the coin. King Herod, taking after Adam: the "woman-pleaser".

"TAILS" Your Fear of Man

However, while initially intending to have John killed, Herod failed to do so because *"he feared the multitude"* (v. 5), and there you have it again! The CIYA "tails" side of the coin, seen in King Herod's "fear of man".

So while the mistress' approval was important to the king, it did not rise to a level above the "fear of man" he experienced when contemplating what the *multitudes* would think of him if he killed John. So Herod decides <u>not</u> to kill John … at least not *yet* (v. 5).

It wasn't until after delivering his lust-filled promise to Herodias' dancing daughter and her request for the head of John the Baptist on a platter, that Herod does a reverse back flip. He sorrowfully complies with her request and has John beheaded. Why? *"… Because of his oath and because he didn't want to back down in front of his guests, he issued the necessary orders"* (v. 9, NLT).

Wow! Talk about a double-minded man being tossed to and fro! In this story, we see that the CIYA levels operating in King Herod made him virtually, DSM IV diagnosable.

"TAILS" Your Fear of Man

Since it is theorized that Herod personally liked John, we notice that the CIYA caused him to go against his own personal preference of preserving John's life, by instead ultimately having him beheaded. Herod's CIYA concern about his "reputation" (as it related to the opinions of those noble men and leaders sitting with him at dinner) won out at the end of the day, above his own preference and above that of the multitudes.

From these facts we can derive a few principles as they relate to the degree and probability of someone making decisions based on the "tails" side of the CIYA: the "fear of man".

First, we can postulate that pleasing someone that "does something for you" (Herodias in this instance), can and will cause you to set aside your own personal preferences, in order to stay in their good graces.

Second, the perspective of the *multitudes* creates a higher probability that the "fear of man" will cause your conduct to side with the multitudes, even when it conflicts with the desired action of a significant other (Herodias). Or, put another way, the "fear of man" most often operates on the side of "the majority".

Third, the higher the "man" is (or men are) in status and/or prestige, the more likely the "fear of man" (or men) will prevail on the side of status/prestige, even if the opposition is greater in number. Or, put another way, even if the group is smaller in number, its members' status or prestige can overcome greater multitudes of "commoners" comprising a much larger group.

Here's another "kingly" example: In 1 Samuel 15, after King Saul rebelled against the directive of the Lord, the prophet Samuel confronted him and declared it was all over, the Lord had taken the kingdom away from him (v. 26). In response to the loss of everything, we see Saul's primary concern was not with getting right with God; it wasn't even with trying to keep all that he had obtained, possession-wise, in his kingdom; but rather, it was with attempting to positively "manage" the views of the people after his public rebuke and demotion by the prophet.

After Saul's acknowledgement *in passing* that, *"I have sinned",* by his second breath, he went on to grovel to the prophet: *"Yet honor me now, please, before the elders of my people and before Israel, and return with me, that I may worship the Lord your God"* (v. 30, KJV).

Saul's main concern was "the fear of man" or how he "looked" before the people; especially after the rebuke-filled interaction they had all no doubt, just witnessed. So he wanted Samuel to "cover" for him by showing him honor, as demonstrated by Samuel walking beside Saul yet again, before all the people.

Now, look closely at this: in his rebellious-- witchcraft practicing-- spirit of divination-driven-- *controlling* state, Saul used the "religious pretense" of worshiping "the Lord your God" (Samuel's God, not Saul's God), to control Samuel's conduct.

Saul no doubt knew, that he could *take advantage of* Samuel by using "religious pretenses" to *control* his behavior. This control was exercised by Saul so that he could try to "save face" by presenting a counterfeit unity to the people. Walking "together" in front of the people implied that Saul, despite the public rebuke, still held his usual place of honor.

"TAILS" Your Fear of Man

Now look: if the spirit of control worked on the Prophet Samuel, it has and will-- continue to work on you.

In Matthew chapter 21, Jesus was in the temple when the chief priests and the elders of the people questioned Jesus' authority (v. 23). Instead of answering them directly, Jesus turned the tables and asked them a question, *"'I'll tell you who gave me the authority to do these things if you answer one question', Jesus replied. 'Did John's baptism come from heaven or was it merely human?'"* (v. 25, NLT).

This was really a fairly simple question. It wasn't even multiple choice, just "true" or "false". Pick one side or the other: Was John sent from heaven, or from earth? Was his work of baptism a work of God, or not? *Rudimentary* … no?

Had the religious leaders co-signed with the baptism of John, they would have had to co-sign with Jesus. If they refuted John, the people watching this discourse would have disapproved of them.

The Bible says these religious leaders, standing in ostensible authority, *attempted* to reason through some kind of response to Jesus' question, but in the end answered, *"We cannot tell"* (v. 27) due to their *"fear of the people; for all hold John as a prophet"* (v. 26).

In John chapter 7, the Jews were seeking to kill Jesus because they just couldn't handle all the attention He was receiving. However, the people themselves were divided: Some said He was "good", while others said he was a "deceiver" (v.12). As a result, the Bible says, *"But no one had the courage to speak favorably about Him in public, for they were afraid of getting in trouble with the Jewish leaders"* (v. 13, NLT).

After Jesus cast out the moneychangers and started teaching daily in the temple, the chief priests and other leaders wanted to destroy Him. Yet, they didn't even try because they were afraid of how the people would respond (Lu 19:45-48).

Theologians say Nicodemus came "by night" to ask questions of Jesus, undoubtedly so that he would not be seen of the people (Jn 3:2, KJV); and when Joseph of Arimathaea sought the body of Jesus he did so "secretly" for fear of the Jews (Jn 19:38, KJV).

"TAILS" Your Fear of Man

Several other Biblical characters, even some members of the Hall of Faith (Heb 11), had the CIYA weakness of "fearing man" in one context or another. Interesting to note, is the fact that this most often occurred when the Lord had given them some great extraordinary, faith-driven, destiny pursuing directive, or assignment to carry out for the Kingdom:

Abraham: Feared man lying twice about his good looking wife Sara, saying she was his sister (Gen 12:11-12 & 20:2);

Isaac: Just like his father Abraham, had a good-looking wife, and just like his father did with Sara, he lied about Rebecca, saying she was his sister also (Gen 26:6-11);

Jacob: Was afraid of facing his brother Esau after stealing his birthright and his blessing (Gen 27:36 & 32:11);

Moses: Was afraid that he would be killed on the spot if he requested an audience with the king of Egypt; so he initially made excuses in an attempt to get out of his assignment of delivering the children of Israel out of the hands of Pharaoh (Ex 4:1 &10);

Shammua, Shaphat, Igal, Oshea, Palti, Gaddiel, Ammiel, Sethur, Nahbi, Geuel (better known as, the "Ten Spies"): Were afraid of the giants in the Promised Land and because they allowed themselves to be controlled by the spirit of fear, they, and millions of others never entered in and fulfilled their God-given destinies (Nu 14:4-15, 32-33);

Joshua: Initially feared when confronted by a conspiracy of five enemy kings and their valiant forces (Josh 10:8);

Queen Esther: Initially feared the risk of being put to death by the king upon entering his court; but to her credit she overcame her fear (Est 4:11);

King David: Ran away from King Saul for fear of his life (1 Sam 21:10); and later abandoned his kingdom and all that he had, based solely on the report of his son Absalom's treason (2 Sam 15:14);

King Solomon: When anointed and appointed king, because of his youth, feared the responsibilities of the position of authority he had been given governing over man (1 Kings 3:7-9), until he was reassured by his father to "fear not" (1 Chron 28:20);

Elijah: Despite the mighty work of God seen on Mount Carmel and despite slaughtering over eight hundred prophets, of Baal and of the groves, felt so threatened by Jezebel that he ran off in fear. In fact, it got so bad for Elijah that at one point in time, he just wanted to die (1 King 19:2-3 & 10);

Gideon: While in hiding from the Midianites threshing wheat (Judges 6:11), destroyed his father's altar to Baal, at night, for fear of his father and the men of the city (Judges 6:25, 27); and then before using him to deliver the children of Israel from the enemy, the Lord seriously downsized the number of men in his army, eliminating those who were fearful or afraid (Judge 7:3);

Jeremiah: Was told by the Lord, *"Be not afraid of their faces: for I am with thee to deliver thee, saith the LORD"* (Jer 1:8, KJV);

Eziekiel: Was told by the Lord, *"...be not afraid of them, neither be afraid of their words...nor be dismayed at their looks"* (Ez 2:6, KJV); and

"TAILS" Your Fear of Man

<u>Isaiah</u>: Admonished, "... *fear ye not the reproach of men, neither be ye afraid of their revilings*" (Is 51:7, KJV).

This same theme is prevalent in the New Testament, starting with <u>Joseph:</u> who was afraid of what the people would think if he took Mary the mother of Jesus for his wife, knowing she had become pregnant out of wedlock (Matt 1:20).

In future chapters, we will see other examples throughout the gospels where people made decisions based on their "fear of man" or what they anticipated others would think of them, rather than the inherent right or wrong of the decision to be made; and without any consideration of the Lord's perspective or position on the matter.

Please understand that it's not just that "faith" and "fear" cannot comfortably co-exist. Rather, it's that "fear" is the antithesis of "faith". There is the Spirit of faith (2 Cor 4:13); and there is a spirit of fear (2 Tim 1:7). And yes! There it is again, yet another anti-to Christ, alive and working in our midst.

140   *"CONTROL FREAK"*

"TAILS" Your Fear of Man

The Bible says: *For God hath **not given us the spirit of fear**; but of power, and of love, and of a sound mind* (2 Tim 1:7, KJV).

*For ye have **not received the spirit of bondage again to fear**; but ye have received the Spirit of Adoption whereby we cry, Abba Father* (Ro 8:15, KJV).

*God is love…There is no fear in love; but **perfect love casteth out fear; because fear hath torment**. He that feareth is not made perfect in love* (1 Jn 4:16-17, KJV).

Ain't that the truth? *"Fear has torment"*.

How many times have you been tormented by your fears? How many times have you been tormented by your fears as they relate to future events in your life? How many times have you been tormented by the fear of loss of a relationship? The fear of what someone would think of you if you did this or that? How many times have your fears caused you to do crazy things and stay in crazy situations?

"TAILS" Your Fear of Man

Operating your life under the "spirit of fear" means torment and emotional bondage. This torment or bondage is seen in four primary areas of our lives:

1. FEAR OF LOSS of people/relationships; and/or status, position, or success;
2. FEAR OF LOSS of possessions/material wealth;
3. FEAR OF LOSS of good health, or physical safety for both yourself and your loved ones; and the
4. FEAR OF LACK of provision/employment/business opportunities, future income or financial security.

When you're operating or making decisions based on fear you are not perfected or matured in God's love. As a result, you may allow yourself to be *controlled* by an individual who is exercising the spirit of divination over your life by playing off of, or *taking advantage of*, your CIYA "tails" weakness.

If the enemy can get you to function out of fear, that's exactly where he wants you. It's not just that you start doing really stupid things like sinning; but more importantly, it's that you don't end up taking those actions of "faith" the Lord would have you take in response to any of the issues listed above. When operating out of the "spirit of fear" you are unable to respond to adverse circumstances "in faith" because you're too caught up, too bound up, and too tied up, in fear. You will never have any victories if you remain in that condition.

Here are a few examples of how "opportunity" afforded to the "fear of man" can *control* a person's conduct:

It's the fear of losing a position in ministry, such as sitting as a board member on a non-profit corporation. And as a result, you're afraid to stand up to the Chairman of the Board who is doing something contrary to the Word of God even though you are accountable to the Lord and it's your duty as a Board member to do so.

It's those family members and friends who always have unsolicited advice for you. Despite the fact that you see absolutely no fruit in their lives, you're still afraid of what they'll say about you if you don't carry out their directives.

It's the angry spouse that uses outbursts of wrath to control you by making you fear or cower in his/her presence. All the while, you never once realize that when you respond by compliance to their fear tactics, you only embolden them to use that same fury against you in the future.

It's deciding to lie on a job application in order to save your house because you're being threatened with foreclosure and you fear becoming homeless.

It's allowing anyone to threaten you in *any* manner that causes you to fear; and as a result, forces you to conform your behavior to their demands, no matter what they are.

You can be sure that whatever you do when acting out of fear, will be anti-to Christ, or the opposite of what God wants you to do. In those cases it's the spirit of control that's pushing the envelope in your life, playing on the CIYA and wrecking havoc with its kissin' cousin.

So don't be deceived!

You must realize that "fear" in any form or fashion is straight from the pit! Making decisions based on your fears is straight from the pit! Allowing the "fear of man" to cause you to do what someone else threatens or demands that you do ... *or else* ... is straight from the pit!

"TAILS" Your Fear of Man

Honestly consider these questions:

1. Do you act in ways you know *another person* wants you to act, in order to try and keep them happy and/or for fear of getting them mad?

2. While in the process of making decisions about your own life, does your consideration what other people would/could possibly think, frequently determine the outcome?

3. Are you more concerned about what others think, feel, and/or may say about you, than what the Lord thinks, feels, and says about you?

Throughout the Bible it says we are supposed to "fear God" not man. The word "fear" generally means to *"reverence, venerate, to treat with deference or reverential obedience"* (1 Pe 2:17, KJV).[31]

God has given countless admonitions, in countless situations for His people <u>not</u> to "fear man": *The fear of man bringeth a snare* (Prv 29:25, KJV); *The LORD is on my side; I will not fear: what can man do unto me?* (Ps 118:6, KJV); *The Lord is my helper, and I will not fear what man*

---

[31] Strong's #5399, transliterated "Phobeo".

shall do unto me (Heb 13:6, KJV); *Fear not them which kill the body, but are not able to kill the soul: but rather fear Him which is able to destroy both soul and body in hell* (Matt 10:28, KJV). [See also: Deut 1:17, 1:29, 7:18, 18:22, 20:1, 31:6; Josh 1:9, 11:6; Prv 3:24-25; Is 31:4, 37:6, 51:7; Zeph 3:13; 1 Pe 3:14.]

It's a weakness in your character if you continue to allow your life to be governed by the "fear of man" because as Christians:

1. We walk by faith (2 Cor 5:7);
2. We live by faith (Hab 2:4; Ro 1:17; Gal 3:11);
3. Without faith it is impossible to please Him (Heb 11:6);
4. The only reason we obey Him in the first place (if you think about it), is *because* of our faith; and
5. With more faith demonstrated in our lives, it would mean less sin, more vision, more divine communication and more manifestation of the power of God in order to fulfill our God-given destinies.

To "walk" by faith encompasses every decision you make and every plan of action you execute towards fulfilling your destiny in life. To "live" by faith means everything you experience in life is filtered through the eyes of faith and not just your natural perception. Joined together, walking and living by faith covers every aspect of your life, encompassing the present experientially, as well as the future, determinatively.

In fact, when we waver between walking in faith and walking in fear or doubt, the Bible says we should *not expect to receive anything from the Lord* as we remain in that feeble condition (Ja 1:6-7, NLT).

Wow! Now that's scary, too.

We all know from personal experience that fear is debilitating, immobilizing, and stressful. We know it is hard to think straight, let alone function, when fearful. As a result of being afraid, many people stay paralyzed and never move forward to do anything with their lives; especially not any "venture of faith", even when it's the Lord who is clearly directing the move.

The spirit of control would like nothing more than for you to base your greatest life decisions, on your fears; or, in an attempt to avoid, or pacify your fears. When you allow another person's opinions, desires, directives, or demands to dictate your conduct and you do things out of the fear of not pleasing and/or getting along with them, you have now lifted your relationship with that person, above your relationship with God. You have effectively set them up as little gods or idols on the throne of your heart and pushed God to the side.

In short ... you've pulled an Adam.

Since we know fear is not from God, we have to decide whether or not we are going to allow ourselves to give-in to fear, when making various decisions in our lives. The Lord wants you walking in faith; the spirit of divination wants you walking in fear. Now that you know what side the enemy operates on, as opposed to what side the Lord is on, it's time for you to take your position.

Whose side are you on?

Living and walking by faith is a mandatory prerequisite for you to fulfill the plan of God for your life. Allowing yourself

"TAILS" Your Fear of Man

to remain in bondage to fear and "the fear of man" assures that you will never make it there.

And so it was for Adam. He knew better, but the CIYA-- that desire to "please man", or woman in his case (the "heads"); <u>and</u> his fear of losing Eve's love and affection if he didn't eat of the fruit (the "tails"), overcame his desire to please God and follow His directive. That's *why* he fell.

So, choose "tails"? You lose also.

"CONTROL FREAK"

CHAPTER 12: An "Emotional Link" Ups the Game

We've described how the spirit of control works in our interpersonal relationships, but we also know that not every interpersonal relationship we have is exactly the same type or quality. We have love relationships. We have people we like. We have people in authority over us whom we respect. We have good neighborly relationships. We have people we would never *choose* to hang out with, but for varying reasons, we must at least try to get along with them.

Not just *anyone* can control you in *every* situation. Think about how many times you've run into a pushy salesman. Someone who wanted to *control* your behavior to the point of buying a vacuum cleaner, a car, a long distance calling plan; yet, you didn't allow yourself to be *controlled* into the sale. You simply said, "Nah, man, I don't need a vacuum" and walked away.

Yet on the other hand, at any given point of weakness, the spirit of control can work through, say, a make-up salesperson at Nordstrom's. This someone you've never even met before. Yet, this is someone who somehow was able to cause you to buy more of the frills that you really didn't need, with more of the money that you really shouldn't have spent.

What you should know is that the spirit of control has far more chances of continuing success when you have some kind of "emotional link" with the person, whom via the spirit of divination, is trying to control your behavior. An "emotional link" is usually present in love relationships, familial relationships, with people whom you have an emotional bond, a "soul tie", or even a love/hate relationship.

"Emotional links" are also found in relationships with people whom you respect or admire, those who have authority over you, experts in certain fields or areas that you work in, or any other person(s) who you may hold in high regard.

An "Emotional Link" Ups the Game

Even people you utterly despise may harness an "emotional link" that can facilitate *control* over your behavior.

Due to the CIYA, you generally seek to "please" and prefer people with whom you have an "emotional link" ("heads"); for *fear* you may lose them if they no longer approve of you, or remain a part of your life ("tails"). An "emotional link" causes you to be even more susceptible to the requests, demands, directives or *control* of these kinds of people. It causes you to more readily comply with the spirit of divination influencing their conduct, of trying to *control* yours.

Assuming you're not an ongoing emotional nightmare standing alone all by yourself, you can usually tell when there is an "emotional link" that you have with someone else in your life. If another person can elicit an emotional response out of you by their words or actions (whether good or bad), then an "emotional link" is likely present.

In other words, if you have people in your life who are able to "push your button(s)" and utterly ruin your entire day by something they did or said, then an "emotional link" is clearly present. If there is someone who can be so nice to you one minute, that you feel like you're in seventh heaven; and then be so mean to you the next, that you're all of a sudden down in the dumps, hopeless and depressed, then an "emotional link" is clearly present.

If someone else's perspective, thoughts, feelings, ideas or proposed directives for your life are automatically adopted by you and "owned" to the point that they become yours to unquestionably carry out, then an "emotional link" is clearly present.

Here are some "ends of the spectrum" examples to make certain the "emotional link" concept is clear: We don't care what the bum on the street thinks of seeing us drop a piece of trash, as much as we care about our spouse getting mad at us if we don't pick up our socks. We care more about our co-worker's opinion of what we're wearing, than the grocery store clerk's opinion. We do things to be respected by our supervisor, more than the trash collector. We want to be loved by our children and family members, more than our nosy obnoxious neighbor. Got the idea?

An "Emotional Link" Ups the Game

So when I say an emotional link "ups the game", it's the same as saying, "ups the ante". When you really love someone, or are extremely emotionally attached to them, or have a special relationship with them that involves "emotion" or high intensity feelings of attachment or affection, or even negative emotion, you're usually also highly concerned about their opinions and feelings, their welfare, their happiness and *their* overall perspective, about *your life*.

In these instances the spirit of control will play on the CIYA, causing you to do things to secure, or try to keep secure, those interpersonal relationships with the people you love such as your spouse, family members, children, siblings and/or the people you respect like pastors, leaders, long time Christians friends, etc.

After all, these are the people in your life that are *supposed* to be looking out for your best interests, right? So for very legitimate reasons, your guard may be down when dealing with them. The question is, does your guard go so far down that you do what they want you to do, in opposition to what God wants you to do?

An "Emotional Link" Ups the Game

In these special interpersonal relationships, the "emotional link" makes the ante go up. Or, in other words, it makes it more difficult to resist the spirit of divination working in and through those other people's lives, while they're seeking to control yours. This is true even for those kinds of relationships that you know are certifiably "no good" for you to maintain.

Now that's <u>not</u> to say that we wouldn't go back and pick up the trash we dropped in front of the bum, or feel uncomfortable having no makeup on and wearing dirty sweats on a bad hair day in line at the grocery store. Nor, would it mean that we have absolutely no concerns about making the trash collector's job harder by leaving a large dried up Christmas tree on the sidewalk for pick-up, or that we wouldn't experience any concern about our obnoxious neighbor being annoyed by our barking dog.

For our purposes, just beware that when you are called on to resist the spirit of control the ante will go up-- or it will be harder for you to resist when it involves people with whom you have an "emotional link".

An "Emotional Link" Ups the Game

Here's a good example of an "emotional link" in play, it involves the latest reoccurring theme for divorce I hear nowadays. It's when a spouse (say the husband in this example) starts a Facebook account and through this endeavor, he inevitably reconnects with his old high school sweetheart.

Within just a few fond commemorative communications, he is ready to abandon his wife of nine years and their two children and to go back to a relationship he had over twenty-five years ago when he was a sixteen-year-old boy. That's right "boy"… b-o-y.

Naturally, the wife is absolutely devastated. It is quite difficult for her to compete with the memories of a years-past, testosterone-laden relationship, whether it was ever sexual in nature or not.

But "fear not", the husband assures the wife, "If it doesn't work out, I'll be back to you and the kids."

In response, the rejected, rug-just-pulled-out-from-under-her, wife, crying uncontrollably, nods and affirms that she and the children will be there for him if he ever decides to return to the family.

The wife's response of leaving the door open for the runaway dog to get back in the house-- is clearly evidence of an "emotional link". She is striving to maintain the status quo or "security" of that interpersonal relationship and in this case, at any cost.

Naturally, no one in the wife's position ever wants a divorce. Just as in any other "emotional link" situation: no one wants their child to hate them; no one wants to be disowned by their sister or brother; no one wants a co-worker to gossip about them; no one wants their in-laws to speak badly of them to their spouse.

No one wants to lose, or even risk losing a relationship with anyone they love. So we do our best to "secure" those relationships with which there is an "emotional link". Unfortunately, many times that means doing what the spirit of divination, working through that other person directs us to do, to the exclusion of what God want us to do.

An "Emotional Link" Ups the Game

In this situation, once things don't work out with the high school sweetheart, absent any form of repentance on the husband's part, there would be somebody else next, and then there would be another, and another, unless and until the husband repents.

From the husband's perspective, his plan for the wife's life is to get her to do whatever he needs done in order to facilitate his agenda. He first wants a quickie divorce; and then he wants his wife to spend the best years of her life waiting around for him, just in case this (the craziest thing he's ever done in his life) doesn't pan out.

If the wife remains compliant in this "emotional rollercoaster" type of relationship, she will continue to exist in a state of emotional bondage to her unfaithful husband. Even though he's long gone in both heart and body, everything in the wife's life will still be "all about" him: "Does he still love me?" "Is he coming back?" "When will he come back?" "He sounded nice on the phone this time when he called the kids, I bet he'll be coming back soon!" "When will he stop having sex with that other woman?" "When will he realize he loves me more?" "What can I do to make him love me again?"

An "Emotional Link" Ups the Game

This level of *control* can go on and on for days, months, and years, totally consuming the wife's heart, mind, body, soul and strength. Throughout the remainder of the wife's life she'll be expected by everyone to continue to fervently pray about someone who may end up living out the remainder of his life as a reprobate. Note also, that there will be members of the Christian community, those who have been amply "Christianized" who will all encourage her to remain in this debilitating condition, just waiting for him to come home.

There's obviously nothing wrong with praying, but what happens many times is that *the wife gets mad at God* for not answering the prayers she's been basing on the Scripture everyone's quoting to her: God, "hates divorce" (Mal 2:16, NKJ) and as a result, she backslides, thinking God doesn't love *her* anymore.

Then a few months later, news comes of the husband having a "love child" with his Facebook sweetheart, and snap! It's all over for the wife. "Another one bites the dust" at the hand of the spirit of divination. God's divine plan for her life is never reached. She's yet another Christian casualty.

An "Emotional Link" Ups the Game

It's almost as if her God-given life's purpose was readily expendable. The wife ends up living the remainder of her days on earth, doing nothing but having been *controlled* emotionally and mentally by this situation, and never once again, having the strength to do anything for the Kingdom.

Yet, all the while, the Lord had a better plan for her life than that!

Do you see how "it" works?

Let's reverse the roles and take a look at another example where we'll see different circumstances and yet arrive at the same outcome: namely, a victory for the spirit of control.

Consider the husband, who has for decades studied the Word of God, who knows the Word of God, who teaches the Word of God and who fancies himself a "pastor" and a "Christian Counselor". While highlighting his own "model" marriage, he spent several years counseling other couples on how to Biblically deal with their varying marital issues; including advising offended spouses on how to handle or cope with adultery, or the unfaithfulness of their spouse, in

An "Emotional Link" Ups the Game

one form or another. You know the routine: "You must forgive", "God hates divorce", "You must do everything you can to try and 'save' your marriage". Whenever giving advice on how to deal with the hurt and pain caused by the philandering spouse's actions, he'd counsel, "You must crucify it all and give it up to God", etc, etc, etc.

This was and still is, generally, all Biblically based counsel of course. But how does this husband, who has held himself out as somewhat of an "expert" over the years respond when his wife goes out on him?

Like a madman!

His "Christianity" and everything he'd ever learned, ever taught and ever counseled to others, flies right out the window when it's time for him to apply it all to his own life.

Moreover, his immaturity in the Lord is seen not only during the *initial* stages of the discovery and his recovery over the affair, but continues for years on end. He is unable to control his tongue, his actions, and his emotional state; let alone, *forgetting those things behind* and moving on with his own life.

"CONTROL FREAK"

An "Emotional Link" Ups the Game

Even though the carnal appeal of this husband's story has waned over the years (most people considering it a story that's *long been told* and is now *way too old);* he yet, maintains his "cause" by continuing to engage other carnal people to do his bidding and push his agenda, since his own credibility in the "Christian Community" has long been lost.

Oh sure, he'll tell you he's right with God and emotionally fine. Yet, anyone with common sense would beg to differ; and the facts continue to demonstrate otherwise. It's not just the fact that he's a hypocrite: responding in ways to his own offense, unlike what he demanded from those he had counseled in the past. It's not just the fact that he has become such a dreadful witness for Christ: gossiping, dividing, biting, devouring, and being vindictive and bitter. But for years now, this husband has tried and tried in every way he can fathom, to put down, pull down, tear down, and bring down the "other man" and anyone associated with him. Though he'd never admit it, his whole meaning in life has now been reduced to carrying out this vindictive agenda.

The spirit of *control* is triumphant again!

An "Emotional Link" Ups the Game

Yes, this husband had been sinned against, but *sooooooo what?* Join the ranks of real soldiers and stop whining, it only makes you look bad. And please don't make me pull out Matthew 18:21-35.

The Lord and Savior that I know, allows people to repent of their sin, be forgiven, and best of all, be restored.

Neither the wife in the first example nor the husband in the second will ever fulfill God's plan for their lives. The spirit of divination has just commandeered them to live out the rest of their lives so consumed with their offense, that they'll have nothing left to give to the Lord's agenda.

When there is an "emotional link" attached to the chink in your armor (CIYA), your ability to combat the spirit of control gets more difficult and complex. As you continue to lose the battle against the spirit of control time and time again, you eventually form a pattern of behavior resulting in a very serious relational dysfunction.

For the Christian, the most dysfunctional relationship to be caught up in is an "idolatrous" relationship. That's when a

An "Emotional Link" Ups the Game

person's "emotional link" is functioning on its highest power setting.

An "Emotional Link" Ups the Game

"CONTROL FREAK"

CHAPTER 13: "IDOLATRY"
Worship of the Creature

Could it be that the LORD-- whose very name is *"Jealous"* meant a great deal more than we have ever understood when He said, *"I am a jealous God?"* (Ex 34:14; Deut 4:24, 5:9, 6:15, KJV).

Could it be that God is so jealous over us, our affections, our love, our attention; over who or what we love; and over who or what has captivated our hearts and minds, that when we choose to give our heart, mind, soul, body and strength over to another "human" to the point of loving them more than God (in any circumstance, including spousal or familial love), that it becomes a type of *idolatry* in His perspective? That actually breaks His heart?

Right-e-o!

"IDOLATRY" Worship of the Creature

"And they that escape of you shall remember Me among the nations whither they shall be carried captives, because I am broken with their whorish heart, which hath departed from Me, and with their eyes, which go a whoring after their idols" (Ez 6:9, KJV).

"If any man come to me, and hate not his father, and mother, and wife, and children, and brethren, and sisters, yea, and his own life also, he cannot be my disciple" (Lu 14:26, NKJV).[32]

Yet, "relational idolatry" is so very easy to get caught up in. We see it in husband/wife, parent/child, girlfriend/boyfriend, friend/friend, employee/boss, and all sorts of other kinds of relationships. In fact, there is no interpersonal relationship in your life that is exempt from the *relational idolatry* possibility.

I hope you take this next statement in the right spirit, but, you know what? We're all a bunch of wanton adulterers

---

[32] The word "hate" in this passage should be understood to mean, "loving ones relatives less than the Lord" (*Hebrew-Greek Key Word Study Bible*, AMG International, Inc.) Or put more simply, you should *not* love your relatives more than the Lord.

and adulteresses. Yep, that's what James says (Ja 4:4); and if you're really honest with yourself, you'll confirm this truth.

Like it or not, our hearts are "whorish" (Ez 16:30, KJV), adulterous, idolatrous. If it's not a person; then we *go a whoring* (Lev 17:7, 20:6; Nu 15:29; Jud 2:17; Ps 73:27, 106:39; KJV) after money, position, possessions, sex, alcohol, drugs, pornography, shopping, or worst of all, the idolatry of self! Or, least recognized of all, the idolatry of our own "agendas", *especially* when ministry related.

Unless we purposefully and intentionally seek to maintain the Lord on the throne of our hearts, we as human beings, all have our default option set on "idolatry".

When "idolatry" happens we then automatically enter into a dysfunctional relationship with that person to whom we've given this "inordinate" amount of affection. It's something similar to that of Adam and Eve, where Adam prized and cherished Eve's love and approval more than God's when he was tempted to sin.

"IDOLATRY" Worship of the Creature

The reason you are so weak and unable to resist, and/or so out of control with someone you "idol", is because you've given your heart, soul, mind and body to him/her to a degree that exceeds that which you have given to God; and therefore, with regard to that relationship, you are in blatant disobedience to God.

Then you wonder why you're "so messed up?"

Guys do this too, but as for women, we *always* seem to fail in this area. It's like there is no such thing as the *discretionary* giving of oneself, especially in the area of romance for women. It's always over the top, over the hill, just jump off a bridge. We throw caution to the wind and we're in-- heart, soul, mind and body.

The problem is that to whomever you give that degree of your heart, mind, soul and strength, they have now been empowered and enabled to *control* you ... just like that! [33]

You're wrapped around their big, little pinkie, in no time. It's done!

---

[33] Snap your finger right now for purposes of sound effect.

"IDOLATRY" Worship of the Creature

"'You can't control yourself,'" announces the LORD and King. "Just look at all of the things you are doing! You are acting like a prostitute who has no shame at all" (Ez 16:30, NIRV).

"'How weak is thy heart,'" saith the Lord Jehovah, *'seeing thou doest all these [things], the work of a whorish woman, under no restraint'"* (Ez 16:30, DBY).

That's why you've got to check your default setting every single day, by asking yourself: "Is my heart with Him, or with something else, or with *someone else* more than Him?"

Like it or not, God created you; <u>and</u> He created you to have your deepest love relationship with Him and Him alone. You were never created to love anyone else more than Him. So forget all those old romance movies you wasted your time watching. They've royally messed up your thinking!

Your love for others was never intended to usurp your love for Him, or His care for your personal wellbeing. From the beginning, He intended on being and *becoming* (Ex 3:14)

"CONTROL FREAK"   171

everything to you and for you. He is your provision (Jehovah-jireh), your healing (Jehovah-rapha), your protection/defense (Jehovah-nissi), your peace (Jehovah-shalom), your comfort and guidance (Jehovah-raah), your joy (Jehovah-shammah), your right standing before with God (Jehovah-tsidkenu). He is the great "I AM" (Ex 3:14, KJV) the *Becoming One*, the One who becomes all you will ever need in any given situation.

Unlike what the world tells you, you were never created to look to anyone else to "*make* you happy". Look, they're not even doing a good job at that! For a person falling into idolatry, "happiness" is always short-lived. Once the bondage locks-in, the "happiness" immediately ... *fizzles out.*

We are to worship the Creator, not the "creature" (Ro 1:25, KJV). The term "creature" or "creation" encompasses any person: men or women, boys or girls-- including our own selves, and/or any other "thing" on the face of the earth.

The "heads" side of the CIYA, satisfying our innate need for belonging, worth and value must be derived from the

Creator, not from the other *created things or people* that we come into daily contact with here on earth.

Give it to them to handle? Eventually, you're sure to get dropped flat and end up lame just like Mephibosheth (2 Sam 4:4).

Unfortunately, the death of that *interpersonal relational dependency* (CIYA) is not so easily crucified. A continuing work of the Holy Spirit needs to take place in order to root out the CIYA permanently. Admittedly, it is a rare and difficult path to follow and few there be that find it; <u>but it is the key</u> to a life of freedom from those to whom we have given the power to control and/or manipulate our personal, emotional, mental and spiritual well being.

More importantly, it is the key to living a life pleasing to God. It is the key to maintaining your level of saltiness, always being a vessel fit for the Master's use. It is the key to maintaining a balanced emotional, mental and spiritual life. Ultimately, it is the key to fulfilling God's assignments for your life here on earth.

"IDOLATRY" Worship of the Creature

If your response to that statement is, "My life is too complicated to be used by God." "I don't have the time, energy, nor inclination for that kind of intense pursuit after God." That only means that you're already so seriously enveloped in a life of dependency on others, that you cannot see, nor fathom your own way out.

You have no clue what the detrimental effect of worshipping another person has done to your mental, emotional, spiritual, and possibly even, physical wellbeing. And I'll tell you something else; you're exactly where the enemy would have you.

Think about it: the enemy would love absolutely nothing more than to have you continue to yield and focus your life; your heart, soul, mind and body; your emotions and all your energies on preserving your dependency on other sinful human beings, rather than on the Lord and the work of His Kingdom.

When you're in that condition of bondage, the enemy says, "Aaaah, perfect. That's exactly where I want him/her, serving them hand and foot. He/she will stay like that for years! Ok minions, let's move on to our next conquest."

"IDOLATRY" Worship of the Creature

The enemy uses the spirit of control to manipulate human beings, even "Christians", to detrimentally affect your life in this way. This is especially true if you've placed them on the throne of your heart and pushed the Lord to the side. The spirit of control then causes those whom you *idolize* (or have an unhealthy, interpersonal relational dependency on) to sin against you, hurt you, damage you, and/or say or do things that manipulate or *take advantage of* your weaknesses, in order to *control* your every move.

After you're all dried up spiritually (having been severed from the True Vine), and after you've suffered all the hurt and damage delivered at the hand of your idol(s), and after you've been tapped out of all your strength and energy and are unable to get yourself back together to do anything useful for the Kingdom of God; you stay *stuck* right there, hurt and offended. Unless repentance takes place, the only thing you have the ability to do anymore, is to recount and re-live all those hurtful hateful events while continuously licking your wounds for the rest of your life.

Most people can never get over the offenses they've suffered at the hand of their idols. Those people who dropped them, rejected them, abandoned them, hurt them, were unfaithful to them, or did not otherwise fulfill the promises or responsibilities that they *should* have.

But listen, in the end, it's not about how mean or wrong they were for mistreating you. It's about the fact that *you failed* to place the hedge, or proper "heart boundary lines" in those relationships, the way God had originally intended.

Take a look at a few translations of Proverbs 4:23:

Keep your heart with all diligence, For out of it spring the issues of life (NKJV).

Above everything else, guard your heart. **It is where your life comes from** (NIRV).

And keep watch over your heart with all care; **so you will have life** (BBE).

Guard your heart more than anything else, because **the source of your life flows from it** (GWT).

Since your life source stems from your heart, and since your heart is supposed to be given fully and completely to the Lord, the reason you've lost all your strength, power, self-control and motivation, is because you haven't kept your guard up.

If you want *real* "life" you need to guard your heart in a secluded, remote location, to be "held in trust" first and foremost, for Him.

Any unhealthy dependency on human beings (or the idolatry of man) is nothing but a recipe for more hurt, pain and grief. It's a perpetual cycle akin to the "cycle of abuse" found in "dysfunctional" relationships. People get caught up in these hurtful cycles because they continually fail to maintain the "heart boundaries" that the Lord (since the creation of man), had always intended to be maintained.

The minute they get out of one "dysfunctional" relationship, they jump into another. There are both men and women out there that simply cannot exist without having a "significant other" (or idol) either on hand, or in the works.

As a side note: Psychologist, therapists, or counselors just love to "tag" or define people as "dysfunctional". As if somehow that means they've earned their fifty-minute *hourly* rate of pay. Yet, when you think about it, they haven't really told us Christians anything new. Dating back to the Garden, this same pattern of behavior has continued throughout generations and has yet to cease.

The CIYA of Adam caused him to choose acceptance by Eve over God's directive. Eve, then automatically became a substitute "god" or *idol* in Adam's life. This allowed the spirit of divination the ability to easily control Adam's behavior, which was then motivated to please Eve, over God. Thereafter, time and time again, over and over, throughout generation to generation, man has chosen other people and/or other things over his/her Creator.

So the reality is that we've all been "dysfunctional" to one degree or another from the start! "Dysfunction" is no doubt a part of our sin nature. The idolatry of human beings, is yet another anti-to Christ where we resort to worshiping grossly inferior man, instead of the only wise God. All the while never once realizing, that man will suck you dry, chew you up, spit you out, and then have the audacity to say:

"What's *your* problem?"

"IDOLATRY" Worship of the Creature

Now realize that our great omniscient God already knew all about the weaknesses of fallen man, and so He provided us with an alternative to our dependency on humans for their love, approval, acceptance and admiration. Namely, becoming dependent on the Lord Himself and Him alone for all of those things.

The enemy, on the other hand, never wants you to get to the point of placing and maintaining God on the throne of your heart. Why not? Because the enemy cannot manipulate God; he cannot control God; he cannot tell God what to do; he cannot stumble God; and he certainly cannot trick or deceive God. With God remaining on the throne of your heart, as you maintain a heightened level of divine communication with His Spirit, those same insights and capabilities transfer to your benefit.

If you're saying, "Yes, I see this happened in my life" and you're wondering, "Why or how did this ever happen to me?" Here's a little roadmap on how idolatry usually occurs:

First, it starts off with your innate desire to be loved, recognized, appreciated, cherished, and acknowledged (the "heads" side of the CIYA). In order to obtain, maintain and/or increase the love, admiration, respect and positive perception that others have of us, we make decisions and take actions that we think will keep those relationships viable and in good standing. In addition, many times out of fear of loss of that relationship or love, we try to make sure we do things that will not cause other people to get mad at us, think badly of us, gossip or say harsh things about us (the "tails" side of the CIYA).

Then, once you get "emotionally linked" to, or fall in love with someone who has characteristics of a "taker" or "deceiver"; or someone who is very "needy" or "high maintenance" (the kind of people that have a way of consuming your life, your attention, your emotions, your affections, your strength, your very being), in no time flat, God gets displaced from the only position He knows or will ever accept in your life … namely, "first".

Anytime we allow any person or thing to take precedence, dictate, and govern our actions in direct opposition and in contradiction to the Holy Spirit, that person now rules and reigns in our hearts in place of God. *While they promise them liberty, they themselves are the servants of corruption: for of whom a man is overcome, of the same is he brought in bondage* (2 Pe 2:19, KJV). This bondage can last for a minute, an hour, a day, months, years, and even decades of a lifespan.

On the other hand, once you get on board with His original intentions, the Lord will bring the right people and the right relationships into your life. At which point, it will be *your responsibility* to maintain the "heart boundaries" He originally expected you to maintain. In the meantime, you must first place Him and keep Him placed, on the throne of your heart, removing any and all other people, pursuits, or pet sins that you've allowed to take over that position.

Since the CIYA causes you to more readily fall into "idolatry", you should also contemplate another "idolatry" possibility that you may have overlooked. I don't want you to think that the CIYA relates only to "individual" human beings because that would be a very limited perspective.

Don't forget about the human beings comprising organizations, churches, ministry, country clubs, social groups, women's groups, sports groups, City Council, the

PTA, the rotary club, etc. They too, present a CIYA factor that cannot be ignored.

The CIYA as it relates to any organization creates a dependency on two things: the leaders in the organization <u>and</u> the purpose driving the organization.

"People" run organizations, churches, ministries, clubs, AA, the PTA, and all other groups or movements. Indeed, organizations cannot exist without the people who operate or are in leadership, over them. So when the CIYA causes a person to become emotionally dependent upon an organization, they're dependent upon both the people who run the organization, as well as the purpose that drives that organization.

In these situations there is a compounded need to belong, be acknowledged, loved and accepted, especially by the leader or leaders of the organization because: (1) they *are* the leaders (and since first grade you wanted to be acknowledge by your teacher); and (2) most often times, they lead an organization that has a worthy purpose.

"IDOLATRY" Worship of the Creature

When you pour yourself into an organization with a worthy purpose, you are at risk of transferring your pure unadulterated "service to God" into an adulterated "serving of the purpose" of the organization, rather than God. While serving God and serving the purpose of an organization may be one in the same for a season; many times, at different forks in the road, during the transition periods of life, they may not.

If you have a CIYA, like most people do and at least one idolatrous relationship (as most people do also); the bondage of your heart, mind, soul and body, as it relates to that idolatrous relationship, may cause you to do anything necessary to maintain it at all costs. This is true even though the idolized individual or organization is visibly and undeniably detrimental to "you", the "servant".

Yet, there remains an intense desire in you to maintain your relationship with the *idols* in your heart, even though that person or organization is certifiably "no good" for you. So as a matter of course, you may overlook, excuse, and justify the failures and wrongdoings of the person(s) or organization that you *idolize*. You may even justify your own questionable conduct of staying attached to that person or organization, by adopting *your idols' views* in order to explain to others *why you remain* in the relationship.

All of this mental wrangling is done in order for you to maintain your "idolatrous" master/servant relationship in "good standing".

Yes, I'm using the term "good" loosely and I'm using the term "master/servant" like a slap in the face, intentionally.

Due to the idolatry, you in essence, end up working in cooperation with the *spirit of divination,* which via your idol, has been sent to steal, kill, and destroy your life. This idolatrous relationship may be utterly ruining your life: stealing your joy, consuming your heart, nullifying your personality, confusing your mind, contaminating your peace, and tapping out any strength you had to serve the Lord.

As a result, you cannot live your own life autonomously, as a healthy and content individual, without continuing to be yoked to your idol(s)-- which, by the way, are generally, exploitive, sick, abusive individuals. Idolatrous relationships provide an open door to which the spirit of divination enters in rather swiftly; takes over *control* rather quickly; and destroys "destiny" rather proficiently.

You may even know and readily admit that the relationship is no good for you. But for *some unknown reason* (Ha!), you cannot find the inner strength to break away. The *unknown reason* should be obvious by now.

If you have placed an idol on the throne of your heart and have given yourself over: mind, body, soul and strength, to that person; position; or that thing, like drugs, alcohol, or pornography; you no longer have the anointing that breaks the yoke of bondage available to you (Is 10:27). As a result, you must continue to serve that idol (or one just like it), until you break away from its control or die; whichever comes first.

You gave "your all" over to the idol; and just like Pharaoh, who held the children of Israel in bondage ... he/she or it, will *never let you go!*

As a result of your idolatry, you have lost the internal strength to recover from this condition without repentance

<u>and</u> deliverance, the success of which will be solely based upon your own obedience.

You *need* a Deliverer!

Believe me, I know:

One day, while sitting on the floor of a rather large master bedroom closet, I found myself crying my eyes out after having yet another hateful emotional and physical altercation with the same man. As it was so many times before, this interaction had again left me in the usual "emotional basket case" condition.

As I began to recount the hateful things that were said to me, I started in on my usual course of believing them as "truth" (just as I had always done in the past). As I continued to pierce myself through with the emotional pain of recounting those words (not knowing at the time that I could choose to "reject" instead of "receive" those hateful remarks), I was voluntarily contributing to my own weakened condition.

"IDOLATRY" Worship of the Creature

Then, all of a sudden something happened differently than had happened before. Namely, I started *talking to myself.*

Now, you know what they say about talking to yourself ... it can be a sign of insanity, right? But no, I was never admitted 5150!

I did however, start asking myself questions like: "Who is this person sitting on the floor of my closet? Who is this emotional wreck? Where is your personality? What happened to who you were, who you used to be? Your identity is nowhere to be found. Come to think of it, I really don't think I like you ... whoever you are."

"That's right; I don't *know* you and I don't like you!"

I realized that, "I" didn't exist anymore. My entire life revolved around a person who was sucking the very life right out of me, exploiting me and taking advantage of me in every possible area; and I said to myself, "This is *messed up!*" [34]

---

[34] Quiet honestly, I used other "words" back at the time. As you may know, a person is much more carnal when they're living in idolatry.

"IDOLATRY" Worship of the Creature

All of a sudden the light came on … "Wow! Oh no!"

I said to myself, "I *think* I'm being abused!"

"Who me? … Abused?"

"Nah, not *me*" …

"Really?"

You see, unlike most people who follow a lifetime pattern of abusive relationships, I'd never been in an abusive relationship before. However, I knew all the signs and symptoms of those kinds of relationships, due to having a Master's Degree in Counseling Psychology.

So I started recalling everything I'd learned in Graduate School and I then took a long hard look at the facts and circumstances in my situation (what he was saying and doing) and then at myself (how I was acting and responding). Then, once I "tagged" what was going on with that "abused" terminology, I began to feel my heart start to beat faster and faster, harder and harder …

"IDOLATRY" Worship of the Creature

I was starting to get *ticked off.*

I said to myself, "Now wait just a minute." I paused. I got up and took a look at myself in the mirror. I really didn't know her, I knew who she used to be; but as to the face I saw in the mirror that day ... I had to say, "Who the heck are you? And btw, you look like an absolute mess!"

It's hard to explain, but at that moment in time I realized, a very deep internal evaluation had to be made. After living several years in the same cycle, I finally realized that all the crying in the world was not going to get this person to stop mistreating me; and that all the crying I had done to the Lord about this situation, was not going to get this person to stop mistreating me either.[35]

At that point I knew I had to make a choice to either continue living in a constant state of emotional upheaval (while trying to win the affections and favorable treatment of this person *like I had been doing*), or I could try to make a change for the better ... *at least for myself.*

---

[35] The Lord will allow your idols to mistreat you for as long as they remain your idols. Once you're ready to repent, He will be faithful to deliver you from their clutches.

"IDOLATRY" Worship of the Creature

This was a decisive point in my life where I had to ask myself a series of questions:

"Am I going to be a "victim" and act like this *every day* for the rest of my life, or what?"

"Am I going to go around the rest of my life living with the symptoms of an abused woman: lifeless, despondent, no personality, walking on egg shells, battered and confused, emotionally weak and needy?

Was I actually going to allow myself to become just like all the women in this condition that I had either met before and/or that I had read about in my psychology books?"

"Or, am I going to do something about it?"

"Am I going to receive this 'victimization' role?"

"Or, am I going to fight against it?"

Truthfully, there was a brief moment in time that the decision was really "touch and go". It could have gone either way. You may not realize it, but it's actually much

"IDOLATRY" Worship of the Creature

easier to remain a "victim" than it is to dig deep and ask God for the strength you need to fight your way out of that role.

After all, no one would blame me, right? I'm a Christian, right? I'm supposed to love unconditionally, right? I'm supposed to trust the Holy Spirit to change other people, right? He was the one in sin, right? God knew, right? God would avenge me … right? I'm supposed to submit to my husband, even if he does not obey the Word (1 Pe 3:1) *r-r-r-r-r-right?*

With all my "Christianization", which really amounted to nothing more than the "religious brainwashing" of an "enabler" character trait; and with all the ways I had been deceived in order to get into that position in the first place; and with my own CIYA still functioning in full swing at that time, the decision could have very easily been to stay right there, in that pathetic situation.

But then something stirred up a fire in my heart.

As I looked at my dismal condition and began to remember who I used to be, my heart started pounding harder and harder as I paced the bathroom floor. I said aloud to myself: "Oh hail no! This just does <u>not</u> suit my personality *at all.*"

I then concluded my note-to-self conversation declaring, "This is <u>not</u> gonna happen! This is not gonna happen to me!"

And then *the fight* in me-- came out!

No, not to beat people up, not to fuss and fight and start throwing things, but to change the situation *while I was still living in it.* And as a result, I began to fight my way out of it and by the grace of God the enemy was fully and completely defeated and in the end, I got the victory!

It reminds me of King David; he was betrayed and had lost everything (his family, possessions, position, he was even about to be stoned by his own once loyal men); as a result, the Bible says he was "greatly distressed". Yet, instead of buying into depression, giving up on what the enemy had stolen, and "throwing in the towel" David "*encouraged himself* in the Lord".

"IDOLATRY" Worship of the Creature

That means to me, that David must have been talking to himself too! He sought the Lord and under His guidance and direction he went after everything that was taken from him ... and David *recovered all* (1 Sam 30:6-19, KJV).

Every person in these kinds of situations has to come to the same "defining moment"; and just like David, you've got to tell yourself, "I ain't goin' down like that!"

If a person does not have Christ in their life to give them the power to break away from idolatry, they will forever live in an unending cycle of similar relationships. That's right, one right after the other, with the same pattern of behavior, the same oppression, the same bondage and the same yoke that never allows them to live out the plan God has for their life freely.

You must decide to fight, or otherwise you will go down. You must fight to change the CIYA. You must fight to rid the idolatrous relationships from your life once and for all. You must fight to remove the spirit of divination's use of your interpersonal relationships to control "you". You must fight in order to ever arrive at your God-given plan, purpose and destiny in life. It's a battle over your own "source of life", so you can't quit now.

So where do you stand?

Strike that! (That was a trick question.) You cannot *stand* on both sides. You will either stand on His side, or you will continue to fall on the other.

If you refuse to repent of "idolatry" you are refusing to lay hold of the plan that God has for your life and live it out to the fullest extent possible. Those idols you've set on the throne of your heart will continue to hurt, stumble and offend "you", unless and until you straighten out the mess you've made.

If you choose to stand and fight; you've made the right decision. It's a very rough road to recover from idolatry, but it's really the only option you have in order to make something out of the remainder of your life.

If you're now willing to loose those chains, allow me to give you some direction on exactly how to "break free".

CHAPTER 14: Breaking Free

▄▄▄▄▄▄▄▄▄▄▄▄▄▄▄▄▄▄▄▄▄▄▄▄▄▄▄▄▄▄▄▄▄▄▄

"Recover My Heart, O Lord"

Recover my heart, O Lord, from sinful man

So that he cannot hurt me, discourage me, control me,

make me mad, upset, cry, or feel down,

Or, make me contend, or compare, or boast, or compete,

Nor stoop to his level of immaturity, by allowing him to

engage me and stumble me

Or, cause me to disregard as nothing

The gifts and talents that You, O Lord,

have placed inside of me

And in so doing, adopt his opinion of me, over Yours.[36]

Breaking free from idolatry will always cost you something
… it will feel like it is *literally* breaking your heart. In fact, it

---

[36] May 6, 2009.

has to. Your heart must be broken to be freed, because it has been wrongfully affixed to an idol. How else did you think you'd break free? Microscopic surgery?

You see, some people *think* they live free just because they live in America. Ha! That's a lie. In reality, most everyone ("Christians" included), live in bondage to either people or organizations; to alcohol, drugs, pornography, spending, gambling, lying, cheating, striving for possessions, power, position, etc. If none of the above, then they live in bondage to the CIYA, the opinions of man, seeking affirmation, respect, love, adoration and "good press" from others. Or, if none of those either, then they live in the least admitted bondage of all: bondage to "self".

The only truly free people living on the planet today are very few and far between. They are those people who are not in bondage to anything or anyone, including "self". They are free to serve God with the entirety of their body, soul, mind and strength; they are able to hear the voice of God and distinguish it from the spirit of control; and thus, they are able to be directed by His Spirit to complete each and every task or assignment as He wills, each and every day of their lives.

Breaking Free

When we are fully dependent on the Creator (like we were created to be), we then have the capability, by the power of the Holy Spirit to be emotionally, mentally and spiritually free; unburdened by the dictates, preferences, demands, manipulations, desires and control of others. When we are untainted by the spirit of divination, we are free to do whatever God would have us to do; we are free to become whatever God would have us to be.

This is but a foretaste describing the "quality of life" the Lord has for us. The experience itself is indescribable!

So our *mark to press towards* (Phil 3:14, KJV) is to rid, or crucify, as much dependency on man (idolatry) and the approval of man (CIYA) out of our lives as possible. Though it is unlikely that anyone will ever achieve *total and complete* elimination of the CIYA (as the proclivity or inclination will always present you the temptation), we all can at least move in that direction, pressing towards that mark. In so doing, we then have a better chance of becoming all, doing all, receiving all, and fulfilling all, that God has planned for our lives.

Breaking Free

This "idolatry" giant is huge however, and it takes a lot of ammunition to slaughter. The weapons of our warfare necessary to take this giant out will be presented in the remainder of this chapter. The specific application will come later, but you can get started by working on the following:

(1) A solid working knowledge of God's Word;

(2) Consistent obedience to His Word by "doing" His Word; and by "doing" His personalized directives to you; *even when* it hurts, or costs you love, acceptance and/or approval from another; and *especially when* it crucifies one of those dependent idolatrous relationships;

(3) Maintaining the good fight of faith, by stepping out and not being afraid to do the impossible under His leading, guidance and direction; and by

(4) Drawing on the power of the Holy Spirit to perform all of the above.

Without these essential factors combined and working in unison, your unhealthy dependency on the love, approval, and admiration of other people will never come to an end.

Breaking Free

Yes, you can go to therapy and psychologists and talk about your relationships with your multitude of counselors, ad infinitum. Yes, you can even read about them; there are probably enough pop psychology books on "co-dependency", or pop "psychiantry"[37] to create a huge one-topic library. But there is absolutely nothing you can ever do to get yourself out of that continuing cycle or pattern of behavior until you become dependent on God first (ridding idolatrous relationships); and then asking Him to help you shore up the CIYA.

Going forward, with the guidance of the Holy Spirit, you need to start to plan the following:

First, you must cut off the "emotional link" that allows these other people to pull you around like a dog on a leash and you must retrain and refocus your energies. Most likely you will need to spend some time fasting and praying in seclusion to break these kinds of emotional chains.

Please do not confuse this with not loving someone anymore. The decision you're making is to become a

---

[37] "Psychianitry" is mixing Psychology with Christianity, and giving the former, preeminence.

better, stronger person for yourself and no longer feed into this dysfunction. This, therefore, is actually the most loving thing you can do for both yourself and them.

The word "'agape' ... *translated charity means benevolent love. Its benevolence, however, is <u>not shown by doing what the person loved desires, but what the one who loves deems as needed by the one loved</u>. Citing John 3:16: God gave not what man wanted, but what man needed as God perceived his need … God's love for man is God's doing what God thinks is best for man, not what man desires.*"[38]

So in a nutshell, the word "agape" is really "tough love" by definition. I know you've been told that "agape" means "unconditional love", but when people hear that phrase they think it means that it's "ok" with God for you to do whatever *you* want to do, including sin up a storm and that He doesn't care one way or the other because He unconditionally loves you anyway, anyhow, no matter what you do.

---

[38] Strong's #26, transliterated "Agape", Lexical Aids to the New Testament; *Hebrew-Greek Key Word Study Bible*, AMG International, Inc. Publishers.

Breaking Free

"Yes!" God loves you like that, but "No!" You don't get to *practice sin* with His blessing, all the while thinking you're going to make it to His divine plan for your life, let alone to heaven! *If* you're *really* a child of God, you will be chastened, rebuked and corrected *whenever* you get out of line (Prv 3:12; Heb 12:7-13).

We all need to learn to appreciate and cherish the Lord's rod and His staff; His loving hand of discipline for what it is, namely, invaluable to your spiritual growth and crucial for you to achieve your God-given destiny. If you're not being chastised on a regular basis, then you need to be concerned that you're not really one of His children, you're only a "make-believer".

The issue you're working on is not your "love" for people, it's your weaknesses (the CIYA), that giant, you've yet to conquer. So don't make it about them, it's about you becoming a stronger man or woman of God, so that He can do something meaningful with your life.

Second, you must come up with new ways to respond to the same old situations. You've probably had several years of experience with many of these relationships under your belt already. So what you need to start doing, is recall the usual verbal responses you received in the past; make a list and ask the Holy Spirit to help you figure ways to re-frame the issues (as will be discussed later) and present them in your response with a different perspective and attitude; a good positive report, that does not buy in to their controlling perspective.

Third, you must plan your steps for the next time an old familiar situation arises, so you can immediately implement your new way of dealing with it.

Fourth, we're not wrestling against "flesh and blood" and so as you take this new ground, realize that these people are not really the enemy. So instead of the usual battle weapons, like guns, knives, tanks and your own strength and abilities, ingenuity and strategies, you're instead going to:

(1)   Actively use your faith in God;

(2)   Continue to demonstrate your faith in the Word of God;

(3)   Listen to what God says first and foremost;

(4)   Draw wisdom from the Holy Spirit;

(5)   Draw application from the Holy Spirit;

(6)   Draw power from the Holy Spirit;

(7)   Keep a tight grip monitoring your thoughts and mind; and

(8)   Becoming keenly aware of your emotions and feelings, while <u>not</u> allowing your conduct to be governed by them.

<u>Lastly</u>, your ability to exercise self-control when confronting the spirit of divination requires one very crucial remaining component: Namely, your own crushing life experiences; the level of "self-control" necessary, will only come by the crushing events in your life, some of which you are facing right now. *"Though He were a Son, yet learned He obedience by the things which He suffered"* (Heb 5:8, KJV).

In order for you to do anything about responding differently to the spirit of divination, there must first be a crushing; or, a series of crushings in your life. It is necessary for your "flesh nature" to become so crucified and ripped out of you, that you are able to respond differently than your previous patterns of behavior. If you haven't gone through anything serious and painful, you won't catch this, nor will you be able to perform what you're about to learn because you likely have no handle on your own "flesh nature".

Jesus said, *"Verily, verily, I say unto you, Except a corn of wheat fall into the ground and die, it abideth alone: but if it die, it bringeth forth much fruit"* (Jn 12:24, KJV).

I do promise that there is a purpose for the pain: it's to make you more like Him; it's to rid those trivial flesh responses that you really could live without expressing; it's to bring your life into submission and subjection to His Spirit so that at some point you too can say, *"… I do always those things that please Him"* (Jn 8:29, KJV).

One day I received a phone call from a man who told me that he went out on his wife and committed adultery. He told me how he had tried and tried to communicate with her, but that she wouldn't talk to him anymore. He was sorrowful and repentant and at a total loss as to how he could win his wife back.

To me, there is nothing more loveable than a repentant person trying to find an answer to make up for their wrongdoing against others and get back on course with God. I'm thinking the Lord sees it the same way.

So he goes on asking me all kinds of questions: what I think she's thinking; how I think she feels; how he can get her to talk to him so that he can fully apologize and ask her forgiveness in person. So, I proceed to give him advice on these issues, because even though I didn't know her, I did know what she needed to hear.

Towards the end of the conversation he says, "Thank you so much for your time, you've helped me a lot, but can I ask you one more question?" I said, yes of course (I'd already been talking to him for who knows how long). He says, "Then when I get to talk to her, what do I say to her? Everything I say ... it doesn't work, it only makes it worse."

I thought for a minute and said, "Well I hope someone has told you this already: you have cut off the relationship with the girlfriend; you have to change your phone number; did you find yourself a new job yet? I hope someone also told you that you don't cut it off with the girlfriend just to get your wife back, you cut it off to get right with God, if He wants to give you your wife back, great. But I hope somebody told you that, too."

He said, "No, nobody told me to do any of that." I said, "Well you've got do that. Then after you do, send her a text that says something like this: 'She's out of my life, I repent, I changed my phone number, I'll never speak to her again, I only love you, and its over for good.'" I said, "Send her a text like that."

He said very quietly and demurely, "Oh" ... "Ok"…

LOL! Guys are so cute when they're clueless about what a girl needs to hear in these kinds of grim situations.

After that conversation I hung up and laughed myself silly! Saying, "Lord you are sooooo funny! I would *never have known* what to tell that adorable guy, unless it had happened to me."

"All praise to the God and Father of our Lord Jesus Christ. He is the source of every mercy and the God who comforts us. He comforts us in all our troubles so that we can comfort others. When others are troubled, we will be able to give them the same comfort God has given us. You can be sure that the more we suffer for Christ, the more God

will shower us with His comfort through Christ" (2 Cor 1:3-5, MSG).

God will take your crushing and He will use those painful experiences to make somebody else's crushing easier for them to handle.

"Do you wonder why you are having to experience some great sorrow? Over the next ten years you will find many others afflicted in the same way. You will tell them how you suffered and were comforted. As the story unfolds, God will apply the anesthetic He once used on you to them. Then in the eager look followed by the gleam of hope that chases the shadow of despair from the soul, <u>you will know why</u> you were afflicted. And you will bless God for the discipline that filled your life with such a treasure of experience and helpfulness." [39]

---

[39] *Streams in the Dessert*, January 11th excerpts, by L.B. Cowman, Copyright © 1966. Used by permission of Zondervan Publishing House. All rights reserved.

Breaking Free

Don't forget this isn't about you! In the big picture, this is not about you soldier! Had it not been for the crushing I had experienced, I wouldn't have had a clue of what that guy's wife wanted to hear. If I had always been in some happy-go-lucky "godly" marriage relationship, I just wouldn't have had a clue.

The Lord will give you deliverance from your idolatry, I guarantee! And, yes, it will be painful; emotionally, physically, and mentally ... I guarantee that also.

But what else are you going to do with your life? Are you going to willingly and voluntarily give the rest of your life over to the enemy to *control* "you" forever?

The answer is obvious.

CHAPTER 15: The Principle of Diametric Opposition

"Secret Places"

"I will give you the treasures of darkness, riches stored in secret places, so that you may know that I am the LORD, the God of Israel, who summons you by name (Isaiah 45:3).

When God takes you to a depth of soul experience be alert to new truths and new perspectives. During these times God often leads us to amazing new discoveries. It can be a storehouse of unexpected riches for the soul.

The Principle of Diametric Opposition

Bible teacher F. B. Meyer once observed, "Whenever you get into a prison of circumstances, be on watch. Prisons are rare places for seeing things. It was in prison that Bunyan saw his wondrous allegory and Paul met the Lord and John looked through heaven's open door and Joseph saw God's mercy. God has no chance to show His mercy to some of us except when we are in some distressing sorrow. The night is the time to see the stars."

He will always reveal treasures from these secret places if we are willing to walk through the process patiently."[40]

It wasn't until I was "delivered" from living in an idolatrous relationship and lived very alone for over a year or so, that I finally figured out that this "spirit of control" (we've all been talking about for the last several chapters), even existed.

---

[40] Excerpts from January 12, 2011, *Today God is First*, Daily Devotional. Reprinted by permission from the author: Os Hillman, an international speaker and author of more than 13 books on workplace calling and faith at work. To learn more visit www.MarketplaceLeaders.org

"CONTROL FREAK"

The Principle of Diametric Opposition

Sure it had been present in my life before, for years actually, forever really … but it hadn't been discernable. I hadn't been able to consciously "feel" its affect, nor "see" its effect in my life until one day, after over a year of total "alone time" with the Lord, "it" tried to creep back in.

Now when I say I was "totally alone", I don't mean I was a monk in a monastery never speaking to anyone at all for years. What I mean is that there was a period of about one to three years, during which I was stripped of everything I had ever worked for: my dream house and the nearly one million dollars of equity I had in it; my law firm income came to a complete halt after a client left me holding the bag of a $250,000.00, debt he owed me for attorney's fees; I was on unemployment, going through famine; I had previously been written out of my inheritance; my once perfect credit score was now shot; my marriage was finally over (but not until being forced through a gruesome court trial and several other motions and appeals); I had continued to be estranged from my once very close family; my "Christian" girlfriends, especially those to whom I gave the most when rolling in the dough, began dropping off like flies; and I had deliberately changed churches.

I had two future events that I expected would pull me out of my financial tailspin. The first was a brain injury case I had worked very hard on with another law firm; and the second was in relation to the $250K debt that I was owed.

As I waited for these two "ships to come in" to save me in the midst of my financial storm, I suffered two more very serious blows to the gut. My two ships capsized.

As we move into our third Law School lesson: "Civil Procedure 1", allow me to explain some of the details:

I had been working with another law firm to help handle the brain injury matter because of their trial experience and because the funding needed for expert fees to litigate that kind of a contingency case, are exorbitant. The defendants had brought two motions for summary judgment that I, alone, did all the "hard work" on to oppose, while those at the other law firm only reviewed and provided input.

The Principle of Diametric Opposition

A motion for summary judgment is an attempt to get your complaint and all of the causes of action contained therein, thrown out entirely. If you represent the Plaintiff on a contingency basis as I did; and the defense brings a motion for summary judgment as they did; if the defense prevails, your entire case and all the work you put into it (that you never got paid for ... *yet)* is all over.

That's right, O-V-E-R! You get absolutely nothing for your efforts; neither does your client. So needless to say, it was relatively imperative that I win.

After the partners at the other firm reviewed the work I did in opposition, one of them voiced his concern that he didn't like my argument as to a few of the causes of action that I had included in the complaint. In fact, he told me we were going to "lose anyway", so he wanted me to just give up and agree to dismiss those causes of action by stipulation with the other side.

Well, I didn't agree and I told him that, to the contrary, I was going to win them. He in turn, told me that I was not. He actually went so far as to wager a bet against his own case, his own client, and myself, by saying that if I won those causes of action, he'd buy me lunch.

To that I said, "You're on!"

I had spent countless hours researching and writing and working with expert testimony to oppose those two motions. In addition, I had to make about four or five court appearances in order to get the ruling on the motions for summary judgment and get a trial date set (which the partners never thought I'd get either).

In the end, I won everything; none of the causes of action were dismissed and I got a trial date. So ... it was time for lunch!

Or, so I thought.

However, the partner (the sore looser one) never paid his bet. Instead of buying me lunch, shortly after winning the motions, unbeknownst to me, all three partners had begun conspiring to remove me from the case. As I tried to get them to work with me to get the case ready for trial, I came upon resistance and accusations about my being "hard to work with".

I couldn't get them to do much of anything in preparation for the trial date and when it came to the end of expert deadlines, the partners at the other firm wanted to continue the trial, amend the complaint and re-open discovery.

As you might have expected, I disagreed with their case "strategy". We just won on motion for summary judgment, to re-open discovery would put the case at risk of another motion for summary judgment; the clients had suffered way too long; it was a perfect time to go to trial because there was a new insurance defense counsel who didn't know the case as well as the one on maternity leave; and naturally, I wanted reimbursement for the approximate sixteen thousand dollars in costs my firm had already advanced, as well as my estimated two hundred thousand dollar portion of the attorney's fees that I had expected to be paid on the case.

Well, the other law firm proceeded to try to pressure me into doing what they wanted. Since I refused, they then pressured the clients into removing me off the case by saying that they simply could not work with me anymore.

I told the clients to go ahead and stay with that firm because I could not support the case any further financially. So the other firm took over the case entirely.

Yes, *exactly.* I got sold down the river by the other firm along with all the expense money my firm had put into the case; not to mention the hours and hours I put into opposing those motions for summary judgment; and not to mention the fact these were my "friends" from law school, one of which was a "Christian".

So I put a lien on the case hoping to someday recover at least *something* for all my effort and expense.

About a year or so later, I get a call from "the boys" in that law firm advising me that the defense had brought *another* motion for summary judgment (after they continued trial and re-opened discovery, and basically did everything I told them not to do). They went on to say that the defense had won this time and that *they* had lost *everything.*

Well naturally, they didn't put it quite that way. They tried to obscure and excuse their defeat and mishandling of the case by pretense and cover up, but believe you me ...

I made the correction.

Ha! The big know-it-alls, acting all along like they knew everything and I knew nothing; their very own uppity case "strategy" wholly and solely tanked the entire case!

Yes! Of course I love it when God shows whose side He is on, it's just the two hundred grand it cost me for His affirmation that hurt. Not to mention the grave loss to the clients.

Just a few months later that same year, I then experienced my second blow to the gut. I had a Promissory Note for the $250K attorney fee debt owed to me by one of my

"Christian" clients that had been secured by a Deed of Trust on a parking lot. Since the Note was set to come due at the end of that year, I began to look for buyers for the land so that I could recover that money.

I already had a working relationship with an attorney whose client owned a building adjacent to the parcel. So I made contact with him and his client was interested; at least to the extent that he ran a title report to check if there was marketable title.

When title came back, lo and behold it revealed that my client actually had *no interest* in the parking lot that he had purportedly conveyed to my firm as security for the $250K debt in the first place! In fact, the deed securing my interest was actually "clouding the title" of the true owner.

So, not only did I lose the sale that I had expected would cover the debt, but now I also had to contact the attorney for the true owner and sign documents over to clear their title, or otherwise risk being sued myself.

The Principle of Diametric Opposition

At that point, suffice it to say that my circumstances and trials were such that I knew that no person on the face of the earth could possibly have the ability to fix them. It would have to be God, or nothing.

In that state, I learned that you don't go around telling people about your problems. After all, what are they going to do about it? They're not God. You got over half a million bucks to throw in my direction to make up for what just happened to me? Or, better yet, a million-five to cover it all?

Furthermore, God had taught me that whenever I'd go and tell people about my troubles, *my true motive* was to seek help or relief from man, because I was tired of waiting for Him to deliver me. So in order to get in line with His loving hand of discipline, I had to stop doing that too.

Beyond that, I realized that every time I was forced to broach a conversation in which one of my pains or losses was the subject matter, *it really didn't help me to talk to anybody about it.* Inevitably, that well meaning, caring person, after praying for me, would make statements that would only make me feel sorry for myself. I realized that their attempts to *sympathize with me,* in the end, were only *stumbling blocks to me.* Their comments only served to dig up, deepen, worsen and ultimately resurrect the hurts and disappointments that I had already tried my best to move beyond.

People who care about you want to help "fix" your problems, never realizing that those problems, are the very things that God wants to make sure you to *go through;* not necessarily get delivered out of. If you try to wiggle your way out of these kinds of situations before you successfully go through them, you're just going to have to go back around the mountain again.

With that revelation, I knew I had to just *get through* whatever He wanted me to, and that meant to *stay in the place* that He wanted me in (no matter how uncomfortable), so that He could change me and eventually get something meaningful out of my life.

The Principle of Diametric Opposition

So in short, I stopped trying to "save" my life; I surrendered; I submitted to the circumstances; and I lost the attitude about it. Even if you're not rebellious and you're just hurt, sometimes you've just got to go through being hurt. It's not the end of the world to be hurt. Remember, you're not going to die because you're hurt. "Hurt" per se, is not terminal.

So I eliminated talking, crying, whining, complaining, reporting and/or answering to anyone but the Lord. As a result of not trying to "save" my life anymore, my "quality of life" improved significantly.

While spending years in that state, no one really ever gave me any advice or suggestions or directives on what to do about my situation. After all, they didn't even know I had a "situation" going on in the first place. They were all clueless!

God had given me the grace to rise above my circumstances to the point where no one thought anything negative was going on in my life. I wasn't being a phony either, I was just submitted to the circumstances and resolved to the fact no human could help my situation. I believe that the Lord had intentionally made sure of that! So I gave up on "humans", to the extent that I stopped communicating with them about my trials, hurts and pains ... period.

When you are removed and separated from being with and around a bunch of people all the time; from living with a spouse for several years; from socializing with plenty of friends and family; from sharing your "business" on a regular basis with others-- and all of a sudden you're totally alone? Well, at first you go through a phase of feeling sorry for yourself because you're "all alone" and thus, arguably, *"lonely"*.

Now don't get me wrong, I had plenty of godly friends and pastors readily available to me, but I didn't want to go talk to them. Again, why bother? What are you gonna do for me? *Pray?*

Nice and appreciated, however: (1) For the reasons already mentioned, I was well over telling people about my problems, especially, if it was so they could pray for me; <u>and</u>

(2) I wasn't in the "prayer" stage anymore, I was in the "worketh patience" stage at this point (Ja 1:3-4, KJV).

The answers to my prayers for guidance and direction out of this storm were being given to me on a daily basis in the form of Rhema Word utterances or teachings and/or promises out of the *Living* Word received during my daily reading. He had already said, "I got this" in several different ways, so I knew I was going make it out of this storm, recover all <u>and</u> be better off than I had been, going in.

He's just like that you know.

Since He had already revealed my miraculous future through His Word, in my mind, it was done; even though in "the natural" it was not. Yet, from my perspective, while in the "endurance" phase of this "process" (Heb 6:15), all I had to do was <u>whatever</u> *He said,* <u>whenever</u> *He said it,* while waiting patiently for the manifestation in "the natural" of the promises He had already given me. If I needed prayer for anything, it was for the grace to do just that, but I didn't want to go through the long drawn out explanation.

The Principle of Diametric Opposition

When a person is "alone" and "lonely" it forces them to make the decision to either: Go out and generate some company or activity of any type, quality and/or quantity in an attempt to help themselves get out of their uncomfortable situation ... Or, a person can take a step back, forget the toiling and not waste any energy on the directives of others; endure and bear up under the pressure they feel when *they think* they should be actively doing something to help themselves, but circumstantially, they're not being allowed to; and learn to wait patiently for only His directives, all the while leaning on Him in order to bear up under the pressure of inactivity.

Once the obvious correct decision is made; and once you get beyond the "pity party"; and once you've been upheld by the Lord's grace; and once you've maintained your sanity in solitary confinement, then all of a sudden you start to say ...

"WOW! Unbelievable! This 'alone'... You-and-me-only exclusive relationship thing absolutely ... ROCKS LORD! This is sweet!"

The Principle of Diametric Opposition

As a Christian, for you to be alone, is really not the bad experience that the world tells you it should be. I didn't have to *think* about anybody else; I didn't have to *take care* of everybody else; I didn't have to *clean up* after anybody else; I didn't have to *get along* with anybody else; I didn't have to *care* if anybody liked me or loved me; I didn't have to cook dinner; dress up; put make-up on; check-in, check-out or check-up… *on anyone.* Nor did I have to deal with another person's bad attitudes or mistreatment, which sought to spoil my bliss! And no … my financial circumstances had not changed one bit, but I sure had.

I want to encourage you, if you're at that stage right now, ride it out! Ride the pony, assuredly it's a bumpy ride in the beginning; but learn to appreciate your freedom and the blessing of only having two voices speaking into your life in this season, yours and His. Once you break into a gallop, you'll be all right.

When you're completely alone like that there is a certain solitude that practically forces you to get to know God better than you would ever have otherwise. You get to know His voice much better, by default actually, it's because you have no one else talking to you or speaking into your life!

When you get into very heavy trials or situations where every decision you make could mean either life or death, blessing or cursing, you realize that *you cannot risk* listening to anyone else's input but His. I didn't want to risk making the wrong move or decision at any given opportunity, and thus, delay my coming out of this storm.

So by circumstances and necessity, this was the time when I began to develop a sort of "flow of communication" with the Lord that was constant and ongoing, untainted, unchallenged and uninterrupted by any outside sources.

This was the manner in which understanding, illumination and revelation were downloaded into my spirit. This is how the Holy Spirit would provide me with the directives that He used to lead and guide my life in the path He wanted me to go, without interference from others.

The Principle of Diametric Opposition

After that growth period, I had my first conscious encounter with the "spirit of divination" when Lord directed me to start teaching a Bible Study on Saturday nights. "It" tried to come in and *control* my decision about who would lead worship.

A friend of mine who was very accomplished in that area, offered to lead worship and I accepted. Once a few people heard "through the grapevine" who was going to lead worship I started to get phone calls, not only questioning my decision, but telling me that this person absolutely could <u>not</u> lead worship at *my* Bible Study because of his "past". Yet, in his "present" the friend was a worship leader who had been restored and was leading worship at a legitimate Bible teaching church under the authority of a Senior Pastor.

Now understand a few significant points: (#1) this was *my* Bible Study, these people who were calling me had nothing to do with it; (#2) none of them were on my non-profit Board of Directors; (#3) none of them were pastors under whom I was in authority; (#4) none of them were donors to the ministry; (#5) these were people I hadn't seen for months, or hung-out with for years; (#6) none of them did anything to ever help me when I was going through my trials, but instead did things to oppose me; and (#7) none of them were going to even attend the Bible Study themselves.

Notwithstanding all of the above, they were dead set on doing something about my decision. They were intent upon pulling out all the stops to make sure this worship leader did not lead worship at *my* Bible Study.

So I started getting all sorts of calls and threats and condemnation, from the lot. Statements were made such as "I can't believe you would do this" "I would expect more out of you" "Don't you know who he is?" "Don't you know what he's done?"

"Don't you *know* what he's done?" "Don't you know *what* he's done?" "Don't you know what he's *done*?"

I probably heard that same question a hundred times. Of course I knew what he did … I knew the whole story, and probably better than they all did cumulatively.

The Principle of Diametric Opposition

After I hung up the phone with all these contentious interlopers, I was unable to readily go back to my usual secluded-- ark of peace and solitude existence. I just couldn't get these conversations out of my mind: It was their words, their implications, their intimidations, their doomsday predictions, their demands, their threats, their expectations, and their ultimatums.

Some of them were so intent upon succeeding in *controlling* my decision on the issue, that *I* was even accused of having an affair with the worship leader! There were physical threats made towards him too. The level of *control* these people were trying to exert over me with regard to this one decision had consumed my heart and mind. All of a sudden, my peace, joy and serenity had all been stolen.

And I was like, "Whoa, Betsy! What on earth is that Lord? I kept asking the Lord, "What is that?" "What is that?" "What on earth is that Lord? I don't know what it is, but I <u>do</u> know I <u>don't</u> like it … but Lord, *what is it?*"

The Principle of Diametric Opposition

Within the day of asking, I started hearing in my mind or thinking these words to myself: "the spirit of divination" "the spirit of divination" "the spirit of divination" "the spirit of divination" "the spirit of divination".

Oh ok … great, so what the heck is that? Yes, of course I'd heard those words before, I knew about the scripture in the book of Acts, but I didn't really know what all it *meant;* until I looked "it" up, read, and researched "it". That's when I realized that the spirit of divination was straight from the pit of hell. That's when I knew "it" was something trying to control me and my decision about worship.

The Spirit of God and the spirit of divination are diametrically opposed to one another. "Diametric Opposition" means: absolutely in opposition; to contradict or oppose; or, antithetical.[41]

That's not to say that the Spirit of God couldn't totally annihilate the spirit of divination if He wanted to; they are not equal opposites. It's only that the workings and goals of the

---

[41] Wiktionary

one, are in contrast to, contrary to, opposite of, or diametrically opposed to the Other.

So I readily came to the conclusion that the spirit of divination was trying to use both the "heads" and "tails" sides of the CIYA, in hopes that I could be intimidated out of allowing this person to lead worship at my Bible study.

"It" wanted me to be afraid of what these meddlers would say about me to others; what they might say or do to my Bible Study attendees; what they might say to others about what they now considered my own "highly questionable" spiritual condition; and of course, "it" wanted me to be concerned about losing them all as "friends".

Since the spirit of divination is not of God at all and rather, "it" is another anti-to Christ, then that automatically tells us that anyone operating under "its" influence is undoubtedly trying to get us to step outside of the will of God.

So once that light went on, it was very easy to decide what the right thing was for me to do. Namely, *exactly opposite* of

The Principle of Diametric Opposition

what the spirit of control wanted me to do. Or, in other words, implement: "The Principle of Diametric Opposition".

While in the beginning we had only been talking about him coming to lead worship one night or another, with nothing definite, I now had *insisted* that he come lead worship that first opening night. This was despite the fact that he had received so much flack over this controversy, that he himself, even wanted to put it off for a few weeks. But somehow I just instinctively knew that if we didn't do the exact opposite of what "it" wanted us to do, that "it" would continue to haunt us.

The "Principle of Diametric Opposition" (a term I made up, so you won't find it in the dictionary), says this:

Whenever you realize that the spirit of control is seeking to get you to do, or not do, something, *anything;* in order for you to sufficiently and successfully oppose or resist that devil, you must consider doing the exact opposite of what the spirit of control wants you to do. In those cases when you are not able to do the exact opposite, you must just resist and stand firm, refusing to give in to "its" demand(s) (Ja 4:7 and Eph 6:14).

In other words, when you really don't know for sure what the Lord *wants you to do* in any given situation; it's sometimes good enough to know what the Lord *doesn't want you to do* in order to resolve it.

So what did I do?

First, I told that entire group of prying personalities to never call me again. This put a decisive end to a few long-term associations and as a result, I kissed "it" good-bye. And so it was, opening night of the Bible study with four bodyguards at each entrance, my friend led worship. The "Principle of Diametric Opposition" had been executed.

Now, whenever I run across somebody with the spirit of control in operation, demanding that I do this or do that, in most cases there is one thing I know for sure … *I just do the opposite.*[42]

This is not done out of rebellion, but rather because I refuse to allow my conduct to be controlled by an evil spirit, one that opposes the leading and guiding of the Holy Spirit. I knew in this particular circumstance, I was to resist that thing just like I would the devil himself; because technically it was just the enemy using an ignorant group of "Christians" to try and *control* me.

After that first highly aggressive Control Freak situation occurred, I started to notice others, though not so intense, though not so aggressive. In fact, I started to notice the presence of the spirit of control working in some people who I loved and who I knew genuinely cared about me; but who nonetheless, were trying to get me to do certain things that I knew I should not do.

---

[42] There will be discussion in later chapters regarding circumstances when a person should <u>not</u> employ the Principle of Diametric Opposition.

The Principle of Diametric Opposition

Many of those things were the usual things people do when going through a trial to seek to "save" their lives, but by that time the Lord had already trained me that those were not the responses, nor the conduct, He was looking for *out of me*.

If I had complied with that kind of influence and control, I would never have grown in the direction that His Spirit was leading; and as a result of my stunted growth, I would have never gotten to the place of fulfilling His plan for my life.

I then began to review my life even more intently, as well as the many personal interactions I had experienced with others in the past. I realized that many of the bad decisions I had made in my life were actually "Control Freak" driven.

I also began to regularly sense and feel "its" working not only in my own relationships, but also in other people's relationships that I observed as well. At first, when I saw "its" influence at work, I didn't say anything, I didn't interrupt, I didn't make any correction, I didn't call "it" on the carpet; I just *observed* and later talked to Him about those observations.

"It" has therefore, been a *secret topic* of discussion between only Him and I for years now; but at this point, our secret is being shared with you.

Whether you are currently in a long-term, extremely controlling relationship; or whether you only feel controlled when the mother-in-law visits, what I want to know is if you think you have ever *felt* "it" before, for yourself?

In order to assure that you stay on board with this discussion, next up is a little taste of how the spirit of divination "feels" when at work in your life.

CHAPTER 16: Can You Feel "it"?

▬▬▬▬▬▬▬▬▬▬▬▬▬▬▬▬▬▬▬▬▬▬▬▬▬▬▬▬▬▬▬▬▬

"But solid food is for the mature, for those who have their powers of discernment trained by constant practice to distinguish good from evil" (Heb 5:14, ESV).

Being aggressively confronted by the spirit of divination helped me become more intent and focused on walking in the Holy Spirit and being led exclusively by Him, and nobody else. That experience caused me to check-in with the Lord a lot more often, especially when I realized someone was trying to *control* me. You will learn in later chapters that this "Check-In" process is necessary in order to ask His confirmation, direction and wisdom, whenever confronted with any Control Freak situation.

Some time after receiving this "spirit of divination" revelation, the Lord said to *"Go forth"* out of the ark (Gen 8:16) and I started back to interacting with a select few people more "normally". You know, communicating more regularly, telling people *how* I was doing, *what* I was doing; sharing vision and discussing where the Lord was leading me in the future; mentioning the directives God had given me to carry out and the corresponding decisions that needed to be made in order to do so.

In short, sharing a little bit more of "my business" if you would, to a select few people who I thought I could trust with that information. As time progressed and people started to re-emerge and new relationships were formed, these people started talking, suggesting, directing and speaking into my life on the various topics and issues I had raised; and I began to listen.

What's important to realize, however, was the fact that *I was not asking* for their input, it was always just readily "volunteered". I was not going around looking for advice or help on how to carry out the directives the Lord had given me. I had only started opening up with people sharing what was going on in my life; but once that information was conveyed, the advice came rolling in.

Can You Feel "it"?

This was the point when very loving, well meaning Christians started volunteering their input about the various decisions I had to make. They began directing me on what I should or shouldn't do, in order to achieve my goals and/or in response to my various circumstances.

These interpersonal interactions caused me to start to feel this kind of pressure that was familiar, but that I hadn't experienced during those years when I was all alone in the ark going through my storm. As I started to consider all of their opinions, suggestions and advice (much of which was not in concurrence), I began feeling this internal pressure like … well ... it was like … *I* was all confused now!

I had been totally clear in my mind with what the Lord had directed me to do, until I went out into the world and started talking to people about it! As I mentioned already, even your very close friends and especially your loved ones with whom you have an "emotional link" can influence your life and get you to take actions that the Lord does not want you to take.

Now, I don't want you to believe for one second that this means they're demon possessed, or not saved, or that they don't have the Holy Spirit dwelling in them, either. That's what is so sneaky about the spirit of divination.

"It" is not an indwelling spirit in a Christian. The Holy Spirit does not share space with the spirit of control like spouses who are at odds with one another, yet still living in the same household.

However, our flesh nature many times attracts, manifests, and then allows or "gives place to the devil" (Eph 4:27, KJV). The word "place" means, in this metaphorical context: "the opportunity, power, **occasion for acting.**"[43]

The truth is that most "Christians" functioning in today's society are "giving place to the devil" on a regular basis and in countless areas of their lives: gossiping, deceiving, not forgiving; it's displayed in their fits of rage, their lack of love, their hatred, contention, selfish ambition, jealousy, envy, comparing and competing … the list goes on and on.

Furthermore, the spirit of control plays upon the flesh or sin nature of the individual, especially their pride; and uses it as a spring-board to cause them to think that their opinions,

---

[43] Strong's #5117, transliterated "Topos".

directives, advice, or resolutions to *your* problems, are absolutely positively the *only thing that you should ever consider doing.*

Indeed, if you do not agree with them or fail to take the action they direct, they become personally offended. They then proceed to tell you how wrong you are and warn you of the doom and gloom that will shortly be forthcoming in your life, due to your failure to honor their advice or directive(s). This is the spirit of control now pumping up the volume (or intensity) in that relationship, because you didn't succumb to "its" first attempt to control your behavior.

Yes, these are people in your life who you love, respect, admire and by whom you want to be well thought of, loved, respected and admired (CIYA). By their "giving place" to that controlling spirit's influence, they can then be used to control "you". "Its" goal is that you too will "give place" and join-in under "its" direction and control, so that ultimately, "it" can influence not only your own actions, but "it" can then use you to influence others' actions as well.

It's like that old shampoo commercial, where they showed that same longhaired brunette woman washing her hair in those tiny pictures that multiplied, and multiplied, and multiplied. It illustrated the compounding manifold effect that took place when everyone who used that same hair product each shared "it" with a "friend".

In later chapters, we will go through many Biblical and common day examples so that you will begin to see "it" more clearly; but before we do that, as best as words can describe "it", I want to explain the experience of how the spirit of divination *"feels"* when in your presence, or when present in the company you keep.

Realize first, however, that I'm very hesitant to use the word *"feels"* because most Christians know that we are not supposed to be governed or ruled by our "feelings", but rather, by the Word of God. I do not disagree with that line of teaching.

Notwithstanding, the English language does not have a word that describes how the Spirit of God that indwells a true believer of Christ senses, or experiences, or discerns spiritual matters. I mean there's really no *one* word for it. "Discernment" isn't sufficient to describe how "it" *feels*, or what you can expect to sense in "its" presence or under

Can You Feel "it"?

"its" influence; nor does that one word describe the affect and/or effect of being confronted by the spirit of control.

So permit me if you would, to redefine the word "feel" to intentionally exclude all "feelings" of the flesh, like anger, hatred, envy, jealousy, etc.; but to intentionally include all the ways in which a genuine believer indwelled and baptized by the Holy Spirit recognizes, discerns, experiences, senses, or "feels" spiritual matters, as it relates to both the *affect*, as well as the *effect,* of a "spirit of control" encounter.

The difference between "affect" and "effect" is this: "affect" has to do with your emotional state, or the feelings you experience as a result of being confronted by the spirit of divination: fear, anxiety, worry, dread, condemnation, etc. Whereas, "effect" is like "cause and effect"; the "effect" of the spirit of divination relates to how "it" influences you to act, perform, or what it causes you *to do* in opposition to the Holy Spirit.

In sum, when encountering the spirit of control, expect "it" to "affect" you, or *make you feel* something negative and expect "it" to also try to "effect" you, *to take some action or to do* something. Also realize that the "affect" is the stimulant to your carrying out the "effect". Put another way, you *feel* so bad about "it", you do whatever "it" wants you to do in an attempt to rid those negative feelings.

Now, be careful that you aren't limited to thinking that the spirit of divination will only come in like a Mack truck, incessantly rolling back and forth over your life. It may come in as a very brief, seemingly non-confrontive suggestion, or offer, made by a person who really is (from their own perspective), looking out for your "best interests".

Furthermore, you can expect to experience the affect and effect of the spirit of control in differing levels of: *intensity; duration;* and *frequency.*

As it relates to "affect": ***intensity*** is measured by just how *bad* "it" "*feels*"; ***duration*** relates to *how long* "it" "*feels*" bad; and ***frequency*** relates to *how often* this bad "feeling" takes place.

As it relates to "effect": ***intensity*** is measured by the gravity of the conduct or action "it" is directing you to perform; ***duration*** is measured by how long you would be expected to carry out or continue that action or directive; and **frequency** is measured by how often you would be expected to carry out or continue that action or directive.

Here's a real life example that will make these concepts more clear:

I have someone who has worked with me for years on my radio program. He only means good in everything he has ever done for me; his help has always been a godsend.

Early one New Year, the radio program was moving to a new date and time and to several new stations. In short, the radio program was now going to "the big dance" (if you follow basketball), at least for the Southern California area.

Like the great producer he was, he had evidently done some research on other radio programs airing on other stations during that same time slot. While arguably, "looking out" for me, he sent me an email with a link. Without opening it, I could tell by reading the link that it contained information on someone else's radio program.

Can You Feel "it"?

After I got the email and realized what the link likely contained, I refused to open it, go to it, or read anything about it. I knew this was a spirit of divination tactic that could have been used to control me to the extent that "it" could have influenced me to "give place" to my flesh to try and *compete* with another radio program.

Or worse, I could have been distracted from hearing the Lord's voice and how He wanted to revamp my program for the upcoming premiere, by opening myself up to the influence of what the other talk show host was doing. I didn't want to be controlled or influenced by what someone else was doing (my alleged "competition", if you will). I didn't even want to know who he or she was, and to this day, I still don't.

What I did know was that my focus needed to stay on Him and doing what He wanted me to do. So I wrote my producer back saying, *"I didn't open the link. I never give the time of day to that kind of thing. No one is able to compete with me for what God's giving me because there is no competition for that. ☺"*

"CONTROL FREAK"

Can You Feel "it"?

[I was later told by someone of an often-repeated statement made by Vin Scully, "Be yourself, you have no competition!"]

In response, my producer wrote me back with a very simple, "Amen!" His godly response to my initiation of kicking "it" to the curb, quickly sealed the deal.

In this example, the "affect" was operating at minimal levels of intensity, frequency, and duration. There was only one suggestion (frequency) made via email, which was quickly snuffed out by my very simple response. There was no high level confrontation, no fight (low intensity); and there was no ongoing argument about it either (duration). Once my response was sent back, the pressure or expectation for me to look at the link stopped. The producer did not re-send or re-demand that I take any further action. As a result, there was no "effect" whatsoever from this interaction; "it" did not get me to take any action at all.

Now, that is a very lightweight, minimal (affect/effect) example of the spirit of control coming in with a suggestion to take my mind and thoughts off of the Lord. "It" wanted to direct my ways on this *other path* intended to get me sidetracked by consuming my mind in worthless thought about the "competition" or "comparing" radio programs, which could have resulted in my taking actions outside of His will.

If I would have done what was suggested, I may have tried to copy or mimic that host; or I may have thought that I should include certain features the other program carried, in my own program, none of which the Lord was directing me to do with the program He had given to me.

However, an "untrained" person's usual course of action would be to simply comply with the request and review the email link. This would be due to the pressure or expectation experienced or *felt* by the radio personality when the producer sends a link that he expects to be looked at and commented about.

Naturally, the "untrained" radio personality wouldn't want to discourage or cause a conflict with the producer and no doubt, would desire to keep him happy and working on the program. So, in order to avoid "rocking the boat" the radio personality would normally comply with the producer's well-meaning directive.

Can You Feel "it"?

How subtle of an example is that?

Now, in order to best illustrate the other end of the spectrum, allow me to take this same example and manufacture some additional circumstances. This way, you can imagine "feeling" the affect and effect of the spirit of divination at work, in that same situation, but at much higher levels of intensity, frequency and duration.

Let's say that I refused the email as I explained earlier and that my producer had instead responded: "Hey look, *I am* the producer of this program, and if you want *me* to continue working with you, then you need to consider *my* input. I've researched this radio talk show host, their program is very successful, they are clearly going to be our competition; and I think we need to implement some of their format in your program. Look, if you don't want my input, maybe you need to look for someone else to work with."

BAM! The *intensity* level rises to the top. This producer is now going to quit unless I do what he says. The "affect" on me is worry and concern about my program not doing well against the "competition" and/or not going forward as scheduled because I lost my producer.

My thoughts stop working on planning the program's premiere and I can't hear any direction from the Lord anymore. Instead, my mind is consumed with thoughts such as, "What on earth did I say that hurt his feelings?" "What can I do to smooth things over?" "What am I going to do now? The program is supposed to air in two weeks. Who can I find if he quits on me now?" "If I lose him, I'll have to re-work everything!"

I begin to stress, worry and become upset at the threat that my program won't ever make it to the "big dance".

Affect! Affect! Affect!

As to my "quality of life"? Well, it's now in the tank.

An "untrained" radio personality wouldn't have the wherewithal to respond, "Since the Lord is directing me to do this program; and since I'm the one who is accountable to Him to do His will; I hope you can appreciate the fact that

Can You Feel "it"?

I must take all of my directives from Him. I want to thank you in advance for your understanding."

No. Instead, what would most likely happen because of this pressure or expectation (or affect), the radio personality would take the producer's suggestion; look at the email, spend time considering the "competition" and then implement various similar features into his/her own program (effect); thereby turning it into a copy-cat radio program that the Lord neither wanted, nor needed!

If I had done that, I would have lost His backing for the program. The Lord would have said, "Look, that's *not* what I wanted to do with the program, so have a fun time with *your* program, I'm out!"

Had that been the case, the spirit of control coming in at a higher level of *(intensity)* or "affect", would have caused the "effect" of changing the radio program's features for every time it aired *(frequency)*; until the program went off the air *(duration)*; which, no doubt, would have been some time in the very near future because the Lord was no longer the One guiding the way.

Are you with me?

The affect is the "feeling" part of encountering "it" and the "effect" is your reaction, or the actions taken in response to that "affect" or feeling. Realize therefore, that every spirit of control encounter you face may vary from one extreme to another and anywhere in between; but nonetheless, no matter what the intensity, frequency, or duration, realize that you are still encountering "it".

As we continue down this line of teaching, it will be helpful to determine how "it" *feels* by making some distinctions between experiencing or "feeling" the Spirit of God <u>vs.</u> experiencing or "feeling" the spirit of divination:

<u>Distinction #1:</u>

When the Holy Spirit is leading you to do something, such as a good deed for another person, <u>it is rarely ever done upon that person, or any other person's request for you to do so</u>. Rather, it is usually in situations where no one has asked you to do anything. The Spirit of God makes the suggestion internally, shows you the way or resource to use mentally and you feel a pressure to obey and perform emotionally, or you otherwise risk *"feeling"* like you're disobeying God.

On the other hand, when the spirit of control is trying to get you to do something, <u>"it" always uses another person to deliver the directive.</u> "It" has to! Because "it" doesn't dwell within you like the Holy Spirit does!

When the spirit of divination is at work, a person *feels* some sort of mandatory obligation, or pressure to comply, or duty to perform in order to please, pacify, obey, or obtain the approval of another person. This is either to "please man" and/or based on a "fear of man" and thus "it" always plays into the CIYA of the person being controlled.

You really don't want to do whatever it is and you really don't necessarily believe God is telling you to do it either, no matter how "right" it seems to be. Nonetheless, you think you must perform for this person, husband, wife, mother-in-law, boss, child; or this organization, church, or ministry, because of something that was said, or something that they expect from you, or because you *fear* some negative repercussions from them if you don't do whatever it is they want you to do.

Can You Feel "it"?

Their demand or input is what motivates or causes you to act or do something (effect). You feel pressured to do it in order to please that person (affect), or meet their expectation of you, or even your own expectation of yourself (which is all motivated by the CIYA). Your compliance to their directive, expectation, or demand, secures that you will be seen favorably in the eyes of the other person or people.

Distinction #2:

The "affect" of the Holy Spirit directing your actions is joy, peace, strength and focus in carrying out the directive, even if it was a hard thing for you to do.

On the other hand, the "affect" of the spirit of control working in your life is that you *feel* controlled and condemned and saddened, sometimes even afraid, it's as if you did something wrong, or would be doing something wrong, if you did not comply with "its" demands.

When, in reality, you haven't done *anything* wrong! Yet you still feel troubled, you still feel unrest, even fear and dread.

Can You Feel "it"?

Your mind is consumed with this personal interaction. You're replaying what was said or done in your mind, the gestures, the rolling of the eyes, the scoff they made, the walking away in a huff; all performed by the person who "gave place" to the spirit of control to be used in their life, in order to try and influence yours.

The instant replay of some of these interactions can literally consume you mentally, emotionally and/or spiritually for days, weeks, months, even years. You're not free, you're consumed with what this person said or did. You know what they want you to do; but it's <u>not</u> something that you really want to do. You could resolve the pressure in an instant by simply complying, but it just doesn't really *feel* right to do that either.

What happens is that the interaction then becomes used by the enemy to control your heart, soul, mind and strength; or as previously defined, all of "you". You're now <u>not</u> focused on God and what He wants you to do, you're only focused on that person and what *they* want you to do.

So you just keep thinking about this person and this situation, its always bothering you, it's always in the back of your mind. You're consumed; it's a steady pressure, it's like a cloud glooming over your head, it's an oppressive damper on your life. You're neither at rest, nor at peace because "it" is there, "it" is *still* there. You're not free in your emotions, mind, or body; instead, you're just tense, agitated, disconcerted.

It's similar to how the contentious person feels after having yet another fight with somebody they love: guilty, wrong, condemned and sorry it happened. It's similar to that, but not exactly the same because it doesn't require an actual "fight" per se to take place; and more importantly, you didn't do anything wrong, you *didn't* sin!

What's happening is that your spirit is struggling against the spirit of control. The spirit of control is now in the lead, gaining territory by taking "you" over. In this state, you are what I call: *"Control-Freaking out".*

Time now, for a quick tangent to cover some new terminology that I will provide you within various sentence structures, including verb tenses, which can be used to describe this *feeling* of being influenced by the spirit of divination. Mind you, very soon, those of us "in the know" will start to expand our own classified language and begin to develop even more phrases to describe when *feeling* or experiencing the "it" phenomenon:

"This is Control-Freaking me out"[44]
"I was totally Control-Freaking out about it"[45]
"It Control-Freaked me out"[46]
"I'm a Control-Freaking mess right now"[47]
"Please, don't even try and Control-Freak me out today"[48]
"Did he try Control-Freaking you out about it too?"[49]
"Are you Control-Freaking mad?"[50]

Distinction #3:

In that "Control-Freaked Out" condition, now all of a sudden you can't seem to connect with God, you feel distant from Him and you don't know why. You check for sin, but you're not in sin. So you *really* just don't know why. "Lord, where did You go?"

---

[44] Present participle
[45] Perfect participle
[46] Aorist participle
[47] Adjectivally participle
[48] Present active infinitive
[49] Adjectival aorist participle
[50] Aorist participle

Can You Feel "it"?

It's not like it used to be when you "checked-in" with the Lord and you could connect and get a quick confirmation or directive from Him. You don't know what the Lord wants you to do now because you feel like you lost connection with hearing His voice, due to this other person's voice you continue to hear in your mind.

The spirit of divination has come into your life and laid hold on your heart, your mind, and your body. "It" has succeeded in consuming "you" with the taped reruns of your interaction with this person, by playing them over and over in your mind. You continue to replay their words and their actions; you recall the pressure-filled statements they made, all the while picturing their facial expressions, their body language, and their scoffs.

Once again, what I believe is going on in the spiritual realm during this time, is a dueling between the Holy Spirit and the spirit of divination. There is a battle over who will consume your heart, mind, soul and body ("you") that is taking place right then and there.

In the natural, all you know is that you're in a situation that is demanding a decision or action; that this person has given you this advice or directive, or made this comment, correction or criticism; and that they have an expectation for you to carry it out or rectify the problem, just as they have advised.

The usual "untrained" effect of this kind of interaction is that you modify your behavior in order to suit, either what you've been told to do, or what you anticipate will be problematic for another person, if you don't do it.

When you comply by your actions (*effect*), in order to rid the negative feelings you're experiencing *(affect),* you give-in to the spirit of divination's *control* over your life. Once "it" succeeds in controlling you, then many times you become angry, you feel unappreciated, you feel as if you've ... *been taken advantage of.*

Distinction #4:

Distinguish yet again, when the Spirit of God tells you to go and correct someone (in love of course); but you *feel* pressure because you're not a Pharisee and you don't *feel* comfortable doing that kind of thing and so you really don't want to do it; therefore, "Lord, please use somebody else."

Can You Feel "it"?

Nonetheless, the Holy Spirit continues to impress upon your heart that *you're* the one He wants to use. You can't get the thought out of your mind and you know you won't be at rest until you get this done.

When the Holy Spirit is at work, you feel led and yes, sometimes even pressured or pushed to do something. That thing you are being impressed to do by the Holy Spirit, however, *may not necessarily please man,* but is usually solely motivated by obedience to God and it forces you to stretch yourself out of your comfort zone.

The distinguishing factor here is that, *it is not motivated by people pleasing, or fearing man, or trying to make people like you, or accept you, or doing what they (people) want you to do* (the CIYA). Indeed, it's quite the opposite. You don't expect this person will like you, or even want to be associated with you anymore once you follow through on the Holy Spirit's directive; but nevertheless you know you must obey God rather than man (Acts 5:29).

The contrary occurs when influenced by the spirit of control. In those cases, *we do exactly what that person wants us to do in order to relieve the emotional pressure and try to rid the negative feelings we're experiencing; and/or in order to eliminate the risk they will be mad, not love us anymore, gossip about us, or disown us.*

So in short, we give in.

We mistakenly think that if we do exactly what they said we should do, or do what we think they'd want us to do, that we will be relieved from the pressure and stress in the relationship; and that everything will go back to a peaceful state in our own hearts and minds.

The devil is a liar!

That's the enormous mistake we all make. The cause of your emotional stress is not this *one incident* with this *one person*, with which *you think*, if you just do what they say it will all be good, amicably resolved and go away.

No, it's not that simple. The real cause of your unrest, pressure, and stress, is the spirit of control at work in your life!

Can You Feel "it"?

If you don't figure out how to deal with "it" alone, after this incident you're dealing with today with this person, there will be a different incident tomorrow with another person. Then later, another incident with another person will occur; and another with another; and another with another, and another with another, ad infinitum. (Don't forget the shampoo commercial!)

The issue isn't trying to get your husband, or boss, or best friend, or pastor, to just stop "being" like that. The issue is that you need to learn how to resist and deal with people who "are" already like that <u>and</u> who "aren't" ever likely going to change.

Here are some common examples of ways you may think or respond when you *feel* the pressure of the spirit of divination:

My best girlfriend will be jealous if I don't include her.
My boyfriend will get angry if I don't come over tonight.
My sister will feel slighted if I don't get the same thing for her that I got for myself.
My neighbor will get mad if I park in front of their house.

"CONTROL FREAK"

Can You Feel "it"?

My pastor expects me to always be available to serve in that ministry.

My prayer partner will think I'm backslidden if I cut off the relationship.

My in-laws will be mad at me if we move closer to my parents.

Now, you fill in the blanks:

My wife hates when I _____, so I never _____.

My husband will love me more if, or when I _____.

My boss is impressed whenever I_____.

My dad hates it when _____, so I never_____.

My mother will be happy if I _____, so I always _____.

The list is infinite! Remember, the real issue is the jugular itself! It's that spirit of divination, which remember, we are intent upon taking out! O-U-T!

Distinction #5:

The spirit of divination also uses people to foster self-doubt when you're faced with making a decision and/or carrying out a directive in obedience to the leading of the Holy Spirit.

Can You Feel "it"?

Remember, the spirit of divination and the CIYA first came into contact with one another as far back as the Garden of Eden when the serpent commented: *"Yea, hath God said?"* (Gen 3:1, KJV)

Likewise with you, questions will start to come through other people (via the spirit of divination), in an attempt to confuse the issue or directives the Lord has given you: "Did God really tell you that?" "Are you *sure* God is leading?" "I don't *think* that scripture applies, to your situation; but this one does" "How do you really *know* that you're hearing God's voice?"

You may know the Word of God really, *really* well, but after you start talking to someone who is being used by the spirit of divination to deceive you and take you off track, you start to question whether or not you're right and whether or not God's Word really does apply to this situation. You then may start to question your own knowledge and application of the Word of God, in even the most obvious situations.

For example, say you have been married to a man for several years and he refuses to get a "real" job and contribute financially to the household. Year after year, it's one delay after another, one excuse after another, but still no income.

You *know* that the Bible says, *"...when we were with you, we commanded you this: If anyone will not work, neither shall he eat"* (2 Thess 3:10, KJV); <u>and</u> *"If any provide not for his own, and specially for those of his own house, he hath denied the faith, and is worse than an unbeliever"* (1 Tim 5:8, NKJV).

So on the one hand, you know that there is something wrong with what he's doing. Namely, he's *controlling* your life by forcing you to carry all the financial burdens of the entire household on your shoulders; but on the other hand, you can't start acting disobediently yourself in response. I mean, what are you going to do? Lose everything you worked so hard for and deliver an ultimatum to him saying, "Look, if you don't work, I'm not going to either?" That would be irresponsible ... *wouldn't it?*

So you start questioning and even doubting a very clear application of the Word of God to that situation and continue to live your life being *controlled*, held in financial bondage.

Can You Feel "it"?

Are you with me?

Now, let me throw another little wrinkle into this example. What if your pastor said you could divorce over this? Yet, you've always been taught that "Biblical grounds" for divorce was limited to only a few situations (Matt 5:32; 1 Cor 7) and this unfortunately, is not one of them.

On the one hand, the husband is clearly in sin before God and financially abusing the wife; on the other hand, the counsel from the pastor goes too far, there isn't any Biblical authority to divorce a man who only married a woman for "her money". It's rather sad, but true.

Even when we get "godly" counsel, we still need to be very careful which "spirit" we're listening to because you and I will be personally accountable to God for every decision we make. *So then each of us shall give <u>account of himself</u> to God"* (Ro 14:12, KJV).

We are not going to be able to stand before God and blame our pastor, husband, wife, or "godly" Christian friend, or anybody else, for giving us bad advice, especially when we knew better for ourselves.

Can You Feel "it"?

Distinction #6:

Understand what I'm <u>not</u> saying. I am not saying that the spirit of control's leading is a feeling of pressure and it feels bad; and that the Spirit of God's leading is a sense of freedom and always feels good. No, no, no!

I am <u>not</u> saying that whenever the Spirit of God is telling you to do something that it always feels good! Don't misunderstand and try to over-simplify complex concepts. Remember, this is a hard thing to put into words.

You will *feel* pressure in Holy Spirit led instances. In fact, many times what the Spirit of God tells us to do is uncomfortable and we actually *don't want to do it;* and yet there is a continuing pressure we will experience and if obedient, that pressure eventually drives us to take action.

When the spirit of control steps in to the game, the "affect" is to feel a similar type of pressure. It's *similar* to the type of impression or pressure we *feel* to do something that the Holy Spirit wants us to do. I'd imagine that's because both the Holy Spirit and the spirit of divination are just that … spirits! One Holy and the other unholy; both of them, looking to lead and guide our lives. So the sensation or pressure felt, the impressions and impulses to act, are essentially quite similar.

If you cannot determine whether or not the conduct directed, is either bad or good by the written Word of God; then many times it will be very difficult to tell which Spirit (or spirit) you *feel* is pressuring you to act.

Take this next example that illustrates both the Spirit of God and the spirit of control, playing their differing roles, in the same person, within the same relationship. In order to increase our reading enjoyment, let's pretend that you're that same person:

The Spirit of God is prompting you to open up a conversation with a co-worker about Jesus. You're totally uncomfortable and you don't want to do it *at all*. It's just so much easier to live your Christian life holding onto your own fire insurance policy, than to risk being mocked or rejected by someone else about it. So you respond, *"Oh no, not today Lord! I'm way too busy and besides, You know my heart, I really don't even like that person."*

Can You Feel "it"?

Nevertheless, because the *pressure* continues, and the door is so obviously open, you eventually obey the Holy Spirit. Despite your once rebellious attitude, the Spirit of God is faithful to give you the right approach and the right words; and as a result, your co-worker gets saved and starts going with you to church and lo and behold, over a very short period of time, you begin to see fruit.

Without a doubt, you know that was Him (the spirit of divination obviously wouldn't want to influence you to evangelize anyone into the Kingdom). Yep, that was the Holy Spirit's work in action; it was right and you *feel* great about it. You even start liking the person a little more too. Wonderful!

Next, enter in the spirit of control, to whom you unwittingly, "give place". "It" causes you (the new evangelist), to trust in your newly energized spiritual pride (since the Lord just used you to lead someone to Him); and now, you believe that you are personally and solely responsible for the growth of that new baby believer co-worker of yours.

As a result, you feel this pressure to make sure that *your* "new believer" gets on the straight and narrow right away. I mean, who better than *you* to take on this much needed responsibility?

So within the month, you proceed to make a list for your co-worker of all these "Christian Rules and Regulations" that you recite, while expecting them to be followed as they walk in their new relationship with Christ: "Pray for at least 20 minutes every morning <u>and</u> every night. Oh, and during your half-hour lunch break too if you can fit it in. Read at least two chapters in your Bible everyday, always go to church on Sundays and mid-week too if you can make it. This is so that you can pay your tithes, which are 10% of your income. You just got a raise, didn't you? You will also need to get into a ministry serving the Lord, we have the children's ministry open. You *like* kids, don't you? You'll also need to start sharing your faith with everyone you see, here are some tracts for you to hand out. Oh and I almost forgot: no drinking, no drugs, or "R" rated movies, no rap music, heavy metal, or love songs of a sexual nature. You need to really be careful of what you read and watch on TV. Actually, a lot of us *more dedicated* Christians ... *well,* we don't even have TV's anymore. So you may want to consider getting rid of yours now too."

Can You Feel "it"?

HA! The spirit of control has just instantaneously quenched this new believer's experience with God. Instead of being a carefree baby believer (at least for awhile anyway), you, via the spirit of divination's controlling influence, have now succeeded in consuming the heart, mind, body and baby-believer spirit, by implementing the expectation that he/she follow all these rules and regulations in order to please both, you and God! Since your co-worker knows you're going to be regularly checking-up on his/her progress, its doom and gloom for them from that point on. The Holy Spirit <u>and</u> the spirit of divination, respectively, just used *your life* on both accounts.

Though *you personally* may have never done this before, you know this kind of thing happens all the time.

Pretty scary, huh? That's the jugular! That's the clandestine nature of the spirit of control. That's what goes completely undetected by the Christian community.

So in summation:

The spirit of divination is a feeling of oppression, bondage, pressure, and a damper on your spirit. You feel trapped, strapped and in bondage to take some action as directed, demanded, suggested, or as commented on by the individual who "gave place" to "it".

Due to the way in which this spirit of divination consumes your thinking over the situation, you lose connection with hearing God's voice. Instead, you are replaying the voice of this person that you feel pressured by in you mind; their statements, actions, directives, demands, suggestions, comments; as well as recalling their more subtle non-verbal communications like their facial gestures, their rolling of the eyes, their scoffs, their huffs and puffs.

You're consumed with pleasing them, getting their approval, making them happy, making them like you, or think well of you; and as a result you can't hear from God at all. Any open flow of untainted, unchallenged and uninterrupted communication with your Creator, is now long gone. All that you can hear now is "white noise"-- strike that! Black noise!

Here are a few good examples of people experiencing "Black Noise":

Can You Feel "it"?

In our first instance, say there is a professional CPA who after practicing accounting for over twenty years, is told by the Lord to leave those old wineskins and start up a ministry serving food to the elderly in his community. This kind of directive can be very difficult for a person to obey when they know they can make a living working as a CPA, but they don't know if they can do the same, laboring exclusively in ministry. Having never been in the ministry before, this CPA expected it to start out slow, at least financially speaking.

In any event, he stepped out and the Lord faithfully provided as he continued for the first few years to build the ministry. During that time, a relative of one of his prior "major clients" whose taxes he used to do for decades calls him in distress. He knows this lady. She is one of the people he would help every once and a while without any expectation of payment, because of her relationship to his "major client".

Her call of distress comes one day while he is merrily continuing to do the work of the ministry. She says she's in desperate need of tax advice and help with filing several past due tax returns. Oddly enough, these temptations to "look back" always seemed to come up whenever the ex-CPA was in some sort of financial strait; but up to this point, he has never looked back and picked up any "side-work" no matter how tempting it was to do at the time.

So during the call she asks him advice on her IRS problems and then asks him to do this CPA work for her (no doubt expecting that he'd do it for free like years past). He tells her that he no longer does CPA work and that he's now in full-time ministry.

After feignedly saying, "Wow, how neat!" She acts as if she didn't hear a thing the ex-CPA just said and she persists. She goes on to tell him how bad her situation is and how unfairly the IRS has treated her and how it seems like he has been *the only person who has ever been able* to keep her records straight.

Then, with a tad bit of whining arising in her voice, she asks him again, *"Won't you please help me ... just this one last time?"*

The pressure begins to rise, the ex-CPA still has good relations with his "major client" and he doesn't want him, to be told by her, that he (the ex-CPA) wouldn't help her. He starts to feel forced to do something that the Lord, on more than one occasion, has clearly indicated that He does not want him to do. Yet he feels obligated, he feels pressured, he still feels like he's expected to resolve these kind of IRS problems for the family.

After a great deal of time spent on the telephone, he is finally able to end the conversation politely without taking on the responsibility. However, to exacerbate (or intensify) the dilemma, he later gets a voice mail from the "major client" personally, asking him to *"Please speak to her and help her"* while leaving him her telephone number to call. (She has obviously made contact with her relative the "major client" and got him to call on her behalf, even after he had declined to provide her with any CPA services.)

The ex-CPA now can't stop thinking about this situation. He can't stop thinking about the fact that his history with this family has created an expectation that he would always come in to resolve these kinds of problems for them; and worse, for free!

He's wondering what the family is saying about him now. He starts to question, "Should I take this last job?" He then goes through several hours of thinking and reasoning; and creating statements or responses in his mind on how he is going to explain to the "major client" (hypothetically, if placed in that position), why he cannot take on this responsibility and disobey God.

He gets so tense that he cannot think of anything else but explaining *why* he really hasn't done anything wrong by declining this job. His neck starts to tighten up, he can't sleep that night as he keeps replaying over and over in his mind, what he said to her when he declined to help. He's wondering how she digested and regurgitated that information onto his "major client" when relaying the fact that he refused to help her. As a result, he gets up the next morning with a "tension" headache of epic proportions.

How will he explain himself to his "major client" if he calls him back today? What if he asks him to take up her matter as a *personal favor to him?* Will he be able to say, "No" then? He starts thinking to himself, "Then, what will I say?" "Then, what will I do?"

Can You Feel "it"?

Our ex-CPA is now, "Control Freaking out". His quality of life is shot, straight down the tubes. He's fretting, worried, consumed. He can't hear from God to confirm or deny *anything* at this point. He's now pressured and confused about what he should do, despite the fact that God has already spoken.

Next, the ex-CPA grabs his morning cup of coffee and starts in on some "stronghold thinking": "Just this one last time won't hurt anybody, I can still keep my ministry work up and if she'll agree to pay, we sure need the extra money. This could actually be a godsend. After all that man has done for me? I don't see anything wrong with doing some work this one last time."

"*Lord,* you don't mind ... do You?"

Due to the fact that he wants this spirit of divination-driven pressure relieved as soon as possible, the ex-CPA is controlled into making the wrong move and he takes the job. The lady shows up at his office with a commanding presence and a smirk on her face, which seems to convey the message, *"I know how to get whatever I want".* So, the entire time the ex-CPA is working, or helping this lady, he's "hatin life". He now hates CPA work and he's regretting having allowed her to bring it back into his life. Furthermore, he can't stand her sense of entitlement to his time and expertise.[51]

Yes, he finishes the job; but afterwards he feels sick to his stomach. Through the entire experience, he knows he's been blatantly disobeying the Lord's directive. Even if she had offered to pay, at this point, he doesn't even want the money.

As a result of his disobedience, the fruit or harvest coming from his ministry efforts are either delayed, or discontinued entirely because people who know they've failed the Lord, oftentimes get so discouraged they just give up the pursuit, thinking they can never recover and go forward.

Here's another example of "black noise": Say there is a lady who works as a "house mother" for a special program serving ex-foster children who are now age eighteen or over (foster adults). The "house mother" is a good woman;

---

[51] Controlling people think they have a right, or "entitlement" to control your time, money, resources and expertise.

she sincerely cares for these foster adults and does everything she can to help encourage them to become productive members of society.

One of the foster adults, with a past of drug abuse and unruly criminal behavior, who has lived a very hard and "wild" lifestyle (where "crazy" is considered "normal"), lives under the supervision of this "house mother". One day when placing her under guidelines or "House Rules", she starts to attack the "house mother" on a personal level. The foster adult calls her names, has fits of rage, blatantly refuses to obey the "House Rules" and threatens to report the "house mother" to her supervisors for mistreatment, etc.

Though the "house mother" has done absolutely nothing wrong, her emotional well-being is immediately rocked by this encounter! She can't figure out how to resolve this problem; or how to make this foster adult's behavior change; how to make sure she doesn't say or do defiant things anymore; how to make sure she doesn't make any false allegations to her supervisor. The "house mother" has been pulled into the emotional drama of what the foster adult considers "normal" and now she has instantaneously become a "Control Freaking mess".

Can You Feel "it"?

Moving on to our last "black noise" example: Say a man has lived with his girlfriend, the mother of his five children, for over fifteen years and yet, has never married. All of a sudden the mother starts a Facebook account and hooks up with someone from her past and starts staying out all night. When she comes home he can tell that she's under the influence of alcohol and/or drugs. The man doesn't know what to do. He's trying to keep the kids together and deal with this "unfaithful mother" situation at the same time.

He has several interactions with the mother of his children during which she gets angry, throws things, calls him every name in the book; threatens that she's going to leave him, or tells him to leave, or says she wants him to take the kids and everybody leave ... "Just leave me alone!"

He doesn't know what to do. So he begins to call every friend he has and he also calls counselors, lawyers, pastors, relatives and family members. He speaks to anyone who will listen to his situation, hoping that someone will help him figure out what to do.

The key to understanding this "Black Noise" situation is that when he makes these calls, you'll notice that he has surrendered all "control" over the outcome of this situation to the mother of his children, even as it pertains to *his own life!*

Of course he can't control what she does, but he still is in control of what *he does in response to it.* But in this situation, the spirit of divination has caused him to lose even the control he once had over making decisions about *his own life.*

In other words, as he relates his problems to others, everything he says revolves around what, "she said" what "she threatened", what "she said she would do if", what "will make her stop" ... "I'm afraid if I do this, she'll do that"...

His whole "world focus" revolves around her. He no longer has any inclination, let alone any ability, to make a decision on how to deal with this situation for himself, separate from her consideration. All of his decisions revolve around what her reaction will be to any decision that he may make in the future. She, via the spirit of divination, is running and controlling his life and his future, and the lives and futures of the children.

Can You Feel "it"?

He can no longer think for himself, direct himself, or get himself and/or his children out of a bad situation without giving deference and consideration to her reaction. He too, is a Control Freaking mess! As a result, his "quality of life" has also hit the skids.

The spirit of divination will cause you to become immobilized via the "Black Noise" generated by these kinds of controlling situations. You'll find that you can't stop thinking about that person, what they said, what they did, what they want you to do. Your emotions are affected, you're down, oppressed, you're not the same person you were before your interaction with this other person.

You're in bondage; you're bound to this situation, bound to the person, bound to their perceptions, bound to coming up with a resolution. And ... you *keep thinking* about it. You can't get it out of your mind; it's a dread, a pressure, a serious feeling of agitation for the conscientious person. You feel like you need closure, it's just bugging you, you need to make a decision, you want this taken care of, you want it over, you want a resolution.

Can You Feel "it"?

It's like a monkey on your back. You're walking around the whole time saying to yourself, "I can't shake this thing!" "I can't shake this thought!" "I can't shake this directive!" You're absolutely miserable; but again, *you* didn't sin. You're the one being responsible; but you feel like you're disconnected in your own fellowship with God and you just can't figure out why.

The *affect* of the spirit of control is experiencing or *feeling* this emotional pressure that some people try to ignore, while still others focus on "it" 24/7 – 365. The *effect* of the spirit of control is to immobilize you into becoming unfruitful for the Kingdom.

In either case, "you" are so completely consumed that you can't do anything else but either think about "it"; or, you remain acutely conscious that "it" is lying in wait, begging for your attention at some point in the near future. Your heart is not free; your mind is not free; your soul is tied up in stress and dread; you have no strength to do the things God wants you to do; you can't even hear His voice, let alone obey it!

Can You Feel "it"?

In short, *you've* become a *Control-Freaking* mess! And that's *exactly* where the enemy wants you!

So there you have it! The foundation has been laid.

We've succeeded in describing, defining, disclosing, explaining, illuminating *and pulling back* the various layers of skin that have been covering the "jugular" for all these years.

Now that the spirit of divination is fully and completely uncovered, we can actually observe and examine "the jugular" vein for ourselves.

Wow! Look! There it is! … Right there, right out in the open, stripped bare, naked and fully exposed for all of us to see.

The only *problem* is …

It's still pumping.

CHAPTER 17: The Table is Set

"You serve me a six-course dinner right in front of my enemies ..." (Ps 23:5, MSG).

The foundation has been laid and the skin has been pulled back, so let's summarize the essential components of our six-course dinner:

Course 1:

Humanity was created with a "free will" and "the power of choice" to exercise that "free will". God intentionally created man this way because God is <u>not</u> a God "of" control, He is a God "in" control. He is a God of love, liberty and freedom. He is a "giver" not a "taker". He wants your heart, mind, body, soul and strength given to Him willingly and voluntarily, in order to fulfill His Kingdom agenda.

The Table is Set

In contradiction, there is a spirit of control/divination at work in the world and more importantly, in the Christian Community. Everything about this controlling spirit is in opposition to Christ, or is anti-to Christ. The spirit of divination is a "taker", a deceiver, a "controller". "It" is so subtle, "it" has figured out a way to *control* you and get you off track with the plan of God, without you ever knowing "it" is at work in your life.

Course 2:

You have a serious character flaw, a "chink in your armor" (CIYA); which is like a two-sided coin. First, you were created with an innate need to be loved, accepted, admired, valued, respected; to be well thought of and well spoken of. This need causes you to be a "man pleaser" (this is the "heads" side of the CIYA).

Second, you've learned over the years to "fear man" or else risk losing the love, affection, admiration and respect (especially of those with whom you have an "emotional link"), should you choose *not* to act or make decisions based on others opinions, desires, or demands for your life (this is the "tails" side of the CIYA).

Course 3:

The spirit of divination's *motive* is anti-to Christ's: it is to gain control over the total "you" and every aspect of your mind, heart, body, soul, and strength; your complete and total existence. The spirit of control attempts to oppose the work of the Holy Spirit in the life of a Believer through their interpersonal relationships, with the ultimate goal of keeping them from ever reaching and fulfilling their God-given destiny.

In sum, "it" wants to control "you" and "it" does so by the use of "Black Noise" in detracting, deterring and eliminating your ability to carry on untainted, unchallenged and uninterrupted communication with the Lord. In that condition, you can never fulfill the purpose and plans that God has for your life, because very simply, you've lost communication with your Commander.

Course 4:

The spirit of divination's *means* are crafty, sly and subtle; so subtle you may not even realize that the spirit of divination is at work in your life through both your

"Christian" and non-Christian interpersonal relationships. The more clandestine *means* used by the enemy are found within your "Christian" relationships. This is where *controlling* "Christians" who have "given place" to the spirit of divination, mislead, misguide and misdirect your decisions and behavior, apart from, or anti-to, the Spirit of God; and most often, without your ever realizing it.

Course 5:

Due to the multiple interpersonal relationships you carry on everyday, the spirit of divination has several *opportunities* to fulfill or consummate its evil motive. Specifically, the spirit of control first influences others who "give place" to "it" and then in turn, they are used to influence, or control your emotional condition (affect) and ultimately, your behavior (effect). While functioning under this type of bondage and control, you will never be able to fulfill your God-given assignments, purpose and plan, because you're being led by the spirit of control, not by the Spirit of the Lord.

Each and every time you adhere to man's directives and opinions (rather than God's), as it relates to the decisions you make and the actions you take, it's yet another, "mission accomplished" for the enemy.

Course 6:

All of these factors mixed up together create a recipe for spiritual disaster! This is the "jugular" hidden underneath numerous layers of skin. When this type of clandestine control takes place in your life, day in and day out, it's an outright crime!

Until the skin is torn off and pulled away, and the jugular is unveiled, revealed and eradicated, this crime will continue to be perpetrated in your life. "You" are being ripped off of your God-given destiny and most of the time, without ever even realizing it.

There *is* a way out for you, but as is usually the case, we're saving the best ... *dessert* ... for last.

At this point, *the table has been set* with the concepts, principles, tools, and terminology necessary for me to convey the much-needed message of:

The Table is Set

"Jugular Eradication".

However, let's not rush through this fine dining experience we're having together; after all, we've yet to fully digest our six-course meal. It's now time to sit back and relax while we enjoy a little *real life* spirit of divination-driven drama.

During our "Feature Presentation" over the next few chapters, you can start to absorb, assimilate and synthesize your feast by thinking, recalling, reflecting and applying each component of the meal you've just been served.

It won't be long now. I eagerly anticipate that you'll soon find yourself *backed into a corner*, blinded by the glaring lamp of interrogation. When that happens, please realize I wasn't necessarily *meaning* to ruin your dinner.

For whatever discomfort you may experience throughout the upcoming pages of drama, I assure you, I'll make it up to you when it comes time to serve dessert.

CHAPTER 18: Affect Drives Effect

■■■■■■■■■■■■■■■■■■■■■■■■■■■■■■■■■■■■■■■

*"And it came to pass, as we went to prayer, a certain damsel possessed with a **spirit of divination** met us, which brought her masters **much gain** by soothsaying"* (Acts 16:16, KJV).[52]

Starting off with a topic very close to the hearts of all of us; namely, "money" <u>and</u> the *feelings* of "security" which seem to accompany anyone with ... *a lot of it.*

Would you be at all surprised to know that just about everyone on the face of the earth, at one time or another, in one instance or many, has been subjected to "the spirit of

---

[52] In this passage the Bible states the damsel was "possessed" with the spirit of divination; and therefore, the need for Paul to "cast out" the spirit of divination arose in this case. This however, is not in contradiction to our previous *indwelling* discussion. As it relates to Christians the spirit of divination is "given place" in a Christian's life (not given "possession"); and then that Christian is used to influence and control the behavior of others.

control" at work in their lives as it relates to money and/or using money in order to try to *feel* "secure" about their lives and/or their futures?

Here in Acts we see a girl possessed with the "spirit of divination" who was being used to control people's spending habits. More specifically, the people were paying money to her master to willingly become the victims of her soothsaying gig. They were drawn to this girl because they wanted her to tell them what was going to happen in their futures.[53]

Why did they want to know their future?

Well, why does anyone want to know his or her future? Obviously, so they can try to "control" it, silly. Remember, the word "divination" is defined in part as: "man's attempts to control the world *and the future* apart from the true God."[54]

---

[53] The word "soothsaying" means: to act as a seer, to deliver an oracle, prophesy or divine (Strong's #3132, transliterated "Manteuomai").

[54] Vine's Expository Dictionary of Old and New Testament Words, Copyright © 2001, Thomas Nelson, Inc., Nashville, Tennessee. All rights reserved.

Affect Drives Effect

Haven't you ever realized, what people *really want* ... even more than money? People want *control* "over their futures" so that they can feel *in control,* over their own, out-of-control lives. Having money is just an adjunct to this underlying aspiration.

In this case, the master was able to *control* the spending habits of the people by making use of the spirit of divination working through this damsel and her predictions of their futures. The people who were paying the master were themselves, attempting to *control* their own futures by desiring to know what was *going* to occur.

In case you didn't know, "money" and "the spirit of divination" have been operating hand in hand, having this ongoing tryst for ages. Restated: "money" and "control" are so often times, intimately associated.

The reality is that money controls the world and the people in and of the world. The Bible says, "We know that we are of God, and the whole world lies under the sway of the

---

wicked one (1 Jn 5:19).[55]

The Bible also says that, *"... the **love of money** is the root of all evil"* (1 Tim 6:10, KJV); <u>and</u> that, *"**money is the answer for everything** (Eccl 10:19, GWT); or, ... **money answers [or responds to] all things.**"*[56]

Admit it! There's just something about money that causes people to think, if they had it, or if they had more of it, their troubles would be all over.

Worldly thinking says, "You've got a problem?" Just throw money at it. So we shouldn't be surprised by the way the world attempts to use money to *control* people and the circumstances going on in their lives.

Additionally, while there is really no such thing as unwavering "security" for anyone in this world and the only thing secure for a Christian, is their relationship with Christ

---

[55] The word "world" in this context means: the world system, world affairs, and the aggregate of things earthly, the whole circle of earthly goods, endowments riches, advantages, pleasures (Strong's #2889, transliterated "Kosmos"). The word "sway" in this context means: lies in the power of the evil one, i.e. is held in subjection by the devil (Strong's #2749, transliterated "Keimai").

[56] Strong's #6030, transliterated *"aw-naw' "*.

and His faithfulness, the fact of the matter is that we all like the "feeling" of *thinking* that our futures are "secure".

Most people *feel* secure *if and when* they have money. The reality is, however, that you can have billions of dollars but be terminally ill, so it's not just all about money. There are several areas, in addition to finances, in which we all would like to *feel* secure.   Here's a summary:

Financial Security- not having to worry about money now or in the future, for yourself or you family;

Provisional Security- having more than enough to feed the family, to provide or meet all of the other material needs; and even some extra to put away for a "rainy day";

Job Security- always having gainful, meaningful employment that gives you purpose and fulfillment;

Physical Security- being healthy, cared for, pampered, free from bodily injury, illness, disease, hurt, or crime; and

Relational Security- being assured that you would never lose the people in your life that you love and that they would always love you, never leave or abandon you; and certainly never hurt or reject you, or do anything else to ever injure or damage you.

Affect Drives Effect

Just try to imagine what it would *feel* like if you were completely and confidently "secure" in every possible area of life. Just imagine if you could rest assured that you would *never again* be tried or tested in any area. Your rent or mortgage was assuredly always to be paid; you always had money to pay your bills; you could go shopping whenever you wanted to and buy both your "needs" and your "greeds"; all the people in your life were there to stay for good, they were never going to forsake you, betray you, disrespect you, gossip about you, or dump you; you would never lose them to a horrible accident, or death; and you and your family members, as well as the other people you loved, were always going to be healthy and safe wherever they went, so you never lived in fear of anything bad, accidental or criminal, happening within your circle.

Wouldn't that then make you at least *relatively* happy? LOL!

Come on, admit it, *feelings* of "security" are a great big deal. Feeling "secure" is the antidote for feeling "fearful" or "insecure". The word "security" encompasses a degree of protection against danger, loss, and criminals. In its most simplified sense, "security is protection against our losses and hurts."[57]

However, "security" is a feeling, not a fact.

We can safely conclude that the information the damsel, via the spirit of divination was conveying to these people, no doubt controlled their *"feelings* of security" (affect); as well as their future actions, as they related to the substantive content of her divining rhetoric (effect).

Each and every one of us, if given the real opportunity, would want to control the future events happening in our lives, as well as the lives of others in order to *feel* "secure". Actually, it's something we are constantly striving to achieve, at least to the greatest extent possible.

We all do many things in an attempt to control our own futures: we save money for a rainy day; we go to college so we can get a better job; we get married so we can have a family and children; we start businesses so we don't have to work for someone else the rest of our lives; we get saved, so we will end up in heaven instead of hell. The list

---

[57] Wikipedia

goes on and on and this is all perfectly "normal".

Just like we have 1-900-TAROTCARDS today; the people back then who were paying money to this girl's master were really very "normal", just as normal as any heathen on the planet would be that's doing this today.[58]

The point to be made in this story is that until Paul cast the spirit of divination out of her, she was being used to play on the desire of the people *to know*; and therefore arguably, attempt to *control* their own futures.

The same thing was going on with the false prophets in Old Testament days. In the book of Jeremiah the false prophets were saying, *"Ye shall not see the sword, nor famine; but I will give you assured peace in this place"* (Jer 14:13, KJV). In the book of Ezekiel, while speaking of the false prophets, the Lord said, they *"have seduced my people, saying, Peace; and there was no peace"* (Ez 13:10, KJV).

---

[58] As a side note: If you consider yourself a Christian and are paying for your future to be told by one of those tarot card readers, you need to repent. Now! (See, 2 Chron 33:6; Micah 5:12; Gal 5:20).

Affect Drives Effect

Common to both passages in Ezekiel and Jeremiah was the fact that the prophets' words gave the people (who were all living in disobedience to God), a *false sense of security* (affect), by prophesying good things in and for their future; and as a result, their conduct (of failing to repent), was being *controlled* as well (effect).[59]

"Affect" drives "effect". Our, "emotions" or "feelings" drive or motivate our "actions" or "behaviors".

If left "unchecked" most people automatically determine what actions they should take, based on how they *feel* about a given thing, person, or situation. If you like a pastor's message, you donate. If you want to belong to a club, you pay the dues. If you're mad at your sister, you won't show up to her birthday party with a present. If you appreciate your neighbors, you'll give them a gift at Christmas. If you're afraid of getting cavities, you'll pay to go have regular check-ups with your dentist.

---

[59] This is Biblical support of a concept we've already covered. The spirit of divination "affects" our feelings, which in turn drives or "effects" our actions.

Affect Drives Effect

We take action based on our feelings because that's how we make ourselves feel "right" or "secure" about our lives and about bettering our future condition. However, there are times when the spirit of divination can cause us to "feel secure" (but under false pretenses); and in so doing, drive or *control* our behavior.

When someone via the spirit of divination "controls" or sways you into a "false sense of security" by their words, directives or counsel, "it" can cause you to start operating "off guard". When you finally figure out what they told you was utterly false, you're far worse off than you were before you took their consoling advice and/or carried out their directives.

Take our husband committing adultery example. People, who get caught committing adultery, as a general rule, initially lie and deceive. Even when confronted with solid "evidence", people who get caught in adultery generally continue to lie and defend their lies. In fact, instead of admitting their sin, in response, they usually throw the same accusation back at the faithful spouse just for "sport".

Affect Drives Effect

So if the wife confronts him, he is going to lie to her about the affair until the cows come home and their residence is located in the city. If the wife chooses to believe her "divining" husband and disregard the "evidence", this will cause her to function under a "false sense of security" and behave in ways that indicate her marriage relationship is "secure" when in reality, that's hardly the case.

So the risk to that wife, as she continues to cook and clean and carry on intimate relations in the bedroom, is that she can be far more damaged in the end, by operating under this "false sense of security" which has been dealt to her at the hand of the spirit of divination.

What if the wife contracts a sexually transmitted disease from the mistress via her husband? Dependent upon the disease, that "false sense of security" operating in the wife, could literally mean her death. So how's that for an abrupt end to God's magnificent plan for her life?

Yet, this all could have been avoided if, number one: the husband hadn't been such a spirit of divination-driven pansy, and just told her the truth up front. Or if, number two, the wife had the sagacity or discernment to spot "it"

<u>and</u> the sufficient strength or knowledge to eliminate "it". In which case, she wouldn't have been deceived into a "false sense of security" believing the lies that the spirit of divination was peddling through the husband's denials.

She would have then been able to better face the facts and evidence and handle the blow from the beginning (instead of living in an emotional fantasyland for however much longer she did). She likely would have <u>never</u> voluntarily agreed to her continuing role in this <u>counterfeit</u> "husband and wife" relationship and as a result, her pain toll at the end of the day would have been greatly minimized.

Whereas now, after living for years in her "false sense of security", not only does she have the adultery to deal with, but she also has the compounded sins and ill effects related to the husband's denial of the affair while they continued to live as "husband and wife" thereafter.

Affect drives effect.

On the flip side, there are some women who actually would rather maintain a "false sense of security" by intentionally *keeping themselves* in the dark. I've seen this in my office on several occasions; women who have been married for 15, 29, 35 years, who felt their marriages were totally "secure" until they found out their husband was having an affair.

Yet, even after finding out, many of them still did not want to know anything about it, let alone deal with the situation. They'd much rather continue to live in the "false sense of security" offered to them by the spirit of control, most often due to financial reasons.

This avoidance or "denial" type of conduct then places the wife at worst risk than if she would have just dealt head-on with the situation when it was first discovered and figured out how to support herself (with the Lord's guidance); and not stayed in a loveless marriage "just for the money".

What usually happens in these cases, as the wife (still being supported), waits for the husband to become the faithful man-of-God she's always prayed for; ten or twenty years pass, the children are grown and gone and then all of a sudden, the pansy husband gets up enough courage to leave. He divorces the wife and gets remarried.

Then, once sufficiently caught off guard (and its not hard to do when living a life of delusion), "it" will do what "it" does best. Get a firm grip on the rug you've been standing on, rip it out from under you with a force so severe it will catapult your whole life soaring into the air-- causing you to experience an "emotional free fall" down, down, down, for years thereafter. In which case, you'll always end up suffering more collateral damage than was necessary.

In these cases, the wife ends up wasting the best years of her life because once she gets visibly dumped (when in reality, she had already been emotionally dumped for several years), due to her age, she now has little to no job opportunities, let alone hopes for a new love relationship in her future. The enemy chalks up another life, sucked dry, chewed up and spit out.

Whichever response is taken by the *controlled* party (wives in this case), know this: The spirit of control can lull you into a false sense of security with "fictitious words", creating "fictitious feelings" which will drive your actions or behaviors into living out a "fictitious lifestyle" for the rest of your "fictitious life".

However, God's plan for your life, no matter what you've gone through, is in *no way* "fictitious". Jesus spoke "death" to very few things; in fact there's only one that I can think of right now. It was that fig tree He came across when He was hungry. While in His state of humanity, it "faked Him out" or caused Him to *think* it had fruit, when it really didn't (Mark 11:13-14). The curse He commanded against the fig tree represents the putting to death of hypocrisy, phoniness, or falsity, in situations or relationships that are based on pretense or fiction.

So you'd be trippin' if you think you're going to live a "fictitious" fake or phony life, and at the same time, be fulfilling God's plan.

Back to our story about the damsel: Once Paul casts the spirit out of her, the master got very angry about losing his stream of income and threw Paul to the magistrates of the city for causing "trouble" (Acts 16:20, KJV).

Isn't it funny how a person's definition of "good" and "bad" varies when it comes to money? Casting out a demonic spirit by Paul, was defined by this master as "trouble". Yeah! Trouble for his bank account I'd say.

Affect Drives Effect

This same kind of thing will happen in the unfaithful husband situation. He'll take money from the family coffer to set up house for his next family (robbing Peter to pay Paul) and the husband will rarely ever see this as being "wrong" either. In cases such as these, the unfaithful husband is usually just "buying-time" while transferring money and assets to set up his new life and getting things situated with his new aficionada before he is ready to literally "fly the coop". Once "the gig is up" and the relationship is over, that's when "trouble" really starts. In divorce court that is, where everyone finally realizes that it really was, *all about the money*.

So wake up to the fact that "it" is at work everywhere, especially as it relates to "money" being used to cause you to *feel* a "false sense of security" in order to *control* your behavior. The spirit of divination will generate and convey misleading information in order to cause you to *feel* secure, but always under false pretenses.

Let's cover a few Biblical examples as confirmation of this ongoing tryst between "money" and "control" and then afterwards, I'll start driving up your street with that interrogation lamp I mentioned earlier.

CHAPTER 19: Judas Points the Finger at Mary

"Then took Mary a pound of ointment of spikenard, very costly, and anointed the feet of Jesus, and wiped His feet with her hair: and the house was filled with the odour of the ointment. Then saith one of His disciples, Judas Iscariot, Simon's son, which should betray Him, **Why was not this ointment sold for three hundred pence, and given to the poor?** *This he said, not that he cared for the poor; but because he was a thief, and had the bag, and bare what was put therein. Then said Jesus, Let her alone: against the day of My burying hath she kept this"* (John 12:3-7, KJV).

In response to Mary's sacrificial act of worship, Judas poses the question aloud to the group, *"Why was not this ointment sold for three hundred pence, and given to the poor?"* (Jn 12:6).

Judas Points the Finger at Mary

Here we see Judas Iscariot indirectly criticizing Mary for purportedly wasting costly ointment on Jesus, when in reality, no act of worship is ever *wasted on Jesus.*

Do you see "it"?

Judas was trying to control the conduct of the woman and her alleged misuse of the costly ointment by this negative, derogatory, yet intensely "religious" comment.

Indeed, Judas' argument was very reasonable. In a religiously economic sense, he was saying, "We could have taken care of more poor people with the money we would have gotten from selling this ointment".

After this statement was made, any reasonable "untrained" person would no doubt agree and conclude that it would have been better to help *more* people, than just that one person … Jesus ... Who really didn't seem like He needed any help anyway.

To the "untrained", what Judas said was the "right" thing to do and what Mary did, was just plain "wrong".

Judas Points the Finger at Mary

There are three other instances recorded in the gospels that have a very similar theme as it relates to a woman with an alabaster box who also used very precious ointment on Jesus (Matthew 26:7, Mark 14:3 and Luke 7:37). Was this the same woman each of these times?

Well, there is argument that Mary the sister of Lazarus was the woman in John 12, Matt 26, and Mark 14; but not in Luke 7 because the woman in Luke 7:37, was referred to as a "sinner" and Mary the sister of Lazarus, was not considered as such.

Yet, in two of the four instances, the one that clearly identifies "Mary" and the other which clearly identifies the woman "sinner", that woman poured the ointment on Jesus' feet (Jn 11:1 & 12:3; Luke 7:38); as opposed to the other two instances where the woman poured the ointment onto His head (Matt 26: Mark 14:3). Now, we're not going to spend any time resolving these issues; I only raise them so that you know of their existence.

The point to be made for purposes of the spirit of divination and its role with "money", is that *in each and every one of these four instances*, when the valuable ointment was expended on Jesus as an act of worship; somebody, in fact *somebody different* in each of the four instances, had something critical to say about it!

In the first three instances the woman was criticized, and in the last instance, Jesus Himself was criticized. Let me tell you, the spirit of divination has always got something to say, someone to say it through, and someone to say it to!

In John 12:5: it was <u>Judas</u> who said: *"Why was not this ointment sold for three hundred pence, and given to the poor?"* (KJV).

In Matthew 26:8-9: it was "…his <u>disciples</u>" (plural) who said, *"To what purpose is this waste? For this ointment might have been sold for much, and given to the poor"* (KJV).

In Luke 7:37: it was the <u>Pharisee</u> who had invited Jesus to dinner who, *"…spoke within himself, saying, This man, if He were a Prophet, would have known who and what manner of woman this is that touches Him: for she is a sinner"* (KJV).[60]

---

[60] Leave it to a Pharisee to criticize Jesus our Savior, for receiving worship from a sinner woman.

Judas Points the Finger at Mary

In Mark 14:4-5: less identifiable people are mentioned and referred to as, "… *some that had indignation* within *themselves, and said, Why was this waste of the ointment made? For it might have been sold for more than three hundred pence, and have been given to the poor. And they murmured against her*" (KJV).

Of extreme importance as it relates to "the jugular" is to note that it wasn't just that evil thief Judas who made this same type of *controlling* condemning comment. Even "the disciples" (plural), made the comment.

This fact substantiates that both good and evil people, Christians and non-Christians alike, can be influenced by the spirit of control to criticize and condemn how you spend *your* money and/or resources on Jesus and His Kingdom.

Honey, I'm home! … I just drove up the block, parked in front of your house and now, I'm knocking at your front door.

Are you ready to answer for this?

Judas Points the Finger at Mary

The teaching point we learn is this: **There are people in your life who criticize you about how you spend, use, or give your money, wealth and/or other valuables away; whether to the church, to ministries and/or to other people in need.**

They say things like:

"You give too much to that church, you won't have enough for your own bills."

"Why are you wasting your money helping that person? You should be thinking about taking care of yourself and your future."

Or say, you just got a raise and you tell a close friend about it and they respond, *"That money can be put to use for a really good cause, like the one I've been supporting."*

Or, after sharing how you met the financial need of a person they don't know and/or don't like, your sibling responds: *"Gosh I sure hope you'll be able to afford your rent this month! Don't come begging to me."*

"CONTROL FREAK"

Judas Points the Finger at Mary

Suppose you tell your spouse about a financial blessing that the Lord, out of the blue, told you to give to another person, they respond, *"So how long are you going to keep doing that?"*

Just as in the case of Judas, we see that the mere posing of the question, without even saying Mary was "wrong" outright-- can create a sense of condemnation. It can create a feeling in the "giver", that you did something wrong, even when you really didn't.

How's that light? Bothering you yet?

These are Biblical and real life examples of how the spirit of control tries to thwart, condemn and prevent your worship of Jesus, through your giving to the work of His Kingdom, or to people in your life as He directs.

Now, let's go a little deeper and consider this: There is no doubt, that the Spirit of God was the One who led Mary and/or the other women to expend their costly ointment on Jesus, because in each instance, Jesus defended the act of worship.

Judas Points the Finger at Mary

So based on the "Principle of Diametric Opposition", we can safely conclude that it must have been the anti-to Christ, or the "spirit of control" that caused everyone from Judas (the evil one), to the disciples, to other unidentifiable people, to criticize this conduct by providing a religious pretense of how the asset should have been used. In the instance of the Pharisee, that same controlling spirit was used to criticize Jesus Himself for receiving worship from a "sinner".

Hence, we learn that we need to watch out for those people in our lives who criticize our giving spirit (which is of God), and how and where we spend our own hard earned money! It's really the spirit of control/divination (that "taker") at work in the lives of the people you know, that does not want the Kingdom of God to be financed, or for you to receive the blessings of being a "giver" by sowing and giving to others.

This same type of conflict often happens when one spouse doesn't "believe" in giving, tithing, or donating and the other spouse does.

Here's an example: Say a wife wants to tithe to the church and give to the work of the Kingdom and the husband doesn't. Even if the money is only coming out of the wife's paycheck, her husband still forbids her to do so.

So does she acquiesce to this demand in order to please him and/or for fear of losing his love and affection? Does she "submit" to him according to the Bible and not give anymore? Or, does she go ahead and tithe?

In this case, let's say the wife overcomes the spirit of control and she decides to continue to give, despite her husband's distain.

What happens next, is that controlling spirit now must pump up the volume (or intensity), in an attempt to control the wife's giving, by adding more pressure on the wife to stop.

In this example, the husband starts accusing the wife of "liking" the preacher, in some improper or inappropriate way, because she has continued to give despite his hot displeasure.

Judas Points the Finger at Mary

When that occurs, does the wife stop giving so that husband doesn't think she's secretly infatuated with the minister?

Or, does she still continue to give?

You already know the right answer.

CHAPTER 20: Judas and the Thirty Pieces of Silver

Not meaning to pick on Judas necessarily, but remember how the religious leaders paid him money for information on the whereabouts of Jesus in order that they could gain *control* over Him; capture, judge, and ultimately crucify Him?

So let's not forget how Judas' love of money, caused him to sell Jesus down the river, for thirty pieces of silver (Matt 26:15).

Our next teaching point is: **Watch out for those people in your life who either, love money; or who, when under financial pressures themselves, are likely to sell you out too**.

Judas and the Thirty Pieces of Silver

Did Judas' criticism of the woman with the alabaster box, give us warning of the greed that was going on in his heart?

People whose choices in life always tend to be based on money, how much something costs; how much they will make; how much someone else has; how much money, assets, or other valuables you have; comparing assets to assets and debts to debts, etc., these are the kind of people you do <u>not</u> want in your life, no matter how much you claim to love them.

These kinds of people are continually providing a comparative financial analysis of themselves, as it relates to anyone else who just got something "new". These kinds of people only care about how they can gain access to the money or assets held by others, in order to benefit themselves. These kinds of people are usually stingy, selfish, always looking out to assure that they get something out of a relationship, even when the "party" is being held for *someone else's* birthday.

When the money runs dry, they cut and run, leaving you holding the bag ... the *empty bag.* When you suddenly find yourself in dire financial straits, they don't bother to offer you a dime. Indeed, you'll never hear from them again, unless and until you, and you alone-- all by yourself, find someway of refilling your moneybag. Hopefully by then, you've learned the lesson that all along they were nothing but big "nobodies" in your life.

The Bible tells us that Judas was the one holding the moneybag (or the distributor of the money); and that he would steal the money and keep it for himself. *"This he said, not that he cared for the poor, but because he was a thief, and had the money box; **and he used to take what was put in it**"* (Jn 12:6, NKJV).

The teaching point we learn is that: **People in your life who are "in charge of the money" often times seek to exercise** *control* **over you by their means of distribution of that money.**

Just like Judas, there are people in your life who are "holding the moneybag", who also try to control your behavior because of that fact. This can take place in several different arenas:

Judas and the Thirty Pieces of Silver

First, we have the work environment. People who are employed in the corporate or business world when directed by supervisors or business owners to do wrong, oftentimes choose to comply rather than risk being fired and lose their paycheck. This happens all the time, in varying degrees, where a person's integrity is "sold out" for a paycheck.

When your supervisor or the owner of your company directs you to do something in violation of the Word of God, you are being tested on the issue of loving God over loving money. If you fail the test and are controlled by money, or the risk of losing your income, the spirit of control has gained new territory in your life.

You may argue, but I have a wife and a family to feed; I have a mortgage, a car payment and bills to pay; so *I had to do it,* otherwise, my family wouldn't make it.

To that position, I would respond … *all right* Mr./Ms. wanna-be Jehovah Jireh, simmer down for just a minute, just one minute. *This is a test!*

You know the Scripture, *"where your treasure is, there will your heart be also"* (Lu 12:34, KJV). This is a test to see how that scripture plays out in "real life", in *your own* "real life" in particular. You've got to refuse to do wrong and let come whatever may. God is your provider and He will take care of you.

Think about it, if those are the kinds of people you're working for, you probably don't like your job anyway. God sees and knows your heart and the fact that you've been wishing and praying that you had a better place to work, or a better way to earn money. It just may be that God is intentionally putting pressure on your godly character and integrity, in order to move you out of a place that you would not otherwise move from voluntarily, because of all those financial responsibilities hanging over your head.

That very thing happened to me after becoming a lawyer while working at my first job with a law firm. In order to share this story in proper context, we now move into our next Law School Lesson: "Civil Procedure 2".

A year or so after I started work at my first "attorney" job, the owner of the firm placed a file on my desk telling me to draft a motion to have an adverse "default" judgment of about $50,000. set aside by the court. This default judgment was entered because neither he, nor the other associate attorney assigned to handle this case, had bothered to show up for trial.

To "set aside" a judgment meant to remove the adverse judgment and permit the matter to go forward and be heard by a jury, or court trial. The owner of the firm marked the file task as: "HOT" (meaning this needed to be done right away) and set it on my desk.

After looking at the law, I couldn't figure out any way to get the default set aside, without being forced to misrepresent the facts, or lie to the court. So I went to the owner of the firm (who obviously knew all of this already; I was the "rookie" he was not); and I asked him what he had expected me to use as the basis to prevail on the motion.

In response, he conveyed, in his oh so very special, previous public defender lawyer-like manner ... exactly *how* I could lie to the court. So I took the file, walked out of his office and went back to my desk and sat down. I had been saved for a little over three years and I suppose it was time now, for a "heart check-up".

Judas and the Thirty Pieces of Silver

You should also know that at this time, I, as many of you, had a mortgage and plenty of bills to pay. What you don't know, is that it took me seemingly forever to get this job in the first place, because I had no prior law firm experience at all.

Yet, at the same time, I really didn't like working there because of how the firm was operated and how the people and clients were treated. This assignment however, was the first time I had personally been asked to use my God-given skills, talents and education to do something wrong; to lie to the court under penalty of perjury.

The first thing we all do in these kinds of moments of testing is engage in what I call, "stronghold thinking". So let's go on a little teaching point tangent on that topic for a few minutes:

I base my use of the term: "stronghold thinking" out of the Bible where it says, *"For the weapons of our warfare are not carnal, but mighty through God to the **pulling down of strongholds**. Casting down imaginations, and every high thing that exalteth itself against the knowledge of God, and*

bringing into captivity every thought *to the obedience of Christ"* (2 Cor 10:4-5, KJV).

The term "stronghold" is defined as: *A castle, stronghold, or fortress. Anything upon which one relies on; the arguments and reasoning by which a disputant endeavors to fortify his opinion and defend it, against his opponent.*[61]

Whoa-- what does *that* mean?

Very simply, this is just another anti-to Christ situation, where God wants you to think a certain way (Josh 1:8, Ps 119:15, Phil 4:8); and the enemy wants you to think the opposite. The spirit of divination is our enemy; "stronghold thinking" is how the enemy wants you to think. The dispute or combat, is based solely on your mental faculties, reasoning abilities and argumentative capacity. No one ever gets physical-- it's only in your mind.

A "stronghold" is the enemy's way of trying to get you to construct and create arguments and justifications in order

---

[61] Strong's #3794, transliterated "Ochuroma".

to *reason your way* <u>out of</u> doing things the way God wants them done.

"Stronghold thinking" consists of mindsets that you have formed over the years that when faced with a temptation to do certain things the enemy's way <u>vs.</u> God's way; they cause your reasoning, deductions and conclusions to follow the same pattern or response <u>against</u> doing things God's way, time and time again.

In my law firm example, "stronghold thinking" would go something like this: "I must lie like my boss says, or I'll lose my job, then I'll lose my house, and then ... I'll become homeless."

Despite knowing the temptation we face is directly against God's Word, we began to contemplate the situation, and think about the pros and cons related to the outcome of each possible scenario: To sin or not to sin, that is the question.

After you've spent enough time "stronghold thinking" it through (meaning, as much time as it takes for you to choose sin over God); you go ahead and sin, all the while justifying your sin with and through your own "stronghold thinking" proficiencies.

This explains why you respond the same sinful way over and over again when being tested in any given area. It's because there is a "stronghold" in your thinking pattern which has limited or excluded the other available "godly" options with which to respond; and thus, has kept you responding in the same old sinful way.

The enemy wants you to think in ways that will cause you to arrive at decisions that defy and undermine the Word of God. When you get on board with the enemy's way of "stronghold thinking" it will create destructive sin patterns of behavior in your life. These sin patterns are based on your inability to see any other way to deal with a situation, except this one way-- the enemy's way, the sinful way.

"Stronghold thinking" dates all the way back to the fall of man in the Garden of Eden, that's where the serpent threw his first "one-two punch" combination at Eve. Man has been taking the same "one-two punch" beating, ever since.

The serpent first approached Eve and the conversation went like this: *"Yea, hath God said, Ye shall not eat of every tree of the garden? And the woman said unto the serpent, We may eat of the fruit of the trees of the garden: But of the fruit of the tree which is in the midst of the garden, God hath said, Ye shall not eat of it, neither shall ye touch it, lest ye die. And the serpent said unto the woman, Ye shall not surely die: For God doth know that in the day ye eat thereof, then your eyes shall be opened, and ye shall be as gods, knowing good and evil"* (Gen 3:1-5, KJV).

The first thing we see is the serpent approaching Eve under the "cloak of religion" pretending he wants to talk about God: *"Yea, hath God said..."* In reality, the enemy only wanted to get closer to Eve through this interpersonal conversation, in order to throw the first, of his "one-two punch" combination.

The first punch of the enemy _for all of us; will always be_ either questioning, or outright undermining what God said (or the Word of God).

Judas and the Thirty Pieces of Silver

The Lord clearly said, *"Ye shall not eat of it, neither shall ye touch it, lest ye die"* (Gen 2:17, KJV). To the contrary, *"The serpent said unto the woman, Ye shall not surely die"* (Gen 3:4, KJV).

Punch number one … executed.

In the situation Eve faced, as well as all of the situations that we face, the enemy's first punch will be to undermine the truth of God's Word. If the enemy succeeds, you will automatically become distracted, lose focus, and go off course. It's just like when you're in a boxing match; the first punch is always just a jab to distract your focus, but it's the second punch that has the force to bring you down.

The second of the enemy's "one-two punch" combination, is in getting Eve to "stronghold think" her way into believing (wrongfully believing), that *it would be better for her* if she chooses to sin instead of doing things God's way.

The serpent assured Eve, *"Ye shall not surely die: For God doth know that in the day ye eat thereof, then your eyes shall be opened, and ye shall be as gods, knowing good and evil"* (Gen 3:4, KJV).

Judas and the Thirty Pieces of Silver

The basis for all "stronghold thinking" is illustrated in thoughts that go something like this: "I will be better off if I do this." "It will be better for me, in this situation, if I do that." "This will make me, or my situation better than it is now if I only..."

After receiving the enemy's "one-two punch" combination, "stronghold thinking" is exactly what Eve engaged in right before she took the fall:

*"And when the woman **saw** that the tree was good for food, and that it was **pleasant** to the eyes, and a tree to be **desired** to make one **wise**, she took of the fruit thereof, and did eat, and gave also unto her husband with her; and he did eat"* (Gen 3:6, KJV).

If you take a close look at these bolded words in the Hebrew, you will realize that they all have "thinking" or "reasoning" or "conclusionary thought" components to their definitions:

saw: to see, look at, **inspect, perceive, consider;**[62]

pleasant: desire, wish, **longings of one's heart,** lust, appetite, covetousness (bad sense) thing desired, **object of desire;**[63]

eyes: of physical eyes as showing **mental qualities;**[64]

desire: to **covet,** take pleasure in, **delight in;**[65] and

wise: To act circumspectly, act prudently, act wisely, **to prosper, have success, to cause to prosper;**[66] (thus arguably, bettering her position in life).

The words: "saw" "pleasant" "eyes" and "desire" show clear indications of the thought, reasoning, deductions and/or

---

[62] Strong's #7200, transliterated "Ra'ah".
[63] Strong's #8378, transliterated "Ta'avah".
[64] Strong's #5869, transliterated "'ayin".
[65] Strong's #2530, transliterated "Chamad".
[66] Strong's #7919, transliterated "Sakal".

conclusions that Eve derived from engaging in the "stronghold thinking" process.

The thrust or force of the enemy's second punch comes after participating in, and then concluding the "stronghold thinking" process against the will of God. This is what causes a person to go down, or chose to sin. Here's the enemy's "one-two punch" combination in a simplified format:

Punch #1:   **YOU** can, will, should, could, ought to:

_____;

(Fill-in the blank with anything defiant to God's Word);

Because,

Punch #2:   It will make **YOU** happier, better off; or **YOU** need, deserve, should have; or it would only be fair if:

_____

(Fill-in the blank with whatever you expect to gain from sinning).

When the "one-two punch" is delivered to a "stronghold thinker" they always go down for the count while flashing their Fake ID (or license to sin), by disobeying what God said.[67]

In a nutshell, "stronghold thinking" is when your mind starts coming up with all these reasons to justify why you can go ahead and do ... what you already know, or strongly suspect in your mind, that the Lord doesn't want you to do.

Experientially, "stronghold thinking" is seen in Christians who report they are "struggling" with a certain sin issue. When in reality, there is nothing substantive to this concept of "struggling" with a sin, except as seen in that person's "stronghold thinking" aptitude and competence.

It's not the sin itself, fighting you in a struggle. You aren't literally struggling with a bottle of vodka; or struggling with the illicit sex that you want to have outside of marriage. There isn't some universal "struggle" to sin, because many

---

[67] Even though the directive not to eat of the fruit was given to Adam (Gen 2:16-17); and even though the woman was deceived (1 Tim 2:14); we can still use Eve as our example for this one-two punch "sin model". Eve knew the commandment of God and she knew her conduct of eating the fruit, would be in violation of that commandment.

other people can just throw the bottle away, or never show up at Motel 6.

So when someone tells me they are struggling with a sin, I say, "What's that mean?" How are you literally struggling with the pornography on your computer screen? Are you taking hold of your computer monitor, picking it up and forcefully moving it back and forth in order to manufacture some kind of visible struggle?

No ... of course not.

What you're really doing is having several bouts within *yourself* and within *your own mind* (while entertaining your own "stronghold thinking" processes) over taking part in that particular sin. What you're really "struggling" with is your own "stronghold thinking" about that particular "pet sin" of yours and whether or not, to commit it again. In short, you're "stronghold thinking" yourself to death.[68]

Your "stronghold thinking" is fickle. At various times and under various circumstances it can arrive at differing conclusions. On some occasions, after being hit with the

---

[68] *"... sin, when it is finished, brings forth death."* (Ja 1:15, KJV)

"one-two punch" of the enemy, you don't flinch; you stand firm and say "No!" Yet, at other times, you flash your fake ID (or license to sin), and bam! You're down for the count.

If there is any real "struggle" at all, it is in your attempt to find rational, justifiable, "Christian" reasons for you to continue to practice blatant disobedience to God's Word; while simultaneously, not looking like a total pagan and getting laughed out of church!

Notably Jesus, as opposed to Eve, when tempted in the wilderness, never took the time to entertain any stronghold thinking. He just automatically fired back with *"It is written* ... and then cited Old Testament scripture (Lu 4:4, 8 &12).

The way to eliminate "stronghold thinking" is for you stop making decisions over whether or not to obey the Word of God, based on the predicted outcome of any given situation.

Please, let me help here. Just set your mind to do what He says, don't give yourself any other illusory options, and poof! The sin "struggle" is now over.

Ok, that's the end of my "stronghold thinking" teaching point tangent; now back to my peculiar situation at the law firm. You did want to hear the end of the story didn't you?

So remember, the conversation with the firm owner telling me just how to say the lies he wanted said in court, had already taken place. I then go back to my office, sit at my desk and say within myself, "Lord, this guy wants me to lie to a judge under oath".

Ha! As if He didn't know.

Though only a few years old in the Lord, I already had a good grasp on the Bible, I think I was even teaching a Bible study by this time. I knew what my boss said about lying; and I knew what the Bible said about lying. But then, I also knew a few other passages in the Bible about the "master-servant" relationship such as those found in: 1 Peter 2:18-23; Col 3:22-25; and Eph 6:5-8.

So all of a sudden, I'm faced with some additional … *complications,* shall we say? I've got a duty to obey and submit to my master or boss; sure enough; but where do I draw the line?

You, my dear reader, already know the answer to this question.

However, "stronghold thinking" would say: "This is just probably how they do it in the legal field and I'd better get used to it. I mean, we have to win the case; we can't get hit with a judgment just because we didn't show up at court that one time. So I'll just *submit* and do what my boss says and draft the motion."

Punch #1: Undermining God's Word has successfully been stronghold-thought through, to the point of compromise.

The internal discourse continues:

"After all, I've got bills and a mortgage to pay and this is my first real attorney job, which took me forever to 'secure' and I don't want to lose my house. After all the hard work I've put in to get my law degree, pass the Bar Exam and get this job in the first place? That wouldn't be fair to me. *Right?*"

Judas and the Thirty Pieces of Silver

<u>Punch #2: Because it would be better for me if I did</u>, has successfully been stronghold-thought through, to the point of compromise.

The "untrained" attorney would then flash their most recent, cognitively formulated, Fake ID (license to sin) and be down for the count in no time flat, drafting away at that motion and lying through their teeth.

On the other hand, a person unadulterated by "stronghold thinking" would say, when the boss tells me to do something that clearly undermines the Word of God (punch #1); I simply don't do it. Then, when it came to punch #2 (the one that usually takes you down), that punch wouldn't have ever been delivered in the first place.

So stop all of your own "stronghold thinking" and you'll stop going down for the count too!

My next question to the Lord was, "So what do you want me to do?"

That question was <u>not</u> "What should I do?" lie or not lie … come on now! Rather, the question was exactly *how* do I handle *not doing* what I've just been told *to do, by my boss,* especially, in light of the fact that he signs my paychecks?

What I did was take the "HOT" file and place it back in his work pile when he was not there with a note saying something like: "I cannot declare the things to the court necessary to win this motion." All the while, yes-- I knew I could lose my job; and yes-- I did have a mortgage and plenty of other bills to pay; and no-- I didn't have any other source of income.

I didn't get any scripture on handling it this way; it was just an impression or "feeling" that drove me to do something against the proposed wrongdoing. It certainly was <u>not</u> something that made me *feel* good, nor was it necessarily something I *wanted* to do, and certainly no body was telling me to do it either. Sound familiar?

A day or so later, the file was delivered back by a paralegal onto my desk with a note saying: "HOT! Draft and file this motion immediately!" But this time, the words were underlined and double or triple bolded with a black felt tip marker.

In response, I did the same thing I had done the first time (all the while, my heart was beating harder and harder); I returned the file to his desk, in his absence, again saying: "I cannot declare the things to the court necessary to win this motion."

A few days later, I got the same file back, for what would be the last time. After returning the file to my boss, the same exact way I had two times prior, *well* ... you know what they always say about "the third time's the charm?"

All of a sudden ... I was "laid off".

No doubt I wasn't "fired" for his fear of some "retaliation claim" I could have made with the Labor Commission. So "laid off" I went … *on to* ... unemployment.

Prior to this event, I had been sending out resumes trying to find another job for at least three months and though I had a pretty good grasp on God's Word as it relates to what I should and should not do; I was still ignorant about God's *ways*.

"Yes" I wanted out of that job and "yes" I had felt that way for months, but "No" ... "being laid off was <u>not</u> what I had in mind ... *Lord.*" Immediately, I was forced into my first experience with God's supernatural provision.

Yet, within only a few months I found a much better in-house Corporate Counsel job for a women's clothing manufacturer. My new job was a whole lot less stressful, a whole lot more fun, I got paid more money; and *I*, basically was the "legal department". So I had a lot of supervisory freedom over *myself*, not to mention a whole bunch of new clothes.

Had I done what the owner of the law firm wanted me to do, I would have immediately been backslidden and become just like any other lawyer out there with no morals: lying to win, lying for money, lying to get somewhere higher-up in the firm. I would have been controlled by money and who knows *if* and *when* I would have ever recovered from that?

I expound on this example in order to illustrate that if you stay with what He says to do; no matter how scary or crazy it seems, when your actions are based on honoring His

Judas and the Thirty Pieces of Silver

Word, God will back you up! He will not only take care of you, but once you pass the test, He'll then promote you too. There is always a promotion coming after you pass the test. Look at the lives of Joseph, David and the three Hebrew boys.

There are thousands of examples just like this one where "money" is used to try to "control" the behavior or "misbehavior" of people. The list is literally inexhaustible, but in order to solidify the connection between "money" and "control" in your mind, I've summarized a few additional examples below, placing them in an order ranging from the most obvious, to the least obvious:

1. A prostitute paid to perform by her "John";

2. Parents taking away, or withholding money for college, unless their child goes to the college they want, or becomes what they want him/her to be (i.e.) Doctor, Lawyer, Accountant, Teacher, etc.;

3. People who "hold the moneybag" paying the way for everyone accompanying them to dinner, a movie, shopping, or on a trip. Yet, the people receiving these subsidies would

never choose to spend a minute of time with the payor, on any other terms;

4. Women who marry much older men, just for their money. Men, who do the same. Oh and yes, you've got to reverse and exchange partners in both instances (Prop 8 remember?);

5. The breadwinner of the family thinking because he/she makes all the money, that it buys them certain sinning rights against you;

6. People who say they're going to break up with you or leave you, if you don't do what they say with *your* own money; and

7. People who buy expensive items for others in high positions; who in turn expect special favors, promotions, acknowledgement in a group, secured employment for relatives, or a seat on the Board of Directors, etc.

One form of abuse in marriage that gets very little attention is "Financial Abuse". Some people have never even heard of the term, but when you explain it to them, they exclaim: "That's him!" "That's her!"

Judas and the Thirty Pieces of Silver

A good example of financial abuse is when a husband gives his wife $50 a week to feed a family of four, when there is plenty more money in the bank. As the husband is doling out this meager amount, all of a sudden, his usual dull demeanor markedly changes and he becomes very animated. You can hear him counting it out bill by bill, "$5, $5, $10, $20, that's $40 and here's some quarters to make it $50." Then comes the very strict guidelines to the wife on "how to" and "how not to" spend the money.

That's just one manifestation of control in a financial abuse setting, but there are hundreds.

In addition to recognizing how "money" and "control" go hand in hand, we must once again distinguish what is of God and what is anti-to Christ, or against God, as it relates to money:

GOD IS A GIVER!

"God so loved the world, He *gave* His only begotten Son…" (Jn 3:16, KJV)

"Give, and it shall be given unto you; good measure, pressed down, and shaken together, and running over, shall men give into your bosom. For with the same measure that ye mete withal it shall be measured to you again" (Luke 6:38, KJV).

You cannot out-give the Lord and whomever you give to in sincerity and purity of heart, He is going to cover you to the fullest extent and beyond. When we are "givers" we are more like Him.

THE SPIRIT OF CONTROL IS A TAKER!

The spirit of control is selfish and self-motivated, constantly reminding you of your own financial needs, and using kissin' cousin fear tactics in order to change your spiritual "giving" perspective, to a carnal, "Looking out for number One" mentality.

If God is a "giver" and the spirit of control is a "taker", then you automatically know which one of the two traits you should adopt as your own.

WARNING! WARNING!

Judas and the Thirty Pieces of Silver

Just because *you* have sense enough to choose the right side, that doesn't necessarily mean that all other Christians have also adopted the "giving" nature of the Lord. Nor does it mean that when it comes to money, that Christians never "give place" to the spirit of control.

So don't go too far off the deep end and naively believe, that when it comes to money, the spirit of control isn't at work in the church setting just because that's where the Lord Himself, is supposed to be at work.

In fact, you may even have a pastor or church leader that is acting under "its" influence each and every Sunday!

Judas and the Thirty Pieces of Silver

"CONTROL FREAK"

CHAPTER 21: The spirit of divination at Work in Pleas for Donations, Tithes, and Offerings

There are churches, TV ministries and other Christian programming on the airwaves, telling their audiences, "If you give God money, He will solve all the problems in your life."

Whether it's a healing, a financial breakthrough, the restoration of a marriage, the acquisition of possessions, just about anything really; there are those who say all you need to do is "sow a seed" into *my ministry* and your miracle is on its way ... *today.*

Now, understand that there is truth to the fact that as Believers, there is a certain relational authority and expectation that we should have in the area of tithing and giving. There is a blessed assurance that accompanies continued obedience to the leading and guiding of the Holy Spirit by tithing and giving as He directs, especially when someone is a good steward of the money and resources that God has given them. But that's <u>not</u> what we are talking about here.

We're talking about that segment of the population who are listening or watching these programs, who barely ever crack open a Bible, or pray; or who may not even be saved, or go to church. Those who may not have any relationship with the Lord, let alone understand the "Lordship" of Jesus Christ. Those who may have little or no faith working in their lives and may even be the kind of people who are living in the most obvious types of disobedience to the Word of God.

Notwithstanding, these are the same people who are being told by evangelists, prophets, or preachers on the radio or TV, to send money for this issue or that problem in your life; and I'll send you this oil, napkin, or cloth in return.

The spirit of divination at Work in Pleas for Donations, Tithes, and Offerings

Then, once "I" pray for *you*, the Lord will immediately respond to your need, just exactly like you want Him to.[69]

That isn't "Truth"!

You can't make those kinds of blanket statements to a congregation, or over the airwaves to thousands and thousands of people as if it applied to each and every one of them. This is especially true when many of them may be practicing sin that God wants eliminated from their lives and/or may be experiencing adverse circumstances, like "the brook drying up" that the Lord has intentionally allowed, in order to move them to another destination.

Yet, you've got some TV evangelist saying pay this specified amount of money into *my ministry* and within days, your problems will all go away and every prayer that you've ever prayed will be answered.

The devil is a liar!

---

[69] As if they had some personal, "genie in the bottle" rights, with God.

The spirit of divination at Work in Pleas for Donations, Tithes, and Offerings

Since there's not a person on the face of the earth that doesn't want or need something from the Lord, this practice provides an open forum for ministerial abuse. This is especially true with ministers who have large monetary responsibilities to meet on a regular basis. They may have a very difficult time avoiding "giving place" to the spirit of control in this area. They may justify their conduct by their own "stronghold thinking" which contemplates the fact that they are personally responsible to meet these sizeable financial obligations and that "the work of the Lord" needs to continue through their ministry.

As a result, many ministers may use their gifts, talents and charisma to *take advantage* of people financially, especially those who have no other hope or recourse, and desperately need a miracle from God. What we have in these instances are indiscriminate evangelists, prophets and/or preachers, who use enticing speech to try to "control" people into donating to their ministries.

The Bible says it like this: *"Whose mouths must be stopped, who subvert whole houses, teaching things which they ought not, for filthy lucre's sake"* (Titus 1:11, KJV).

The spirit of divination at Work in Pleas for Donations, Tithes, and Offerings

When the Bible gives us this type of stern warning, we know that this *control* tactic must have been working on the hearers back in that day ... *at least in the beginning*.

In our day and age, the hearers of these kinds of messages, if they have the money, at first readily respond and donate in the hopes of getting God to perform whatever miracle they may need. After paying their money, they then expect God to promptly do that which mere man cannot do, as if God's power and abilities were "for hire", as brokered through that particular ministry.

Once these ministers have successfully *controlled* their listening audience into trying to pay God for their miracle (through their own ministry's accounting system of course), the spirit of divination has successfully *controlled* the behavior of this unwary listening audience.

The saddest thing is that when the miracle doesn't come through as promised, the people who gave their money conclude that either: there really isn't a God; or, if there is, He doesn't love me enough to fix my situation like all those other people on TV giving their miraculous testimonies; or, maybe God would work in my life, if I just had *more* money to give Him.

In the most severe cases, these ministers are actually trying to prostitute God. They've yet to realize, however, that every time they make a plea for donations under these conditions, they're really only "giving place" to the spirit of divination and prostituting themselves.

When it comes to donations, tithes and offerings, of course, it's not wrong to provide the opportunity for those watching or listening to the program to give. The Bible clearly teaches that ministers of the Word, those who sow spiritual things, should receive material (carnal) things from the hearers (Ro 15:27; 1 Cor 9:11; 1 Tim 5:17, KJV). So we should all monetarily support our churches, our favorite TV and/or radio preachers, or other ministries and causes in which we believe the work of the Kingdom is being done.

So let's at least "qualify" our audiences first. Let's remind them that many of the promises of financial blessing are "conditional", or contingent upon certain actions that they must take. Let's hit upon the concepts of "Lordship",

The spirit of divination at Work in Pleas for Donations, Tithes, and Offerings

"submission", "laboring in the fields" and "gratitude" before just *assuming* we know what God is doing in everyone's life who is watching or listening; and before *assuming* they're all up for a miracle, a healing, a promotion, or a huge financial breakthrough.

Let's also remind them that the Lord is and will always remain, "Sovereign". He does *whatever* He wants to do, *whenever* He wants to do it. Therefore, just because a person now has some money to donate, that doesn't mean they can now "buy" a favorable response from God, just because they can finally *afford* to do so.

Are you guilty of exercising the spirit of control/divination in order to get donations for your ministry? Do you up-the-game when the finances are low? Having once begun in the Spirit, are you now trying to perfect your monetary donation figures in the flesh?

Just because you may have a very powerful, influential way of controlling the level of giving from the congregation, that doesn't mean that you should exploit your ability by manipulating your audience when asking for donations.

The spirit of divination at Work in Pleas for Donations, Tithes, and Offerings

Just because God has allowed this method to seemingly look successful, and then continue over time-- that doesn't mean God is "winking" at your conduct (Acts 17:30, KJV).

If upon a full and honest examination before the Lord, you now realize you are using a certain tone, a certain choice of words, certain inflections in your voice and certain rhetoric that you anticipate will pull on the heart strings of the people to give more than they would have otherwise, you should be convicted for manipulating your congregation, or listening audience and stop it immediately.

Since the spirit of control is the anti-to Christ's nature, why would you ever want to exercise "it" in *any instance*; let alone in order to obtain monetary gain?

Do you *really* want money from people that gave to your ministry because they felt compelled to do so, due to your donation proficient "spirit of control" laced speech, or spiel?

Since it's straight from the pit, you'd better not!

The spirit of divination at Work in Pleas for Donations, Tithes, and Offerings

What's worse is that the spiritual leaders who exercise the "spirit of control" in their pleas for money are rolling a stumbling block in front of each and every one of their donors, each and every time they do it!

Here's how that happens:

When the spirit of divination is in operation, it changes a person's pure unadulterated thinking and feelings about giving. Where they once had a sincere desire to give because of their love for God and in furtherance of His Kingdom and/or in appreciation for what the pastor has taught them, they now no longer give for all those good reasons. Instead, they give because they're being manipulated and controlled.

Yet worse, since God "loveth a *cheerful* giver" (2 Cor 9:7, KJV), as a result of the work of the spirit of divination, there is now a "taint of heart" in the person who is giving. The donor's "giving" is no longer borne out of a pure love for God; they have a change of heart due to the pressure the spirit of control exerts on them through their pastor, TV or radio preacher. Their heart was once primed for pure cheerful giving, now it's tainted. That taint then takes away the fullness of their future harvest or blessing!

Where a person at first had the intention to give voluntarily, after the spirit of control comes into play, giving is not voluntary anymore; it has become obligatory, they are feeling "its" force and pressure. So they start giving out of a duty or obligation to comply with the demands of the pastor, or to buy a miracle from God; all the while their heart is begrudging and/or their motives are now tainted.

This is why I tell people if you feel this kind of pressure, do not give! Pressure to give is not of God. Rather, it's the spirit of control at work in the words and manipulative speech used by the preacher or pastor at offering time.

As a "giver", here's how you'll know when the "spirit of control" is at work in the offering/donations process. First, there is a feeling of pressure placed on you, the donor/giver. You will experience a feeling of obligation, of condemnation, of guilt, if you do not give money; or, if you do not give *the amount of money* asked for by the preacher.

The spirit of divination at Work in Pleas for Donations, Tithes, and Offerings

If you love your pastor, that "emotional link" will cause you to give in order to meet the pastor's request and please him; or in fear that he will think less of you if you do not comply with his request (the CIYA).

Many times you will experience a guilty feeling, which forces you to give, <u>in order to avoid feeling bad.</u> (Affect drives effect.)

So it's no longer about your love for God and your desire to further His Kingdom that motivates you to give anymore. You give, not out of love, nor because it feels good to give to Kingdom work; you now only give, *in order to avoid feeling bad.* That type of tainted "giving" ends up being of no credit to you whatsoever in the Kingdom.

In addition, there is also *another way* the spirit of control manifests in this area of giving, but "it" works in reverse, on the backside. It's when people, who after initially resisting the temptation to *not* tithe, "give" anyway like they should. Then *afterwards* the spirit of divination comes in and that person experiences fear-ridden concerns that they shouldn't have given at all. They start to fear that they are not going to have enough for themselves or their own families; and then they regret their own generous God-led giving.

In the end, whether you gave or didn't give, you still feel bad about it, for either: (1) not giving at all; or (2) not giving enough; or (3) even when giving enough, you feel bad because you start worrying that you won't have enough for yourself or your family. (The latter, is the spirit of divination working on the backside.)

On the front side "it" was working through the pastor's pleas for donations; on the backside, "it" attacks the person who came up under the "effect" of that controlling spirit, did what it said and yet *still feels bad* about it! (The negative "affect" of the spirit of control then continues.)

By sharp contrast, a person will know when they have the right, untainted heart for giving. It's when they feel no pressure or obligation to give; but rather, they *want* to give out of their love and gratitude for what God has done for them through those ministries that have touched and blessed their lives.

The spirit of divination at Work in Pleas for Donations, Tithes, and Offerings

You couldn't stop them from giving even if you tried. In fact, these people many times think, or wished, or prayed that they had made more money to give to certain churches or ministries. They give beyond mere tithing numbers and still wish they had more money to give after that. Now, that's a "cheerful giver".

Up next, is our last and worst case scenario about the relationship between "money" and "control". This is when a person attempts to use "money" to "control" the power of God Almighty Himself.

Yikes!

The spirit of divination at Work in Pleas for Donations, Tithes, and Offerings

"CONTROL FREAK"

CHAPTER 22: Attempting to Control God with Money

━━

In Acts 8:9-24, we see the story of Simon the sorcerer and his encounter first, with Philip and then later with Peter and John. The Bible says of Simon, that he *"...for a long time had been using <u>sorcery</u> to <u>bewitch</u> the people, giving out that he himself was some great one. To whom they all gave heed, from the least to the greatest, saying, This man is the great power of God"* (Acts 8:9-10, KJV).

The word "sorcery" means: to be a magician, to practice magical arts.[70] The word "bewitched" means: **to throw out of position, displace,** to amaze, to astonish, throw into wonderment, to be amazed, astounded; *to be **out of one's mind, besides one's self, or insane**.*[71]

---

[70] Strong's #3096, transliterated "Mageuo".
[71] Strong's #1839, transliterated "Existemi".

Attempting to Control God with Money

Simon the sorcerer was a magician who had everyone in Samaria believing he was some great man of God who had supernatural powers; but in reality, he was just playing a bunch of phony tricks and games, deceiving the people.

Simon was using sorcery to throw the people off course, or out of the position God wanted them in; and in so doing, it brought so much turmoil into their lives, that they felt like they were "going out of their minds".

We all know from personal experience, that when we get off the Lord's straight and narrow path, things can get very stressful and upsetting and that circumstances can cause us to grope for various sources of "relief" *other than* what's found in the Lord. That was Simon's setup.

While in that "mental" state or condition, the people of Samaria naturally looked for some relief ... *in Simon*, of course. (It's called a vicious cycle.)

Simon's sorcery caused the people to depend on him for counsel and advice to better their situations; and this dependency provided Simon a high level of *undeserved* respect and admiration from the people in Samaria.

Attempting to Control God with Money

Now don't tell me for a minute that you've never done *anything* like this for yourself. I'd only have to touch upon one example to prove you wrong; after which, I'll just move on.

You know what they say about people *before* they get married? You know, those newlyweds who all of a sudden have a "personality transplant" and change dramatically *after* the vows have been spoken? You know that the word "hypocrite" in the New Testament means "actor", "stage player", or "pretender", right? [72]

Get it?

Moving on now, Simon was acting or pretending in order to get approval from the people. He wanted them to think he was greater than he really was. He was commanding respect and admiration from the people that he really did not deserve. Sound familiar? Yes, there was a CIYA motivation to Simon's conduct.

We do the same thing all the time, we are concerned about what people think of us, we all want people to think highly

---

[72] Strong's #5273, transliterated, "Hupokrites".

of us, we all want to be admired and respected, loved and honored (the CIYA). So don't bag on Simon for being just like you are.

Come on and admit it! This is an important key to this teaching and the transformation of your own behavior. We must all honestly examine ourselves. You should intentionally start thinking and acknowledging before God the various things you do so that others will like you, love you, admire you, or respect you.

Once you start *admitting* … then you can start *repenting*, at which point, He'll start *transforming*.

Consider a modern-day example of Simon the sorcerer, found in an alleged woman of God and a self-proclaimed prophetess, one whom you'll find present in many church settings today. She uses her self-professed prophetic gift to "divine" other Christians.

In so doing, she places herself in a position of authority, telling others what God allegedly said to her, about them; what glorious things she has seen happening to them in a vision and/or what will be the outcome of their magnificent

Attempting to Control God with Money

God-given destinies and future.

In the beginning, the content of her divination is always positive and superficial: "You're anointed with the Spirit of God", "God is going to use you in a mighty powerful way in this ministry", "The Lord has shown me a vision of you serving in the most wonderful place" "It's a very high position that He's going to be elevating you to in the future", "Just be faithful"... etc.

In essence, the alleged "prophetic word" has absolutely no substantive, let alone prophetic, content. Absent the "Christianization" aspect, it's little more than what you might find in the astrology section of Cosmopolitan magazine.[73]

This "divining" inspiration carried out by the false prophetess, has resulted in her own personal gain. She now has gullible "Christians" surrounding her at all times. These are people who would not have otherwise given her the time of day, had it not been for her "divining" them all along. They are now found talking to her, inquiring of her, consulting her, hanging around her, following her advice; taking and accompanying her from place to place. They

---

[73] Assuming, of course, Cosmopolitan has an Astrology section ☺

can be seen regularly standing in wait, just hoping for another <u>counterfeit</u> forecast about their own anticipated future grandeur.

They have all been, *thrown out of position.*

Once they're hooked, she then goes into "taker" mode and uses these people, their resources, their time, and their energy, to suck them dry with the things she needs from them to either *do* for her, or to *give* to her.

Notwithstanding the fact she's clearly become a burden, they continue to communicate with her, serve and honor her. They stick around in anticipation that she may tickle their ears once again with how great and wonderful they are and how enormous and breathtaking God's plan for their lives is really going to be.

If they don't watch it, they can become so consumed in meeting the demands of this "divining" relationship that they never end up hearing the *real* voice of God *for themselves*, ever again!

Attempting to Control God with Money

When it gets to the point where her "divining" never comes true, or they get tired of the one-sidedness of the relationship, or when they try to stop adhering to her variety of control tactics, she then seeks to regain the attention and control she once had by forecasting harmful, negative, "doom and gloom" consequences for such misconduct.

This is another very sad example of how the spirit of divination unwittingly controls the lives of other well-meaning Christians. They think they're just being *nice* "Christians", when in reality-- they're just being *taken*.

Now, back to Samaria. When some *real* competition rolled in to town, namely Philip, who began preaching about the Kingdom of God, many people got saved *including* Simon the sorcerer. After getting saved, Simon began to follow Philip around witnessing God's miracles, signs and wonders performed through Philip's life.

Peter and John then arrive and lay hands on the new converts so that they would receive the "gift" (or baptism) of the Holy Spirit. When Simon witnessed this event, he wanted that power for himself.[74]

Once Philip showed up and everyone started getting saved and healed, the people of Samaria's attention that was once focused on Simon, took a nosedive. Simon's prior lofty standing in the community was over! O-V-E-R!

So no doubt in an attempt to re-gain *control* over his audience, Simon wanted that same power the apostles had demonstrated at his disposal. So he figured he'd just offer them a little capital, in order to buy that "power" for himself. His intention, no doubt, was to use it to resuscitate his once enjoyed preeminence and status.

Oftentimes, we too try to control God and/or the power of God with our money.

Some people think if I give money to God, He must give me His power for whatever *I* want to do with it. If I give this

---

[74] Simon, having a past in bewitching the people for personal gain, may have seen this "power" as a new angle that he could use to regain the admiration and respect from the people as he once had. (You know that fleshly "old man" dies hard.)

money to the church or to the poor, or to this worthy cause or ministry, I can buy the gift of teaching, prophecy, or healing. I can buy a "not guilty" verdict and get my son out of jail. I can buy my daughter off drugs. I can buy my wife's love back. Or even worse, like Simon, I can buy God's power in my life to demonstrate it in *my* "ministry".

Yikes!

"But Peter said to him, "Your money perish with you, because you thought that the gift of God could be purchased with money! You have neither part nor portion of this matter (ministry), for your heart is not right in the sight of God. Repent therefore of this your wickedness, and pray God if perhaps the thought of your heart may be forgiven you" (Acts 8:20-22, KJV).

The apostles rebuked Simon because something God was giving away as a free gift to new converts (the power of the Holy Spirit), he was trying to purchase with money.

While the Lord does perform all the miracles mentioned above on a regular basis, it is never because you paid Him for it. You can't pay God to cause the Holy Spirit to indwell you (1 Cor 6:19), nor come upon your life in power (Acts 1:8); nor can you purchase whichever spiritual gift(s) (1Cor 12:4-11), you wish to make use of for *your* ministry; nor can you pay Him to manifest His glorious presence in your life or at your Sunday church services.

God demonstrates His power as He pleases; in and through whomever He pleases; whenever and wherever He pleases, period. Again, it's called "Sovereignty".

It's just like what happened with King Saul: at one point the Spirit of God was with Saul (1 Sam 11:6); yet at another, after practicing "rebellion" or witchcraft, He was long gone (1 Sam 16:14).

Notwithstanding, there are some pastors, preachers, teachers, church leaders and other para-church ministry leaders, who try to imply or even expressly state, that you *can* control God with your money.

Now, don't misunderstand: again, it <u>is</u> right to adopt the nature of God and be a "giver"; it is right to tithe and give to your church and other ministries that you believe are furthering the Lord's Kingdom agenda (we already covered that).

The point to be made in this chapter, however, is that you cannot buy the power or presence of God like bubble gum out of a candy machine. You cannot throw money at God and expect to purchase His gifts, talents, anointing, or power. These things are not for sale. That's why Simon's heart was not right.

Yet, we have people today who think that, contrary to the Word of God, they can buy or purchase the power of God, or good standing with God, and/or the salvation of God, or the "gifts" of God, with their money, deeds, or other charitable giving and/or moral living (Titus 3:5; Eph 2:8-9; Is 64:6).

To Simon's credit, he received this correction from the apostles and asked them to pray for him. Here again we see that you can be "saved", but still not adequately transformed out of your prior thinking, conniving, and manipulative behavior patterns, to keep yourself from "giving place" to the spirit of divination.

Attempting to Control God with Money

So, to sum up the "money" and "control" duo, we've learned that the spirit of divination often uses "money" to gain "control" over people, their feelings, their actions, their resources, and their money; but, that neither money, nor the spirit of divination's use of the same, can ever control the Lord, nor a person's receipt of His gifts, talents, miracles, anointing, or power.

Would you now like to next see how "it" works in other very familiar religious settings?

CHAPTER 23: The spirit of divination at Work in Religious Settings

----

Just as the spirit of divination uses money to control people, "it" also uses "the Word of the Lord" to control people as well.

"The LORD said unto me, The prophets prophesy lies in My name: I sent them not, neither have I commanded them, neither spake unto them: they prophesy unto you a false vision and divination, and a thing of nought, and the deceit of their heart" (Jer 14:14, KJV).

"They have seen vanity and lying divination, saying, The LORD saith: and the LORD hath not sent them: and they have made others to hope that they would confirm the word" (Ez 13:6, KJV).

The spirit of divination at Work in Religious Settings

The Amplified says, "*They have seen falsehood and lying divination, saying, the Lord says, but the Lord has not sent them. Yet they have hoped and made men to hope for the confirmation of their word* (Ez 13:6, AMP) ... "*because with lies you have made the heart of the righteous sad, whom I [the LORD] have not made sad...*" (Ez 13:22, KJV).

If there's anywhere that a Christian should be able to feel safe, it should be in a church or other religious settings among the brethren, *right?*

Wrong!

The spirit of divination works in and through some of the most unexpected people, in the most unexpected places, including but not limited to, the church folk sitting in pews.

The word "divination" in both Ezekiel 13:6 and in Jeremiah 14:14, is the same Hebrew word that is translated "witchcraft" in 1 Sam 15:23, which was used when Saul was dethroned.[75]

---

[75] Strong's #7081, transliterated "Qecem".

The spirit of divination at Work in Religious Settings

In these passages we see the prophets or spiritual leaders of the day, making statements that they claimed were from God: "*Thus saith the Lord…*" In contradiction, God Himself was saying that they were *not* of Him at all.

Put yourself in the place of these false prophets for a minute. Think about the pressure that was on them to say something positive in order to win the people over; and think of the rejection they'd experience if and when they failed to do so. Where do you think that came from?

Correct! Their CIYA.

We see that the false prophets themselves were subject to the spirit of control because they wanted to be liked and accepted by the people, like Simon the sorcerer. So while everybody was blatantly practicing sin, while they all were in big trouble with the Lord, they pretended that *everything was gonna be all right in Christ.*

The teaching point we derive is that: **People in positions of spiritual leadership may claim to be representing God's Word or the Lord's perspective on your situation, when in fact, they really are not.**

The spirit of divination at Work in Religious Settings

In order to "control" your conduct, the spirit of divination may use some person with some level of spiritual authority over you, whether real or imagined, to make statements claiming to be "of God" when they really are not.

Therefore, you should never be surprised, shocked, or amazed to see some spiritual leader in your life telling you something is "from God," when it really isn't. In those cases, it's really from that lying spirit, the spirit of divination, who is presently just "name-dropping". Or, throwing God's name around saying: *"Thus saith the Lord"* in order to get you to respond exactly how "it" wants you to.

In common day vernacular, we might hear someone say to us: "God said" or, "The Lord would want you to..." or, "That's not of God" or, the "Word of God says you're supposed to..."

Whenever anyone quotes the Bible or says, "God said" or "The Lord spoke to me and told me that you should...", many times, their name-dropping of "God" or "the Lord" is intended to give more weight or credibility to their statements; and when the spirit of divination is involved, it is ultimately meant to *control* your behavior against God's will.

Understand now, that there's nothing wrong with this when the directive really is from the Lord; but on the other hand, there is certainly something wrong when the directive is from the spirit of divination.

"Name-dropping" JEHOVAH is a means by which the spirit of divination's influence can become more compelling on the person receiving the advice or directive than it would otherwise be, had His name not been throw into the mix.

Then, if the person speaking into your life is a respected representative of God: a pastor, teacher, preacher, other church leader, or just someone that's been a Christian longer than you have, you end up with a very forceful influence that can be used to control any well-meaning Christian's behavior, apart from the will of God.

So be very cautious of those people who indiscriminately throw God's name into every situation. More often than not, they're just looking to garner some authority over your life that they wouldn't have otherwise.

The spirit of divination at Work in Religious Settings

Hence, our next teaching point is: **You cannot let just anyone speak into your life.**

When I use the word "anyone" I intentionally mean to include the following categories of people:

"Christians" who are either your spiritual leaders officially; or who have unofficially taken you under their spiritual wing.

"Relatives" spouses, fathers, mothers, in-laws, young children, grown children; especially, people who have taken it upon themselves to oversee, monitor and/or supervise your walk with the Lord, or control your behavior in other venues by use of religious jargon.

"Friends" who brought you to the Lord and whom for the rest of their lives will try and act like they've got some sort of spiritual edge, authority, or superiority over you.

"Pastors" especially those who only "show" for the "show" but never mingle with the sheep, let alone get to know any of them. They don't know "boo" about you, your gifts, or talents, your circumstances or your situation. They certainly know nothing about what God's leading you to do, such as: separate from your spouse, start a business, leave a job, serve in a different area of ministry, change your career, or start up a ministry of your own, etc. Yet, they've got plenty of, *"thus saith the Lord"* advice, without any of the indispensable facts-- so watch out! (Prv 18:13,17).[76]

"Christian Counselors" who aren't really providing "Christian" counsel at all. They use psychology instead of theology to try and solve your problems. Or pastoral counselors, who grasp the first scripture they can think of that matches the subject matter of your problem, who then hastily throw it out and send you on your way "In Jesus name" so that they can rush off to make their 12:30 luncheon appointment.

"Anybody Else" sitting in the pews of the church, from an usher, to a deacon, to a heathen. Those who know you well, as well as those who hardly know you at all. Any one of them can make it *their business* at any given time, to "speak into your life".

---

[76] This statement is made to the exclusion of those with genuine prophetic, or word of knowledge, gifting from God.

The spirit of divination at Work in Religious Settings

When I say, "speak into your life" I mean that you just can't go to *anyone* and certainly not to *everyone* and tell them all your troubles; and then do whatever they say or recommend that you do in order to solve your problems. We touched on this concept previously.

When you get "a word from the Lord" or advice, or a directive from someone, then the first thing you must do is see if God confirms the advice. You cannot just "trust" the advice is really from the Lord, merely because they have some title or leadership position over you; or because they call themselves "Christian"; and certainly not just because they proclaim, *"Thus saith the Lord..."*

In fact, when someone gives you "a word from the Lord", it is many times only a *confirmation* of what He's already disclosed to your spirit. Assuming of course, you're in communication with Him at the level and intensity you should be; which is again, a topic we've already covered.

God uses prophets, pastors, teachers and other gifted Christians for counseling inquiries in three primary ways: (1) As confirmation of what the Lord has already spoken in your spirit; (2) As correction for your conduct by using the right application of God's word; (3) To answer questions you have about God's *ways* in order to confirm or correct what you should do in any given situation; and/or (4) to encourage you in ways on how to seek the Lord for yourself, in order that you might receive your own personal confirmation directly from Him.

I am against any type of *long term* "Christian" counseling relationship because they far too often foster a dependency on the limited Christian counselor, instead of the limitless, Wonderful Counselor. There are people who come in, session after session to just talk, never once "doing" what they've been directed to do to help their own situation.

Once a person is given the Word that applies to their issue, it is now time for that person to be a "doer" of the Word (Ja 1:23, KJV). They shouldn't come back for *more* counsel until they have implemented what was directed for them to do the last time they were there.

In any case, you cannot hang your "Christian hat" on the unconfirmed words of another person; especially if that person is saying the opposite of what God has shown you.

The spirit of divination at Work in Religious Settings

There's just nobody on the face of the earth that this hasn't applied to at one time or another. The spirit of divination is much more difficult to overcome when "it" is influencing your spiritual leaders to influence you, because you have a tendency to conclude: *"Oh they should know better than me; after all, they are my spiritual leader".*

I don't care if it's a pastor, Christian leader, gifted psalmist, or just someone who has been a Christian longer than you have, you cannot take advice or counsel from just anyone; nor can you *lean to your own understanding* and be confident that you are walking in the will of God based solely on someone else's input.

You've got your own relationship with the Lord, use it! Don't be lazy like so many Christians are and as a result, be forced to confer with "flesh and blood" to confirm your path. You must check-in with Him and wait on Him, until He shows you. Remember, He's the only One with "the plan". He's the One Whom you'll ultimately be required to give an account to for what you did with the life He gave you.

"CONTROL FREAK"

The spirit of divination at Work in Religious Settings

One Sunday as I was sitting in church waiting for the service to start, there was a couple sitting behind me who were well known for their work on Christian television. Now, I wasn't *trying* to overhear what was being said (within just a few inches of the back of my head), but it was very difficult not to.

I overheard people from that church, who personally didn't know this couple from Adam, complementing them from one end of the sanctuary, to the other. Sure, expected ... *I suppose*. But, then they also started giving this couple unsolicited advice about their ministry: What they should do, where they should take it, talking about the vision and providing input for the future direction of the couple's TV program, etc. etc. etc., *when again*, they didn't even know these people from Adam.

In that situation, the spirit of control stepped in, uninvited, seeking to direct already successful Christians, on how to run their ministry in the future. At the end of the conversation, these church people proceeded to give out their own business and ministry cards to them, while explaining "the vision" for their own ministries and how any monetary support that the couple may "feel led" to provide would be greatly appreciated.

Have you ever seen "it" before in that context? Have you ever witnessed how members of our Christian Community go around giving unsolicited advice and input to others, telling them how to run their lives, their children, the businesses, their marriages, their churches, and even their ministries?

With our next teaching point we learn to: **Consider the potential motives of every person or spiritual leader who speaks into your life because they may be deceitfully seeking to fulfill their own agendas.**

In Ezekiel we saw the spirit of divination giving false directives, which ultimately *made the righteous sad.* Why? Because they were false and never came to pass. In Jeremiah, we saw the spirit of divination also giving false directives which were motivated out of *deceitful hearts.* In both instances, the directives were *alleged* to be coming from the Lord, but they really were not.

The spirit of divination at Work in Religious Settings

While we can never judge the motives of someone else's heart, the Bible does say that, *"out of the abundance of the heart the mouth speaks"* (Luke 6:45, KJV). Therefore, we can sometimes get a brief glimpse of what's going on in a person's heart, by the words they make use of in order to further their own agendas.

I personally witnessed a real life Ezekiel, *"making the righteous sad"* situation that happened one day in a church office. One of the key helpers to one of the pastors had decided that the Lord was moving her out of state in order to go through an open door of ministry. This opportunity was a "divine fit"; it was something "right up her alley". So she made a counseling appointment with the pastor she had been serving under to tell him the exciting news.

Shortly after leaving that appointment I spoke to her and she told me that, in response to her news, the pastor told her: "That's not of God!" The young lady was devastated because the pastor did not support her step of faith, which she truly believed was directed by God. What's worse, she was now even more concerned about making the move because of the negative comments made by that pastor.

The spirit of divination at Work in Religious Settings

What's even worse than that, is the fact that she spent less than ten minutes talking with the pastor before he made his bold, *"Thus saith the Lord"* proclamation. He clearly didn't even spend enough time with her to listen to the whole story of how God was showing her where He wanted her to go.

Naturally, I encouraged the precious young lady to follow the Lord, not man and she went anyway, thank God! But just think of how many Christians in those same kinds of situations are being misled by the counsel of their spiritual leaders; and as a result, they then miss where the Holy Spirit had really intended to take their lives.

In Ezekiel it says that the righteous people of God were saddened, yet the Lord had never intended for them to be in that condition and no wonder. It's bad enough when you have a situation that causes you to seek out godly counsel for confirmation; but when you're told by a person in spiritual authority over you, something diametrically opposed to what God really wants you to do, what a mess that becomes!

The spirit of divination at Work in Religious Settings

In those instances, even when the person goes with the directives of the Lord and dumps the ungodly counsel, great sadness and disappointment are unavoidable, because "it" continues to undermine that person's faith and exploit their doubts throughout their whole "ministry" experience.

I personally had an example of a Jeremiah, *"out of the deceitfulness of their own hearts lies were spoken"* situation that happened to me:

I was serving in a church for a year or so, helping all the pastors, church employees, and other volunteers in different tasks that needed to be done. I liked the variety.

I got along very well with all the pastoral staff, leadership and church staff who were laboring on a daily basis, or "holding down the fort" so to speak. It was just the wife of the senior pastor who didn't seem to take kindly to my presence at the church.

Though she didn't know me from Adam, on several occasions *it appeared as if* she was intentionally undermining whatever I did, in some way or another. She

The spirit of divination at Work in Religious Settings

used to direct others to have me removed or excluded from areas where I spent a lot of time fulfilling my volunteer duties, whenever she or her husband were around. There were several things that happened over time that I wouldn't bother to recite, because I'd rather not bother to recall.

What is important for you to appreciate is the fact that when you are a woman going to a church, you're automatically serving under the first lady of that church. When the first lady's conduct clearly indicates, time and time again, that she doesn't want you around, this can cause any "untrained" person to leave that church immediately (effect) because of their "hurt feelings" (affect).

Remember, affect drives effect.

In fact, that's exactly what had happened to a very nice woman right before me. Though I never asked about the details, whatever transpired was so bad that she never showed up to an event that she planned for the church. She just left the church and never came back.

In my case, however, since I knew about the spirit of control, I didn't get hurt, nor did I automatically run out the door to go find another church. Instead, I asked the Lord what He wanted me to do in response to these various situations whenever they arose (and there were several over time).

For each incident, He would always confirm that what I perceived was *correct;* and that He *knew;* and that I should just *rise above it;* and that He wanted me to *stay* at that church, despite the despising.

So the teaching point we learn is: **the spirit of control can try to offend or hurt your feelings (affect); in order to get you to leave a church setting (effect); before it is the will of God for you to do so.**

So I did what He said without even flinching and best of all without attitude! The reason it was so easy for me, as opposed to the other lady that left, is that I had been gravely mistreated by people in the past who I really loved and cared about, so these incidents with a first lady I didn't even know, had *barely* made a blip on my radar screen. Plus, when you know it's the Lord telling you to do something while you're under fire, it makes it a lot easier to handle.

The spirit of divination at Work in Religious Settings

Time passed and then during the last few months I was there I sensed a stirring. The "spirit" of the church itself, had changed. I didn't look forward to being there anymore like I used to; and yet, it had nothing to do with this situation with the first lady.

I had completely overcome her issues and I did my best to cater to her level of maturity by continuing to honor and respect her position of authority in the church. Within just a few weeks, some other totally unrelated things started to happen around the church that indicated to me that He was preparing me to leave.

The very last encounter I had with the first lady was once again, indirect, just as all the times before. It came after I had been asked by the leaders of the men's group to help out at a men's event, which I gladly agreed to do. So I went out shopping for what was needed, found some great things within the budget, and brought everything back to the church office. By early the next morning one of the pastors called me and told me to, "Take everything back, because the senior pastor's wife would be handling the event."

The spirit of divination at Work in Religious Settings

There were people at the church who, by this time, had seen this kind of thing happen to me so many times before, as "godly" as they were, they could no longer suppress their words or facial gestures in acknowledgment that something *wrong* was definitely going on. They offered to help me take everything back, offered me a gas card; or tried to "make it up" to me in some other way. I declined all such offers; I was determined to ride this all the way out and without a sinful attitude.

Concurrently with that situation, there was a Women's Leadership Group formed at the church. Naturally, given the relationship I had with the wife, I had never expected to be a part of her Leadership Team and of course, I was correct.

However, once the various leadership appointments were "made public" to the congregation, many of the women in the church began to ask me, "Why didn't they pick you?" "Why aren't you in the Women's Leadership Group?" "You should be a leader more than _____" (such and such a person).

I mean, I knew *"why"*, God had shown me *"why"* every single time some incident had occurred in the past. But beyond that, it wasn't just this malfunction with the first lady, or my not serving in the Women's Leadership Group that was the problem; it was because the Lord had much bigger things planned for my time as it related to my own ministry.

However, after the "Women's Leadership" team had been publicly announced, every single time I went to church I had to deal with these same kinds of inquiries. I did my best to minimize or avoid these conversations and to watch my facial expressions when responding, because I had always been told that I didn't have a very good "poker face".

I refused to say, imply, or even let my facial gestures say or imply, anything bad to anyone about this first lady. I had gone this far in total victory. I had made it to an "advanced" testing level and I was determined not to fail now.

So I asked Him directly, *"Lord, am I staying at this church? Or, are You moving me? And, if I'm leaving, do You want me to do anything about this before I go?"*

The spirit of divination at Work in Religious Settings

In other words, I was asking the Lord if I should let her know that I *knew* what she had been doing all this time; or should I just move on and let Him handle it?

Look, its one thing to know what's really going on, and just not say anything to that person, because you're confident that God's got your back and He's got a purpose and a reason to allow all of this to happen to you. I'm good with that; it carried me through this situation for well over a year or more, without stumbling.

It's another thing, however, to allow that person to carry on what they're doing and hurt others (who aren't as strong as you are); while they continue to *think* you're an idiot, totally oblivious to what they've been doing to you the whole time you were there "serving" them. From my perspective, "Go ahead, be carnal", but at the same time, I want you to at least know that *I've always had your number.*

Additionally, when the person to be corrected is arguably "untouchable" to the point where the Lord has no one to use to correct them in their sin; that can cause a person like me to ask Him, *"Do You want me to do anything about this?"*

The spirit of divination at Work in Religious Settings

This is usually the case in so many of the incidents where pastors are committing adultery. The entire staff knows, but there's no Nathan on the inside without the CIYA to confront the sin. Personally, I didn't care one way or the other what the Lord directed me to do. Oddly enough, I didn't even feel like I had a dog in this fight.

So my question was, *"Lord should I tell her I know, on my way out the do'?* [77]

After making these inquiries, lo and behold this time His answer was different than before. "Yes!" He was moving me and "Yes" He wanted me to say something too.

The spirit of divination had failed in its attempt to use offense (affect), to move me out of that church (effect), when "it" wanted me to go. The Spirit of the Lord wanted me to stay so that He could allow me to be mistreated a bit more and then use me for this last assignment, *before* I went.

How did I know for sure?

---

[77] "Door" intentionally misspelled for rhyming pronunciation effect.

The spirit of divination at Work in Religious Settings

Well, the morning I posed those questions to the Lord, I just so happened to be in Third John. That passage speaks of Diotrephes *"who loved to have the preeminence"* (v. 9, KJV). In order to maintain that position, he was basically throwing all of the good fellow-workers out of the church.

BAM!

I then, pulled out a commentary to 3 Jn 1:9-10, and it clearly gave me the answer to the second part of my question when it stated: *"All we know about Diotrephes was that he wanted to control the church. John denounced (1) his refusal to have anything to do with spiritual leaders (2) his slander of the leaders (3) his bad example of refusing to welcome any teachers, and (4) his attempt to excommunicate those who opposed his leadership. Sins such as pride, jealousy, and slander are still present in the church, and when a leader makes a habit of encouraging sin and discouraging godly actions, he must be stopped. If no one speaks up, great harm can come to the church…"[78]*

---

[78] The Life Application Bible, TLB, New Testament Life Application Notes and Bible Helps © 1996 owned by assignment to Tyndale House Publishers, Inc. All rights reserved.

The spirit of divination at Work in Religious Settings

BAM again! It was clear as day to me.

This is the standard way the Lord speaks to me: I pose a question, I read through the various sections of the Bible that are already set to be my devotional reading for that day; the Holy Spirit applies the Word to my situation; and thereby confirms His directive. Done!

So in my mind, it's done!

The next question was, "What should I do about advising the pastors under whom I'd been serving about my intentions?" I decided it was only fair and respectful to forewarn them of what I was going to do, and how.

Now here's where it gets good, this is where the *spirit of divination* comes into play with my pastoral leaders. I call one pastor and he says "Wow!" Are you sure it's God? I say, "Yes, positive". He says, "You've got to do what the Lord tells you, Janet." So we said our "goodbyes" because obviously, I wasn't coming back to that church.

I then call the next pastor.

The spirit of divination at Work in Religious Settings

After telling him my plan, the next pastor says, "Janet that's not of God!" "I can't believe you're going to do this." "What are they going to say to me? I'm the one that brought you on the inside." "You're gonna burn a bridge", while referring to the senior pastor and his wife as people in "high places".

Do you see the spirit of divination directing me not to do what God clearly had told me to do? Do you see by his comments, how this last pastor was more worried about *his standing* with those in "high places", than my standing in obedience to the Lord, who is "exalted above all the earth?" (Ps 97:9, KJV).

I responded to that last pastor by politely saying, "I wasn't calling to *ask you* if I should do it, but just out of respect to *tell you* that I was going to do it, so that you wouldn't be blindsided by the news".

This kind of thing takes place both inside and outside of the church on a daily basis. These are people trying to *control* you by saying that God would want you to do this or that, but in reality it's not God at all. Rather, it's what *that person wants you to do for their own benefit* and they're just throwing God's name into the equation because that way, they think you'd be more likely to do it if, "God said so".

So I again, was faced with another defining moment.

Remember, the spirit of divination tries to play on self-doubt and your insecurities by making subtle suggestions such as, "Did you really hear God, or not?" *"Yea, hath God said?"*

Since those kissin' cousins are both diametrically opposed to what God had for me, I had to stamp "it" out and follow the Holy Spirit by implementing: "The Principle of Diametric Opposition".

In this case, since the commentary was already written for Third John, it was a very easy thing for me to do. I simply drafted an email, referred to and quoted word-for-word directly from that commentary, put it together with a few choice and very respectful words of my own ... pressed the "send" button and it was done!

I didn't care what relational bridges burned down with those people, especially "Christians" like that. I chose to keep my connection with the Lord firm, rather than risk Him deciding that He can't trust me to carry out *any directive* that He wants accomplished through my life.

So are you going to obey man or God? In every single solitary spirit of divination-driven situation, that will be the ultimate question.

Two very cool confirmations related to the whole incident happened just a few weeks after I left that church. First, this sinister person who had been trying to find out where I was living, who I was hanging out with, and where I was going to church, came to that church *looking for me.*

LOL! I was long gone by then.

But what if I would have stayed?

The second blessing, which I believe was directly related to the fact I had passed that *particular test*, came after I found a new church. The first lady of my new church had an automatic love and interest in me, far beyond what you would "normally" see. After just a few weeks of going there, the senior pastor (her husband) came up to me one night after service and said, "My wife really likes you, I mean she *really, really* likes you."

I walked out of that service that night and said, "Lord, what was *that* all about?"

The Spirit spoke to my heart saying, *"As much as the last first lady hated you; this first lady is going to love you."*

Wow! It was like the Lord was rewarding me for passing that previous testing experience, by giving me a new first lady to make up for my previous mistreatment. As always, when the Lord asks you to do something for Him, He always gives you *way more* back in return.

This new first lady is a true woman of God, gifted, anointed and discerning. When you see her in action, she tends to the flock as if she had all of the time, care, and love in the world to lavish on them; and indeed she does, because it's the Lord's strength and love visibly working through her life. What an example.

Many months later a prophecy was given that our destinies were tied together; I expectantly await the full manifestation of that Word. In the meantime, I have been treated with more favor, honor and respect in that house of God than anywhere I have ever attended church before.

This goes for all children of God, when you pass the test, you get the promotion!

Next up, the spirit of divination's dirty ... "work" ... continues.

"CONTROL FREAK"

CHAPTER 24: The spirit of divination "At Work" in the Business World

━━━━━━━━━━━━━━━━━━━━━━━━━━━━━━━━━

"Don't become partners with those who reject God. How can you make a partnership out of right and wrong? That's not partnership; that's war. Is light best friends with dark?" (2 Cor 6:14, MSG).

The spirit of divination is also "at work" in your professional and business relationships. There are people in the business world calling themselves "Christians" who want to partner-up with you on various business ventures, ideas, deals, or "visions". You may not know them that well; many times, not even well enough to know their last name.[79]

---

[79] I had a woman call me one day who said she gave over $400,000 to a man for investment purposes. When I asked, she couldn't even tell me his last name without saying she'd have to look through some paperwork.

The spirit of divination "At Work" in the Business World

Yet, after a little "Christian lingo" is thrown around for a while and after they tell you that they're "Christian too", an otherwise astute businessperson may not even bother carrying out their own "due diligence" or investigation of the business proposal. Instead, after experiencing a time of intense "fellowship", they may "throw caution to the wind" while "in the spirit" and end up making a ridiculous business transaction.

You end up hiring them, partnering with them or worst of all, giving them large amounts of money for "investment" purposes, only to later find that they were nothing but "Christianized" scammers.

I've had so many different calls from so many different people over the years, yet all having that exact same theme. They met someone "at church" who said they were "Christian" and had this great "business venture" that was totally "from the Lord" and they asked if I wanted to "invest" so that I could become "financially secure" and I said "yes" and gave them "all of my money" and now "I can't find them".

The spirit of divination "At Work" in the Business World

There are "businessmen" or women, out there playing on your Christian "trust" while trying to convince you to invest in their Ponzi schemes all in "the name of the Lord". Once the deal goes south, those that get "taken" are left groping around. Groping but still hoping ... asking advice from person after person about what to do, how to make the deal work and how to get their money back if it doesn't.

The reason they're forced to call so many people is because no one is willing to just tell them, *"Honey, you just got scammed."* I think that's why I end up getting the calls.

I can't tell you how may women, young and old, highly educated and not, who have called my office over the years talking about these "smooth operator" men, who took their cash for some pie-in-the-sky investment that was a "sure thing". Now their telephone numbers are no good, they can't find them anywhere and they don't know what to do.

Not only do these women end up financially wounded, but some how or another they thought that the dirty businessman really "cared" about them, so they end up emotionally hurt to boot.

The spirit of divination "At Work" in the Business World

Again, affect drives effect. My guess is that some of these women were deceived into thinking that Ponzi actually carried some personal interest in them. This generated *feelings* of affection (affect; and in some instances, possibly even romantic affection); causing them to surrender their money for investment (effect); so that when the returns on that investment started rolling in as promised, they could finally *feel* financially secure (affect, again).

When the deal goes south, these Christians are left dealing with conflict, dishonesty, theft, and embezzlement. This causes them to get distracted and take their focus off working or running their business; eventually, they become so consumed with the loss, that they are no longer *profitable servants.*

This is another type of *control* that the spirit of divination executes in the business realm.

I had a woman call into the radio program one evening to tell me about her business "partner" who she had just found out embezzled $300,000., from the company they jointly owned.

The spirit of divination "At Work" in the Business World

The woman who called didn't know what to do. She didn't want to turn her "friend" into the police because of the criminal record and "jail time" ramifications. In fact, she was so "Christianized" she was going to allow her company to suffer a $300K loss, purportedly "in the name of Jesus".

The devil is a liar!

From a Christian perspective, when you are the owner of a business, you are *really not* the "owner" per se. You are only the "steward" (or manager) of the business, holding it "in trust" so to speak, for the real Owner.

The real Owner is a real Businessman. He expects all of us, His stewards, to "occupy" (or carry on business) until He comes (Lu 19:13, KJV). So unless you have an internal memo straight from His throne, directing the forgiving of a debt like $300K, you are actually co-conspiring with an embezzler to rip *Him* off.

Yikes!

The spirit of divination "At Work" in the Business World

Yet the spirit of divination will cause a woman like this business owner to be willing to *take from* the real Owner and *give to* the embezzler, all "in the name of Jesus."

The Lord Himself, on the other hand, was likely looking to chasten the embezzler; allow her to suffer the consequences of that sin; use it all as a means to bring her to repentance and unto Himself; and then later use her life as a testimony to others inclined to commit the same type of crime. Who knows, she could have been called to start a prison ministry?

Know this, the spirit of control wants to *run* your business … that's right-- straight into the ground, that is.

"It" wants you to join in partnership with "make-believers" who say they are "Christian" so that they can be used to thwart, undermine, and ultimately destroy all of your plowing and sowing in the business realm, *before* you ever get to reap the harvest.

"But thou shalt remember the LORD thy God: for it is He that giveth thee power to get wealth, that He may establish

The spirit of divination "At Work" in the Business World

His covenant which He sware unto thy fathers, as it is this day" (Deut 8:18, KJV).

On the other hand, the Lord wants your business to be operated with love, proficiency, honesty and integrity. He wants to prosper your business so that you can underwrite the work of His Kingdom.

There are an infinite number of ways that "it" is at "work" in the business realm, here are just a few more examples:

There are "Christian" service providers, like General Contractors, Cleaning Services, Auto Detailers, Gardeners and the like, that do shoddy work; and there are "Christian" companies that sell inferior products. When the product sold doesn't work, or the thing "repaired" still doesn't work, they just want their "Christian" brother to overlook and "forgive" that trivial fact, and pay them top dollar for their services anyway.

It's actually gotten so bad that I've heard people say, "I'll hire anyone, *except* if they have a fish on their business card".

If a "Christian" doesn't do the job they were hired to do "right", just like anybody else, they should <u>not</u> get paid until they do.

There are also evildoers in the business world that, via the *spirit of divination,* will time and time again throw your "Christianity" in your face-- in order to try and control you. These are people who seek to take advantage of what they've learned all "Christians" are *supposed* to be like, act like, or allow. They then function with the expectation that you should comply with their demands, no matter how ridiculous or unfair.

How many times have people taken advantage of your "Christianity" in the business arena?

This usually takes place when *controlling* people, motivated by the "almighty dollar", who have absolutely no relationship with God themselves, dare quote you a Scripture in order to get you to comply with their desires or demands.

The spirit of divination "At Work" in the Business World

I had this situation happen once in the courtroom, where the opposition endeavored to use my "Christianity" to try to *control* me. The attorney for the other side wanted me to agree to a trial continuance; since it was not in my client's best interest to continue trial, I politely disagreed.

After several futile attempts by the opposition to convince me that a continuance of trial *was* in my client's best interests, opposing counsel then pulled out the "big guns" and said very rigidly: *"I thought you were a Christian?"*

Ha! How funny is that? As if being a Christian meant I sell my client "down the river" at the whim of the opposition, especially when my client had the edge at trial.

Now, I'm sorry; run that by me again ... exactly *why* should I do that?

Just to be all "Christian" about it?

You've got the wrong girl ... *friend.*

The spirit of divination "At Work" in the Business World

But do you see how the "untrained" might have very easily allowed themselves to be *controlled* by this tactic and think: "Wow! She knows I'm a Christian. I need to be a good witness for Christ. I think I'll give her the continuance even though it may damage my client's position at trial. I'm sure the Lord would agree that my being a good witness is far more important."

HA!

Look, being a Christian in the business world does not mean you give in to everyone's demands, requests, and/or "deals". Nor does it have anything to do with your compliance to what everyone else in that field wants you to do, especially when they're trying to strong-arm you by name-dropping "the Lord" or "Christianity". That's nothing but yet another Control Freak tactic. Yet, everybody is so "religiously trained" nowadays they don't even have common sense anymore!

Your "Christianity" in the business realm is seen in the manner in which you treat your clientele; the quality of services performed and/or products sold; and your integrity,

The spirit of divination "At Work"
in the Business World

which is demonstrated by the way you stand against evil when tempted to do wrong.

You must expect the spirit of control to come in and try to take over your business and professional pursuits too. "It" certainly doesn't want you to prosper financially because as a result, you'll tithe and cause the Kingdom of God to prosper as well.

So the next time a "Control Freak" comes knocking at your place of business, saying they're "Christian" and/or playing on the fact that you're a "Christian", don't be manipulated into doing whatever they request, especially when it's not in your company's or client's best interest.

Next up, the interrogation lamp becomes even brighter. It's now time to take "it" to a *personal level* by an examination of the spirit of divination working in the lives of two very well known "Control Freak" kings.

The spirit of divination "At Work" in the Business World

414 *"CONTROL FREAK"*

CHAPTER 25:
Two Control Freak Kings

We can learn more about the workings of the spirit of divination by a brief examination of the personal lives of two kings: King Saul and King David. Both had plenty of power and money; and yet, both spent plenty of time exercising the spirit of control in an attempt to "fix" the consequences of the sin in their own lives.

King "Control Freak" Saul

The Lord gave King Saul a directive to "utterly destroy" the Amalekites. Specifically the Bible says, *"Thus saith the LORD of hosts, I remember that which Amalek did to Israel, how he laid in wait for him in the way, when he came up from Egypt. Now go and smite Amalek, and **utterly destroy all that they have, and spare them not**; but slay* *both man and woman, infant and suckling, ox and sheep, camel and ass"* (1 Sam 15:2-3, KJV).

The Amalekites were "a type of the flesh" in the Old Testament and God's directive to utterly destroy them, reflects His position about "sins of the flesh" even today in our lifetime. Jesus echoed this same sentiment in Matthew 5:39-40, where He stated that the offending eye and/or hand should be plucked out and/or cut off, respectively.

Works of the flesh <u>and</u> relationships of the flesh have got to go! This is true even if it means getting rid of people, habits, things, possessions and/or whatever other fleshly deed(s) you continue to allow to survive and thrive in your life. You're not going to make it to your God-given destiny while dragging along your vices.

For Saul, the directive was "either do it God's way, or get demoted." Saul disobeyed the directive, claiming he did so because he wanted to sacrifice those things to the Lord that he failed to "utterly destroy". *Not,* a good answer.

King Saul's sacrificial weaknesses caused him to be

demoted by God instantaneously.[80]

Yet, in the natural realm, Saul did not *appear* to have lost control over the kingdom at all. So in an attempt to save what God had already determined was lost, Saul began to act in ways to try to regain *control* over the kingdom, over his life, over his position and arguably, over the entire situation.

This was all done despite King Saul's clear understanding that he was finished and that God was not going to change His mind. Here's what was said, "*... Samuel said unto Saul, I will not return with thee: for thou has rejected the word of the LORD, and the LORD hath rejected thee from being king over Israel. And as Samuel turned about to go away, he [Saul] laid hold upon the skirt of his mantle, and rent it. And Samuel said unto him, the LORD hath rent the kingdom of Israel from thee this day, and hath given it to a neighbor of thine, that is better than thou. And also the Strength of Israel will not lie nor repent: for He is not a man, that He should repent*" (1 Sam 15:26-29, KJV).

---

[80] At an earlier point in time, Saul rebelled against a directive of God in violating sacrificial protocol. It was back then, that he was first forewarned that his disobedience had cost him the kingdom (1 Sam 13:12-14).

Two Control Freak Kings

So even after being told very clearly that he lost his reign through disobedience, Saul continued to try to "control" the situation and turn things back around into his favor and under his command. From that point forward Saul made various attempts to try and murder David, his successor.

Saul was seen throwing javelins at David to try and kill him, during what should have otherwise been, pleasant dinner conversation (1 Sam 19). When David left the palace scene, Saul began to chase him down like a wild animal. In so doing, Saul was compounding sin upon sin. Saul's original sin of disobedience was being compounded by his sin of attempting to kill David, so that he could retain his position in the kingdom.

In short, Saul sought to exercise the ultimate *control* over David, as seen in his attempts to orchestrate his death.

King Saul spent a lot of time, energy and toil trying to regain *control* over his life and his circumstances by murderously pursuing David, despite being specifically told by the prophet Samuel "why" all these bad things were happening to him.

I can just hear him now, can't you? "I can't believe *this* is happening to *me*! All I wanted to do was hold a little sacrifice with the boys."

Don't you love it when people come to you for counsel and say, "I don't know *why* all these bad things are happening to me?" Yet, their ongoing conduct has been in express disobedience to the Word of God. Saul was told plainly where he went wrong but he ignored God the whole time, never once even considering the option of "repenting".

Then, after many unsuccessful attempts at murdering David, Saul eventually tries "inquiring" of the Lord, but the Lord "answered him not" (1 Sam 28:6, KJV).

Huh, *how surprising.*

Whenever the Lord stops answering us, we need to examine whether or not *we* are in the process of adding "sin unto sin" in our own lives. When did we lose contact with God? After contact was lost, what sinful things, if any, did we start doing to try and "save" or take *control* over our own lives and/or the lives of others?

"For whosoever will save his life shall lose it: but whosoever will lose his life for my sake, the same shall save it" (Luke 9:24, KJV).

Saul was trying to "save" his own life, by eliminating David's.

Once Saul's pursuits "in the flesh" to "save" his own life had failed miserably and as the Lord continued to ignore him in his unrepentant sinful state; in total desperation, Saul decides to go straight to a witch to see if perhaps she could improve his chances of "securing" his future.

What's important to note at this point, is that Saul had previously ordered that no one could practice "divination" in the land (1 Sam 28:3). However, when the "going got tough" for King Saul, he threw his own ban against practicing divination-- right out the window, and he ran to a witch to see what she might be able to "stir up" in her cauldron for his personal benefit!

Saul, in this state, became worse than a heathen; groping, desperate, without direction, and without hope; resorting to whatever means possible in order to try to *control* and "secure" his now-- not so promising "future".

In a last ditch effort to try to *control* or change the adverse circumstances in his life, Saul goes to the *witch* of Endor and asks her to conduct a séance to bring the *prophet* Samuel back from the dead.

Wow! Talk about desperate.

He goes to *a witch* to call *a prophet ... back from the dead!*

Who would have ever thought of that? But it worked! Look, the power of witchcraft; the power of divination-- it works.

Samuel comes back from the dead, albeit for a very brief visitation; and after getting mad at Saul about the eternal disturbance, he then states, *"tomorrow you and your sons will be with me"* (1 Sam 28:19). That meant *dead.*

D-E-A-D!

The witch then prepares Saul his very own "last supper" and the next thing we know, he is dead (1 Sam 31:4).

Two Control Freak Kings

In sum, we see that King Saul disobeyed God, and then resorted to every tactic he could come up with to try and thwart his God-determined end by sinning against David. When none of that worked, he committed a most grievous sin of going to a witch to try and help him.

Important to note, is how Saul's sins not only continued to compound (numerically), but also began to escalate in severity. These murderous efforts by King Saul were all done in a futile attempt to keep *control* over a kingdom that the Lord had made very clear was already lost. Saul resorted to the only way he could attempt to "control" and "secure" his own future, *apart from God.*[81]

This is the spirit of control at work in the life of King Saul. Since Saul was trying to fight against God Himself, he was unable to change the course of events in his life. *"If it be of God, ye cannot overthrow it; lest haply ye be found to fight against God"* (Acts 5:39, KJV).

King Saul was therefore a very sinful, yet very unsuccessful

---

[81] Refer back to the word "divination" defined in Chapter 2; *Vine's Expository Dictionary of Biblical Words*, Thomas Nelson Publishers.

Two Control Freak Kings

"Control Freak" king; but a "Control Freak" king nonetheless.

King "Control Freak" David

Lest you think King David was exempt from exercising the spirit of control just because King Saul had picked on him for a season, think again. Take a look at the life of King David a few years later, after he too, gets out of the will of God.

Remember David's sin with Bathsheba? No wait a minute before we go any further ... let's make a correction on the oft told "sin with Bathsheba" story.

Many have taught that David saw Bathsheba "while she was bathing on the rooftop". But go back and re-read your Bible more carefully. It says that it was David who was walking on the rooftop and that he saw her bathing ... not that *she* was bathing on the rooftop. When I heard those teachings, I had always thought to myself, "Who bathes on a rooftop?"

"And it came to pass in an eveningtide, that David arose from off his bed, and walked upon the roof of the king's house: and from the roof he saw a woman washing herself; and the woman was very beautiful to look upon" (2 Sam 11:2, KJV).

What's more likely, is that David goes walking on his rooftop and while looking over the city, he gets a bird's eye view into some window where he could see Bathsheba bathing. The long and short of it is that Bathsheba was not an "exhibitionist" bathing on the rooftop; but that King David was more likely, the very first "voyeur" referenced in the Bible.

The spirit of control enters the picture after the deed was done with Bathsheba and King David finds out she's pregnant. You recall the story, David first tries everything he can think of to *control* the circumstances and force Uriah to sleep with his wife, so that everyone would think she got pregnant by her own husband (1 Sam 11).

First, David brings Uriah back from battle in order to get him to go home and sleep with his wife; but Uriah refuses to do so. When that didn't work, David moves to "plan B" and tries to get him drunk, in order that he would hopefully then go home and sleep with his wife. That didn't work either.

Do you see it? "Control Freak" or what? Here again we see someone in sin against God, trying to manipulate and *control* the behavior of another (Uriah in this instance), in order to cover and minimize the consequences of his own sin.

After that plan fails, King David hurriedly proceeds to "plan C" to have Uriah killed on the battlefield; and that plan works indeed (1 Sam 11:17).

Hence, King David was a very sinful and yet, very successful "Control Freak" king himself.

Now note some additional "Control Freak" commonalities found in the stories of these two kings:

Both kings had a certain amount of power and authority over others; and both kings were in sin: Saul- in refusing to utterly destroy the Amalekites (a type of the "flesh" Old Testament); and David- in committing adultery and murder ("sins of the flesh" in both the Old and New Testament, Ex 20:14; Gal 5:19-21).

The spirit of control kicks-in and starts working in both of their lives, when they were walking in disobedience to God. As a result, they both tried to correct the negative ramifications, or adverse consequences of their sin, by attempting to exercise "control" over other people and circumstances, *apart from God.*

Specifically, Saul sought ways to hold on to the kingdom by trying to kill David; and David sought ways to hold on to Bathsheba, by killing Uriah.

From these two kingly examples, we derive this teaching point: **When a person is walking in disobedience to God, they many times seek to *control* other people and/or circumstances, in an attempt to avoid or minimize the negative impact or consequences of their sin.**

In short, the spirit of control influences the person to add additional sins onto their original sin, in an attempt to try to hide or cover that original sin; which, in the end, only causes their original sin to compound and escalate.

Since we know that your *"sin will find you out"* (Nu 32:23); and that sin separates you from God so that He will not hear you (Is 59:2); and that ultimately, any defiance of God will not go unpunished (Prv 11:21), these kings' attempts to cover up their sin may at first glance *seem,* idiotic. However, if you'd take a close look at your own life when you're practicing a sin that you don't want to repent from, you'll likely see the same pattern of behavior.

When you're in sin like Saul and David were, you're forced to grasp at straws because God is not working in your life anymore. As a result, you have to start trying to *control the people and circumstances* in your own life by employing your own spirit of divination-driven tactics.

As for Saul's life, we see that God refused to answer Saul, ever again. Not only did the Lord take His Spirit from him, but his position of authority, his material wealth, and any other type of honor that He had previously given Saul was gone too.

Two Control Freak Kings

This all took place shortly after the people themselves had added sin unto sin, by asking for a king (Saul), in the first place. *"And all the people said unto Samuel, Pray for thy servants unto the LORD thy God, that we die not:* ***for we have added unto all our sins this evil, to ask us a king"*** (1 Sam 12:19, KJV). The Lord wanted a Theocracy; the people were in sin for wanting to be ruled by a king. The Lord ultimately gave them what they wanted; to be controlled by a Control-Freak king.

As for David's life, after repenting, the consequence of his sin was that, *"the sword would not depart from his house"* (2 Sam 12:10, KJV). And so it was, beginning with the death of his first son with Bathsheba, and continuing through all the troubles he had with his other sons: Amnon raping his own daughter Tamar; and Absalom avenging the rape by murdering Amnon; and then Absalom's treason against his own father ... David's life was full of familial grief after that sin of adultery; the ramifications of which, he initially tried to *control* with "a cover up".

Besides our learning never to add sin unto sin for ourselves, this should also teach us to never pick on people who have sin in their past. Believe you me, they're already suffering enough!

We all have the same kinds of choices as these two kings had to make, everyday. We can either, learn from the error of our way, submit and obey God; or, we can do as they did, attempt to avoid the negative consequences of our sin, by trying to "control" other people and/or circumstances.

This again, is the spirit of divination; "its" work is going on right now at this time, in this day and age. Consider these current day examples:

First, the crimes of "witness tampering" "jury tampering" and "evidence tampering" are all classic examples present in many Mafia cases. This is where evidence is "lost" or "destroyed"; where jurors or their family members are "threatened" or "intimidated"; and where witnesses are actually "murdered" so that they will not, or more accurately, *cannot,* testify at trial.

The secondary crime of "tampering" is committed on top of the original crime being prosecuted. In these situations, the defendant is trying to *control* the outcome of the criminal prosecution for "fear" of imprisonment.

Second, we also see "compounded sin" situations in corporate financial scandals, including the crimes of embezzlement, fraud, or misappropriation. This is when crooked business executives keep two sets of books in an attempt to cover up their crime: the first set reflects the crime, while the second set is used to feign their innocence. In these situations, the defendant is trying to *control* the outcome of a criminal or civil prosecution for "fear" of imprisonment or civil liability.

Third, think about all the people you know who abuse or are addicted to drugs or alcohol. They hide their original sin of abuse, first, by "denial". They then hide their substances from others: bottles under the bed, crack pipes in the sock drawer, and stash in plastic bags in the toilet tank. They sneak money in order to abuse their substances. They lie about where they've gone, or where they're going; and they end up going places they refuse to admit they've ever been. They continue to lie whenever confronted with any "evidence" of their abuse. They try to cover-up even after they've been caught "red-handed". At which point, they then lie all the more, in an attempt to support all of the lies they've already told. This is all done in order to *control* the perception of others who may demand that they give up their "habit" and check-in to rehab.

Lastly, consider this real life example that you've already no doubt heard reported about John Edwards (former Presidential Candidate and Democratic Senator from North Carolina). It aptly illustrates how a person, in an attempt to "control" the perception of others, will add sin unto their original sin, causing the ramifications of their original sin to both compound and escalate:

"A federal grand jury indicted him on charges that he violated federal campaign finance laws by "secretly obtaining and using" contributions from wealthy benefactors to conceal his mistress and their baby while he was running for president in 2008."[82]

Edwards was obviously trying to "control" the voting public's view of himself, or "save" his "reputation" and still

---

[82] *New York Times*, "Politics" section, June 3, 2011.

win their votes, by attempting to hide his affair while running for President of the United States. He no doubt thought that the general public would not vote for a candidate who was having an affair (Ha! No comment).

While the outcome of this indictment is still unknown at the time of this publication; and while I take no position on his "guilt" or "innocence", the point being made is that these *allegations* against Edwards provide a perfect "real life" example of the idea of compounding "sin unto sin" in order to "control" the circumstances or outcome of a situation. They also illustrate how *controlling* attempts to "cover up" sin, can cause the "escalation" of wrongdoing, resulting in far more serious ramifications.

Here's the brief analysis:

The first sin is of course, the adultery; the second sin/crime is the alleged misappropriation of campaign finances, used to hide the first sin. The second sin has decidedly escalated the potential ramifications of the first sin, since committing "adultery", though sinful, is not criminal and cannot get you thrown in jail; but violating federal campaign contribution laws is certainly all three: sinful, criminal, and punishable by jail time.

While you cannot control God or the principles laid out in the Word of God; you can however some times, and in some instances, *control* other people. The odds of your having the ability to control other people (as *allegedly* attempted by John Edwards) are like that of the gambler, sometimes winning and sometimes losing.

Psychology calls it "intermittent reinforcement", which is considered to be the basis for forming gambling addictions. Sometimes you win (it works), sometimes you lose (it doesn't work); but nonetheless, you persist in trying.

"Controlling" others is the same way: there are some people who you can control, while there are others, who can control you. Of those you can control: sometimes, you can't control them; other times you can. Of those who control you, sometimes they can, while other times they can't.

Rarely, do you ever find people in the world who are *never being controlled* by others. More oftentimes, you find people in the world who are *always being controlled* by others. Unbeknownst to many of us, this same kind of *control* is going on in our own lives too-- though it's just a little harder to track.

What about your life?

Are you still uncertain?

In order to relieve any uncertainty that you may still have; let's move a little closer into that bright light of interrogation and that corner that I promised to back you into earlier.

Now's the time to grab your shades.

CHAPTER 26: Modern Day "Control Freaks" in Action

Let's just get right down to it:

We are now going to go through some of the most obvious present day "Control Freak" manifestations, by type or classification of "control".

In the examples to follow, your life will fit into either one, both, or all three of the possible "Control Freak" categories: You'll either be the "Control Freak"; the person who is "Control Freaking out"; and/or you will find yourself in both roles, at varying times, within differing relationships, playing the role of Bi-Controlling/Controlled.

In any case, I guarantee that one or more of these classifications will apply to your life.

Modern Day "Control Freaks" in Action

"ANGER"

Can be used by you to "control" others and/or by others to "control" you:

When Nehemiah sought to rebuild the walls of Jerusalem, the haters tried to use their "anger" to control and dissuade God's work. *"When Sanballat heard that we Jews had begun rebuilding the wall, he **became furious** and began to ridicule us"* (Neh 4:1, GNT).

They tried every "cheap shot" comment possible to bring the work of the Lord to an end: *"In front of his companions and the Samaritan troops he said, 'What do these miserable Jews think they're doing? Do they intend to rebuild the city? Do they think that by offering sacrifices they can finish the work in one day? Can they make building stones out of heaps of burnt rubble?' Tobiah was standing there beside him, and he added, 'What kind of wall could they ever build? Even a fox could knock it down'"* (Neh 4:2-3, GNT).

Instead of being controlled by their anger, their negative comments and ridicule, Nehemiah, after hearing what they said took it straight to the Lord and prayed, *"Hear how they make fun of us, O God! Let their ridicule fall on their own heads. Let them be robbed of everything they have, and let them be taken as prisoners to a foreign land. Don't forgive the evil they do and don't forget their sins, for they have insulted us who are building"* (Neh 4:4-5, GNT).

People with anger problems are very capable of controlling others with their anger. How many times have you heard someone say, *"I can't do that, she'll get angry"* or *"He'd get angry if I say what you're suggesting."* These people then curb or modify their behavior to suit their avoidance related predictions.

Time and time again, people make decisions to do, or not do various things, in anticipation of another person's response of anger. When taken to the extreme this can create a "walking on eggshells mentality" for those who live with and/or work around angry people.

If you find yourself in this type of situation or relationship, realize that even if you "walk on eggshells" *forever*, it will never work! Even if you do everything just exactly how they like it done, people with an anger problem will always find something else to get mad about. It's not because there is any legitimate reason to get angry, but it's because *that's how they are able to "control" your behavior.*

Anger is a very powerful tool that can be used to control other people's behavior. Yelling, throwing, or breaking something; slamming a door, or drawer; hitting a wall, screaming and cussing someone out, are all demonstrations of attempts to *control* the person or persons witnessing these kinds of demonstrative events.

Then, on the flip side, people usually miss the fact that there is another way of demonstrating anger. They miss it because they mistakenly think if someone is not yelling and screaming, kicking and hitting, that they do not have an anger problem.

Not so.

Some of the angriest people on the face of the earth are simply, "ignorers".[83]

---

[83] The word "ignorer" I assume, has some very close root-word relationship to the word "ignoramus", which is a very apropos description of these kinds of people.

Modern Day "Control Freaks" in Action

They intentionally fail to acknowledge that you just walked into the room. If you live with them, they never say "Hi" when you come home; they never even carry on the type of polite communication they would with strangers. Instead, because they're *always* angry, they just pretend that you-- *don't exist.*

"*We despised Him and rejected Him; He endured suffering and pain. **No one would even look at Him - we ignored Him as if He were nothing***" (Is 53:3, GNT).

People who express their anger in this manner hold their fury inwardly and disconnect, disengage, and intentionally cut themselves off emotionally from others. Taken to the upper echelon, this behavior can actually become a type of emotional abuse.

In either case, the person who is controlled by another person's anger is in a very bad place. Due to the CIYA and fearing the wrath of man, the person being *controlled* modifies all of their conduct and behavior to comply with what they believe will minimize or eliminate the wrath. When their actions are being "controlled" like this, they do not have the freedom to do what God wants them to do, absent consideration of what the angry person will think or do in response to God's directive.

Many people with whom you have interpersonal relationships will not like the fact that you have an assignment from God to carry out in your life. If you do not respond as Nehemiah did, you will cower under the pressure of hateful angry people who try to dissuade you from carrying out God's work in and through your life.

"CRYING"

Can be used by you to "control" others <u>and/or</u> by others to "control" you:

On the flip side of an "angry controlling personality", is the person who cries. Where the angry person controls your behavior in a demanding fashion, the person who cries tries to control your behavior by appealing to your sympathetic nature. Whether the cry-er sheds real tears, or crocodile tears, both serve as an attempt to control you, the cry-ee.

In the book of Acts, the men of God travelled several places being both led by the Holy Spirit to travel (Acts 8:29;

Modern Day "Control Freaks" in Action

11:12; 19:21); as well as restricted from travel, by the Holy Spirit (Acts 16:7; 21:4).

In one particular situation, a prophet told Paul that his decision to travel to Jerusalem would cause Paul to be put in chains. The people who loved Paul, didn't want that to happen to him. So during their pleas to get him to ignore the Spirit of God's leading, they *cried* asking him to play it safe and stay with them.

Here's the blow-by-blow:

*"We had been there for several days when a prophet named Agabus arrived from Judea. He came to us, took Paul's belt, tied up his own feet and hands with it, and said, 'This is what the Holy Spirit says: The owner of this belt will be tied up in this way by the Jews in Jerusalem, and they will hand him over to the Gentiles.' When we heard this, we and the others there begged Paul not to go to Jerusalem. But he answered, '**What are you doing, crying like this and breaking my heart?** I am ready not only to be tied up in Jerusalem but even to die there for the sake of the Lord Jesus.' We could not convince him, so we gave up and said, 'May the Lord's will be done.' After spending*

some time there, we got our things ready and left for Jerusalem" (Acts 21:10-15).

The people begged the Apostle Paul, with tears, not to go where the Lord had directed him to go. However, Paul did not allow their "crying" to control his God-given destiny.

The behavior of crying is frequently reinforced and repeated because it is usually a sure-fire way to garner sympathy from an audience. So over time, a cry-er has trained a sort of reflex reaction to cry every time they seemingly are not going to get "their way", in an attempt to reverse the trend and *control* the situation.

You see this a lot of times in relationships where the woman cries, or pretends to be upset about something that the man did wrong. This is usually done in order to elicit an apology, create a guilt complex, force him to change his behavior, or get some kind of feigned affection, some money, or something else out of him.

Take Samson for example: His first wife's tears were able to *control* his conduct to the point of his telling her the answer to the riddle he had wagered a bet on. She, in turn, told her brethren. This Control Freak tactic not only caused an irremediable breakdown in their marriage, but Samson was forced to slay thirty men in order to make good on his loss of the bet (Judges 14:1-20).

You also see children who learn very early on, that crying, yelling, screaming, having a temper tantrum and creating a scene, can serve to put that package of Skittles at the checkout stand into their little hands rather quickly.

When you allow someone's tears to control your behavior, you do so because of the CIYA. After all, you don't want that person to *cry,* you want them *to be happy.* So you're afraid that you'll lose that relationship if you don't "make better" whatever they're crying about. You mistakenly think that by doing whatever they're crying for you to do, that it will make them happy.

Sorry to say-- *you're* wrong.

Here again, even if you do everything just as they want and just how they like it, "cry-ers" will always find something else to cry about. Again, it's not because there is any truly legitimate thing to cry about, but it's because *that's how they are able to "control" your behavior.*

How often have you allowed someone else's tears to cause you to rethink what you wanted to do for the Kingdom of God? It happens all the time.

Take this example: A young man believes God's is calling him to the mission field. He tells this to his fiancée, who happens to be afraid of snakes and spiders and who still wants to be able to shop at the Nordstrom's mid-summer sales event.

So she starts crying, "Don't go" "Don't go" "I don't want you to go. It's so dangerous!" "I don't want you to go! I love you too much!" "I can't live without you, so *please*, don't go; I just can't bare the thought of being without you!" "I'm afraid, honey I'm afraid *for you!*"

Waah waah waaaaaaaaaaah!

Look missionary, if it was God telling you to go; then one thing you know for sure, it's the "spirit of divination" trying to keep you at home.

Modern Day "Control Freaks" in Action

"LIES AND DECEIT"

Can be used by you to "control" others and/or by others to "control" you:

We have the Holy Spirit who leads and guides our lives in all truth (Jn 16:13); and we have *lying spirits*, whose job is blatantly obvious-- to do exactly the opposite!

*"Now the **Holy Spirit** tells us clearly that in the last times some will turn away from what we believe; they will follow **lying spirits** and teachings that come from demons"* (1 Tim 4:1, NLT).

Wow! There it is plain as day, yet another anti-to Christ.

In a court of law, a "lie" and "deceit" are two different things. A "lie" would be an affirmative statement made with an intention to get you to act in a certain way, based on believing it to be true. "Deceit" would be intentionally withholding information that you know would cause the other person to act differently, had that information been fully disclosed.

Modern Day "Control Freaks" in Action

Let's go back to our original, unfailing example of "the sin of adultery" to better illustrate these definitions:

A husband caught having an affair might say, "I'm not having an affair, I never slept with her, I love you!" These are all affirmative statements or "lies" made to discount or undermine the information received by the injured spouse about the affair.

On the other hand, "deceit" is when the husband tells the wife he's going to the office on a Saturday and while it's true he does go there; he just so happens to leave out the part about the rendezvous he has planned in the conference room with his secretary, behind locked doors.

With both lies and deceit, the husband in this instance is seeking to *control* the wife's behavior, by intentionally keeping her in the dark about his extramarital relationship. The exercise of this *control* keeps the good ole faithful wife at her post. Home. Cooking dinner, cleaning the toilets, doing laundry and taking care of the children.

People will lie and deceive you in order to *control* you into doing all sorts of things: from partnering with them in business, to buying a product from them; from getting your telephone number, to even marrying them under false pretenses.

Since Satan is the father of lies (Jn 8:44), it's unnecessary to expound on the fact that lies and deceit are anti-to Christ. Indeed, the lying tongue is something that God hates (Prv 6:16-19).

What many people fail to realize, however, is that whoever lies to you, actually hates you too! No matter what they say when they get caught, understand this: *"Someone who wants to hurt you uses his words to hide his hatred. But his heart is full of lies that cover up his evil plans"* (Prv 26:25, NIRV).

How many times has the spirit of control used lies and deceit to get you off the path of God?

How's about, *every time* you've ever strayed off that path for an answer?

"WITHHOLDING OF ATTENTION AND AFFECTION"

Can be used by you to "control" others <u>and/or</u> by others to "control you:

Whether intentional or not, whether at home or on the job, whether in the pews or on the street, when people who in times past, previously paid you a certain level of attention and/or affection, all of a sudden stop doing so, this too can *control* your behavior.

People, who abruptly stop rendering the affection to you that they once did; or stop paying attention to you as much as they used to, are oftentimes guided by the wrong motives. This kind of drastic change in conduct or treatment can *control* your behavior.

"For instance, suppose someone comes into your meeting dressed in fancy clothes and expensive jewelry, and another comes in who is poor and dressed in shabby clothes. If you **give special attention** *and a good seat to the rich person, but you say to the poor one, "You can stand over there, or else sit on the floor" – well, doesn't this discrimination* **show that you are guided by wrong motives?** (Ja 2:2-4, NLT).

Modern Day "Control Freaks" in Action

Though not the context of this passage, the fact is that people who "come on strong" in the beginning with attention and/or affection are usually trying to get something out of you; or, in other words their "special attention" towards you is usually *guided by the wrong motives.*

This kind of behavior is a way of manipulating the receiving person's heart, mind and affections. Continuing over a period of time, this type of manipulation can rise to the level of utter and complete *control* over a person's life to the point where they're unable to leave the relationship, even if it become abusive.

In fact, if you ever watched the movie "The Preacher's Kid" *carefully* ... you already know how "the game" is played. You could have easily missed this interaction, but I didn't. The day I saw that movie, it succinctly "registered". The light bulb went on as it clarified what I, myself, had previously experienced.

Oh yeah, devil! I will expose "the game" right here and right now ... "*player*".

Modern Day "Control Freaks" in Action

For your information, to be a "player" means to "play" or better yet, "prey" on women and their weaknesses; their desire to be loved, admired, told they are beautiful, valuable, and capable (the CIYA). In sum, to be told they're totally irreplaceable in a man's life.

When you're a "player", you're really just a "predator". You're constantly on the prowl for women who can do something for you: give you sex, money, opportunity, position, status, possessions (for sure), vacations, a nice place to live, a nice car to drive, jewelry, clothing, etc. (Yeah, guys like the "stuff" too).

Now, I don't remember the specifics of who was talking to whom in the movie; but it was the "bad guy" (the one who was abusive) and another guy talking about the girl, the Preacher's kid. I also don't remember exactly what words were used to communicate the message; but what I do remember, is the one male character explaining to the other, the *psychology* behind how to "play" women. Now, while they didn't use the word "psychology", per se, I just knew that's what it was.

Modern Day "Control Freaks" in Action

Taking the concepts from the movie and generalizing them for our purposes, it goes something like this: in the beginning of these kinds of *feigned* relationships, a "player" will continuously tell a woman how beautiful, wonderful, talented, gorgeous, capable, sexy, and outright "hot" she is. How well she cooks, cleans, irons, decorates, paints, sings and/or dances, etc. As to whatever it is she does for a living and/or a hobby, and as to those things she feels are important parts of her life, character, identity, or individuality; the "player", in the beginning, will also unendingly praise.

With his malicious intent concealed, the "player" will continue on this course of conduct day after day; week after week; month after month (and I don't think it ever needs to go any further than a period of months); exclaiming, declaring and gushing over the woman, her beauty, her abilities and her character, as mentioned above, in onslaught fashion.

As a result, in a very short time, the woman gets "hooked". Psychologically, mentally, emotionally, "hooked". "Hooked", heart, soul, mind and body, "hooked". "Hooked" on the "player's" attention, "hooked". "Hooked" on his affection, "hooked". Hook, line and sinker, "hooked". Sinker for sure, "hooked", because next up? She's going *down*.

Next, the characters in the movie went on to explain after she's "hooked", how the "player" begins to do nothing but "dog her out!" The "player" says nothing nice to her anymore, no, never, ever, again.

Worse than that, the "player" starts to tear her and everything about her, down, in a most horrific fashion. He also starts to do other extremely hateful and hurtful things, while committing every type of abuse imaginable. He does things that no one would ever think *anyone* would be capable of saying or doing (with the exception of Dr. Jekyll and Mr. Hyde, of course).

It's real bad; it's like going from heaven, straight to hell.

"Divining" is the only plausible explanation for the "player's" switch from "lover" to "hater" in no time flat; because as far as she knows, there aren't any psychotropic medications that he's failed to self-administer.

Modern Day "Control Freaks" in Action

Understand, that because the woman has been "played" or "divined" for so many months prior, she is no longer in her "right mind".[84] Therefore she continues to allow herself to be subjected to this abuse and mistreatment; and then over time, if nothing is done to escape, she becomes a "victim".

Note however, that had it not been for these beginning stages of being "played" or "bewitched" by the spirit of divination, she would have never ever put up with this abuse in the first place. Absent being "divined" by the "player", at the first sign of a red flag, he and "it", would have immediately been kicked to the curb.

In other words, the "player" couldn't have ever pulled off the abusive behavior he now regularly carries on in the relationship, had he not in the beginning, "played" her with his "bewitching" spirit of divination-driven tactics.

Left unchecked, the "player's" tactics provide him with the *control* he needs to execute his ultimate mission against the woman: to kill, steal and destroy.

---

[84] Refer back to our discussion in Acts 8 about Simon the sorcerer and the definition of "bewitched": *to be **out of one's mind, besides one's self**, or insane* (Strong's #1839, transliterated "Existemi").

Modern Day "Control Freaks" in Action

As a result, the woman is whipped, her life is totally *controlled* by the "player" and many times for a lifetime. She's seen regularly groveling at his feet for that "divining" attention she experienced in the beginning. All the while the "player" goes on about his business of taking and hurting; ignoring and destroying; and never again saying one more nice or kind thing to the woman. That is unless, of course, he suspects she's on to his "game". Then in response to that, he'll just "play" her a little more until she gets back in line with the program.

Yes-- this is an extreme example, but a good one nonetheless. Look out for people who give you "inordinate" affection (Col 3:5); meaning excessive, unreasonable, or inappropriate in magnitude, and then poof! One day it's completely gone. This can be used to *control* your behavior.

Due to your fear of losing the relationship and the attention or affection you once had (CIYA "tails"), your future actions can start to be *controlled* as you engage in behaviors in an attempt to regain your previous position on that bogus "pedestal" you only *thought* you were on.

Modern Day "Control Freaks" in Action

You may start to be nicer to them and give them more attention yourself, asking them, "What's wrong?" "Is everything alright?" "Don't you love me anymore?" "Aren't I doing a good enough job at _____?"

Should that pursuit become your primary goal in life, again you voluntarily leave "you"-- heart, mind, soul and body in the hands of a sinful man or woman. (Don't forget, this happens to the guys too; they're called "gold diggers".)

In this condition, you'll find yourself waking up every morning not seeking God and His will for your life; but trying to figure out ways to regain the "divining" attention and affection of this person. It will never work, however, even if it appears for a brief instance that you are being successful. Believe me, they were over you a long, long time ago. They're just currently being entertained by your persistence.

The only thing this *control* over your behavior will serve to do in the end, is cause you to feel more rejected, become even more hurt (because of your failed efforts); and ultimately you will be exploited and *taken advantage of* by your new idol, the "player".

Now in all fairness, as any well-versed "player" would say in his own defense: *"Don't hate the player, hate the game."*

Good enough, I suppose that's a semi-admission of guilt. Which is actually pretty good for a "player" because usually they'll never admit any wrongdoing, even under the most grievous of circumstances.

The reality is, however, that "players" are nothing but "children of the devil" because their entire way of life is based on a lie. They steal, kill and destroy; lick their chops; and then move on to their next victim of prey.

In Christianity we say: "Don't hate the sinner, hate the sin." For our purposes, that is true, you shouldn't hate the "player" that the spirit of divination used to control "you" with feigned attention and affection.

Just forgive them <u>and</u> *forget them!*

If you don't, that's just another Control-Freak tactic, still being exercised over "you" and your life. Instead, focus on the fact that the spirit of control is at work on "you" and on others; and that "it" needs to be stopped right now!

Modern Day "Control Freaks" in Action

<u>"SEXUAL GRATIFICATION"</u>

Can be used by you to "control" others <u>and/or</u> by others to "control" you:

"Sexual gratification" is a way for women to easily *control* men; while "emotional gratification" (given by men to women), is a way for men, to easily *control* women ... into providing "sexual gratification" to them, the men. Got it?

The most obvious way, in which "sexual gratification" is used to *control* a man, is seen in men who practice the sin of pornography. It's not that they just "practice" the sin—it's that they've become "addicted" to the sin, in "bondage" to the sin; nor can they stop, or help themselves from continuing to be enslaved by the sin.[85]

Eventually, their spouses are no longer able to gratify them sexually; they become angry, hateful people; and their sin must escalate in gravity and intensity, in order for it to

---

[85] I am not going to waste any time arguing over whether or not pornography is a "sin". Give me a break! Look at yourself. No ... pretend like you're the Omnipresent Lord, watching what you're doing next time (if there is a next time); then straight-faced, just try and tell me it's not a sin.

continue to be satisfying. In that state, they are obviously, visibly, under the express *control* of the enemy.

How does it happen? Well, most often it's because the man goes "online" to some porn site and begins "dabbling" when they're mad, or hot under the collar about something; and then, they keep going back whenever they're driven by some emotional "affect". Then, once the act of gratification, or the "effect", pairs up to calm or sooth the "affect", a pattern of behavior is formed; the heart is "hooked" and he can no longer break free of his own volition.

What has always been totally inexplicable to me is why guys get hooked on women, who in reality, don't even know they exist. Look, this woman doesn't even know you, she doesn't even like you, she doesn't think you're "hot" and she doesn't even want you sexually, either.

She's only "playing" while you're "paying". Just like the "player", she is only "preying" on your weaknesses as a man.

In short, men-of-God, you're just being "divined" ... online.

Modern Day "Control Freaks" in Action

While men can get "played" due to their sexual weaknesses and *controlled* into acting like a fool; women can get "played" due to their emotional weaknesses and be *controlled* into having sex with a man their not married to and thus, act like a fool also.

You've heard it all too often, and no doubt several versions of the same: "You know I love you, baby, and if you really loved me, you'd let me..."

Men, who are able to skillfully tap into the "emotional weaknesses" of women, are also usually able to get them in the sack fairly easily. They just say some nice things, treat them good, give them some love, a gift or two, some "divining" attention and affection and, it's done!

So too, in the marital relationship, spouses use sex *all the time* to *control* their spouses and get their way. The most often criticized are the women for withholding sex; their husbands, under protest, citing 1 Corinthians 7:3-5.

While I don't mean to sound over simplistic and while I realize there are certain exceptions, I just gave the guys a big clue on how to resolve this problem: In sum, take care of her "emotionally" and she'll take care of you "physically".

In addition, the spirit of divination will use wives who unashamedly, will use "good sex" to *control* their husbands and keep them "in line" with several different issues, including their overspending. They put on their little "sex kitten" outfit and meow a few times and then get away with over-spending thousands of dollars each month on an ongoing basis. Yes, I've seen it!

You've also got husbands who are no longer interested in their wives sexually, they've gotten too fat, too old, too boring for their taste, or there's some sort of negative sexual history that the couple can't overcome; and so the husband just eliminates that topic from discussion.

The wife is then *controlled* both emotionally ("affect") and physically ("effect") by this kind of situation. Not only does she *feel* unloved, ugly and unwanted, but she is also inhibited from the sexual enjoyment that the Lord intended her to have in the confines of a marriage relationship. Many times, these wives go on to commit adultery only because some other man at least, "wanted them". Once the *backslidden* "effect" takes place, you can chalk up another one up for the enemy.

Whatever the scenario in your life, just realize that "sexual gratification" is another means by which the enemy can use others to *control* "you" and take "you" instantly out of God's will.

You must put a stop to "it"! You'll never make it to your God-given destiny if your focus is on "sexing it up" all along the way.

"THREATS OR ULTIMATUMS"

Can be used by you to "control" others <u>and/or</u> by others to "control" you:

From categorically "abusive" people to the "shy or timid" personality, all individuals at one time or another, may use threats or ultimatums to *control* you. Whether threats of bodily injury to yourself or to others you love; threats that they will leave you, not be in your group, won't support you financially, will divorce you, disown you, tell everybody *about* you, the list goes on and on.

People comply with the threats of others because of the "tails" side of the CIYA. Threats and ultimatums cause a type of mental torment to the person who is being threatened.

In 1 John 4:18, it says, *"Fear hath torment"* (KJV). *"Where fear is, there is pain"* (BEE). *"Fear is crippling"* (MSG). This torment consumes "you": your mind and heart, your thoughts and emotions. You cannot shake it! The threat or ultimatum is forcing your behavior in a direction against your will and/or better judgment.

Abusive people, those who threaten you physically, are the "poster child" example of what I call a "Control Freak Extraordinaire".[86]

If they don't like what you're doing or saying, they'll just slap you in the face; slug you; grab you; pinch you; push you down and/or push you around.

As a side note: while physically abusive people are usually men; guys, don't be deceived into thinking your petite wife

---

[86] A "Control Freak Extraordinaire" functions at the highest level of depravity of all the "Control Freak" species.

who uses hot grease in frying pans to threaten you, doesn't also classify as physically abusive.

Physically abusive people are the weakest link in society today, especially those who don't *"pick on somebody their own size"* and instead, pick on smaller, weaker, women and children. Look, if you're bigger, stronger, taller, and can fight better than another person, and you use that edge to *control* their behavior with threats of violence, you're just a plain ole ultra-pathetic, "Control Freak Extraordinaire".

Consider also, the category of "Control Freaks" who classify as "stalkers". They are people who harass you with unwelcomed appearances, telephone calls, text messages, threats, and unceasing inquiries that place a demand on your behavior and disrupt your peace of mind.

They will follow you around; call you several times a day leaving daunting voicemail messages, text you on multiple occasions, in short periods of time, demanding to know where you are and who you're with. They will show up at places uninvited; email incessantly; send letters, gifts, cards and other messages or communications through others, in order to try and get to you emotionally.

Modern Day "Control Freaks" in Action

Despite the fact you've made it clear to them that you want nothing further to do with them; and despite the fact that any other *sane* person on the face of the earth would have gotten the message; these sick individuals are driven by the spirit of divination to continue to *go after you.*

For everywhere they go, and for everyone they talk to, the subject matter is always the same … *you.*

Yes, of course they have nothing better to do with their own lives; they themselves have been given over to the spirit of control. Therefore, they have nothing productive to live for other than to seek to control, or seek to regain control, over *your* life.

The "affect" of their control is seen when you dread checking your voicemail, emails, or looking at your phone when it chimes with a text message. You wake up in the morning wondering what this person is going to try to do to you today. You are mentally and emotionally consumed; by either what *they said,* or what they threatened; what *they are saying,* or what they are threatening; or what *they may say,* or what they may threaten at any given time in the future.

Modern Day "Control Freaks" in Action

Face it! You are a Control Freaking mess! In this state of existence, you're a complete "nobody" for the Kingdom of God.

Good. Finally. I want you to get mad about it.

Stalking, is the "spirit of divination" being used to terrorize a person's life. If "it" is not put to a resolute stop, many people become physically ill due to the stress caused by this sick spirit.

Know this, "it" will never *voluntarily* give up "its" grip on "you". "It" must be decisively severed out of your life; and it's you my dear, who must give it the axe!

Another classification of threatening "Control Freak" is the person who makes threats to commit suicide if you break up with them. This is an extreme example of the way someone might try to *control* your love and affection.

There are also the "Control Freaks" who may threaten to kill you, your family and kids if you leave them. This is another very extreme example of someone trying to *control* your love and affection.

Modern Day "Control Freaks" in Action

Yet, another classification of "Control Freak" may threaten to withhold or take something from you: their participation, their attendance, their emotional support, or how about ... *the grandchildren*.

Then there's the "Control Freak" who may threaten to expose an adulterous affair if you don't pay them money. In an attempt to avoid embarrassment, or public humiliation, a public figure may actually pay money to those who have threatened to expose that kind of information.

Take the Tiger Woods' case for example: It was reported that one of his mistresses received a million dollars <u>not</u> to sell her story about him.[87]

If that's true, Tiger no doubt thought he was "buying peace".

However, generally speaking, once an extortioner runs out of money, they will always come back for more. Then what

---

[87] *HUFFPOST Sports* article dated December 11, 2009.

466   *"CONTROL FREAK"*

are you going to do? Sue them for breach of an extortion agreement?

To the contrary, in the Daystar Television case, Founder Marcus Lamb and his wife Joni, refused to buy-in to the extortion plot. Instead of giving in to the threat of exposure of the husband's adulterous affair, the couple announced the indiscretion to their audience voluntarily. That was a good move from my perspective, not only legally and practically speaking, but spiritually as well.

In the case of threatening people, realize that they have tapped into the "tails" side of the CIYA, your "fear of man" and they seek to control "you" through the spirit of fear.

If you give into this type of control, you will forever be operating in fear, not faith. Your decisions will forever be controlled by your fears, instead of the kind of faith that pleases God.

In response to the spirit of fear threatening your life, you've got to just call "it" on the carpet. Tell them to "bring it on!" Go to court and get a restraining order; change your address, email, and telephone number and call the police every single solitary time you see them in your path, 9-1-1 on speed dial.

"Confess your faults one to another" (Ja 5:16, KJV) if you did something wrong; and then employ the Principle of Diametric Opposition and turn "it" around! Invite them to "expose" whatever they want to, because the lower they try to bring you down; the higher the Lord will raise you up. Just get it right with Him first.

"GUILT"

Can be used by you to "control" others and/or by others to "control" you:

Statements made by anyone that elicit a feeling of guilt, or obligation that create a weight, or heaviness for you to act in order to feel better or lift the burden, can be readily used to *control* your behavior apart from God's will.

Jesus made it very clear that He was not going to be controlled by the guilt-ridden statements made by both Martha and Mary, when they said, *"Lord, if You had been here, my brother would not have died"* (Jn 11:21 & 32).

Modern Day "Control Freaks" in Action

If you've ever been taught well on this chapter, you know that it was <u>not</u> the Father's will for Jesus to hurry over and save Lazarus from dying. Rather, it was God's will to resurrect Lazarus from the dead, four days later, so that He would be glorified and the people would believe (Jn 11:15, 40, 42).

Your own family members may use a guilt complex on you, in several different ways, in order to try to get you to do something for them. Or, to keep you from doing something for someone else, that they think you should be doing for them.

They too may say things that imply that, "You should have been there", "You should have done something", or somehow, "If you would have been involved or around, this bad thing wouldn't have happened."

The classic example of this is, the old nagging mother who makes statements to her children that make them feel guilty for having a life of their own, for moving out of town, for failing to call every single day, or for whatever your mother may say that makes you feel guilty, condemned, or obligated.

Modern Day "Control Freaks" in Action

Spouses in marital relationships do the same thing. "If you really loved me, you wouldn't go fishing with the guys." "If you had any respect for me, you would always go with me to my mother's house for Sunday dinner".

All these types of guilt "control" tactics are most effective against the well-meaning good intentioned, conscientious type of spouse. Indeed, they never work with "hater" spouses, because "hater" spouses have no conscience.

Ask yourself, how many times do you take actions, not out of pure unadulterated love, but out of pure unadulterated guilt? It's not because you necessarily wanted to do that thing, it's because you knew you'd continue to feel guilty if you didn't. And, you'll do just about *anything* to <u>not</u> feel guilty.

That's got to stop.

<u>"DAMAGE TO REPUTATION"</u>

Can be used by you to "control" others <u>and/or</u> by others to "control" you:

When describing the difference between "reputation" and "character", Coach John Wooden, said, "Your reputation ... is what others think of you; your character is what you really are."[88]

Restated, "character" is who you are when no one is watching you; whereas "reputation" is only who other people *think* you are.

Here are some examples of how a person's conduct can be *controlled* by fear of damage to "reputation":

In order to avoid someone exposing the facts of your past, you may maintain an amicable relationship with certain people you dislike, in an attempt to keep them from telling anyone about *who*, or *how*, you used to be.

---

[88] *Coach John Wooden: The difference between reputation and character,* June 5, 2010 article, DAVIDWARD.com.

Modern Day "Control Freaks" in Action

In order to avoid the embarrassment of someone sending defamatory material to all your friends and business associates, you may agree to pay them spousal support.

In order to avoid harm to your reputation, you may fake being friendly to co-workers, just so they won't speak badly of you to your boss and to other co-workers.

In order to maintain your "loving" reputation at church, you may give-in to the excessive demands for "help" from a congregation member and thus, allow your behavior to be controlled.

The possibilities of threats to your "reputation" are unlimited. Yet, realize that they all revolve around the same issue: your "pride", which btw, needs to hit the cross.

Jesus was, *"despised and rejected"* (Is 53:3) and of *"no reputation"* (Phil 2:7). As His servants, neither you nor I, are above our Master (Matt 10:24). So you can't spend the rest of your life "kissing up" to people who are gossips and backbiters. Jesus never did anything like that.

Modern Day "Control Freaks" in Action

Just look at yourself, look at how it *controls* your behavior. Calculate all the time you've wasted chasing the accolades of some fickle fly-by-night personality that does nothing but speak evil about other people's lives.

Why are you still hanging around with them in the first place?

Answer: Because you "fear man", and you fear what they'd *say about you* if you cut off the relationship (CIYA).

People who threaten your reputation usually don't have such a good reputation for themselves. That's why they say, "Consider the source". Exactly *who* is saying *what* about you? Usually people who "talk smack" about others, are not respected for anything anyway.

Don't you know? Although scores of carnal people listen to them; no one really respects them, or anything they say. And even if they did, who cares? If your conduct is right before God, He will fight your battles and take care of your haters. *No weapon* formed against you shall prosper! (Is 54:17, KJV)

Modern Day "Control Freaks" in Action

The worry, fretting, and concern over being spoken evil of, is flat out *controlling* your life! It's consuming your heart and emotions, thoughts and mind; and "you" feel absolutely miserable about it. It's made you a Control Freaking mess!

As a result, you're doing exactly what the enemy wants you to do by giving all your energies over to worrying about your "reputation" and trying to monitor, the unmonitor-able: (i.e.) what people are saying about you. This is all done, in lieu of getting anything productive done for the Kingdom of God.

That's also got to stop, today.

"A RELIGIOUS SPIRIT"

Can be used by you to "control" others <u>and/or</u> by others to "control" you:

A "religious" condemning spirit can be used to control you, especially if you are a Christian who wants to do right before the Lord. This "religious spirit" is calculating and dominating. "It" insists upon you, conforming your behavior to some religious principle "it" dictates, for which the application is either totally inappropriate, or highly questionable under the circumstances.

The "religious spirit" works best on Christians who have yet to develop sufficient spiritual knowledge and discernment to catch this repulsive thing when "it" shows up. They know *something* is wrong with what they're being told to do (even though scripture is being quoted), but they just can't quite put their finger on it.

This one is the worst!

Here's an example: During the first month of a Christian couple's marriage, the wife (who had only been a Christian for a few years), receives the first telephone bill since living together with her new husband. The bill reflects that several 900 calls had been made from the phone line at the family residence.

The wife, at that time, has no idea what a 900 number is; she asks her husband about the bill, and he says he doesn't know anything about it either. The wife calls the phone company who confirms that the calls came from the residence. So wife decides to dial one of the 900 numbers listed on the phone bill and she sickeningly finds out what it is for herself.

"Yuck, that's odd", she thinks to herself. She then tells her husband that the number was to a *pornographic* phone line. He continues to deny his involvement, despite the fact that no one else has access to the residence. As a result of his denial, this wife is "lulled into a false sense of security" and caused to believe it was just some mistake made by the phone company.

A year and a half goes by in a marriage that was clearly never right from the beginning; still unbeknownst to the wife, the husband has brought sin into the marriage. As a result, the marital "relationship" only continues to deteriorate because the sin is not being confessed or dealt with properly. The husband continues to totally and fully deny any sinful conduct on his part and the wife remains clueless; never once suspecting that her "Christian" husband, who is in "leadership" at the church, would ever be carrying on like this.

Eventually, some additional "damning evidence" is discovered by the wife which causes a "Christian counselor" to step into the picture. After being confronted by the counselor alone, one-on-one for a time, the husband finally confesses. The wife, still having absolutely no idea that any of this perversion was going on in her home, is then brought in to the room. The counselor, now intending to facilitate an admission from the husband to the wife, including all of the incidents that were going on right under her nose, tells the husband to start confessing.

The bomb drops!

All this excruciatingly painful information, including the gruesome details, comes out-- all at one time, all within just a few minutes, in one significant blow. The wife is emotionally distraught, visibly upset, crying, angry, yelling at the husband, cussing from time to time, and otherwise voicing her utter disgust, upon hearing the details of the numerous incidents confessed to her by the husband.

She is absolutely furious over learning about this grandiose deception that had been taking place in her home over the last year or so. She's a "Christian" now; she would have *never* married someone practicing sexual sin.

Modern Day "Control Freaks" in Action

She was tricked and now ... *she's ticked.*

In a hasty response to her emotional upheaval, she is immediately rebuked by the counselor and told how she needs to "forgive" the husband, "Now!" *So that she can be right with God* and work on saving the marriage."

That's right, before ever giving her a chance to process all the information contained in the confession she just heard; the spirit of divination, playing in and through the counselor's "religious spirit", placed an immediate mandate on the wife to forgive now, right then and there, right on the spot! "It" also told her to correct the expletive language she had just been using.

The wife, totally confused with this demand, looks at the counselor with eyes of bewilderment; her head cocked to the side is shaking, "No". The wife refuses to obey this counselor's command, as if she were some highbred golden retriever.

She has yet to even process all of the events that just got confessed moments ago. "Forgiveness" is the last thing on her mind ... her head is still spinning from all the details she's just been told; and, she's got questions of her own that need to *finally* be answered.

Another bomb drops, for each answer she receives; and while the details of the various incidents are still being disclosed and confessed, in an attempt to force "its" "forgiveness agenda" straight down her throat, the counselor again, takes the focus off the husband and puts it back onto the wife by telling her again that she, *"Needs to forgive"*.

Then, when no reply is made by the wife, in a move of spiritual pride (instigated by the spirit of divination), and in an attempt to get some leverage and control over wife's alleged "misconduct", the counselor starts quoting several scriptures on "forgiveness", explaining to the wife that if she doesn't forgive, <u>she</u> *is never going to be right with God.*

The focus has now totally moved from the real issue: namely, the husband's living a "double life" and it's now the wife who is under "Scriptural fire".

This counselor's ineptness, insensitivity, and utter foolishness, is compounding her grief. This makes her even more upset than she is already about her husband's multiple incidents of unfaithfulness. In response, the wife, in a fury calls the counselor "an idiot" and walks out of the room.

Though she was ignorant that this was the work of the spirit of control, pushing "its" "religious spirit" agenda at the time, the wife just knew, "Something is wrong with this picture". So she refused to budge and comply with the counselor's demand, all the while thinking to herself, "How senseless, the Lord knows my heart. It would only be meaningless words, repeated like a robot, in order to please this counselor." So she again, rightly refuses to play "doggie" and comply with the counselor's second "forgive" command.

In this situation, the counselor was trying to "control" the wife's behavior via this controlling "religious spirit" working through him. At this point in time, it was really the husband who needed the correcting and the wife who needed the consoling.

The spirit of divination was actually able to use this ignorant counselor as one of "its" "play toys" to inflict even more grief on the wife than she was already experiencing. The real issue was the husband's perversity; but the counselor was focusing on wife's alleged "sin" of not forgiving, expecting her to recite meaningless words to the counselor's satisfaction. When the wife did not obey this directive, the counselor then condemned *her response* to the pain, classifying it as "rebellion" on her part.

*"Study to shew thyself approved unto God, a workman that needeth not to be ashamed, **rightly dividing the word of truth**"* (2 Tim 2:15, KJV). For, *"they that are unlearned and unstable wrest (twist), as they do also the other scriptures, unto their own destruction"* (2 Pe 3:16, KJV).

The spirit of control working through the life of this "Christian counselor", who, without any compassion or understanding of *how and when* to apply scripture, twisted or "wrest"-- which literally means "tortured"[89] -- the scripture with his: "Forgive" dictate to the wife. This was especially grievous conduct since it was given at a time when she had yet to process all the painful information she just received and stand back to her feet.

---

[89] Strong's #4761 transliterated "Strebloo".

Modern Day "Control Freaks" in Action

The "religious spirit" is hateful, critical, and controlling. Due to "its" malicious work, not only did the wife have to deal with the hurt she was experiencing with regard to her husband's unfaithfulness; but she also had to deal with the foolishness of this self-proclaimed Christian counselor that should have known better about how to deal with hurt people *before* he ever took on the responsibility in such a role. Instead, the counselor joins with the husband and *also* hurts the wife and she ends up worse off than she was before the couple ever got "counseling" from this "religious spirit".

Though one could argue that the wife should not have cussed or called the counselor an "idiot" -- *well* ... that's just the "religious spirit" at work again!

For it is far better for the wife to have fought off the spirit of divination in whatever way she knew how at the time, than it would have been for her to comply with "its" foolish "religious" demands when her heart was not ready.

If she had complied, she may have then forever operated under the influence of this "religious spirit", feeling condemned for her own legitimate emotional response to the news of the demise of her marriage, as if *she* had done something wrong. And worse, "faking" her "Christianity" from there on out, in order to meet the expectations of others in the Christian Community operating with the same "religious spirit".

The "religious spirit" has higher regard for a person's feigned outward piety, instead of their inward human reality. Put another way, a "religious spirit" doesn't care if someone is hurting on the inside, "it" only cares that someone is acting "right" about it on the outside.

"Woe unto you, scribes and Pharisees, hypocrites! For ye are like unto whited sepulchres, which indeed appear beautiful outward, but are within full of dead men's bones, and of all uncleanness" (Matt 23:27, KJV).

If you are a person who takes on the role of counseling others, be careful because *"the measure you meet against others will be measured back to you"* (Matt 7:2, KJV).

"COMMENTS AND OPINIONS"

Can be used by you to "control" others <u>and/or</u> by others to "control" you:

Here's where your interpersonal interactions provide an unending source of input and advice that can be used to *control* your life:

"If I were you, I'd _____" (insert whatever you best remember being said).

"If I were you…" "If I were you…" "If I were you …"

The minute someone says, *"If I were you…"* in response to your situation, immediately and automatically the spirit of control engages and triggers an internal pull for you to do whatever *he or she* said you should do.

From the brief statement, "If I were you…" to the tongue lashing dissertations, lectures, dictates, demands, phrases, and comments, of others; no matter the frequency, duration or intensity, all are intended to *control* your behavior.

Modern Day "Control Freaks" in Action

People who try to micromanage your life with their condemning and/or condescending input can both "effect" and "affect" "you". Here are some examples:

"You're too stupid to go back to school" [Causing a forty-five year old mother to feel hopeless and give up on her dreams of the education the Lord wants her to have so He can use it at some time in her future.]

"You're not that good at sewing" [Causing a soon to be capable seamstress to stop the sewing hobby she loves, which would have been used for Kingdom purposes at some time in her future.]

"You're just a "Disneyland Dad" [Causing a father who is admittedly weak in the area of discipline, to just accept that role, even though the Lord has shown him he needs to work towards change.]

"You don't know how to keep your things in order very well, do you?" [Causing a person to feel condemned for not being a good steward of the possessions God has given them; and then never thinking they deserve anything more from the Lord in the future.]

Modern Day "Control Freaks" in Action

"You don't make enough money to support this household!" [Causing a man to feel emasculated by his wife; lose his motivation to work and harbor bitterness and resentment against her.]

"I guess cooking is just not your forte" [Causing a person to be forced to buy take out food, instead of cooking, whenever this person comes over for dinner.]

"Look, don't pass the ball to him" [Causing someone playing a sport to lose confidence in his abilities and feel excluded.]

"If you knew how to type, this would go a lot faster" [Creating undue pressure and anxiety to finish a clerical task, and causing that person to make even more typing errors.]

"How long have you been trying to pass that test?" [Causing a person to give up trying to ever pass the SAT, a Notary exam, the Bar exam, or Real Estate License exam.]

"You're a bit inexperienced in the bedroom, here's a 'How to' book- you really need to read it." Or better yet, *"Let's*

watch these flicks together, I know that they'll help you."
[Causing a person to feel totally inadequate and unloved, and even more fearful and incompetent in the bedroom than before.]

"You did what?" [When you explain that in obedience to God, you quit your job. You then feel like you did something wrong, despite the fact it was God who led you to quit.]

"I can't believe it!" [When you tell someone how your ex-husband continues to fail to pay the child support, they think you desperately need to survive. This statement causes the "affect" of anger to well up in you, when prior to that you were going to simply trust God for the provision you needed.]

"I can't wait until you're done with that." [When you have been directed by God to serve in a ministry; this statement causes you to think about quitting the ministry sooner than God is ready to release you, just so you can go "play" and go shopping with your commenting girlfriend.]

Modern Day "Control Freaks" in Action

"When will they ever get the message?" [When you share with a friend that you have been trying to end communications with a very needy person whom the Lord actually wants to remain in your life to stretch you. The comment takes you out of the Spirit, and causes you to join in frustration and say, "Yeah! I wish they'd just leave me alone".]

"He did what? ... What again?" [When you share how your unsaved family member failed to invite you to yet another family event, for this, the hundredth time. After the comment is made it causes you to buy into carnal feelings and offense, and express resentment towards that person, when the Lord would have you act differently. You *were* doing just fine. At least *before* the comment by your well-meaning friend was made.]

The people whom you want to think highly or well of you (the CIYA) can control you with their comments. This is especially true if they are people who you know have a sin pattern of gossip, or saying bad things to you about others. You may be afraid that if you don't keep them in your good graces they'll do the same to you, so you comply with their demands.

Get that cord-cutting mechanism ready for this area as well.

"GOSSIP, BACKBITING, COMPLAINING, HATEFUL WORDS, CRITICISM, AND FALSE ACCUSATIONS"
Can be used by you to "control" others and/or by others to "control" you:

This category is probably one of the worst. This is when you have one person talking to another person about a third party (or person). It's when Person-A goes to Person-B and talks about Person-C in a derogatory, hateful, accusatory, critical manner. It's gossip.

The Bible calls these people "whisperers" (Ro 1:29). Their conduct is considered, "backbiting" (Prv 25:23, KJV); "devouring" (Gal 5:15, KJV); "sowing discord" (Prv 6:19); "evil speaking" (Eph 4:31); they are considered, "hateful and hating one another" (Titus 3:3, KJV).

Person-A, in expressing their sinful perspective to Person-B about Person-C, does so (whether they know it or not and whether they'd admit it or not), in order to "control" the behavior of Person-B as it relates to Person-B's future treatment and/or perspective of Person-C (the one being evil spoken of).

This scenario happens a lot in relationships where Person-B has a lot of "clout": power, position, money, or resources. Person-A comes in, no doubt desiring to benefit themselves from Person-B's status, and therefore starts "hatin'" on Person-C, so that Person-B won't like or talk to Person-C anymore; and/or will decide to exclude Person-C from a party, an inheritance, a business deal, a family dinner, a job, a ministry opportunity, or whatever.

In fact, the only reason Person-A (the hater) talks to Person-B (the clout holder) about Person-C (other than catering to their own carnal nature), is so that Person-A can indirectly "control" Person-B's future perspective and treatment of Person-C.

People that backbite, gossip, and imply wrongdoing about other people's conduct, do so in an attempt to control the behavior and/or perspectives of those they are gossiping to. They do this in order to exalt themselves in the eyes of whomever they are talking to, over and above, whomever they're talking about.

Modern Day "Control Freaks" in Action

Yes it's weak, it's pansy, it's carnal; and yet it's *controlling.*

Whether it's just one brief encounter, or a pattern of conversations continued over time; at some point, "it" will successfully control the treatment of, and the perspectives held about Person-C, by whoever heard or overheard the wicked evil speaking, vomited up by Person-A, to Person-B.

Make a diagram if you need one.

"DEMANDS FOR TIME AND ATTENTION"

Can be used by you to "control" others and/or by others to "control" you:

There are some people in your life who are constantly placing demands on your time and attention. Though at times, these "demands" may not appear as such-- *they may not appear* as outright "demands"; but rather, as very polite requests such as, "Would you please?" or, "Is it possible that you could..." or, "I would love it if you would..." etc.

Modern Day "Control Freaks" in Action

One of the ploys of the enemy is to get you so consumed with the way other people foolishly waste their time, that you too will waste your time, your days, and your years here on earth doing nothing substantial for the Kingdom. The *control* factor is found in your thinking that you must cater to their requests when it comes to *their* scheduling or consumption of *your* time and attention.

They want you to accompany them to stupid movies, to lunch appointments or meetings, located in Timbuktu-- or to other events or outings that have no real meaning or purpose. They want you sit with them and listen to their life story (for the seventh time), or visit with them, or just hang out and do nothing in particular, "I just want you to be there".

Generally, they want you to go places and do things with them that deep down inside you know are nothing but a waste of your time. These are people that are doing nothing for the Kingdom's sake. They're people that you're not even able to minister to, because they don't "receive" from anybody. So you know there will be no fruit or edification out of the encounter; and therefore, you know that you have far more important things that the Lord would rather have you doing, with the time they want to take from you and waste.

These are people who want you to spend hours with them on the telephone; and once you're done with the conversation, they then start making up other things to keep talking about in order to hold you on the line. They email, Facebook, Twitter and text all day long, <u>as if because everyone else on the face of the earth spends their time this way</u>, that you should too-- it's perfectly "normal".

These are people who would never even think of turning their iPhone off, or placing it on silent. "Time Management" to them, has no meaning; they're notorious for allowing the "tail to wag the dog". When you say that you are unable to comply with their demands on your time, they act shocked and amazed and begin to interrogate you as to, *"Why not?"*

If you're foolish enough to respond to that question, they then begin to re-work *your* schedule in an attempt to *show you* how you actually can, fit them in.

Modern Day "Control Freaks" in Action

Many times I have had other attorneys (the opposition), or clients tell me how to schedule my time to meet their demands or deadlines. I've had people insist that their event required my attendance. When declining an offer to go on an outing, or maintain a relationship that I already determined *lacked edification*, people have gossiped about my being "too good" for them now.

In short, these people are used by the enemy to try and manage your "daily calendar" by determining whether you really need to go to this appointment or that meeting; why you need to spend so much time in prayer, or in the Word; or if you should go to the gym, to church, or to the beach. They ask things like, "Why would you ever want to just stay home and relax, *alone?*"

They want to decide how you should spend each waking moment of the time God has given you here on earth; and thus by running your schedule, they literally run your life.

Don't let this happen to you, *anymore.* Redeem the time you have left to serve the King!

Modern Day "Control Freaks" in Action

<u>"NON-VERBAL CUES"</u>

Can be used by you to "control" others <u>and/or</u> by others to "control" you:

The serpent when challenging the Lord's words, said to Eve in the Garden, *"'You won't die!'" the serpent **hissed***" (Gen 3:3, NLT). Though the serpent's "hiss" is not found in all translations, it is true that one audible sound, like a "Tchssssh" ... which really isn't even a word at all, can send a message of disdain that can be used to *control* the conduct of another person.

Here's some good example of non-verbal cues:

You've heard how husbands and wives, or parents and children, sometimes describe giving one another, "the evil eye" haven't you?

If a couple gets asked to dinner by another couple, but one of them doesn't want to go, it just takes one flash of "the evil eye" for the other spouse to decline, or at least put off the invitation to another time.

Modern Day "Control Freaks" in Action

Parents with good disciplinary skills don't have to say a word to their kids, but just give them "the evil eye" and they stop whatever they're doing wrong, right there on the spot.

In both instances, nothing had to be said, but just "that look", caused a modification or *controlling* of the behavior of someone else.

Likewise, there are several non-verbal cues such as "the evil eye" that can also send a message of dislike, disdain, or disgust to the recipient, all of which can be used to *control* your behavior.

The rolling of the eyes sends the message, *"What an idiot?" "How stupid." "Whatever!"*

A scorning look of disapproval is a way of controlling, or stopping someone from doing something.

Ignoring the presence of another person, ignoring their comments or questions, will many times successfully control another person's behavior. They'll either get mad (affect) and/or they'll stop talking or acknowledging the ignorer anymore (effect).

Modern Day "Control Freaks" in Action

Looking up in the sky in another direction sends the message, *"Look, I am totally checked out of this conversation and just waiting for you to shut your mouth so I can move on."*

Refusing to look into the eyes of someone who is talking to you means, *"I don't care who you are, or what you're saying."*

A person's body position turned in the opposite direction, shrugs of the shoulders, folded arms, etc., can be used to send you a message of control. There's a whole science to "body language" that I'm not going to delve into. Just realize that non-verbal behavior can send a message that can *control* the observer.

Your mind then replays what it "saw" in real life, like on a movie screen. When recalling the non-verbal interaction and watching the replay in your mind; that scene can cause you to conform your behavior to the message that was conveyed.

Modern Day "Control Freaks" in Action

The point to be made is that a person can control you without ever having to say one word! This is yet another point of recognition, scheduled for future termination.

"MONEY, POSSESSIONS, AND POSITION"
Can be used by you to "control" others <u>and/or</u> by others to "control" you:

We've covered the topic of money already in great detail, but don't forget a person may threaten to take not only their financial support away from you, but also various <u>possession(s)</u>: a car, a house, an inheritance; or <u>position(s)</u>, a promotion, or a job, a role in leadership at the church, or a ministry opportunity, if you don't comply with their controlling demands.

"THE CATCH-ALL CONTROL CATEGORY"
Can be used by you to "control" others <u>and/or</u> by others to "control" you:

This "catch-all" control category is for you to fill in the blank with people and their characteristics that you now realize have been used to *control* your behavior. Any one thing, or any combination of things that we already covered; can be used by the spirit of divination to control your behavior.

Maybe you have a wife who is "depressed". The world revolves around her depression, her mood and how she feels from one time to another. Your entire family life and that of your children's can be *controlled* by mom's moods.

Maybe you have someone in your life that is addicted to drugs or alcohol; your entire life is *controlled* by their misconduct and your attempts to keep them off drugs, out of the bars, not going to parties, and staying away from other bad influences.

Maybe you have someone in your life that has no other friends but you; they consume your time, your attention and your activities. You're not even married to them; you don't live or work with them; yet, *they* are *the first thing that you think of* when you wake up each and every morning. That means Control-Freaking trouble!

It may also be racism, discrimination, or bias that has been used to control your life. In these types of "catch-all" control situations, you have to ask yourself: "What am I doing for God besides allowing my entire life to be consumed with this issue or perspective?" Or, "Why am I still spending all this energy "babysitting" someone who is bent upon his/her own destruction?" Or, "How is this person's influence negatively affecting and/or effecting my life?"

The worst spirit of divination case I've ever seen is when genuine Christians who had been cursed by a voodoo practicing relative years prior, spent their lives as "shut ins"; believing and walking in "the lie" of being cursed for life, instead of "the truth", that no one can curse what God has blessed (1 Jn 4:4 & 5:4; Nu 22:12).

So realize that the possibilities are infinite!

Now that we've covered some generalities, let's go a little deeper and get into some specificity. If you're not backed into a corner as of yet, you soon will be. Up next, it's all about "you".

CHAPTER 27: The spirit of divination at Work in Your Interpersonal Relationships

----

You've now got the principles. It's time to apply them to some of the scenarios going on in your own life. But first, let's do a quick review:

Controlling Christians have "given place" to the spirit of divination to work in and through their lives, by invitation. They are grossly deceived people, never once realizing that as they continue to try to control the people and circumstances in their own lives, in absolutely every instance, they are actually being used as a "play toy" of the enemy.

There are certain general character traits that controlling people all have in common and it makes no difference whether they are heathens, carnal or mature Christians. Controlling people being governed by the spirit of control are always in a fuss. They're upset about something someone did, failed to do, or is presently doing. "Contention" is the mark on their lives; because they're so busy trying to control everyone associated with them, naturally there is resistance to that control. As a result, controlling people are always upset about what this person did, or that person said, or how they wanted this to work out and it didn't; whose fault it was and how this wouldn't have happened if someone would have only done what *they* had told them to do, and so on and so on.

People, who seek to "control" other people, are functioning under the spirit of control/divination whether they realize it or not <u>and</u> whether they'll ever admit it or not.

What must they admit? Well, number one that they have a primary negative character trait of being "controlling". Number two, that this "controlling" character trait makes them an ally of the enemy, notwithstanding the fact they call themselves "Christian".

Controlling Christians are actually more detrimental to the Christian Community than people who are merely walking in the flesh; like fornicators, drug abusers, pornographers, etc. Indeed, controlling Christians may not be practicing any outward sin that anyone can readily pinpoint; in fact many of them live the most stringent, Pharisaical, outwardly sanctimonious, legalistic lives on the planet. Nevertheless "looks" can and will be deceiving.

People who try to control others are not following or trusting God; no matter how much they profess to the contrary. God is love, not control! Therefore, the transformed life of a mature believer should reflect His nature, not the nature of the enemy.

You can break the yoke of *control* by acknowledging and adhering to the fact that the relationship between the Lord and any other person in your life, is *rarely ever* any of your business. *"Who are you to condemn God's servants? They are responsible to the Lord; so let Him tell them whether they are right or wrong. The Lord's power will help them do as they should"* (Ro 14:4, NLT).

With that said, let's move to some examples that have been categorized for your perusal, this time by *type* of

relationship. Realize that the spirit of control and the various ways "it" may manifest in your life is not exhaustive, like something I can list for you in a concordance. Rather, as I mentioned before, because of the number of interpersonal relationships you have and because of the number of situations that occur in your life each day, the manner in which the spirit of divination can manifest is exponentially unlimited. Therefore, I'm forced to limit the number of categories to *ten types of relationships*; and to limit the number of *real life examples to ten* in each category.

Furthermore, for each "type" category, I have tried to present examples from the most obvious to the least obvious. Therefore, you should expect to be able to see the spirit of divination at work most easily at the beginning of each category, and less clearly towards the end of each category. By presenting them in this order, I am intentionally "training" you towards recognizing "its" subtleties.

Finally, you should assume that the Spirit of God is guiding the decision or conduct that the spirit of divination is

The spirit of divination at Work in Your Interpersonal Relationships

attempting to change or modify. So in each of the examples that you'll read, you will see people trying to make *your* life *their* business. Only names have been changed to protect the innocent ... or rather, *ignorant* that is.[90]

Category #1
The spirit of divination at Work in Your Spouse:

Threats of murder and/or suicide to yourself or others you love, should you dare leave the abusive spouse. This can control a person to the point of remaining in an extremely detrimental relationship for several years of their life.

Talk about ruining a God-given destiny!

The minute someone threatens you like this, the first thing you must do is devise a plan to implement the Principle of Diametric Opposition. However, you must execute it very

---

[90] Remember most people don't know any better; they're oblivious to the fact that this controlling spirit has been using them as a tool of the enemy to derail the unwary child of God.

wisely and carefully. You must strategically plan a way in which you and your loved ones can escape unharmed.

Yes, I'm talking "witness protection" tactics, if necessary.

Abusive spouses/people, those who hit, beat, push or manhandle their mates, children, parents, or others. They impose their *control* over nearly every action of their victims. Abusive people many times carry on daily interrogations, from a minute-by-minute accounting of a person's whereabouts, to questions about their choice of clothing and jewelry, and why they're wearing perfume or cologne. They monitor cell phone and text use, they dictate how and when a person is to go shopping and do chores around the house. They make inquiries about exactly *when* a person got to work, who they *saw*, who they *talked to* and *what they did* there all day long, etc. For every activity they reportedly engaged in, the person is then interrogated about every thought and/or feeling experienced with regard to the same. The more information provided, the deeper the interrogation becomes.

The spirit of divination at Work in Your Interpersonal Relationships

People who subject themselves to this kind of treatment cannot think or do anything independently, or for themselves, let alone for the Lord. Everything they do is controlled by, or filtered through, their anticipated future interrogation sessions with their abuser.

Possessive behavior seen in boyfriends, girlfriends, fiancées, or spouses; they monitor your behavior when away; or if present, they watch and then question your every move ... *all the time.* They sneakily stand in doorways of the residence you share; turning corners, in on your conversations or conduct with others, spying, stalking, peering, watching. They make inquires about: who you looked at, who you talked to and for how long, who you smiled at, demanding to know why you were so nice to a certain man or woman. The very subject matter of their questions, coupled with their tone and innuendo, are all stated in an attempt to try to *control* your behavior.

In the beginning, a person may think these initial signs of possessiveness in a potential mate are "cute" or "endearing". They may foolishly think to themselves, "Wow, they must really love me." But once the light comes

The spirit of divination at Work in Your Interpersonal Relationships

on in the morning, you'll wake up and realize you married a bonafide Control Freak!

Outbursts of wrath can control the behavior of everyone living in the same household. It causes people to feel uptight and uncomfortable while existing in such a threatening environment. The inhabitants are constantly forced to walk on eggshells; all the while their minds are consumed, *"Do this so he won't get mad"* or *"Don't do that because she will get mad."*

Many people, especially children who live in these types of environments, develop anxiety disorders, twitches, speech impediments, ulcers and the like.

Accusatory questioning of your feelings towards, and about your relationships with other people; accusing you of adultery or homosexuality, or of loving someone else more than them can control your behavior and cause you to cut off good edifying relationships, in order to satisfy your accuser.

508   *"CONTROL FREAK"*

The spirit of divination at Work in Your Interpersonal Relationships

Spouses that lie and deceive or "lull" you into a "false sense of security", in order to maintain the benefits of the marital relationship that they would otherwise lose in an instant, had they been honest.

Spouses refusing to get a job, or help around the house, or contribute in any way; people who never got married to form a "joint union", but just wanted a "maid/cook/hustler" or a "sugar daddy". This type of control leads to oppression for the working or contributing spouse; similar to what the children of Israel suffered under the hand of Pharaoh.

Spouses who make derogatory statements about your friends and family members, can control you to the point of causing you to cut off those relationships, or minimize future contact.

Spouses who tell you how to act when you accompany them to a business dinner or event can control you. They give directives about what you should say and do when in the presence of certain "important" people. They warn, *"Don't say anything stupid like you did last time."*

The spirit of divination at Work in Your Interpersonal Relationships

Spouses who withhold sex and/or affection can cause a type of emotional control over the other spouse; and promote the sinful states of anger, bitterness and feelings of insecurity.

Category #2
The spirit of divination at Work in Your Ex-Spouse:

The Ex who doesn't understand the meaning of "divorce" or "it's over" and continues to hound you with emails, voicemails, texts and other means of uninvited personal interaction. You live in a constant state of unrest, just waiting for the arrival of yet another communication.

It's the Ex who continues to call and question you in order to get information on your activities and whereabouts, under the pretense of calling you about the children. He/she begins to ask questions about your life, your job and other things that have absolutely nothing to do with the kids. You end up complying with his/her interrogation in order to "keep the peace".

The spirit of divination at Work in Your Interpersonal Relationships

The Ex who threatens to "expose" you, or embarrass you, or say such-and-such about you to your friends and family if you don't get back together with them, do what they say, or pay them the settlement amount they demand. You comply with their demands, reasoning you'd be worse off in the end if you didn't.

The Ex who sends threats and/or ultimatum messages to the other spouse, through their children, causing the children to feel like they must take one side over the other. For example, *"If your dad would ever pay support you could get some new tennis shoes."* Or, *"I'm going to take your mom back to court if she keeps doing this."* You then become pressured or *controlled* not only by the threat, but also by the children who were used to deliver it.

It's the Ex who allows their new spouse to "talk smack" about you while in front of *your* children. When they come home from visitation they tell you everything that was said in their presence. This information can then control your behavior in defending yourself and explaining to your children *why* what was said was not right, not fair, and/or not true.

The spirit of divination at Work in Your Interpersonal Relationships

The Ex who intentionally withholds child or spousal support, in order to "get a charge" out of seeing you fret and struggle financially, can control your behavior. You begin to get angry and cuss them out, both in and outside of their presence.

The Ex who withholds court ordered child visitation to the other parent, can control their emotions, get them angry, and cause them to reciprocate the behavior.

The Ex who fails to exercise their own court ordered visitation, without consideration or notice to the other parent can cause them to be forced to rearrange their schedules to accommodate, now, keeping the kids for the weekend.

The Ex who continues to bring you back into court, month after month, year after year, when they've already lost several times over. This is an indicator that the Ex is still trying to *control* your behavior by re-gaining your attention, even if it's in a negative context.

"CONTROL FREAK"

The spirit of divination at Work in Your Interpersonal Relationships

The Ex who never moves on from your past relationship, and continues to try to fit into the circle of friends that they met through their association with you. In so doing, they can still gossip about you and what you're up to with those acquaintances that also know you. Though you have long removed yourself from your Ex and associating with anyone from that group, there is still an attempt to hold on to and control at least, *your memory.*

As they continue to gossip about the relics of your life, they never once realize that they too, have become relics themselves.

Category #3
The spirit of divination at Work in Your Friends and Acquaintances:

Advice given by a friend, that once you refuse, causes them to harp, nag, rebuke, scold and get mad at you. Even if you never give in to their demands, you still get controlled by spending an inordinate amount of time on the telephone with them, talking about it, explaining your own decisions and actions, making excuses and trying to get them to change their opinion of your decision. All the while you fear that they'll start to talk badly about you to someone else, or you'll lose them as a friend if you don't eventually do what they're directing (CIYA).

You decide to get married and your best girlfriend becomes livid because no one wants to marry her. So she starts to put a guilt trip on you for not calling, texting and emailing her like you used to when you were both single. After you get married, you avoid her like the plague (effect), because she couldn't even handle the courtship phase. Whenever there is contact, she's always trying to make you feel bad (affect), for not having time for her anymore *like you used to.*

You're a handsome successful businessman, attending a gathering and introduced to another man who begins looking you up and down. His face practically disfigured by comparing and competing, he then asks, *"So what do you do for work?"* Instead of telling him the whole truth, you downplay your answer in an attempt to afford him some relief from his barefaced envy. You've been controlled.

The spirit of divination at Work in Your Interpersonal Relationships

You tell a friend you're starting to write a book. They very innocently ask, *"Who's going to publish it?"* Since you don't know the answer to that question, you can be pulled off track thinking that you need a publisher *before* spending all the time and effort it takes to write a book. So you quit writing because you don't have a publisher.

A simple question from someone who may be legitimately concerned about a dire financial situation you're facing says, *"Do you think you're gonna make it?"* This statement alone causes you to focus on your fears and become concerned about things you hadn't even been concerned about before this conversation took place.

A complaining comment by a friend during a lunch date like, *"They always take too long to bring the check here"* can cause you to feel like *you're responsible* to get up and get the check from the waitress in order to put an end to your friend's irritation.

Your Christian friend asks you questions like, *"When's the last time you went to that church?"* Or, *"I don't like his teaching, do you?"* Or, *"I'm moving to another church."*

The spirit of divination at Work in Your Interpersonal Relationships

These kinds of questions and statements may control your behavior by creating an expectation for you to do the same.

You go out to dinner or on a date with someone who ignores you the whole time; but has plenty of attention, considerate words and kind responses for every other good-looking skirt they encounter. This can have a controlling affect on your emotional wellbeing and cause you to feel inferior, unloved, angry and unattractive.

Your friend asks, "Where are you going on vacation this year?" Yet, you hadn't planned a vacation, nor could hardly afford one. This affects your emotional state and you start to feel sorry for yourself because you've been deprived of a vacation, yet again this year, especially after you've been working so hard.

God has shown you that He wants you to attend Bible College. You tell a friend who for years, has been miserable, discontented, backslidden and groping for direction in his own life. He responds to the news in a negative tone saying, *"I went to Bible College too, but I guess you can see where it got me."* This derogatory comment may cause you to reconsider the Lord's directive for your own life, thinking: "If it didn't do anything for his life, it likely won't do anything for mine either."

Category #4
The spirit of divination at Work in Your Parents:

Any kind of monetary threat; to withhold allowance, school tuition, gas for the car, write you out of a will/trust, etc., if you don't do whatever they want you to do, is a Control Freak situation that can cause you to comply with parental demands that may be out of the will of God.

A parent advising you should not quit your job and start your own business because of the "security" of the corporate paycheck you are now regularly receiving. This advice can be motivated by the parent's fear of having to support you should you fail at the business the Lord has told you to start.

Statements made to give you a "guilt complex" such as, *"Well if you ever had time to visit me, you would have known this was going on"*, can cause a person to feel guilty (affect) and do anything in compliance (effect), in order to try and rid that feeling.

Your father telling you that your deceased mother would *"Never want you to..."* do this or that (you fill in the blank), can control your behavior into complying with the expectations of someone who may have already been dead for decades.

Your stepfather (or stepmother), who makes derogatory comments about your biological father (or mother): those comments invite, or "control" you into "taking sides" with them by making your own similar derogatory comment, or risk feeling uncomfortable if you don't.

Your biological father (or mother), who makes derogatory comments about your stepfather (or stepmother): those comments invite (or control) you into "taking sides" with them, by making your own similar derogatory comment, or risk feeling uncomfortable if you don't.

The spirit of divination at Work in Your Interpersonal Relationships

When at your house for a celebration, your mother is non-stop instructing, advising and directing you on how to cook, clean and host a party. This is *not* your first party, you're forty-nine years old. Yet, if you don't comply with everything she says, you're afraid she'll ruin the festivities.

When talking to your parents about choosing a college, you share that you believe God wants you to go abroad to become an exchange student. But because your parents want you to stay close to home, near them, they start talking about "swine flu" and "mad cow" disease. These kinds of comments open the door to the "spirit of fear" and even if the student goes abroad, it can cause him/her to carry this fear throughout their journey.

While getting dressed for a special formal event, you're totally excited because this time, you found a dress that you really love. You just know the Lord led you to find it and you feel totally blessed. Your mother-in-law comes in while you're admiring it in the mirror and says, *"Honey that color never looked good on you."* This statement can cause you to dejectedly hang the dress back in the closet and look for something else to wear.

The spirit of divination at Work in Your Interpersonal Relationships

Your father always wanted you to be *"Daddy's little girl"*, so you never got to learn how to fish, throw a baseball, hike, or ride a motorcycle, because you always had to "act" like a little princess.

Realize that no matter how old you are, parents still have a very special influence that other people will never have in your life. Children (even fully grown into adulthood) will forever seek to be loved, accepted and approved of by their parents (CIYA).

Category #5
The spirit of divination at Work in Your Siblings:

At the time of death of a parent, one sibling seeks to take control over the estate or inheritance, in an attempt to exclude the other from receiving what the deceased parent had intentionally left to them. Should they succeed, not only have they controlled the behavior of the eliminated sibling, but they have also controlled or thwarted the desires of the deceased parent.

The spirit of divination at Work in Your Interpersonal Relationships

Your older brother who constantly advises you on business (whether solicited or not) can be controlling whenever you get together to "talk shop". During each interaction you have with him, he expounds only on his successful business ventures, predictably, leaving out all the "rough spots" he experienced along the way. His advice can be used to control your own business management practices in an attempt to compete with his success, even though his way of doing business is "shady" at best and certainly not the way the Lord would have you operate your business.

Your family has been running in every direction and you think it prudent to spend Thanksgiving at home this year with just your immediate family members. Your sister exclaims, *"You're not going to Thanksgiving at Aunt Miriam's?"* You respond, *"Not this year"*. Your sister says, *"Oh, really ... why not? What happened?"* As if to imply you did something wrong that you need to account for and/or had been intentionally excluded from the family event. This can cause you to go through a list of reasons and details explaining *why* you have made this decision, which when concluded, will still never be satisfactory to her.

The spirit of divination at Work in Your Interpersonal Relationships

The Lord tells you to purchase a house and you take your brother and sister on a tour and they say, *"Wow! It seems like it's too big for you, are you sure you should buy it?"* You then reconsider the blessing that the Lord wanted you to have, by backing out of the deal.

Your siblings' comments on the value of every Christmas present you've ever bought for anyone in the family. This is done in a sarcastic manner, which makes you feel guilty for earning twice as much money as they do. These comments cause you to "dumb down" your giving the next holiday season, in order to try and meet with their approval.

Your sibling makes comparisons between your children and their children for the sole reason of indicating how their "parenting skills" are superior to yours. They say things like, *"When Johnnie did that, I just whooped his bee-hind and he never did it again."* These kinds of comments are used to control your behavior, because they imply that you should do the same.

The spirit of divination at Work in Your Interpersonal Relationships

Your sister never celebrates your birthday with you, not a card, not a text, nothing; yet she always celebrates with your other sister when it's her birthday. This can cause you to feel rejected and respond "in-kind" by never celebrating her birthday either.

You get a new car and some snide comment is made by your sibling related to your being *undeserving* of such a nice ride. This comment causes you to regret the purchase every time you start the engine, now considering it an excessive expenditure.

Both you and your brother have had weight problems all of your lives, but over recent months, you've been successful at sticking to your diet. You meet for a lunch visit and because you haven't seen your brother for a while he comments, *"Wow! Your beer belly is almost gone, bro! But you know how that goes, I don't think you'll keep it off this time either. You might as well go ahead and share this Schlitz malt liquor with me like old times."* This little bit of "truth" spoken in the face of temptation, coupled with an "emotional link" and the appeal of re-living the good ole days, can cause you to order a beer for yourself, blow your diet and get drunk with your brother, all *for ole times sake.*

Siblings who continue to remind you of your past, your failures, or the regrettable decisions you made in your life: this is done in an attempt to position themselves, their lives and their decisions, as superior to yours. This too can control your behavior; either you don't want to talk to them, or ever be around them anymore; or on the flip side, you are always trying to seek to regain their approval by your actions.

Category #6
The spirit of divination at Work in Your Children:

Elder Abuse has become more and more prevalent today; striking, neglecting, cussing out, financially abusing, or the physical mishandling of an elderly parent, in any manner whatsoever, is obviously controlling behavior.

Telling a parent "I hate you" can cause a parent to be so hurt that they begin to allow their child, no matter what age, to "run the show" in hopes that they never say that again.

The spirit of divination at Work in Your Interpersonal Relationships

Whining and crying for candy in line at the grocery store causes a mother to both: *buy* candy she wasn't otherwise going to buy and *give* it to her child (for whom it has no nutritional value); all in order to avoid the condemning stares of those bystanders in the check-out line.

Making incessant demands for cell phones, clothing, computer games, TV's, laptops, make-up, jeans and shoes, can control a parent into purchasing for a teenager, exactly what they want.

After disciplining your child, they declare, *"I want to go live with dad!"* can cause a parent to stop disciplining.

From the rolling of their teenaged eyes, to cussing and talking back; walking off in a huff and slamming the door; and then blasting their music in the bedroom can control a parent's mind causing them to think: *"Was I too harsh? Should I go apologize and try to make up?"*

Parents nowadays, especially single parents, make monumental decisions, where to move, where to work, what events to attend, when to do chores, when to go to church, who to invite to a party they're having, all based upon the input and opinions of their ten or twelve year old children. If the immature minor child, who has no mental capacity to make these kinds of decisions is not in agreement with the parent, it doesn't happen.

Teenagers who use the ole "Johnny's parents are letting him go…" to the party; to the dance; to the mall; to the movies, etc., is a way of trying to control you, the parent, into doing the same.

Any lie, deceit or withholding of pertinent facts or information from a parent; can be used to control the parent's behavior and "lull" them into a "false sense of security", allowing their child to do whatever he/she wants to do.

For example, your fourteen-year-old daughter says she's spending the night at Sara's house, but intentionally fails to disclose that Sara's parents are both out of town ("deceit" remember?) While you've allowed your daughter to spend the night with Sara before, you would never have done so had you known Sara and her twenty-year-old brother, had been left home alone by their parents.

You find drugs or alcohol or cigarettes or condoms on your fifteen-year-old child, in their pockets, purse, or bedroom. You ask them what they're doing? They respond, *"Gosh, dad, what's your problem? You drink too!"* This same response and "reasoning" provided by the teen, can cause a parent to allow their teens to continue to "act" like adults in several different areas.

Category #7
At Work on the Job in Co-Workers:

Your immediate superior says, *"If you don't think you can get this project done on time, I know someone else who can."* This pressure can force you to set all other responsibilities aside, including a special school event your child expected you to attend, all in order to show your boss, that you really were, "The right man for the job!"

The spirit of divination at Work in Your Interpersonal Relationships

A supervisor makes sexual advances and innuendos towards you every time you come in contact: You're afraid you'll lose your job if you report the incidents, so you go about your entire workday walking in fear and intimidation; trying your best to avoid yet another interaction with him/her.

You work for a church or a ministry and find out that one of the co-workers you love dearly has improperly taken money out of petty cash. She confesses and admits what she did, but to you only; and then she asks you, "not to tell anyone", while begging you for a loan to make up for it.

Business executives, who so badly want to be recognized and acknowledged (maybe even your own boss); who then take credit for everything you thought of, worked on, and completed. When someone else finds out it was really you who did the work, the boss steps-in and points back to himself, while minimizing your efforts. You get so angry you go home "ticked off" and take it out on your wife; she then screams at the kids; and they then go out into the backyard and kick the dog.

The spirit of divination at Work in Your Interpersonal Relationships

Not being invited to go to lunch with the "in crowd" can control your behavior and cause you to be offended and act distant and aloof from the group; or worse, cause you to "kiss up" to the group leader so that you'll be invited to go the next time.

Being told about another co-worker's personal life and problems can and will control how you feel about them and the way in which you treat them in the future.

Co-workers who you know have an axe to grind with you but who never say a word; they just watch you, examine, question, and monitor your every move. They seem to keep some sort of "mental note" of your breaks and your lunchtime. Going and coming back from the restroom even causes a raised eyebrow. This peering personality can then control everything you do, or even *think* about doing, while you're on the job.

Any look of disapproval can control your behavior; from not coming in through a certain door; to not placing files on a certain desk, or in a certain way; to not using a trash can

The spirit of divination at Work in Your Interpersonal Relationships

or paper shredder; to even not using the lunchroom or restroom when you need to.

The rolling of the eyes by a co-worker when the manager passes your workstation can cause you to feel as if you need to side with your co-worker's disrespect of the supervisor and make a confirming gesture yourself, or roll your eyes back at them as well.

Any gesture or facial expression of any kind whether positive or negative can be used to *control* your behavior on the job.

Category #8
The spirit of divination at Work in Church Members:

A religious leader's complimenting of your service, or the need for your service, can sometimes turn into an expectation that you will always continue to do this or that in the future. This causes you to feel like you cannot leave that ministry and serve elsewhere, even if it's the Holy Spirit telling you to do so.

The spirit of divination at Work in Your Interpersonal Relationships

You feel like you're drying up at the church you're attending. You're not a church hopper, but you're "bored in the Lord" and your attendance at church has become more religious than loving. You pray about it, God leads you to another church and He confirms the move. This means you must leave all your great friendships at your old church. Yet, you're afraid to obey Him because of the "emotional link" you have with all of those people who are expressing how very sad they all are to see you go. This can undermine, delay, or even totally thwart your obedience to the Lord's directive to "move on".

Church members who tell you how "God has blessed" them with this money making business venture and suggest you get involved, so that you can "be blessed too!" Yet, in reality the only reason they want you involved is because you have the venture capital they need. You comply with their invitation expecting to "be blessed" just like they purportedly have been, but you end up losing everything you gave them.

The spirit of divination at Work in Your Interpersonal Relationships

Christian mothers who tell you that you should put your child in the same Christian school as they did, because it's simply "the best" school in the area. You comply and then later find out that they were getting a discount and really just needed another carpool member.

Leaders who have you take on some responsibility that they say is your "gifting" from God; but it's really only to help them out of a jam. Your compliance is obtained by use of the "gifting" compliment, even though you never bore witness to the compliment in the first place.

The Lord has led you to exactly where He wants you to hold a Bible study. Yet, the numbers do not appear to be increasing and it's costing the ministry money at that location. One of the regular attendees of the Bible study says, *"Not too many people showed up tonight, why don't we move the study to my house?"* This comment can be used to cause you to disobey where the Lord has clearly indicated He wants the study to be held.

Your small group leader says, *"We missed you the other night."* This statement implies that it's now time for you to

The spirit of divination at Work in Your Interpersonal Relationships

answer, or give an account of where you were in order to not be looked down upon, or suspected of backsliding.

A lady in your congregation compliments your outfit and then says, *"I could never wear that kind of thing to church."* Having once thought you were wearing a great, fairly conservative outfit (at least when you first put it on); your mind now, instead of being focused on the Lord during worship, is consumed with trying to figure out what she *meant* by what she *said*: Did she mean her figure wasn't right for the outfit? Did she mean the color was wrong for her? Is it too flamboyant for her taste? Is it too low cut? Does she think it's too "sexy" for church?

Church members who ask Church Leaders a series of questions such as: *who* is in *what* position at the church, or *who* carries *what* title, or what responsibilities does he/she have, etc.; and then, after the answers are provided, they comment about whether or not *they agree* with the respective appointments and assignments; thus implying that changes need to be made if they don't.

The spirit of divination at Work in Your Interpersonal Relationships

When just one person calls the church office to complain about something and it actually changes the course of the Senior Pastor's decision on the matter, you've got a "Control Freak" issue. If just one comment or complaint can be used to change the course of a decision made by the church leader (who is presumptively being led by the Holy Spirit Himself), then it is incumbent upon me to ask, "Who's guidin' this ship, captain?"

Category #9
The spirit of divination at Work on the Streets:

You catch your next-door neighbor (who has always paid you a tad bit more attention than you were comfortable with) time and time again, peering into your home looking down through one of your skylight windows. You are now forced to either cover a window that shouldn't be covered; remain a victim of the voyeur; or move from that residence.

People who beg for money with signs saying, "God bless you" or "I'm a Christian", may create additional pressure on another Christian to give.

The spirit of divination at Work in Your Interpersonal Relationships

People who hand out tracts all the while saying, *"The end is near, make your salvation sure!"* This kind of conduct can either cause people to come to the Lord purely out of fear; or, cause them to be more repelled from the Lord, due to the "evangelist's" condemning approach.

Road rage incidents are the spirit of control driving in fifth gear, turbo boost. They obviously make people angry and upset (affect) and then cause them to engage in very risky driving maneuvers (effect) as an outward expression of their rage.

Going to the make-up counter at Macy's, after the sales person says, *"We can do something about those bags under your eyes",* can certainly force a sale.

Your child is having fun going to karate class and while referring to him/her, another parent comments on how his child *"used to have a sloppy side kick too".* This can cause a parent to begin to criticize their child about their side kick and even threaten that if they don't work on it and make it better, they'll be taken out of karate class.

The spirit of divination at Work in Your Interpersonal Relationships

Calling customer service at the electric company while trying to figure out why your bill is so high; and then encountering a clerk who puts a condemnation trip on you for how much electricity you used this last month. This can actually cause you to apologize for what may have been a mistake in the reading of the meter the month prior.

While shopping at the five-and-dime, you find a great sale on your favorite night cream. So you buy several containers and the clerk at checkout gleefully comments, *"Wow! I see that you're trying to look younger."* This comment can cause you to resent the clerk (someone you don't even know) and feel guilty for taking advantage of the sale.

You have served as senior member of the train club for several years. Then some brand new member comes in, criticizing the club and its policies and tries to revamp and/or undermine all of your previous work. What was once a fun hobby has now turned into a dreaded experience. You really don't even want to go to train club anymore.

"CONTROL FREAK"

The spirit of divination at Work in Your Interpersonal Relationships

The Women's Committee at the Country Club has asked you to head-up and oversee the "Ladies High Tea" event. However, it seems like every single person who is supposed to be "helping" you, is actually directing you on *how to do, what needs to be done.* You end up doing your best to grant and fulfill all of their suggestions and directives. Or, you end up spending and wasting an inordinate amount of time explaining to them why you haven't taken their advice, all in order to make sure they don't get mad and refuse to attend the event themselves.

Category #10

<u>The spirit of divination at Work in</u>
<u>Others Circumstances and Situations:</u>

At the airport you hear the people behind you in the security line huffing and puffing because, from their impatient perspective, you're taking too long to get your shoes off and put your things through the x-ray machine. This causes you to feel rushed, stress out and as a result you make several apologies; when in reality, you're actually moving along at a pace that is "normal" given the circumstances.

At the company Christmas party a co-worker says, *"My wife could really use that"* about some gift that you received in the white elephant exchange. This comment provides the expectation that you'd offer it to you're co-worker, so he can make his wife happy.

"You're not obeying Scripture", says a friend when you decide to miss church one Sunday to finish a major project that the Lord has directed you to do. So you disobey the Lord, delay completion of the project and "religiously" attend the church service, all the while knowing and feeling like you're actually doing something wrong ... while sitting there *in church!*

Depending on the content-- getting and reading your own mail can be a means of controlling you, especially if it relates to overdue debt, court papers, or hate mail, etc.

Accusations of being a homosexual made by someone who wants to gain your undivided attention (or control your affections), or wants you to spend all of your time with only

The spirit of divination at Work in Your Interpersonal Relationships

him/her, can cause you to cut off close ties with your same sex friends, even when *nothing like that* has ever gone on.

At the carwash they do a shoddy job on your car, but you don't want to "make a scene" in front of everybody else by saying something about it. So though dissatisfied (affect), you go home and do the work you just paid someone else to do, all by yourself (effect).

At the baseball game when the people in front of you refuse to sit down. You say nothing, but you become infuriated to the point of leaving the game before it's over.

At the gym when someone cuts in line for the Stairmaster but you're too intimidated to tell him or her that *you* were actually next (CIYA). So you wait in line another twenty minutes for a machine; or, you just give up and go home, saying to yourself, *"It must not have been the Lord's will for me to work out today."*

At the beach your wife is watching you squirm, as you struggle to keep your eyes off of all of the scantily clad women. By the end of the day, you realize you never really enjoyed the outing because you felt like every blink of the eye was prohibited by your wife's supervisory conduct.

In the Board Meeting someone suggests you take on an extra task because you're, *"Just so good at it"*. Even though you already have way too much on your plate, you fulfill their expectation due to their compliment.

So now, how are those shades of yours performing? Has the lamp of interrogation penetrated your UV lenses yet?

I'm sure that throughout the course of all the illustrations I've shared above, that they were either "on point" with your own life, or you at least saw yourself and/or others "in-principle". I'm sure you'll agree that the ways in which the spirit of divination can be used to influence your emotions (affect) and behavior (effect) are immeasurable, truly unquantifiable.

In order to specifically tailor what you've learned both in-principle and by example, it's now time to take your sunglasses off and ask the Holy Spirit to open your eyes and give you revelation and application to your own life's interpersonal relationships and circumstances.

Take a legal pad and on one side of the ledger write, "Controlling others" and on the other side of the ledger write, "Controlled by others". Now that you realize the multitude of methods that can be employed to *control* behavior, you're now going to list at least five to ten of the most significant interactions that you can remember under each heading.

There are two points to keep in mind during this exercise while determining what should make your lists, as it relates to you being *controlled* by others:

First, whenever a Control Freak tactic is in play, <u>if</u> it causes you to act outside of the Lord's will when complying, then you're being controlled.

Second, if your compliance is done out of your own weaknesses (CIYA), and not intentionally, knowingly and willingly, then you're also being controlled.

The spirit of divination at Work in Your Interpersonal Relationships

Now pray, and ask the Holy Spirit to recall people, events and circumstances, in which you've either been *controlling* and/or been *controlled*.

Then BAM! There they are, in your mind.

Now, make your lists.

After completing this exercise the question will still remain:

"What, if anything, are *you* willing to do about it?"

CHAPTER 28: Backed Into a Corner

Admittedly, my intention all along has been to get you to this point ... *backed into a corner.*

Manipulative <u>and</u> controlling ... aren't I? [91]

After you've checked in with the Holy Spirit and asked Him to apply what you've learned thus far, this is the point where your own life should be backed so far into a corner, that you're now desperately looking for a way out.

No matter which way you turn, you now recognize the spirit of divination at work your life. "It" is either trying to get-- to you; or work-- through you, or both.

---

[91] ☺

Backed Into a Corner

Now remember, we haven't really been talking much about control issues related to sin; nor the type of control exercised when a parent, for example, keeps their toddler from running out into the middle of the street. What we've been talking about all along, is the type of *control* exercised over your life that opposes the Lord's direction, guidance, and will for your life.

Therefore, if at this point you are still attempting to *innocently* ask, *"What's so wrong with being controlled by others?"*

I would suggest that you stop your "stronghold thinking", go back to Chapter One of this text and start reading it all over again. If you make it to this point a second time and still don't get it, try another book.

If you argue, "I see how being *controlling* is a sin because the spirit of divination is anti-to Christ, but I really don't see why *being controlled* is such a sin", then let's review:

When you gave your life to Christ it was for Him to take the driver's seat, not man. Allowing yourself to be "controlled" by others, puts man in the driver's seat of your life, not

"CONTROL FREAK"

God. You will never fulfill your God-given destiny if you allow man to continue to control your life. You are disobeying God each and every time you choose to follow the directives of man, over the directives of God; especially now, since you have gained the knowledge and understanding discussed in this text (Lu 12:42-48).

As for every one of you who are still "on board", you should have digested your six-course meal by now. Throughout the stories and examples we have reviewed, you have either actually seen yourself and/or others in your life (or glimpses of the same).

So of which class, or classes, are you now a member?

(1)   Are you a First-Class *Controlling* Christian;

(2)   Are you a Second-Class *Controlled* Christian; or

(3)   Are you a Bi-*Controlling/Controlled* Christian (which includes both first and second class conduct, with different people in varying situations).

If you're not quite sure, I'll next further explain and define some of the characteristics of each class and I'll do so to the extreme; just to make sure you know what you're aiming at, when you begin to fire.

First-Class Controlling Christians:

We have all had "controlling" friends, family members or relatives. You know, a mother-in-law or a girlfriend that always has "the answer" for what *you should do* in any given situation?

These are truly amazing people you know … *really*.

Why? Because many times they have absolutely no experience or education in *any* given area; yet they are able to give you advice and tell you what to do about your finances, your marriage, your legal problems, your personal problems, your troubles at work, the struggles with your parents, or children, etc.

What I find most fascinating about Controlling Christians is how highly they must think of themselves (Ro 12:3), to give the kind of directives or advice, or make the kind of comments and/or gestures, that they do.

Backed Into a Corner

Realize that underlying all of these control tactics is a person's prideful opinion that you should care more about what they think about your life than: (1) what you think; and more importantly, (2) what God thinks.

Wow! That *really is* something else. That's why they're so amazing.

It's as if their opinions should bear more weight in your life than the Lord's, or as if you have absolutely no sense on how to run your own life.

I'm sorry, again please, "*Who* are you?"

There's something about being around Controlling Christians that always makes you feel pressured, there's always a stress or strain going on about something or someone. It's never peaceful.

Just think about why you've ever experienced being in a state of unrest. It's always because you would prefer to have some level of control over other people and/or circumstances.

Backed Into a Corner

I've had the most controlling people contact my office trying to use any and every tactic possible to try to make me take their case, call their ex-spouse, call-in a favor owed to me for their benefit, take a type of case in an area of law that I don't practice, work for free, find them another attorney who will work for free, etc. They've said things like, "I thought you were a Christian" "Aren't you a lawyer? "Aren't you supposed to help people with their legal problems?" "I'm going to talk to my pastor about this" etc. etc. etc.

Now look, if you're *really* a Christian and you admit and know you've got your own *controlling* personality trait, now is the time to kick the habit! Not only is it carnality-ridden and extremely unattractive to your countenance; but you're also siding with the devil whenever you try to control the behavior of other people!

At this point, to all of you admitted first-class *controlling* Christians, though I shouldn't even have to mention it again: There is a dire need for some serious repentance.

You are being used as a "play toy" of the enemy to get other people in your life to do what you want, not what God wants. You may make the excuse that you know better than they do, but that's just your pride. Your controlling behavior is actually handicapping those people you claim to "love" from getting closer to the Lord for themselves and maturing to the point of learning to hear His voice, not yours.

So stop reading now and get it right, if you haven't already.

<u>Second-Class Controlled Christians</u>:

As to our second class of *controlled* Christians, you first need to take a serious look at how you relate to others in your life. In order for you to ever get rid of any controlling person in your life, you must take a long hard brutally honest look at yourself, and ask the question, *"What might I be doing to solicit advice, counsel, or input from others?"*

If you're the type of person who goes around all day telling all your "problems" to everyone you see, naturally as good well meaning people, they're all going to give you advice to try and help you solve your problem(s). Indeed, it is a rare conversation where someone expresses a problem to another, that advice is not given to help solve that same problem.

So first off, stop sharing your problems with people! And stop asking for advice or counsel, or saying, *"What should I do?"* from everybody you run into, <u>especially</u> when you haven't even bothered to spend any time with God asking Him the same exact question.

Stop looking to man to solve your problems. You don't ask from people, you ask from God. Then the Lord will use the people He wants to answer your requests, according to His timing.

Second, is there anything about "you" or about your life that begs for counsel or advice from others? Meaning (and I don't know how to put this any kinder), *"Are you, or do you appear to be, a total airhead?"*

Do you go around *looking like* you have absolutely no direction about where you're going? And even if you got there, you wouldn't remember why you went there in the first place? Hopefully that's not you, because that's not a problem this book is designed to fix.

There is, however, a certain segment of the Christian population that is meandering around from one church service to another, and from one spiritual conference to another, looking to be "charged up". While there's nothing wrong with not yet knowing your assignment, the problem for many is that they're not even bothering to seek Him to find out. They're just going from one spiritual high to another, but still not on track with the Lord's plan.

Expecting the plan of God for your life to be tied up in a red bow like the "Lexus Christmas Sales Event" and presented to you on a silver platter, like the head of John the Baptist, just isn't going to happen. So stop lolly gagging around and start redeeming the time that you have left here on earth.

After we eliminate whatever actions or statements that you may be making that create an "open door policy" for outside influences to effect your decisions and actions; we then need to look at the people in your life that are the most influential and/or controlling since we'll be getting some artillery prepared for them soon.

But first, as to all of you second-class *controlled* Christians; understand that the people who are being used to *control* you divide into two groups: Type-A Controllers and Type-B Controllers.

Type-A Controllers: Consist of your relationships with "reprobates" who very simply, must be removed or cut off from your life, or they will continue to hinder your progress.

Type-B Controllers: Consist of relationships you must learn to manage by making "heart boundary adjustments", so that you won't ever allow yourself to be controlled by them again in the future.

Type-A Controllers: are generally evil, deceitful, abusive, taker-user types, haters, backbiters and gossips; they are always comparing and always competing. They're jealous, envious, always looking out for their own interests. They are the outright ultimatum types who say, "You need to do this!" Or, "If you don't do this, something [negative] will occur" (you fill in the blank).

Type-A's can only function well in their own little "kingdoms" in which they rule. They have subjects who are attached to them by blood, fear, desperation, or personal gain. They always refuse any correction and make excuses to justify their ongoing sinful behavior. They are "reprobates" (i.e. lost causes). They rarely, if ever, see any validity to your point of view, because theirs is always better than yours. Duh! Hello!

In the past, you have allowed Type-A Controllers to control your behavior, your conduct, and your emotional reactions. They have been able to make you an emotional basket case at the drop of a hat. Type-A Controllers need to be fully and forever "relieved from duty" in your life if you ever expect to truly be led by the Spirit of God.

You cannot listen to the advice or counsel of people who already are honing in, pushing their agenda and/or their opinions in and about your life. You must cut them out of your life, lessen or minimize contact, and then all of a sudden become, "unavailable".

No ... I don't care if you've known them for 30 of your 50 years of life. You cannot hear and obey God with controlling, pressuring, spirit of divination-driven people trying to take you off track to do what *they think is right* about the situations in your life. So stop all your "stronghold thinking" about it.

Backed Into a Corner

I've seen it time and again. The person (which happens to be you in this instance), doesn't even realize the affect and effect of hanging around with these Type-A Controllers. You don't even see the madness! You won't see the madness, unless and until you are removed from them for a period of time; <u>and</u> deprogrammed. *Seriously.*

When you first try to cut off any Type-A Controller from your life, you can always expect them to turn up the heat in an attempt to keep you in their clutches. During the last stages of "breakaway" from reprobates, they'll start "making up" things to accuse you about because they can no longer put you into a state of emotional upheaval.

Whereas before, they could always point to your own sinful behavior in response to their abuse, now they are forced to employ the art of "gross fabrication" in order to try and control your behavior because you've since stopped sinning; throwing things, slamming doors, and cussing, etc.

When a reprobate has nothing they can point the finger back at you about, expect Type-A Control Freaks to then manufacture or "make up" sins to accuse you of because they've got nothing else "on you" to try to *control* your behavior anymore. Also expect the *type* of accusations to escalate and include some of the most grievous sins, ones that you would never even dream of ever committing. Expect it!

When this happened to me, the Holy Spirit said, *"Don't be moved, this is a good sign."*

You've come to a great point in your walk with the Lord when you're trying to get out from under the command of the spirit of divination so that you can be free; free to totally and fully serve Him, and the Type-A's in your life don't have anything "true" or "real" to accuse you of, anymore.

Hallelujah!

"Blessed are you when they revile and persecute you, and say all kinds of evil against you <u>falsely</u> for My sake. Rejoice and be exceedingly glad, for great is your reward in heaven, for so they persecuted the prophets who were before you" (Matt 5:11-12, KJV).

So *if* ... no, that's *when* this happens to you too, don't you dare be fooled. Don't be condemned. Don't even bother to defend yourself. Yes that's right! It's just another Control Freak tactic.

God's got "the plan", not your Type-A Controlling friends or relatives. So free "yourself" up as soon as you possibly can. Then step back, wait a month or so, then experience and enjoy the peaceful existence that had escaped you for all these years. I promise, you'll be so glad that you did.

Type-B Controllers: consist of salvageable relationships. Either it's a husband or wife; mother or father; sister or brother; a life long friend; or some close relative that is not technically, "cut-off-able".

It could also be your own personal issue, or bondage to the relationship; and so it's more *your* problem of giving yourself over to them in the extreme, heart, mind, soul and body, above what you've given over to the Holy Spirit and that's what is causing them to *take advantage* of you.

These relationships are salvageable, but the Type-B Controller still needs to come off the throne of your heart. Depending on who it is, this may mean a time of separation from the relationship; fasting and praying for the idol to be removed; learning to monitor or "guard your heart" (Prv 4:23; KJV); and your thought life (2 Cor 10:5); and learning more about tapping into God's strength to draw the "heart boundary" line and then tow and hold that line, once it has been drawn.

After that, you must learn other tactics to disengage their controlling influence in your life. I have a whole chapter coming up for both Type-A and Type-B Controlling people with the specifics on how you need to respond to their control tactics in the future. Best of all, it will be without sinning!

Bi-Controlling/Controlled Christians:

If you're a Bi-Controlling/Controlled Christian, that means that in some relationships you *control;* and in others you are *controlled.* In either case both discussions above apply to you and you should act accordingly.

After having made your Controlling vs. Controlled lists, you must now take the opportunity to repent and ask the Lord to empower you to remove the influence of the spirit of divination from your life; *in toto.*

Backed Into a Corner

As previously mentioned, we pulled back all those layers of skin covering "the jugular" and I'm sure you'll agree that "it" is *still* pumping in your life.

Yet now, something has changed inside of you. It has become abundantly clear that there's something desperately wrong with the fact that "the jugular" is still alive in your life. Now, you see "its" ill affects and effects. Now, you want to do something about "it". Now, you're determined to free yourself from "its" clutches.

Perfect.

Once you come into agreement and ask the Lord to empower you to make the necessary "Control Freak" corrections in your life, then you will be ready to face your very own …

defining moment.

CHAPTER 29: Your Defining Moment

As a Christian, your defining moments of life will always present the same age-old question: "Who are you going to please or obey; God or man?"

We now have a few questions for you to honestly answer:

Are you ready to give up your attempts at *controlling* anyone else in your life ever again?

Are you ready to stop allowing others to exercise *control* over you?

Are you ready to instead move to the Lord's side of this anti-to Christ dilemma, and allow only the Holy Spirit to lead, guide, rule and reign in your life?

Or, are you still afraid that you'll be gossiped about, disowned or demoted, should you refuse to comply with the directives of others? If you are still intent on "pleasing man" in order to "keep the peace" and "not rock the boat", all the while defying the Lord's will, you're still not getting it.

You cannot please God and "play patty cake" with the spirit of divination at the same time. *"They that are in the flesh cannot please God"* (Ro 8:8, KJV).

Therefore, "... *fear not them which kill the body, but are not able to kill the soul: but rather fear Him which is able to destroy both soul and body in hell... Whosoever therefore shall confess Me before men, him will I confess also before My Father which is in heaven. But whosoever shall deny Me before men, him will I also deny before My Father which is in heaven. Think not that I am come to send peace on earth: I came not to send peace, but a sword. For I am come to set a man at variance against his father, and the daughter against her mother, and the daughter in law against her mother in law. And a man's foes shall be they of his own household. He that loveth father or mother more than Me is not worthy of Me: and he that loveth son or daughter more than Me is not worthy of Me. And he that taketh not his cross, and followeth after Me, is not worthy of Me. He that findeth his life shall lose it: and he that loseth his life for My sake shall find it…"* (Matt 10:28-39, KJV).

The themes found in this passage, actually encapsulate the crux of this entire text:

1. Don't fear man, fear God;
2. Don't deny the Lord, or you too will be denied;
3. Don't expect your stance on the side of God to create peace in every relationship; indeed expect division or the severing of relationships (the sword);
4. Expect the severing to occur even with those in your own household; those who should love and support you, but who will now become your enemies (in a sense), due to your breaking free from their control;
5. If you should choose "not to rock the boat" with those in your household or the people very close to you, while undermining the will of God, you aren't worthy of the Lord;
6. If you don't bear this cross of separation you are not worthy of Him;

7. If you decide to continue to live your own controlling life and/or a life being controlled by others, you will lose your life;

8. If on the other hand, you choose to lose your life (your will and your agenda in order to accomplish His will and His agenda; and thus, shore up the chink in your armor CIYA); you will find *real life,* a "quality of life" reflective of that abundant life lived in and through Him; and,

9. If you "love" or "prefer the desires" or "choose to please" people (including your closest family members) more than or instead of Christ, don't call yourself a disciple; you're not worthy of Him.

So now you're thinking that the Lord is a bit extreme, are you? Realize that He has made the same commitment to you, that He asks you to make to Him. Not only has He said He will never leave you or forsake you (Heb 13:5); but when faced with preferring His own mother and brethren over others, here's what He said in Matthew 12:46-50:

"While He yet talked to the people, behold, His mother and His brethren stood without, desiring to speak with Him. Then one said unto Him, 'Behold, Thy mother and Thy

brethren stand without, desiring to speak with Thee.' But He answered and said unto him that told Him, 'Who is My mother? and who are My brethren?' And He stretched forth His hand toward His disciples, and said, 'Behold My mother and My brethren! For whosoever **shall do the will of My Father** which is in heaven, the same is My brother, and sister, and mother'" (KJV).

Jesus was intimating that the kind of people who get His attention first, are those who "do the will" of the Father. He has given this same priority to your relationship with Him and there is great reward for this kind of commitment to God:

"Then Peter began to say unto Him, 'Lo, we have left all, and have followed Thee.' And Jesus answered and said, 'Verily I say unto you, There is no man that hath left house, or brethren, or sisters, or father, or mother, or wife, or children, or lands, for My sake, and the gospel's, But he shall receive an hundredfold now in this time, houses, and brethren, and sisters, and mothers, and children, and lands, with persecutions; and in the world to come eternal life'" (Mark 10:28-30, KJV).

The Lord has <u>committed Himself</u> to making up for anything you gave up or lost while obeying and following Him. This includes relationships and possessions, with a one hundredfold return and in this lifetime! Wow, what a promise!

This promise however, doesn't apply to everyone. If you haven't left or given up anything, you don't get the hundredfold return. But, if like most of us, you have, or even if you're now willing to do so ... it's bank! A huge promise!

The reason you must take action to totally eradicate the workings of the spirit of divination in your life is so that you can bring all of "you"-- your mind, your thoughts, your heart, your emotions back-- into a state of peace; and as a result, attain clear uninhibited communication with God. In that state, at any given time, you will be ready and available, fit for the Master's use.

If you decide <u>not</u> to eliminate the effects of the spirit of control working and directing your life, "you" will be consumed with the pressure to do what "it" is demanding of

Your Defining Moment

"you" in one situation after another, in one relationship after another, until death do you part.

Once you're committed to moving forward with taking "it" out, then defining what "the victory" in your life will *feel* like and *look* like is the next critical thing to do. Once you know that, you will assuredly know when you've obtained it.

For example, there will be times when you have a spirit of control encounter and even if you do not give in to the controlling directive, you can still carry the "Black Noise" (or the thoughts, feelings, emotions and pressure to act about the incident) around with you for hours, days, months, even years. That type of end result, does <u>not</u> amount to a victory.

While the fact that you did <u>not</u> take the action "it" wanted you to take, is progression; if you still remain mentally immobilized thinking about the interaction with that person; that, in and of itself, is a crime. It's a rip off of your mental and emotional peace and freedom and therefore, that's <u>not</u> accounted as a victory.

Your Defining Moment

This battle is not just for you to refrain from taking any action led or directed by the spirit of divination; but the mark or goal is to be *totally un-affected* and *totally un-effected* by each and every "Control Freak" incident that occurs in your life in the future.

You should no longer be taken off track, stumbled, delayed, or become emotionally disturbed or disrupted in any way. While there will always be an acknowledgement that you just confronted "it" yet, again; you will soon become so proficient at taking "it" out, that there will be very little else to say about the encounter.

In order to achieve this end, a new response strategy, one that you will soon be learning, will need to be employed on a consistent basis. Understand that eliminating the spirit of control from your life will not be like a once-and-for-all removal of an ingrown toenail. Rather, it will be more like an insect eradication, something you'll always need to watch closely so that "it" will not come back into your life and be allowed to re-infest. Your spirit of divination monitor must always be left "on" in expectation of your next eradication encounter.

Your Defining Moment

"Be sober, be vigilant; because your adversary the devil walks about like a roaring lion, seeking whom he may devour. Resist him, steadfast in the faith, knowing that the same sufferings are experienced by your brotherhood in the world" (1 Pe 5:8-9, KJV).

Finally, realize that there will be things you must actively "do" and "say" in order to eliminate this controlling spirit from your life. You cannot just sit around and *pray* and hope it will go *away*. You are dealing with evil, coming at you in an indistinguishable package. So expect to expend hard work and effort. Expect to be required to "do" and "say" something on a consistent basis, in order to get and maintain the victory.

Now that we've got that straight, if you're ready to carry out your decision and if you're ready to stand by it, even when it hurts (and it will); there is one more key point to cover before I give you the tools to extract "the jugular".

In fact, this is such an indispensible key to your success, if you fail in this directive, your mission cannot possibly be accomplished.

CHAPTER 30: Take "it" Out-- Without-- Sinning!

In order to have victory over the spirit of divination, you must eradicate, or "take out" the jugular-- but you must do so *without* sinning. *"Don't let evil get the best of you, but conquer evil by doing good"* (Ro 12:21, NLT).

Therefore, every time you're confronted with a spirit of control situation, you cannot go sinning against the person under "its" influence. You can't be yelling and screaming and cussing them out about how, *"the devil is using them to try and control your life"* and how you've, *"had just about enough of it!"* and how, they don't realize that they're really *"a child of the devil and being used as a puppet for their father of lies, Satan"* and how, because of it, *"you never want to see or talk to them, ever again, in Jesus' name!"*

Take "it" Out-- Without-- Sinning!

If you sin, when you confront the spirit of divination, then you've defeated the whole purpose of the battle. In those cases, it's actually the spirit of divination that gains ground out of the interaction, rather than yourself.

Why? Because "it" got *"you"* to sin!

That's not a victory over that controlling spirit, if "it" got "you" to fall into sin, while you were trying to get rid of "it".

Furthermore, depending on what you did (sin-wise), you may then have to be the one to go apologize and ask forgiveness of the person who was trying to control your behavior. You do not want to fall into that snare either.

Here's a great example of overcoming evil with good. I had a divorce case I handled for a wife whose husband was having an affair, had a child out of wedlock, and was using money from a second mortgage on the family residence to set up his "second family" out of the country.

She came to my office, having always been a stay-at-home mother; married for thirty plus years; not having any experience with handling finances; she never had an official job out of the home; she had never even balanced a checkbook.

Her husband wasn't a Christian and refused to repent. They had plenty of assets and the husband made good money.

So for all these reasons and more, it was very difficult for her to decide whether or not to file for divorce. The easy way out *financially* was to stay married; the hard way out *emotionally* was to get a divorce, because she was a Christian and wanted to keep her family together.

She had one thing on her side, however; that was, God Himself. If you ever find yourself in this kind of situation, don't let anyone confuse you about that fact, and don't allow fear or hurt diminish the fact that in His timing, the Lord will vindicate your situation.

In fact, sometimes God will use us, His people, to make a stand for right, while *not sinning*. Standing up for right, will cause those people you're positioned against, to either, hit up against you and get bruised (for the Lord will help you to stand); or it will cause them to change their behavior.

Take "it" Out-- Without-- Sinning!

Anyway, this litigation went on for a few years. We won everything we tried to win; and then, we continued to win on appeal. It wasn't until years after those victories "in the natural", that I heard the very end of the story from the wife. Though they never got back together, the husband eventually got saved and started attending a solid Bible teaching church.

Realize this, that had it not been for her taking a stand against his sin (which was a very difficult thing for her to do at the time); he'd likely still be living a double life, on his way to hell, *practicing* the sin of adultery!

The funniest thing about this case took place years later when I got a call from a lady who needed legal counsel. When I asked her who referred me, it ended up being my client's now saved, ex-husband. So now I've got my ex-opposition sending me referrals? Boy! Was that a work of God, or what?

If the wife had stayed in that relationship, he probably would have never gotten saved. He would have continued to *take advantage* of her and she would have been miserable the rest of her life. Instead, she grew into this stronger, more confident, beautiful woman of God and she's doing just fine serving the Lord.

You too will have to decide to make a change and then be consistent in enforcing your change. You cannot give way to pressure; you must hold the line, or you will lose every inch of ground in the Promised Land that you ever gained.

It's time to change your way of thinking; you don't have to be like everybody else anymore. You don't have act-a-fool every time someone mistreats you, or fails to do what you want him or her to do. Nor do you have to fall over every stumbling block that is rolled your way, there *is* always the option of jumping over it!

I'm not talking about becoming sinless perfection, but what I am saying is that you cannot fight this foul spirit by becoming foul yourself. You must fight it with class, finesse, dignity, tact, planned and practiced choice words and phrases, and in the power and authority of the Holy Ghost.

Realize that once you start seeing the spirit of divination at work in your own interpersonal relationships, there may be a tendency for you to get angry with the *people* instead of *yourself* (for CIYA), and instead of *the enemy*.

Remember, these people are generally ignorant of what's going on: *"for we wrestle not against flesh and blood, but against principalities, against powers, against the rulers of the darkness of this world, against spiritual wickedness in high places"* (Eph 6:12, KJV).

Fighting the "spirit of control" will not be like a regular battle (soldier against soldier in the battlefield). It's not really about him or her; if that person who the spirit of divination is using to control your behavior is eliminated, another person will step into that role; and then another, and another, and another. Ad infinitum.

So don't get angry with the person. If you want to get angry with *someone*, get angry with "it" first and yourself second. Get angry about how "it" has been used to take advantage of your own weaknesses and emotions (CIYA). Get angry with yourself about how "it" has caused you to give into the whims of others so that they will like, love and accept you, instead of doing what you know is the Lord's will. Get angry about how you've foolishly given everything

Take "it" Out-- Without-- Sinning!

of yourself over to people who, in return, have barely given you the time of day. Get angry enough to decisively, put a stop to "it"!

*"There is therefore now no condemnation to them which are in Christ Jesus, who **walk not after the flesh, but after the Spirit"** (Ro 8:1, KJV).*

*"All things are lawful unto me, but all things are not expedient: all things are lawful for me, **but I will not be brought under the power of any**"* (1 Cor 6:12, KJV).

*"All things are lawful for me, but all things are not expedient: all things are lawful for me, **but all things edify not"*** (1 Cor 10:23, KJV).

Being fed up with yourself, your character flaws (the CYIA), and how or who you've been in the past, is a very significant motivating factor for change in your life.

So, with that said, are you ready?

If so, it's now time to gear up with some new artillery so that you too, can take "it" out-- without-- sinning.

Take "it" Out-- Without-- Sinning!

There are seven pieces of artillery; some slightly used, others likely never been used, for you to now pick-up; get familiar with; become trained in; get proficient in handling; and get equipped to utilize during your next encounter with the spirit of divination.

They include the following:

Weapon #1: "Self-Control"

First and foremost, this fruit of the Holy Spirit (Gal 5:22-23) "self-control", must be exercised in your life in order to govern how you interact, react and respond to the spirit of divination.

This piece of artillery, you've no doubt used at least to some extent in your life before; but have you tapped into it entirely?

"Self-Control" is the virtue of one who masters his desires and passions, especially his sensual appetites"[92] But please don't think of self-control as only being related to sex!

---

[92] Strong's #1466, transliterated "Egkrateia".

"Self-control" is not just a demonstration of restraint as it relates to outward sins; but it also covers the level of discipline that you employ when it comes to the "inner man" (Eph 3:16). Self-control encompasses your anger and all of the emotions that *you allow yourself* to entertain and/or engage in: fear, distress, worry, anxiety, hatred, etc.; <u>as well as</u>, all of the thought processes that you allow to go on in your mind, whatever the content or subject matter; <u>as well as</u> your outward display of those emotions with: your tongue, your tone, your words, your facial gestures, your murmuring and complaining, as well as all of your other clearly sinful actions.

The risk when confronting the spirit of divination is for you to get angry with the person and then say or do something sinful in response to their attempts to control you. We need to make sure we are not brought under the power of anything or anyone that does not edify us or build us up; specifically, these people who have "given place" to the spirit of control and who are now trying to control your life.

So *now* is the time to tap into the depths of "self-control" that the Lord has made available to you and get a tight grip on your perceptions, thoughts, feelings, attitudes, words and actions.

Weapon #2: "Rehearsed Responses" that "Turn the Tables"

"Rehearsed Responses" are planned statements that you have predetermined you will implement in every situation in which you confront the spirit of control. "Turning the tables" is what Jesus did when He wanted to put an end to the moneychangers control over the people, who we're trying to get right with the Lord through their sacrifices.

Yep, Jesus turned the tables … *all the way over*. This is something we will talk more about in our upcoming Chapter entitled, "Escalated Rebuke".

For now, understand that your arsenal of "Rehearsed Responses" is the way for you to obtain and maintain the victory with your words, without ever sinning. Please understand that "Rehearsed Responses" don't come naturally, unless and until you've been adequately trained in "Jugular Eradication Methodology".

Take "it" Out-- Without-- Sinning!

So don't expect to be able to perform these non-sinful responses without some intentional planning, training and determination. They are called *"Rehearsed Responses"* for a reason.

I am certain that you already have identified numerous interpersonal relationships, where the spirit of control has manifest in your life on previous occasions. Controlling people have patterns of behavior that you can anticipate due to your past experience with them. Therefore, you can begin your training by preparing "Rehearsed Responses" to combat the usual statements or tactics that the controlling people in your life have used in the past to control your behavior.

It's much like Daniel who, *"... **purposed in his heart** that he would not defile himself ..."* (Dan 1:8, KJV). You must purposefully plan and prepare your "Rehearsed Responses" to spirit of divination-driven activity *before* you face another one of "its" controlling encounters.

You will need to prepare various sinless responses that are tactful, insightful, "on point" with the issue at hand, and naturally very commanding and powerful. All the while, despite your suave diplomacy, your message of eradication will be promptly and contemporaneously delivered.

Incorporating Scripture or Biblical precepts is many times a good basis for formulating your "Rehearsed Responses". However, there are many times when you cannot think of any Scripture to correct/rebuke the spirit of divination. In those cases, you must use other common day vernacular, to bring the necessary correction.

My motive for coming up with this piece of artillery relates to my earlier discussion about getting mad enough at yourself about your own condition (not the other person), so that *you* will be determined to change *yourself*. You need to prepare new responses for those situations in which you previously have always ended up falling. You need to demonstrate that "you" are in subjection to the Spirit of God. Don't just say you are, show, or demonstrate that you are. The only way to do so in these Control Freak situations, is to be prepared with several "Rehearsed Responses" that you're ready to fire off, whenever placed in enemy territory.

Take "it" Out-- Without-- Sinning!

The Lord *always* provides us a way of "escape" (1 Cor 10:13). We just need to do our part to think of it, practice it, and employ it. You too will need to originate, implement and put your own "Rehearsed Responses" to practice in every new Control Freak situation you face from here on out. So take the time now to seek the Lord's wisdom on the well-known controlling words and controlling patterns of behavior that you've already experienced in the past, with all the well-known "controlling" people in your life right now.[93]

Ask Him for wisdom to help give you some "Rehearsed Responses" that you can have prepared as artillery, ready for the next time you encounter that person. In other words, you should prepare your "Rehearsed Responses" for each of the controlling people in your life with the expectation that they will act the same way towards you, that they've always acted in the past.

This means you will need to be innovative and think! Big time! You will need to break out of the "stronghold thinking"

---

[93] There is a sub-point to Rehearsed Responses, called "Re-Framing the control issue", which we will get to later. Rehearsed Responses consist of a re-framing of your usual response.

"box" and the ways that you're used to responding to these people, both in word and deed. Once you change "you", the other people will be forced to do the same. The goal is that for each Control Freak encounter you face, that your "Rehearsed Responses" will help you to "Turn the Tables" on the enemy.

Here's an example of "Turning the Tables" in a far too often encountered situation:

Say for example there is a husband who is practicing pornography. His wife keeps catching him time and time again, over and over. Each time the husband promises his wife he is going to quit. He claims to be a "Christian" but refuses her numerous attempts to get him to go to church and/or to go with her to pastoral counseling to get some help.

Every time the wife catches him in this sin, her world is thrown into a tizzy. He did it again! He lied again! There is hurt, anger, tears and plenty of yelling and screaming back and forth between the two.

Take "it" Out-- Without-- Sinning!

After months, maybe even years of his continuing to practice this sin and her continuing to catch him in this sin; and his continuing to fail to repent of this sin, or go to church or counseling; and her continuing to be outraged and upset about it, the wife decides to meet with a lawyer and file paperwork for a legal separation.

She comes in visibly upset while explaining everything he was doing, how it was adversely effecting her life, the lives of her children, and how she was in an emotional tug o' war over what she should do about it.

This one issue of the husband practicing pornography had consumed her life for many months on end. She can't think of anything *but*, this situation. She has been constantly wondering, worrying, and thinking about whether her husband was on the Internet looking at pornography; what she was going to do about it; who she can tell to help get him to stop; how she can "catch" him in the future if he continues to lie and if he does it again, etc.

Getting him to repent has become an obsession that has caused her to lose any enjoyment or "quality of life". Since he continues to deny the sin and refuses any help, counseling, or church, the wife feels totally hopeless.

Do you see "it"? The husband's sin has now not only totally controlled his own life, but his wife's life as well.

To put it bluntly, upon meeting with the attorney, the wife was a Control Freaking mess! This is why it's so important to watch out who you "yoke" yourself to, because they can easily take you down.

People in these situations, like the wife, aren't able to see *their own* "madness". They don't see how they are literally held captive by the spirit of divination, heart, mind, soul, body and strength; and how their "quality of life" has been totally swallowed up and consumed by the enemy.

Yet for the observer, here's how "it" is so very easy to spot. It's when a person, such as the wife in this instance, is unable to talk about *anything else* but what the husband has said or done; what he is threatening, and what he is justifying. In short, every thought in her mind, every emotion that she had, every word that she spoke was all about him (the husband), and nothing about Him (her Lord).

All the while she needed confirmation and assurance that she was right with her analysis and conclusions; and that he was wrong for what he was doing (i.e.) lying and not repenting of the sin.

The spirit of divination is seen when the wife is so utterly consumed with the husband's life of sin, that it causes her to be unable to think of anything *but,* his sin; and even when focused on his sin, the wife become totally confused and uncertain about the obvious: "Is pornography really a sin? Because he said it wasn't."

That's what the spirit of divination can do to an otherwise, totally sane person. "It" makes you question yourself over the reality of things that are totally apparent to anyone else not involved in the drama.

I have been asked to mediate several similar matters of this kind. In one such instance, I observed a good example of where the wife "Turned the Tables". She had been referred to my office during a time when, she too, was acting like so many other similarly situated women I had met with in the past, *a Control-Freaking mess.*

I explained to her what I did as a mediator and she decided she wanted to go forward with it because she was at her "wit's end." She had been unable for months and months to get her husband to do anything about his sin. Since she'd already tried absolutely everything, she didn't know what else she could do about this situation, so she came to my office.

I made contact with the husband over the phone while she was there. I explained to him what was going on, that his wife was intent upon filing legal papers; and I explained the role I could play as a mediator to complete the paperwork and keep everyone out of court, if he agreed.

Now, I'm talking to the husband on the telephone, and naturally I'm being very nice, but he stops me mid-sentence and says that he, "Can't talk about it right now" and asks to speak to his wife. I hand her the phone and they talk. But, as you well know, you can usually get the gist of even a one-sided conversation when you're in the same room, though she said very few words.

Take "it" Out-- Without-- Sinning!

After she hung up the phone, she told me that her husband had just agreed to go to church and pastoral counseling. She looked me in the eye and with a sigh of relief, she said, "Wow! That feels pretty good."

Now the tables were turned.

You may not realize it, but sometimes you're the only person in the life of another who is in a position (like a wife) to bring correction in an area that nobody else would have any reason to know about.

Note: nobody screamed or got mad (unlike every other confrontation between them in the past). It was just a determined, strategic action, taken by the wife that turned the tables on the spirit of divination's control. She was no longer going to be controlled by his sin any more. She had taken the driver's wheel of her life, out of the hands of the spirit of divination and given it back to the Lord, Whom she believed had told her to file.

This works! There's something about taking control out of the hands of evil that makes you feel *really good,* especially when you don't sin in the process.

Take "it" Out-- Without-- Sinning!

So prepare to turn those tables over in your own life too. Turn them upside down, just like Jesus did if you have to. But remember, you must do so without sinning.

Weapon #3: Constant "Check-In"

It will be necessary to constantly "Check-In" with the Holy Spirit during any confrontation you have with the spirit of divination in the future. You must employ your "Constant Check-In" artillery with the Lord throughout each and every interaction, before, during and after.

You must function on "high alert" while monitoring your heart and mind: what you're thinking; how your emotional state is being "affected"; and how your actions are being "effected" by each and every Control Freak situation you face.

During these "Constant Check-In" consultations with Him, you'll be asking Him to reveal the answers to these kinds of questions:

Take "it" Out-- Without-- Sinning!

1. What is this person trying to get me to do?
2. What are his/her potential motives?
3. What action(s) do they want me to take (effect)?
4. How am I responding to that pressure, physically and mentally?
5. How do I *feel* emotionally (affect)?
6. Is "it" consuming and/or confusing my heart and emotions, mind and thoughts?
7. What am I saying to others about this situation?
8. Do I feel and/or appear frantic and upset?
9. Is "it" tapping out my strength?
10. Lord, what do You think?
11. What does the Word of God say I should do?
12. Lord, what do You want me to do?
13. What Rehearsed Responses should I use?
14. When should I use them?
15. What tone should I use?
16. What attitude should I employ?
17. How long should I allow this interaction to continue?
18. When should I fire?

Remember, this is not about your personal feelings about the individual. This is not about their feelings either. This is not about what you'll lose. This is not about what they want. This is not about making them happy. This is not about how mad they're going to be. This is not about getting them to stop whining and crying. This is not about getting them to stop yelling and hating you. This is not about how they'll probably never talk to you again. This is not about what will happen if you don't comply with their demands. This has nothing to do with, or about them.

Rather, it's all about <u>Him</u>. Has He said anything about this issue at all, in His Word, or in His still small voice to your spirit? Is your brain or mind cleared out sufficiently to listen and hear what He says on the issue? Or, do you have too much "Black Noise" still going on to readily hear His voice?

Have you already decided what to do without even asking Him? Then that's your pride making presumptions; pretending as if *you* already know what to do. That means you're in a bad habit of leaving Him out of the equation. Self-Sufficiency can be your demise; you will end up sinning in response.

Has He been teaching you on some principle that now, all of a sudden, has shown up in this particular interaction? Then that means you've been trained enough to be tested.

Take "it" Out-- Without-- Sinning!

Take the test, pass it and get promoted to another level of existence!

These are inquires your mind needs to consider, evaluate, and draw conclusions about for *each and every time the spirit of divination rears its ugly head in your life.*

It may seem like a lot of points to cover and consider, but the Lord has made your brain *"superfly".* You can handle this kind of critical analysis every time ... hands down, no problem.

The victory is in your freedom to hear, obey, serve and fulfill God's assignment, plan and destiny for your life; and to do so in the fullness of the anointing and authority He has given you.

Weapon #4: Do Not Respond "In-Kind"

When someone comes at you with "guns a blazing", do not act like they act; or, put another way, do not respond "In-Kind". Another person's approach or attitude towards you does not mean that you have to act just like them!

Take "it" Out-- Without-- Sinning!

Your artillery of <u>not</u> responding "In-Kind" means that you do not buy into the emotion that *someone else has* about any given situation and take it on, or "own it" for yourself. This is a common trap, or ploy, that the enemy often times uses in order to get you to fall.

Here's an example: I was asked to help out at a women's conference with setup one day. While I was putting some water bottles on a table or *setting up,* if you will, one of the leaders of the conference came over to me and with a very hostile tone, demanded to know: who I was, what I was doing there, who said I could be in there and exclaiming, "You need to get out of here, only specially authorized people can be back here at this time!"

BAM! I mean, "it" was thick! I was just merrily in my own little world helping with setup and yet for some reason, I had been singled-out and without question laid-out, for doing nothing wrong. It was like being blindsided on the twenty-first yard line.

I was just there to serve; I wasn't trying to steal anybody's thunder or anything like that, *really.*

Take "it" Out-- Without-- Sinning!

I forgot exactly what words I said in response, but with a very calm spirit and demeanor, though my heart was beating fast (being under attack by the spirit of divination), I answered her questions in a very composed matter of fact kind of way and said: "Janet Carter; helping put water on the table; I was asked to help; and you can check with whomever you'd like to see if I should leave or not, just let me know."

Without saying another word, the leader turned and went off in a huff.

One of the ladies that was right next to me who witnessed the whole incident, complimented me on how I handled it. She explained how she would have "gone off" in response to that lady, if that had happened to her.

After being "allowed" to stay and help, later while thinking through the situation with the Lord, what I remembered to be most important for our purposes, is that I did not respond "In-Kind" to her attack.

We get into these bad habits of responding "In-Kind" to others. If they come at us angrily, we usually automatically respond in anger too (even when we weren't previously angry). If someone comes to you yelling, you respond by yelling back. If someone comes at you with a smart sarcastic attitude, your response is the same.

But, you don't have to be like everybody else!

Why do we think if someone gets in our face and yells at us, that we have to yell back? Why do we think if someone ignores us and doesn't speak to us, that we have to respond "In-Kind" and act just as immature and rudely as they are?

Let me relieve you of this duty right now because you cannot respond "In-Kind" and have the victory in this territory!

If someone can get you to start "Control Freaking Out" and acting as foolishly as they are; if they can get you to throw a pot or a pan, some cruel words, or a flippant attitude; then you're in sin because of their provocation, and you just blew your opportunity to disengage the spirit of divination and extract the jugular.

Take "it" Out-- Without-- Sinning!

No ... not on my watch. You can forget about it!

"This suffering is all part of what God has called you to. Christ, who suffered for you, is your example. Follow in His steps. He never sinned, and He never deceived anyone. **He did not retaliate when He was insulted. When He suffered, He did not threaten to get even.** *He left his case in the hands of God, who always judges fairly"* (1 Pe 2:21-23, NLT).

The last thing we need to happen in these situations is for you to start sinning against that ignorant person, who is being used by the spirit of divination to try to control your behavior; and then, allow "it" to succeed with "its" attempt to control, by causing you to sin.

Weapon #5: Stay "On-Point"

When confronting the spirit of divination, once you have "Checked-In" and discern what "it" is trying to get you to do, or not to do; whether it is an action (effect) or a feeling (affect), or both; your artillery of, "Staying On-Point" will cause you to stick to the "Control-Freak issue" or "subject matter" of the interaction.

Take "it" Out-- Without-- Sinning!

As a lawyer, when there is case law that matches up with the facts of a case you're personally handling, we refer to that legal authority as being "on point". You will need to learn how to stay "on-point" during these Control Freak confrontations. You cannot allow yourself to start in on any personal attacks like, "You always..." or "You never..." and certainly not, "Jo mama..."

The "Rehearsed Response" that you choose to employ, should only address the subject or content of the "Control Freak issue" at hand, always keeping it right "on-point".

For example, if you've been having an issue with training your teenager to care for her clothes better and she's been taking advantage of you doing her laundry; you may formulate a Rehearse Response that is "on-point" such as: *"It sounds like you're just about to ask me to do your laundry dear; but like you said, you're almost an adult now, so I know you can handle it all by yourself."*

Don't go off on calling her an ungrateful slob, talking about how much each and every article of clothing has cost you; and how many times in the past you've done her laundry; and how she's never once said, "thank you"; and how you've seen her take freshly folded clothes, try them on, take them off, throw them on the floor, and then leave them there for days.

LOL! No, no, don't go there. Just stick to the issue (namely, she's old enough to do her own laundry); and "stay on-point" (you're not doing her laundry anymore); and nothing else.

Use a "Rehearsed Response" and tap into your "self control" in order to hold all that long-term emotion down, soldier!

Weapon #6: "Confront with Authority and Expect Attitude"

When you confront the spirit of divination in the power of the Holy Spirit in response, you must *expect attitude* from the spirit of divination; or better yet, from those people who are trying to exercise *control* over your life.

"They are a defiant bunch. Whether or not they listen, at least they'll know that a prophet's been here. But don't be afraid of them, son of man, and don't be afraid of anything

*they say. Don't be afraid when living among them is like stepping on thorns or finding scorpions in your bed. Don't be afraid of their mean words or their hard looks. They're a bunch of rebels. **Your job is to speak to them. Whether they listen is not your concern.** They're hardened rebels"* (Ez 2:3-8, MSG).

The Lord knew that Ezekiel (like most) would have a tendency to be influenced by the people's scoffing, their words and the looks on their faces. The Lord promised to tell Ezekiel exactly what to say, but warned him to be ready, because these rebellious, stubborn, stiff-necked people are not going to like it! Don't even think about being rebellious like them, the Lord confirmed.

When you confront the spirit of divination in the power and authority of the Holy Spirit, "it" is *not* going to like it either!

Therefore, you must expect to get "attitude" from everybody in and through whom, "it" is working. When you *expect* to get "attitude" you can be prepared with an "on point" "Rehearsed Response" that will "Turn the Tables". That way, "it" won't catch you off guard, stumble you, and cause you to sin.

Take "it" Out-- Without-- Sinning!

Weapon #7: "Sing a Song"

There is just something about singing that counteracts negative emotions. This is your last piece of artillery. Its use, is to be reserved for extremely obstinate Control Freak situations. Most often times, it should be employed when you are forced to stay in the presence of a Control Freak, who is adamant about trying to control "you" and your behavior.

Whenever you confront the spirit of divination and your "on-point" "Rehearsed Responses" do not bring a shift in "its" influence and things have gotten so bad that you realize that if you say one more thing, that you may fall; it's now time to "Sing a Song".

The song you sing will definitely <u>not</u> be anything you've *ever* heard, or sung before. *You*, yes *you*, will have to make up the lyrics and possibly even the melody, all by yourself ... right there on the spot! Moreover, in order to stay in line with your other pieces of artillery, the song you make up must also be "on-point".

Take "it" Out-- Without-- Sinning!

This may sound like a lot of responsibility for a new recruit, but if I, someone who can't sing a lick-- can do it, you can do it too. In fact, if you can sing, you've got the edge over me.

The words or lyrics to the song will relate to the "Control Freak" issue at hand and like I said, will need to be "on-point". That's why you'll need to make them up. No one has ever written the lyrics to this song before, because no one has ever been in the exact same "Control Freak" situation that you are now facing.

The melody can be anything you come up with; you can copy another song, or create an original melody of your own to suit your fancy.

Here's an example: Say you have a grown daughter, whom you believe the Lord has now shown you, only spends time with you because you take her shopping and buy her things. If you didn't do that for her, you suspect she'd never even give you the time of day.

You've realized this relationship needs to be corrected because it taps into the CIYA and controls your life. So now, you're ready to stand against the spirit of control the next time your daughter even suggests another, "you-subsidized" shopping spree.

So she comes over early one afternoon for the usual Sunday dinner and says, "Hey there's a big sale going on today at that favorite boutique of yours, wanna go check it out before dinner?"

You deliver your first Rehearsed Response of, "No thank you, not today."

She persists, by saying; "Well, I really want to go to just check it out, not necessarily buy anything. Don't you remember how much fun we had last time?"

You respond, "Yes, we sure did have fun shopping there in the past, didn't we? But I'm just not interested in going back."

In response, she says, *"What?* What did I hear you say? You don't *ever* want to go back there again? What's wrong with *you*?"

Take "it" Out-- Without-- Sinning!

You say, "We _had_ fun, but I don't want to spend my money on that kind of fun anymore. You go on ahead."

In response she says, "What? You're never going to go shopping for clothes again? What on earth has happened to you? What's wrong with you? You always loved to go clothes shopping. _What happened?_"

You now respond, "I'm just re-directing where I spend money, and it's not going to be on shopping for things I don't really need."

In response, she starts explaining how you _do_ have money available and says, she can't believe how you're not going to go shopping anymore, ever again; and again says, "_I_ want to go shopping, but man ... what's wrong with _you?_"

She then goes off with an "attitude" right in front of you, and starts to hold a conversation with herself, about you: mocking your decision, attacking you personally about how ugly the outfit is that you have on, and sending other non verbal cues while in your presence, like rolling her eyes and scowling at your comments.

Take "it" Out-- Without-- Sinning!

You *expected* this remember? "Confront with Authority and Expect Attitude" is one of your pieces of artillery.

You've been operating on constant "Checked-In" and you can feel the "affect" of this interaction; namely, your blood is starting to boil. You're thinking to yourself, "I can't believe this, what a selfish daughter I raised! How did I *ever* fall for this before? Boy "it" sure is ugly".

To each statement she makes thereafter, you respond in the exact same way, calmly stating, "There are just no funds available for that kind of fun anymore." Or, "I'm just re-directing where I spend money, and it's not going to be on shopping for things I don't really need."

Because you are not going to respond "In-Kind"; and because you're going to keep this "on-point"; and because you don't need to judge her ill motives; and because you're not budging; this many times causes the spirit of divination to become childish and go off on a temper tantrum and never come back.

However, this time "it" isn't going anywhere, she's expected by everyone else to be present for Sunday dinner. So "it" is staying right there with her, *in your face*. In this situation, you can't really leave, but you want to get "it" to stop; while at the same time, you'd *prefer not* to have to ask her to leave either.

Yet, she continues on a tirade slamming you with rude comments, mocking your decision, telling you how your clothes are so old and outdated; and saying sarcastically, "Look, trust me, *you really* need to go shopping!" while raising her voice and tone on various words for purposes of emphasis.

You're starting to get really, really angry on the inside, you're heart is pounding and you don't want to say another word because you know it won't *sound* right anymore. So you say nothing, but she begins yelling and screaming, demanding her way and slamming doors; and when you don't respond to that at all, she then calls someone else on her cell phone, right in front of you, and says, "Did you know there was a sale today and can you believe my mom doesn't want to go?"

The spirit of control is obviously digging for an emotional response from you; your "self-control" has been tapped and is functioning at full potential. At this point, the emotional state of "it", as seen in the conduct of your adult daughter, is even out-of-control. Why? Because "it" hasn't found a way into *your* pocketbook.

You're really upset on the inside, but because you've tapped into the depths of "self control", you've been able to not respond "In-Kind". Yet, at the same time you realize you can no longer converse with this individual or listen to what they're saying to and about you anymore. You know yourself all too well, at some point, you will simply "go off".

Those personal attacks have pushed you to the edge; you're just about to blow a fuse; but you can't leave and "it" is not leaving either.

"*Lord,* what do I do now?", you think to yourself in desperation.

What you can do now, within earshot of the person (since she's still present), or at other times, just by yourself (if they've gone into another part of the house where they can still hear you), is to lighten the weight of the interaction by "Singing a Song".

Take "it" Out-- Without-- Sinning!

I've done this so many times I can't even remember all of the songs I've made up. These are not songs that are going to make the charts, but they are going to address the "Control Freak" issue "on-point" and make the necessary rebuke or correction of the spirit of divination at the same time.

Here's an example of some lyrics to use in this particular situation (choose whatever melody you like):

You don't like me anymore,
Because I won't…
Go to the store
And spend money
On you…
Anymore
So you don't like me
Anymore…
So yoooou…. Oh yes yooou…
Don't like meeee, yes that's meeee
Anymore…
Anymoore…
Anymoooore.

Take "it" Out-- Without-- Sinning!

That's it! You're cracking up, right? Me too, that's exactly what we want to happen. After singing a few more bars, you're anger is now gone, because you're laughing at your own song.

While your daughter thinks you've totally lost it, you notice however, that she is *very intently* listening to the lyrics of your song. She knows the song is about her and this Control Freak interaction. So she starts making fun of your song and fun of you; but you don't care (no CIYA for you anymore), and you just continue to sing and laugh, sing and laugh, aloud.

This continues for just a little while longer and all of a sudden, she leaves the room! And "it" goes with her.

You won!

You're no longer angry, you're not mad with her, you're not thinking about what just happened, you're free! It's over, you're not upset anymore and "you" are free to enjoy Sunday dinner with everyone.

Take "it" Out-- Without-- Sinning!

"When the Lord brought back the captives to Zion we were like those who dream, it seemed so unreal. ***Then were our mouths filled with laughter, and our tongues with singing.*** *Then they said among the nations, the Lord has done great things for them"* (Ps 126:1-2, AMP).

Now, a few of you, may at first glance think this sounds kind of silly, and with this kind of example, perhaps it does; and in fact, perhaps it is ... and *perhaps that's the point!*

Let me tell you, if you've ever been forced to live with a Control Freak Extraordinaire, it's a lifesaver. Singing instantly changes an atmosphere of "hate", into-- a total crack-up, especially if you're a bad singer like me.

"Laughter" and "making light" of the emotionally charged situation that "it" created in an attempt to control your emotions and make you fall into sin, *will utterly defeat the enemy!*

Just keep singing the song over and over, with different tones and a different emphasis on different words. You'll find that you kept "on point" with the "Control Freak issue"; you didn't give-in and do what "it" wanted you to do; you rebuked the living daylights out of "it" with your lyrics, <u>but</u> you didn't sin!

Best of all, "you" are FREE! You're laughing at the conclusion of the encounter, instead of being forced to ask the Control Freak's forgiveness, for your usual sinful response, to their usual Control Freak tactics.

Got it? Great!

Your new artillery is now set. You've seen one simple example of how to use it, but in order for you to become more comfortable with your new weaponry, there are many more examples to come. Soon you will be ready to "prove" or test your arsenal in one of your own *real life* "Control Freak" confrontations.

But before I throw you out there to the wolves, let's first enjoy that long awaited dessert I promised you earlier.

It's time to make some decisions: will it be double chocolate cake, or whipped cream, or fresh berries, or ice cream?

Take "it" Out-- Without-- Sinning!

When confronted by the spirit of divination, you will be called upon to combine two of these four dessert options and then serve that dessert combination to "it".

As you will soon see, some of these dessert combinations are much "heavier" than others.

CHAPTER 31: Dessert is Served

"The desire accomplished is sweet to the soul..." (Prv 13:19, KJV).

We always save the best ... *dessert,* for last. At this point, "the jugular", as best as spiritual principles can be put into words, has been revealed, uncovered, and disclosed.

It's now time to take "it" out! O-U-T!

We've got to put the spirit of divination to death in your life for good. "Its" total and complete eradication is mandatory.

However, we're not planning to use battery acid or arsenic to get the job done. No, no. "It" is going to be eradicated more along the lines of how ants or roaches are attracted to a trap and then sweetened, or sickened to death. We too are going to use something sweet.

Dessert is Served

Yes, "dessert" of all things.

It's time for you to learn how to prepare various dessert combinations to be served to the spirit of divination, in order to readily eliminate your next "Control Freak" dilemma. To this end, we will be serving assorted combinations of the following: double chocolate cake; ice cream; whipped cream; and fresh berries.

For each spirit of control situation you face, you will have four dessert option combinations from which to choose. The dessert combination you choose determines, what you will "say" and/or "do" in response to the spirit of divination.

"My meditation of Him shall be sweet: I will be glad in the LORD" (Ps 104:34). During "Check-In" is when you will need to hear from the Lord in order to decide which dessert combination to serve to "it", the next time "it" tries to contaminate your "quality of life".

As we go through the details of our four dessert combinations, you will readily notice that the "heavier" responses also have the most calories.

Dessert is Served

Below are your four dessert combinations. Study them carefully and prepare yourself to choose wisely:

Dessert Combination #1:

Whipped Cream and Fresh Berries: You Say Nothing; and Submit or Comply;

Dessert Combination #2:

Whipped Cream on Ice Cream: You Say Nothing; and then Resist/Stand or Employ the Principle of Diametric Opposition;

Dessert Combination #3:

Double Chocolate Cake and Fresh Berries: You Correct or Rebuke; and then Submit or Comply;

Dessert Combination #4:

Double Chocolate Cake and Ice Cream: You Correct or Rebuke; and then Resist/Stand or Employ the Principle of Diametric Opposition.

Dessert is Served

This might sound confusing at first glance, but what did you think? This was going be-- a no-brainer?

We have a full chapter dedicated to each of the four dessert combinations coming up. Once you understand these concepts and get the hang of using them, it will eventually become instinctive; almost like a reflex action.

But for now, let me give you a brief explanation of each dessert option:

Choosing between serving "**whipped cream**" or "**double chocolate cake**" has to do with <u>what you do or do not _say_</u>; choosing between serving "**fresh berries**" or "**ice cream**" has to do with <u>what _action_ you take</u>.

What You "Say"

Your "**whipped cream**" response of: "**Say nothing**", means just that. There will be certain times when confronted with the spirit of control that in response, you will serve whipped cream and simply, say nothing.

Dessert is Served

Your "**double chocolate cake**" response to: "**Rebuke and Correct**", is when you will need to say something using one of your Rehearsed Responses to bring rebuke or correction to the demand(s) of the spirit of divination.

"Deflect the harsh words of my critics - but what You say is always so good" (Ps 119:39 MSG). *"How sweet are Thy words unto my taste! Yea, sweeter than honey to my mouth!"* (Ps 119:103, KJV).

The Lord will help you make ready to serve this dessert option in the future.

What You "Do"

Your "**berries**" response requires you to: "**Submit or Comply**" with the action the spirit of control wants you to take. You "Submit" primarily when there is Biblical authority directing you to do so, as long as you are not sinning. You "Comply" when you decide, out of meekness (not weakness, the CIYA), to "do" whatever has been requested of you to do, because it does not conflict with the Lord's directives in your life; <u>and</u> it will have no significant or detrimental effect on your destiny or assignment.

Your "**ice cream**" response will be to: **"Resist/Stand or Employ the Principle of Diametric Opposition"**. This is when you know what action(s) the spirit of control wants you to take; but you either resist or refuse to take that action, or you choose to do the exact opposite of that action by employing "The Principle of Diametric Opposition."

Got it?

The Lord knows you've read the book. He knows the goals and intents of your heart to work on this issue. Now, He's ready to give you what you need <u>to "say" and "do"</u> in any given "Control Freak" situation that arises in the future.

He's ready, are you?

CHAPTER 32: DESSERT OPTION #1: Whipped Cream and Berries; Say Nothing <u>and</u> Then Submit or Comply

----

"He was oppressed, and He was afflicted, yet <u>He opened not His mouth</u>: He is brought as a lamb to the slaughter, and as a sheep before her shearers is dumb, so <u>He openeth not His mouth</u> (Is 53:7, KJV).

While there are several examples of when Jesus opened His mouth, responded to and interacted with others; there were also times when He submitted to the torture and pain of the cross and opened <u>not</u> His mouth. No, not at all.

DESSERT OPTION #1: Whipped Cream and Berries; Say Nothing and Then Submit or Comply

There will be certain times when we are called to exercise "self-control" and do exactly the same thing:

"For even hereunto were ye called: because Christ also suffered for us, leaving us an example, that ye should follow His steps: Who did no sin, neither was guile found in His mouth: Who, when He was reviled, reviled not again; when He suffered, He threatened not; but committed Himself to Him that judgeth righteously (1 Pe 2:21-23, KJV).

Jesus, while being accused by the chief priest and elders, was asked by Pilate to defend Himself; but to Pilate's amazement, Jesus answered *"never a word"*, but submitted Himself to the unjust railings and accusations (Matt 27:12-14, KJV).

Likewise, in your life, don't think that every time you *feel controlled* in a situation that it's the spirit of divination trying to exercise control over your life, because many times, your own irresponsible flesh may be to blame. Additionally, don't think that every time the spirit of divination *is* actually

DESSERT OPTION #1: Whipped Cream and Berries; Say Nothing _and_ Then Submit or Comply

trying to exercise control over your life that you are supposed to resist "it".

Yes, now we get to the good part.

While there is that aspect of discerning and sensing and "feeling" that must be drawn into every spirit of control evaluation; _don't you dare go overboard_ with what you now see and understand and haphazardly think that it applies to every situation you'll ever face, ever again in the future.

Many times control or submission to others is indeed ordained by God. So there are some situations where people are undisputedly controlling you, but because of the dictates in the Word of God, you say nothing in response to "it" and you simply submit.

There is a distinction to be made between the spirit of control and God ordained submission. If you are in a situation where God ordained submission is supposed to take place, then your response to that "control" or the directives given by others is to: **"Say Nothing and Submit or Comply".** During those interactions, many times, you

DESSERT OPTION #1: Whipped Cream and Berries; Say Nothing <u>and</u> Then Submit or Comply

are likely being tested in the area of submission, just like Jesus was.

There are lots of situations where we are called to submit to other people in authority over us and/or intentionally comply with the directives of others:

Here is a list of the biggies:

(1) Employer/Employee Relationships;
(2) Husband/Wife Relationships;
(3) Spiritual Leader Relationships;
(4) Governing Authorities;
(5) Other special case-by-case situations and relationships as the Holy Spirit leads.

Let's take a look at each one of these more closely:

<u>Employer/Employee Relationships</u>

"Servants, be submissive to your masters with all fear, not only to the good and gentle, but also to the harsh" (1 Pet 2:18, NKJV).

DESSERT OPTION #1: Whipped Cream and Berries;
Say Nothing and Then Submit or Comply

"Servants, obey in all things your masters according to the flesh; not with eyeservice, as menpleasers; but in singleness of heart, fearing God" (Col 3:22, KJV).

Most people have no disagreement when their employer is controlling their behavior, obviously because they're getting paid. For the most part this is a contractual arrangement; you can quit whenever you want; they can fire you whenever they want, so it is not necessarily a "control" situation. Yet, the spirit of control rears its ugly head in the work environment all of the time.

The Bible teaches us in sum: to submit to both good and bad bosses, work diligently when the boss is present or absent, and not to "kiss up" or be a "man pleaser" (CIYA).

However, your submission stops, where the practice of sin starts (as was explained in my earlier law firm employment example).

DESSERT OPTION #1: Whipped Cream and Berries; Say Nothing and Then Submit or Comply

Husband/Wife Relationships

"Wives, submit yourselves unto your own husbands, as unto the Lord" (Eph 5:22, KJV).

"Wives, submit yourselves unto your own husbands, as it is fit in the Lord" (Col 3:18, KJV).

To "submit" in this context, is a military term meaning to order or "arrange under" or "to place in an orderly fashion under."[94]   God is God of order; so that means, everyone cannot be the Commander-in-Chief, or a Five-Star General.

However, again, even in a husband/wife relationship, if the wife (or either spouse for that matter), is being asked to sin by the other, your submission should stop, when the directive to sin starts.

For example, if a husband wants his wife to help him go rob a bank like Bonnie and Clyde, she should not submit or

---

[94] Strong's #5293, transliterated "Hupotasso".

DESSERT OPTION #1: Whipped Cream and Berries; Say Nothing and Then Submit or Comply

comply, no matter how much debt she's racked up on the Visa card.

If a husband wants to view porn with his wife and she refuses, she has not done anything wrong or un-submissive; she has simply refused to submit to sinful behavior.

When a husband wants his wife to sign tax returns that are fraudulent, false, or misleading; it is not wrong for the wife to refuse to submit, because "each of us shall give account of *himself* to God" (Ro 14:12, KJV).

Those are clear-cut examples where submission would mean sin; so the woman should not submit. However, there are also other situations where the line gets a bit blurred and more difficult to evaluate, such as with issues of disrespect, abusive language, lack of consideration, refusal to work, or contribute to the household, etc.

You even have some women who are so easily offended that they think they have grounds for divorce if their husband called them the "B" word, once. I actually had a

DESSERT OPTION #1: Whipped Cream and Berries; Say Nothing and Then Submit or Comply

call into the radio program from a husband who, in the heat of the moment during an argument, called his wife the "B" word, *one time*. Though he was repentant, she was unforgiving. She was making ready to divorce him. My response to the husband, was that the Prima Donna needed to get over it and forgive him.

Understand that depending on the circumstances, as a wife, you may be called on by God to use any one of the four dessert options in your marital relationship; most often times, this first one.

Spiritual Leader Relationships

"Obey them that have the rule over you, and submit yourselves: for they watch for your souls, as they that must give account, that they may do it with joy, and not with grief: for that is unprofitable for you" (Heb 13:17, KJV).

If the Lord has placed you in a church, or serving in a ministry, whatever the Leader says-- goes. Don't get attitude about it, don't even think you know better about it (even if you do). For whatever reason (which is none of

DESSERT OPTION #1: Whipped Cream and Berries;
Say Nothing _and_ Then Submit or Comply

your business), God has given them the leadership position and placed them in authority over you. Comply, submit, serve and don't have an attitude or "talk smack" about them either.

Now, that's the general rule. The general rule should be implemented unless and until they tell you they want you to do something wrong, or sinful; _or_ when the Lord gives you a "go forward" or "move on" directive, and you leave from under their authority.

In any case, here again, submission stops where sin starts. This reminds me of the Marcus Lamb, Daystar situation and the lawsuits that were brought by previous employees of Daystar. I read a few of the new stories and their claim, as best I remember, was that they believed they were being hired to work in a "Christian" environment; and that they suffered "great emotional pain" while on the job, because they were directed to do things to help hide or

DESSERT OPTION #1: Whipped Cream and Berries;
Say Nothing <u>and</u> Then Submit or Comply

cover up the fact that Marcus Lamb was having an affair from his wife Joni.[95]

This is a perfect example of where those Daystar employees were wrong. Yes, Marcus was wrong for the sin, but the employees should have never helped hide the sin in the first place!

They should have gone to Marcus and confronted him with his sin; if that didn't work, they should have gone to his wife Joni and told her; and if that didn't work … *well* by then, they should have already been fired. Ha!

Now stop it! God would have honored their actions. You *never* have to fear "doing right" in the face of wrongdoing. It's a test! This is where your faith comes in, risking your livelihood, facing your "fear of man" and carrying out the rebuke/correction despite what appears to be the ultimate adverse consequence … your not being able to make your mortgage payment.

---

[95] CRIMESIDER, December 3, 2010, article entitled: *Rev. Marcus Lamb of DayStar TV Faces Unusual Lawsuit After Admitting Affair.*

DESSERT OPTION #1: Whipped Cream and Berries; Say Nothing and Then Submit or Comply

Think about it, what if one of these Daystar employees would have handled the situation differently way back in the beginning? Perhaps there would have been repentance a whole lot sooner; and there certainly wouldn't have been any of these silly "emotional distress" lawsuits.

Marcus Lamb needed someone like a Nathan to do the confronting early on. The Lord gave all of those Daystar employees the ball and they all fumbled.

You're emotionally distressed, Daystar employees, because *you sinned* by covering up for someone else who was practicing sin.

So case dismissed!

Submit to Governing Authorities

"Obey the government, for God is the one who put it there. All governments have been placed in power by God. So those who refuse to obey the laws of the land are refusing to obey God, and punishment will follow" (Ro 13:1-2 NLT).

DESSERT OPTION #1: Whipped Cream and Berries; Say Nothing and Then Submit or Comply

"Submit yourselves to every ordinance of man for the Lord's sake: whether it be to the king, as supreme; Or unto governors, as unto them that are sent by Him for the punishment of evildoers, and for the praise of them that do well" (1 Pe 2:13-14, KJV).

We are supposed to submit to all governing authorities: the laws of the land, police enforcing those laws, court systems and court orders, etc. Only on very rare occasion, should we fail to do so.

Unlike Peter, who cut off the ear of Malchus, Jesus did not resist when the authorities came to the Garden of Gethsemane and "took Him", "bound Him" and "led Him away" (Jn 18:10-13). Jesus acted in submission to the will of the Father for His life.

After being questioned about whether or not Jesus paid His taxes, Jesus directed Peter where to go and get tax money to pay tribute for Himself and Peter (Matt 17:24-27).

In other words, these are situations where you may have the *ability* to resist; but, in obedience to the laws, or the

DESSERT OPTION #1: Whipped Cream and Berries; Say Nothing <u>and</u> Then Submit or Comply

authorities in your life, or the system of justice in general, or by some special directive from the Lord, you submit and comply in that situation. The Lord honors those, who honor these positions of authority.

<u>Other Situations and Relationships</u>

There are other situations and relationships where you may well know that the spirit of control is at work trying to get you to act in a certain manner. So you Check-In with the Lord and tell Him what you see, He confirms it; and yet, He may direct you to overlook it, let it go, or stay right where you are. Sometimes, He'll even tell you to just "take it like a man" (or woman), even though you're being mistreated.

"Be watchful, stand firm in the faith, act like men, be strong" (1 Cor 16:13, ESV).

There are sometimes that God's will for your life, is to take mistreatment; and that mistreatment *is* a type of control. I've been in those kinds of situations, but I Checked-In and said, *"Lord, You do see that, right?"*

DESSERT OPTION #1: Whipped Cream and Berries; Say Nothing _and_ Then Submit or Comply

"Yes"

"Did you want me to do anything about it?"

"No"

So you just "take it like a man", you just take it and "stand" (Eph 6:13, KJV).

We know that everyone will be judged, justly, for everything they have done. But have you ever thought about how exactly the Lord is going to do this?

Have you ever considered the possibility that being mistreated by others may not actually be _all about you_? Have you ever considered that the Lord may intend on allowing you to suffer a wrong, because He may want to use that interaction as supporting evidence for His final judgment _and_ because He knows you can handle it?

"Therefore the wisdom of God also said, 'I will send them prophets and apostles, and some of them they will kill and persecute, that the blood of all the prophets which was

DESSERT OPTION #1: Whipped Cream and Berries; Say Nothing and Then Submit or Comply

shed from the foundation of the world may be required of this generation" (Lu 11:49-50, NKJV).

When that person ultimately goes before the Lord, when the books are opened and the movie screen of their life plays before them; you just may be one of the many characters they mistreated in their story. When the Lord tells them, "You were told, you were accountable, and yet, you didn't listen, you did this instead." He may ultimately intend to use your interaction with that person to support His final determination.

We must realize that submitting our lives to the Lord means that He gets to use our lives for the hard stuff too, not just the great and glorious things. He will use your life to be mistreated, but it will always be for a very good reason.

*"That I may know Him, and the power of His resurrection, and the **fellowship of His sufferings**, being made conformable unto His death"* (Phil 3:10, KJV).

Let's look to our example (Heb 12:1-2) and something that Jesus said about His *life* prior to His *death*: *"No man taketh*

DESSERT OPTION #1: Whipped Cream and Berries; Say Nothing and Then Submit or Comply

it from me, but I lay it down of Myself. I have power to lay it down, and I have power to take it again" (Jn 10:18, KJV).

Speaking of Moses, a type of Christ in the Old Testament (Heb 3:1-6), the Bible says, *"Now the man Moses was very meek, above all the men which were upon the face of the earth"* (Numbers 12:3). Speaking of Himself, Jesus said, *"I am meek and lowly in heart"* (Matt 11:29).

With this first dessert combination when you, "**Just say Nothing and Submit or Comply**", realize that the spirit of divination is *not really controlling you* because you *could* choose to respond either way to "it". But just as Jesus submitted to His own death on the cross, you too *choose* to respond how God wants you to respond, which when serving this first dessert combination, happens to be in submission.

While it may *appear* as if you are being controlled (just like it *appeared* with Jesus), you're really not-- because you're going to allow this to happen too. In Jesus' case it was a demonstration of His meekness, or His power under control. When you're intentionally demonstrating a spirit of

DESSERT OPTION #1: Whipped Cream and Berries; Say Nothing and Then Submit or Comply

meekness towards an individual, you are not being controlled either.

The key is that you do this out of "meekness" because you "choose" to and it's not done out of any "weakness" or CIYA. When exercising this first dessert option, you don't say anything to the person at all; you just comply.

But before you comply, you "Check-In" with the Lord and make sure your compliance is not done out of weakness, but out of meekness. Then, let them have their way. This type of submission may be what the Lord directs, even when the demanded control is exercised by devils.

Yes, devils.

Remember that interaction, where Jesus Himself complied with the request of the devils He had cast out of that young man, by allowing them to enter into a nearby herd of swine? Though they were obviously under His command, in response, Jesus did not correct or rebuke that request. He just said, "Go" (Matt 8:28-34, KJV).

DESSERT OPTION #1: Whipped Cream and Berries; Say Nothing and Then Submit or Comply

Jesus' compliance to this request was obviously in demonstration of His meekness, not His weakness or inability to control the situation. After all, He had just cast those devils out of the young man.

This, **"Say Nothing and Submit or Comply"** dessert combination is used in situations where you know you could put a stop to the control someone is trying to exercise over you, but *you allow it* to go on. You don't get angry or mad or resentful; that's weakness, not meekness. You don't become a Control Freaking mess! You've "Checked-In" with Him and this is the chosen dessert option He wants you to serve.

However, there are three important considerations *before* ever serving this particular dessert combination: (1) that the situation is not sin and/or does not undermine the Word of God; (2) that it doesn't cause another person to sin; and (3) that the situation does not detract or derail you from your God-given destiny or assignment.

DESSERT OPTION #1: Whipped Cream and Berries; Say Nothing and Then Submit or Comply

Here are some examples of: **"Say Nothing and Submit or Comply"**:

Maybe it's a situation with your grandchild: You know they're crying in an attempt to get you to adhere to their demand for yet, another cookie. You "Check-In" with the Lord, He says its "ok" and you go ahead and give them the cookie; despite the fact you know, that those big blue eyes have just, controlled your behavior.

It may be a situation with your parents and the fact that you now realize that your parents use "guilt trips" to control your behavior. Yet, you also know that the Bible says:

"Honour thy father and mother; (which is the first commandment with promise;) That it may be well with thee, and thou mayest live long on the earth" (Eph 6:2-3, KJV).

"Children, obey your parents in all things: for this is well pleasing unto the Lord" (Col 3:20, KJV).

Therefore, you may permit the "guilt" to cause you to take actions that you may not otherwise take (even when you don't think they are necessarily from God); but since He says its "ok", you go on ahead.

It may be a situation with anyone else with whom you have an interpersonal relationship and you know the Bible says:

"Let nothing be done through strife or vainglory; but in lowliness of mind let each esteem others better than themselves. Look not every man on his own things, but every man also on the things of others" (Phil 2:3-4, KJV).

"Submitting yourselves one to another in the fear of God" (Eph 5:21, KJV).

"As we have therefore opportunity, let us do good unto all men, especially unto them who are of the household of faith" (Gal 6:10, KJV).

There may be other people who have been in your life for a long time, or yet others who are merely passing through, but at one time or another, with His consent, you may choose out of meekness to submit yourself to their request under the same rule of thumb: (1) the situation is not sin

DESSERT OPTION #1: Whipped Cream and Berries; Say Nothing and Then Submit or Comply

and/or does not undermine the Word of God; (2) it doesn't cause another person to sin; and (3) the situation does not detract or derail you from your God-given destiny or assignment.

So you let your girlfriend *always* choose where you eat out for dinner, *every time.*

You allow your neighbor to borrow milk and never replace it, again and again.

You give-in to your co-worker's obnoxious personality and just let them ramble on and on, without cutting off the conversation.

Get the idea?

Good.

So with our first dessert combination, as you see, there is very little commotion or conflict. But, let's now throw a few more calories into the equation by choosing some rich ice cream to serve to "it" and see what happens next.

DESSERT OPTION #1: Whipped Cream and Berries; Say Nothing <u>and</u> Then Submit or Comply

"CONTROL FREAK"

CHAPTER 33: DESSERT OPTION #2: Whipped Cream on Ice Cream; Say Nothing and Then Resist/Stand or Employ the Principle of Diametric Opposition

In situations where you **"Say Nothing and Stand or Employ the Principle of Diametric Opposition"**; the spirit of control will come in and address you in some manner, using either verbal or non-verbal communication which expresses "its" desired action. You simply refuse to give "it" the time of day, so you **"Say Nothing"**, that's nada, zero; and you do the **"Exact Opposite"** of what "it" wants you to do.

DESSERT OPTION #2: Whipped Cream on Ice Cream; Say Nothing and Then Resist/Stand or Employ the Principle of Diametric Opposition

Here are a few Biblical examples of when Jesus served up Dessert Option #2:

They murmured about Jesus inviting Himself, to eat at the home of Zaccheaus, because he was a 'sinner'. Jesus said nothing to them in response, but went anyway and that day Zaccheaus got saved (Lu 19:1-9).

In John chapter 6 it says, *"Therefore when Jesus perceived that they were about to come and take Him by force to make Him king, He departed again to the mountain by Himself alone"* (Jn 6:15). It wasn't time for Jesus to be made King, it was time for Him to suffer and die on the cross for our sins. He did not allow the desires of the people, no matter how nice they were, to thwart the plan of the Father for His life here on earth.

Wow! Take a very close look at this situation because it's pretty amazing. The people were trying to control Jesus to the point of making Him "King"-- it was obviously a promotion. In response, He just said nothing and split.

DESSERT OPTION #2: Whipped Cream on Ice Cream; Say Nothing _and_ Then Resist/Stand or Employ the Principle of Diametric Opposition

We learn by this example that the spirit of control can work in even _seemingly_ "good" or positive ways that are still contrary to the plan of God. Only those in total submission to the Lord, have that level of meekness necessary to _disallow_ themselves to be raised up at the beckoning of man. Look, not just anyone can do that.

Dessert Option #2 should almost always be employed with abusive relationships. There are several different kinds of abuse:

(1)   <u>Physical Abuse:</u> when bodily injury or threat of bodily injury, contact, or control is present;

(2)   <u>Verbal Abuse:</u> which has two components. First, where harsh demeaning words _emotionally_ damage a person, making them feel as if they're a "nobody"; and second, where words are intended to inflict _mental_ anguish, such as living under threats, fear, or ultimatums;

DESSERT OPTION #2: Whipped Cream on Ice Cream: Say Nothing and Then Resist/Stand or Employ the Principle of Diametric Opposition

(3) Financial Abuse: when money is used to control your behavior (which we've already covered in great detail);

(4) Spiritual Abuse: can range from someone calling into question your "Christianity" or your commitment to God, in an attempt to control your behavior to their benefit, to the more severe case, like what happened in Waco Texas;

(5) Sexual Abuse: which, *includes* forcible rape situations, as well as others, based on demands for sex, criticisms in performance, comparisons with other sexual partners, lack of emotional connection and the like.

The first thing to know, is that if you're in one of these relationships you must get out. Now! It is never smart to enter into a verbal conflict with an abuser; they will tear you up and spit you out-- in no time flat. What's worse is that

DESSERT OPTION #2: Whipped Cream on Ice Cream; Say Nothing and Then Resist/Stand or Employ the Principle of Diametric Opposition

any verbal conflict you have with an abuser, will only cause them to get more abusive and violent towards you.

It's better not to talk at all, but just do the opposite of what they're demanding of you. Many times, for your own safety and sanity, that will mean leaving not only their presence, but obviously, leaving the relationship entirely.

The fact is, you should already know by now that your verbal confrontations and conflicts with this person have gotten you absolutely nowhere ... *fast.* Remember what they say about the definition of "insanity", it's "doing the same thing, over and over and over, and yet, expecting a different result". *You* need to change *your "usual" response* and instead of battling a power that has proven itself too strong for you to handle, it's time for you to get up and get out! And, **"Say Nothing"** while you're doing so.

Stop your "stronghold thinking" about it and stop worrying about what other people will say. You've read enough of

DESSERT OPTION #2: Whipped Cream on Ice Cream: Say Nothing and Then Resist/Stand or Employ the Principle of Diametric Opposition

this text to know it's the enemy controlling your life. So get out and get yourself together.

I had a call from a woman on the radio that had been involved in her first physically abusive relationship, which had been going on for almost two years. After a recent more serious incident occurred, she went to the police to file a report against the man. At which point, the man filed a civil restraining order against her; and she in turn, filed the same against him.

The District Attorney refused to prosecute her criminal case and so she was left with defending and prosecuting the consolidated civil restraining order matters, in pro per, against the boyfriend's Beverly Hills attorney.

She was calling to ask me if she should even bother to hire a lawyer for the civil case because, she reasoned: "She shouldn't have to spend money on an attorney since she was the 'victim'". She also mentioned still having fond feelings for this person, and concerns over his health and

DESSERT OPTION #2: Whipped Cream on Ice Cream; Say Nothing and Then Resist/Stand or Employ the Principle of Diametric Opposition

welfare. In fact, she admitted that she went out of her way to continue to do "nice" things for him despite and subsequent to, this last episode of abusive behavior.

It was an extended conversation, but the long and short of it from my perspective was, that she was looking for confirmation that she did not have to put up her best fight against him in court; though naturally, she didn't say as much outright.

It seemed as if she wanted me to advise her that she didn't need to hire an attorney; and that she didn't need to fight to defend her position in court, which would have allowed him to basically "get away" with this last episode of physical abuse.

Christian women staying in abusive relationships are not only being controlled by the actions of their abusers; but are also being controlled by the "religious spirit" of control. They use Christian concepts and scripture, such as

DESSERT OPTION #2: Whipped Cream on Ice Cream: Say Nothing and Then Resist/Stand or Employ the Principle of Diametric Opposition

"forgive" and "love" to justify their decision to stay connected with their spirit of divination-driven, heartthrobs.

This is what she was doing.

After confirming to her that everyone would agree the man was abusive, I tried to bring her to the realization that there was something about her that she needed to examine and fix before she entered into another relationship. Each and every time I made any comment that even remotely intimated that she had corrections to make in her own life, the "religious spirit" kicked in to justify and support every single solitary action she continued to take as it related to this man; even up to not wanting to obtain an attorney to make sure she had a good defense and prosecution in the consolidated civil restraining order matters.

It didn't matter what angle I tried to use to get her to examine herself, she immediately shut it down with some Christianized brainwashed commentary, which protected

DESSERT OPTION #2: Whipped Cream on Ice Cream: Say Nothing and Then Resist/Stand or Employ the Principle of Diametric Opposition

her actions and justified her enabling behavior. "It" actually even tried to make me look bad; "unloving" in particular.

I butted up against that "religious spirit" of control working hard and fast in and through her, to the point where it almost appeared as if I was picking on her; but I wasn't. I knew something about what she was doing that she herself had failed to yet realize; but that she was certainly never going to admit to "live" on the air, not that day anyway.

It's the same type of thing I hear all the time, "I have to love him like Christ" "I was only doing what any good Christian woman would do for him" "I must forgive him and show him I still care for his soul" "I had to keep in contact, otherwise I could have been in the sin of, 'holding a grudge'". The list goes on and on and on and on.

That is the "religious spirit" of control, working in the life of the controlled person, justifying the control with Christianese, Christian lingo, Christian principles; but it's

DESSERT OPTION #2: Whipped Cream on Ice Cream: Say Nothing and Then Resist/Stand or Employ the Principle of Diametric Opposition

really all a big cover up for the enabler's weaknesses (the CIYA).

In this case, there was no marriage and there were no children. Therefore, this lady didn't have to stay in this relationship for *any reason* whatsoever; except of course, her own weaknesses. That was the point I was trying to get her to realize.

Now, I'm not condoning staying in any physically abusive relationship; but when you're married to an abusive person, or have children with an abusive person, it makes it much harder to break free. On the other hand, when there aren't any ties like that and you stay in it for years? Well, that's another story.

Abusive relationships are a major wile of the enemy used to control your life. If you're a Christian, you can justify staying in those kinds of relationships with various Christian excuses, all the while claiming your decision is based on

DESSERT OPTION #2: Whipped Cream on Ice Cream; Say Nothing and Then Resist/Stand or Employ the Principle of Diametric Opposition

"godliness" when in reality, it's only based on "weakness" (the CIYA).

Abuse equals control; and ultimately "its" control will take over your entire being! Your entire personality! It won't be just one action that will be under the control of the spirit of divination; it will be your entire heart, soul, mind, body and strength. Over time, eventually, the "you" that everyone used to know, will no longer exist.

People who are living in abusive relationships become unfruitful for the Kingdom pretty early on, because they spend each day in emotional turmoil barely surviving. When they are in that condition perpetually, they can't function well in society; they can't think about anything else but simply trying to endure emotionally, mentally, physically, and spiritually. Ultimately, if the abused person is not delivered from that environment, their entire life will become nothing but an attempt to try and stay emotionally stable enough *not* to commit suicide.

DESSERT OPTION #2: Whipped Cream on Ice Cream; Say Nothing and Then Resist/Stand or Employ the Principle of Diametric Opposition

So if you're in one of these types of relationships, it's time to serve Dessert Option #2, **"Say Nothing and Employ the Principle of Diametric Opposition"** to everything they're wanting you to do and then, get on out of town! No "Dear John" notes, necessary.

Time now to increase our caloric intake, by adding some Double Chocolate cake to our dessert combinations. Here is where sharing dessert starts to get more interesting, innovative, and far "weightier".

DESSERT OPTION #3: Double Chocolate Cake and Fresh Berries; Correct/Rebuke and Then Submit or Comply

CHAPTER 34: DESSERT OPTION #3: Double Chocolate Cake and Fresh Berries; Correct/Rebuke and Then Submit or Comply

----

With this next dessert combination, you are going to ultimately submit, but *before* you do, you are going *to say something* (usually a Rehearsed Response); that will bring correction to that person who is attempting to control your behavior.

Correction and/or rebuke are "Biblical", in both principle and practice, by the way. Yet, many people are so afraid to "rock the boat" that they dare never engage in it.

DESSERT OPTION #3: Double Chocolate Cake and Fresh Berries; Correct/Rebuke and Then Submit or Comply

"Open rebuke is better than secret love" (Prv 27:5, KJV).

"Brethren, if a man be overtaken in a fault, ye which are spiritual, restore such an one in the spirit of meekness; considering thyself, lest thou also be tempted" (Gal 6:1, KJV).

"Brethren, if anyone among you wanders from the truth, and someone turns him back, let him know that he who turns a sinner from the error of his way will save a soul from death and cover a multitude of sins" (Ja 5:19-20, NKJV).

"He who says to the wicked, 'You are righteous', him the people will curse; Nations will abhor him. But those who rebuke the wicked will have delight, And a good blessing will come upon them" (Prv 24:24-25, NKJV).

If you fail to ever correct or rebuke the spirit of divination working in and through the controlling people in your life,

DESSERT OPTION #3: Double Chocolate Cake and Fresh Berries; Correct/Rebuke and Then Submit or Comply

"it" will cause your relationships to "run hog wild". Indeed, if left unchecked, the spirit of control will gain so much territory in your life; that you too may end up like one of those pigs, aspiring to go jump off a cliff (Matt 8:28-34).

If you don't agree with someone and you have good cause, (like a Scriptural backing); you have a duty to say so … without sinning (of course). Otherwise, your failure to correct implies your complicity with the situation.

It's the classic, "Give 'em an inch and they'll take a mile" type of relational scenario. The CIYA is the reason behind your failure to bring correction in these kinds of relationships.

If and when God tells you to correct someone, you'd better do it! The Lord uses His Spirit and His children to correct, His children. Again, if you think about it, whom else does He have? If you're afraid to bring correction to those in

DESSERT OPTION #3: Double Chocolate Cake and Fresh Berries; Correct/Rebuke and Then Submit or Comply

your life to whom it is due, it's because you're still wagging your "tail", fearing man (the CIYA).

Don't worry about how the other person will respond! I can already tell you it won't be pretty. No one ... rarely anyone *whenever* corrected, says: *"You know, you're so right; I really have to do something about that sin in my life. Gosh, thanks for bringing that to my attention, I just love you my brother."*

Ha! Rather, you can expect the usual clawing motion of a wild animal, when backed into a corner, trying to defend itself. *"You're wrong! That's <u>not</u> what I'm doing".* The personal attacks on *your character* or about something that *you do* wrong will always come, shortly thereafter.

Now I'm not talking about turning you into one of those Pharisaical, legalistic "Christians" who can find something to criticize with anything and anyone they ever encounter.

DESSERT OPTION #3: Double Chocolate Cake and Fresh Berries; Correct/Rebuke and Then Submit or Comply

You know who they are, those First-Class Controllers, who have a self-appointed "ministry" to go around correcting everyone who crosses their path, including people with whom they don't even have a relationship.

No! Not what I'm talking about.

I'm talking about Spirit-led correction done out of love and out of bettering the person and your relationship with that person. It usually happens in instances when God is telling you to do it, but *you really don't want to;* yet He continues to press.

As opposed to the current day Pharisee, who is always up and running, just raring to go correct someone, anybody ... where? Where? Where are they? (That's "the flesh" and not at all the Holy Spirit).

When the Lord leads you to approach someone who needs to be corrected, it's to be considered a privilege that cannot

DESSERT OPTION #3: Double Chocolate Cake and Fresh Berries; Correct/Rebuke and Then Submit or Comply

be taken lightly. The way you handle the situation must be cautiously and circumspectly (Gal 6:1). Yet, some Christians sway from this responsibility claiming, "I don't want to judge".

However, when you have the Word of God behind you and you have behavior in clear violation, from either the actions you have witnessed or that they have admitted; and you match-up the two and it amounts to disobedience to the Word of God, that is not judging.

Judging is when you hypothesize about a person's motives for their behavior, whether good or bad. Whenever you correct/rebuke, you must be sure not to judge a person's motives for *why* they're doing what they're doing. You cannot judge the heart, or inward intentions; you can only judge their fruit, their outward actions, or their statements (Lu 6:45).

DESSERT OPTION #3: Double Chocolate Cake and Fresh Berries; Correct/Rebuke and Then Submit or Comply

The best way to **"Correct/Rebuke"** anyone when serving this dessert combination is with the Word of God, just like Jesus rebuked the devil in the wilderness. However, many times you can get caught in a situation or circumstance and are unable to think of a Scripture to use. In those cases you will need to employ Biblical precepts, or "Rehearsed Responses", while using common day vernacular that will bring the necessary rebuke or correction to the situation.

Here are some Biblical examples of the **"Correct/Rebuke and then Submit or Comply"** dessert combination:

The first miracle Jesus ever performed was after being asked by His mother to do something about the wine shortage at a wedding celebration. In response, Jesus said, *"Woman what do I have to do with thee, mine hour is not yet come"* (Jn 2:4, KJV).

Yet we know by the story, that Jesus obviously did something "big time" by changing water into wine; and not

DESSERT OPTION #3: Double Chocolate Cake and Fresh Berries; Correct/Rebuke and Then Submit or Comply

only that, but it was the best wine that the partygoers had tasted all night.

Notwithstanding, when you look at what Jesus first said *before* performing the miracle (or submitting to His mother's request), it was really a rebuke or correction of His mother.

Take a look at a few translations of Jesus' initial correction of His mother Mary:

"Dear woman, why do you involve Me?" Jesus replied. "My time has not yet come" (Jn 2:4 NIV).

"Jesus said to her, Woman, this is not your business; My time is still to come" (Jn 2:4, BEE).

"You must not tell Me what to do," Jesus replied. "My time has not yet come" (Jn 2:4, GNT).

DESSERT OPTION #3: Double Chocolate Cake and Fresh Berries; Correct/Rebuke and Then Submit or Comply

"Jesus said, "Is that any of our business, Mother - yours or Mine? This isn't My time. Don't push Me" (Jn 2:4, MSG).

This is a perfect example of serving Dessert Option #3: **"Correct/Rebuke and then Submit or Comply",** to the request, demand, or directive of another person.

Here's another example, *"And when He was twelve years old, they went up to Jerusalem after the custom of the feast. And when they had fulfilled the days, as they returned, the child Jesus tarried behind in Jerusalem; and Joseph and His mother knew not of it. But they, supposing Him to have been in the company, went a day's journey; and they sought Him among their kinsfolk and acquaintance. And when they found Him not, they turned back again to Jerusalem, seeking Him. And it came to pass, that after three days they found Him in the temple, sitting in the midst of the doctors, both hearing them, and asking them questions. And all that heard Him were astonished at His understanding and answers. And when*

DESSERT OPTION #3: Double Chocolate Cake and Fresh Berries; Correct/Rebuke and Then Submit or Comply

they saw Him, they were amazed: and his mother said unto Him, Son, why hast thou thus dealt with us? Behold, thy father and I have sought thee sorrowing. And He said unto them, How is it that ye sought Me? wist ye not that I must be about My Father's business? And they understood not the saying which He spake unto them. And He went down with them, and came to Nazareth, and was subject unto them..." (Lu 2:42-51, KJV).

Here Jesus was doing the work of His Father in heaven; and His parents came in, interrupted Him and basically wanted to take Him home, and maybe even to the back of the woodshed on the way. He gently rebukes their interruption of Kingdom work and yet ultimately, He submits to them.

Here's another example: After all the other disciples, except for Thomas, had an opportunity to see His scarred hands and body, Thomas said that he needed to see it for himself, or else he would not believe. Jesus complied with

DESSERT OPTION #3: Double Chocolate Cake and Fresh Berries; Correct/Rebuke and Then Submit or Comply

the request and showed Thomas what he wanted to see, and then corrected him by saying, *"Blessed are they who have not seen, yet believe"* (Jn 20:24-27, KJV).

Consider the woman from Canaan whose daughter was grievously vexed by a devil; at first Jesus totally ignored her. Then, He corrected her by saying that, what He had was not for her, it was for "the house of Israel". Yet she persisted.

Jesus then, "pushed the envelope" of politeness and rebuked her by impliedly calling her daughter a dog. In spite of all of that, by the end of the conversation Jesus complied with the woman's request and healed her daughter (Matt 15:22-28).

Here's another: After Judas' identifying kiss of Jesus, Peter drew the sword and cut off the ear of the high priest's servant. Jesus corrected Peter by essentially saying, I don't need your sword, I've got plenty of angels if I need

DESSERT OPTION #3: Double Chocolate Cake and Fresh Berries; Correct/Rebuke <u>and</u> Then Submit or Comply

them, but I must submit to fulfill God's plan for My life (Matt 26:49-54).

With Dessert Option #3, you tell that person you believe they are wrong in their position, and why, and "in love" of course; but you still do what they've asked you to do. All the while remembering our bright line distinction of being certain that what you are asked to do is not a sin; nor causes others to sin; nor substantively effects your destiny or any directive that you've already received from the Lord.

Here are some real life examples of the **"Correct/Rebuke and then Submit or Comply"** dessert option:

This is your classic married couple situation, where the wife disagrees with a decision the husband wants to make. Say there is conflict over which private school the couple should enroll their children into; the closer more expensive school (says wife); the less expensive school that is much farther away (says husband).

DESSERT OPTION #3: Double Chocolate Cake and Fresh Berries; Correct/Rebuke and Then Submit or Comply

The wife (a stay at home mother), thinks she should be the one with more say in the situation, since she is responsible to drive the children to and from school everyday; and since she is more "hands on" when it comes to classes, communication with teachers, homework, extra curricular activities, etc.

The husband (as the spiritual leader of the home and provider of the money to afford "private school" in the first place), thinks he should be the one to ultimately decide what the family can afford.

Now both sides have substantive reasons for their position, both Biblical and practical. Where the spirit of control comes into play, is when the husband gets so irked by the manner in which the wife states her case; that in his anger he doesn't even listen to a word she says and demands his way by yelling something like, "Submit woman!"

DESSERT OPTION #3: Double Chocolate Cake and Fresh Berries; Correct/Rebuke and Then Submit or Comply

This usually happens when the wife thinks she knows what's best and she has become personally offended by the husband's perceived ignorance. She cannot believe her husband could be so inconsiderate, especially given all that she does for him and the children. She cooks and cleans, makes sure they get to school and everywhere else they need to be, on time; and she takes very good care of her husband and his needs.

As a result, the wife cannot fathom how he could ever dream of making her drive that much farther, every day, just to save a few dollars? Due to hours of ruminating over her husband's gross insensitivity and inconsideration, the wife has angered herself to a point of emotional upset before ever releasing the first word used to convey her perspective, out of her mouth.

Ladies, the guys automatically turn off to the "control tactic" of emotion, whining, screeching and nagging, no matter how rational your underlying argument. So it's better to

DESSERT OPTION #3: Double Chocolate Cake and Fresh Berries; Correct/Rebuke and Then Submit or Comply

state your case in terms of suggestions, or questions, *not* demands or ultimatums, like every other "Control Freak" would do in this instance.

State your case unemotionally; use the wit and the personality that attracted him to you in the first place. All the while knowing that at the end of the day, if he doesn't agree, that he ultimately gets to be the *one* to decide. Coming into line with this fact, and getting over it now, will help you to <u>not</u> become a "baggage carrier" along with everything else that you do.

There are however, some husbands who wrongfully call it "disrespect" when a wife (without sinning), simply disagrees with her husband's position. Come on! She needs to be allowed to *voice her opinion and her reasons,* during which, you should at least *pretend* like you're listening and considering her perspective.

DESSERT OPTION #3: Double Chocolate Cake and Fresh Berries; Correct/Rebuke and <u>Then</u> Submit or Comply

Your role is not that of a dictator where anyone whose mouth disagrees with yours must be stopped. Better yet, a smart man, one who is not "dictator-ly insecure", will ask his wife what she thinks *before he* even decides; and while voicing her opinion, he will listen with an open heart.

Look man, you married her; she must have had something to bring to the table. There are a lot of women out there who may have *no experience* in any given situation, but have a lot of wisdom from the Lord. Wisdom from above, wins out over experience from beneath, every single time.

So, for the husbands, it's much better if you inquire of your wife and allow her to speak freely about any issue and not take it as some challenge to your manhood, or disrespect; especially if she disagrees with your perspective. There's something about at least *feeling like you've been listened to,* rather than just automatically shut down, that helps in a woman's role of submission and at least minimizes the

DESSERT OPTION #3: Double Chocolate Cake and Fresh Berries; Correct/Rebuke <u>and</u> Then Submit or Comply

nagging, kicking, and screaming that usually takes place along the rest of the way.

Here's another example: Say you have one of those friends who, whenever you hook up with them to go anywhere or do anything, it always ends up being *all about them*. In other words, they control where you go, where you eat, what movie you see, how long you stay, when you get up and leave the restaurant, how much you tip, when you stop to window shop, what you talk about, even when you take a restroom break … you get the idea.

While lo and behold, for some *unknown* reason, you seem to be the *only friend* this person has ... and no wonder? ("Control Freak", that they are.)

It may be one of your God-given assignments as a good and loving "friend" to find a way to bring correction to his/her "rulership" mentality and just tell them the truth. We

DESSERT OPTION #3: Double Chocolate Cake and Fresh Berries; Correct/Rebuke and Then Submit or Comply

will soon get to a wide variety of ways to do that kind of thing.

This same kind of Dessert Option #3 can also be served in church settings. It is actually a very good dessert combination to serve to "volunteers" who complain so much about the various factors and conditions related to the job they're "volunteering" to do, that you wonder, "Why on earth are you even volunteering?"

I witnessed this at a church where a person's volunteer responsibility was to re-supply the tithing envelopes and pens in the church pews. He didn't want any help from anybody; he wanted to do it *all alone*.

Yet, each and every week, leaders or other workers in the church had to drop everything they were doing in order to listen to him complain about the fact that the supplies weren't exactly as, where, and how, he wanted them to be. They were the wrong kind, in the wrong location, somebody

DESSERT OPTION #3: Double Chocolate Cake and Fresh Berries; Correct/Rebuke and Then Submit or Comply

had moved the boxes where the pens were; if the envelopes had gotten thrown together in a box, somebody else had to reorganize them to go in uniform direction, *before* he could ever dream of starting his "volunteer" work.

He would complain about the difficulties of his task and leave voice mails marked urgent to church staff at 7:00 in the morning about misplaced supplies. He would carry on this same substantive conversation (even though his complaints had already been corrected), for the remainder of each week. The dawning of every new week inevitably brought him something else to complain about.

The spirit of divination working in and through this man caused church staff and other volunteers to become totally distracted from focusing on the "real work" God had for them to accomplish on any given day. This "volunteer" ended up consuming the time and energy of teaching pastors and others church leaders who were either listening to his complaints; catering to his demands; or

DESSERT OPTION #3: Double Chocolate Cake and Fresh Berries; Correct/Rebuke and Then Submit or Comply

wasting their time talking to others about what he was upset about *this week*.

Cumulatively, they spent hours talking to each other about their frustrations with this volunteer (affect); and/or they spent time taking various actions or precautions to correct whatever the issue was he had complained about that week (effect). This foolishness, wasted hours and hours that should have been devoted to Kingdom work, all expended in order that he could continue to "volunteer".

Yet, the leaders thought that the most loving thing to do for this man was nothing; but let him complain and just comply with his numerous demands. What they didn't realize is that he was sinning with his complaining; not getting any credit in heaven for his volunteering; distracting others who were trying to complete their Kingdom assignments; and quite frankly, this character trait of his was no doubt the main reason why he was so lonely in the first place and yet, at the same time, always wanted to work alone.

DESSERT OPTION #3: Double Chocolate Cake and Fresh Berries; Correct/Rebuke and Then Submit or Comply

"Control Freaks" have a difficult time of working in unity and getting along with other people, because everything has to be done *their way.*

Instead of allowing this to continue, what Leadership *should have done* was gently correct him, with something like, *"Hey, maybe we need to move you to something that is less frustrating for you to do?"* Then allow that opening to lead to a conversation about his complaining and how it effected and affected the church staff; and make the necessary correction, instead of allowing that controlling spirit to run rampant in the church office every week.

If he did not receive the correction, then "Plan B" should have been implemented: he simply needed to stop "volunteering" because his volunteering was really *costing* the church in the long run, not benefitting it.

Here's another: It's a mother-in-law that you wish you had a better relationship with, but who continues to make critical

DESSERT OPTION #3: Double Chocolate Cake and Fresh Berries; Correct/Rebuke and Then Submit or Comply

comments about how you're not quite "up to par" with the rearing of her grandchildren; your care for her son (your husband); and the quality of the meals you prepare ... well, "They're nothing like he's used to at 'home'".

I mean she's really a pain.

In your mind, you have great reasons for why you do everything the way you do it. If the truth were told, you're actually a great mother and wife, by anyone's standards, except hers of course. Notwithstanding, in this case you are intent upon submitting because it would be honoring to both your husband and his mother.

So what do you do to eliminate the spirit of control from coming in and controlling your behavior? You may decide God wants you to correct her statements and yet, find some way to still honor her by your compliance.

DESSERT OPTION #3: Double Chocolate Cake and Fresh Berries; Correct/Rebuke and Then Submit or Comply

Therefore, instead of just holding in your frustration and getting angry about the comments she makes and then doing everything she tells you to do with a sinful attitude; you decide to address her comments and correct her misunderstandings; while at the same time, making certain that you exercise "self-control" to the fullest extent possible so you won't blow a fuse!

Since she's coming over for Sunday dinner, you know for sure that she's going to say something derogatory about your cooking. You also know that she's criticized the way you've made mashed potatoes in the past and since you're making mashed potatoes again this Sunday, you ask the Lord for some help preparing a few "on point" "Rehearsed Responses" that will be ready to fire, when the mashed potatoes "Control Freak issue" arises. You then hold your prepared "Rehearsed Responses" under your belt until the whipping begins (whipping of the potatoes, is of course, what I mean).

DESSERT OPTION #3: Double Chocolate Cake and Fresh Berries; Correct/Rebuke and Then Submit or Comply

Here's what you come up with: She always thinks more milk should be put in the potatoes before whipping. So this time you say, "Sorry mom, Johnny can't have that much milk, he's lactose intolerant; but I would love to whip some on the side for you, just the way you like it."

You make a simple, non-emotional statement, which indicates it's not going to happen the way you want, *mummy dearest,* yet with God's wisdom you've figured out a way to comply with her request and honor her at the same time.

Look, the lady is eating at your house and maybe it's not about how everyone else's potatoes are prepared, but rather it's just the way *she likes them for herself.* Selfish? Possibly, but don't take things so personally; you've created a heightened sensitivity to her comments because *you've* never corrected them in the past, so part of the frustration you're experiencing is on you.

DESSERT OPTION #3: Double Chocolate Cake and Fresh Berries; Correct/Rebuke and Then Submit or Comply

So think! Think out of the box, don't allow the history of emotion surrounding a relationship like this, cause you to be stuck in a negative response pattern. Ask God for wisdom and prepare an arsenal of "Rehearsed Responses" ready to fire off the next time she comes over for dinner.

Are you now ready to get even "heavier"? Time to increase our caloric intake to the max!

DESSERT OPTION #3: Double Chocolate Cake and Fresh Berries; Correct/Rebuke <u>and</u> Then Submit or Comply

"CONTROL FREAK"

CHAPTER 35: DESSERT OPTION #4: Double Chocolate Cake and Ice Cream; Correct/Rebuke and Then Resist/ Stand or Employ the Principle of Diametric Opposition

----

Finally! Now we get to the really good "rich" fattening stuff. When you're serving double chocolate cake *and* ice cream that means you're being called on to **"Correct/Rebuke and Resist/Stand or Employ the Principle of Diametric Opposition"** to whatever is being demanded by the spirit of control.

DESSERT OPTION #4: Double Chocolate Cake and Ice Cream; Correct/Rebuke <u>and</u> Then Resist/ Stand or Employ the Principle of Diametric Opposition

You need a higher caloric intake when serving Dessert Option #4 for obvious reasons: energy and focus. This is when the conflict level rises and as a result, things get quite a bit more ... *complicated*.

These are "high end" spiritual battles, where the spirit of divination is coming in like a flood with full force. These are situations where you absolutely cannot give in to "its" demands, or otherwise you'd be feeding the CIYA; disobeying the Word of God; and/or taken off track from completing a specific directive that you've already received from the Lord.

Whenever you **"Correct/Rebuke"** someone operating under the influence of the spirit of divination and you fail or refuse to do what "it" is requesting or demanding of you; what you should expect, is that the spirit of divination will "pump up the volume" either verbally and/or manipulatively.

DESSERT OPTION #4: Double Chocolate Cake and Ice Cream; Correct/Rebuke <u>and</u> Then Resist/ Stand or Employ the Principle of Diametric Opposition

Here is where your artillery of: "Rehearsed Responses"; and "Confronting with Authority and Expecting Attitude" in return, are utilized the most.[96]

This dessert combination will often apply to your Type-B Controlling personalities category: those people whom you cannot readily eliminate from your life such as relatives, spouses, siblings, parents, in-laws, bosses, co-workers, pastors, even Christian friends and counselors.

This is where many times a person, trying to pass judgment on your actions, will try to quote Scriptures in order to control what you do, or condemn what you've already done in any given situation. This is an especially high-risk setting for those "Control Freaks" whom for years, you've bowed down to their every whim and done exactly what they wanted you to do.

---

[96] You will also learn to use another piece of artillery when serving Dessert Option #4, it is called, "Escalated Rebuke". We have devoted an upcoming Chapter to arming you with that weapon.

DESSERT OPTION #4: Double Chocolate Cake and Ice Cream; Correct/Rebuke and Then Resist/ Stand or Employ the Principle of Diametric Opposition

Be warned, they will not like losing that control over you that they've been exercising for years. As a result, expect the heat to be turned up *seven times hotter* when "it" senses you're intent upon breaking free from "its" shackles. Be ready for them to respond "in the flesh"; and nonetheless, you, not return the favor and sin yourself.

The thing you are correcting in their life does not necessarily need to be sin either. It may just be someone trying to control your behavior and you simply refusing to be controlled. You then correct his/her actions and walk away from the interaction, not having complied with the demand.

Once your spiritual eyes get a handle on the spirit of control you will begin to see "it" at work at some level, in almost every relationship *you have;* and/or in every relationship where *you witness* other peoples' interactions; and/or in every relationship in which *you have been told or know* about the things that are going on between the parties.

DESSERT OPTION #4: Double Chocolate Cake and Ice Cream; Correct/Rebuke and Then Resist/ Stand or Employ the Principle of Diametric Opposition

When serving Dessert Combination #4, it is going to take a lot more intentional preparation, wisdom from God, tact and finesse, in order to avoid falling into sin during the time of rebuking the spirit of control while refusing to comply to "its" demands.

In order for you to become proficient in serving this last dessert combination, you will need to clean and polish your spiritual weaponry and tools in the following areas:

(1) Closer communication in your relationship with the Lord, which will yield "wisdom" from the Holy Spirit on demand (or right when you really need it);

(2) "Practice" with varying people in numerous types of situations; where you learn to modify and vary your approach dependent upon results;

(3) "Finesse and Diplomacy" to determine the content of the words to be used; to whom and how to apply them; and what level of rebuke

DESSERT OPTION #4: Double Chocolate Cake and Ice Cream: Correct/Rebuke and Then Resist/ Stand or Employ the Principle of Diametric Opposition

you employ, in any given situation. You cannot use the same tactics on every person. You must become *all things to all men*, that you might win some in this area too (1 Cor 9:22);

(4)   A good working knowledge of the Word of God;

(5)   A good sense of humor;

(6)   Pliability as you refine and fine tune your skills; and

(7)   Lots of tenacity, endurance and brainpower!!

The last thing you'll need to learn in order to successfully serve our "heaviest" dessert, is to develop a technique which is essential to any respectable lawyer's practice of law. The technique is called, "framing the issue of law".

We are now ready for our most advanced Law School Lesson: "Appellate Practice" and an examination of the way "the issues of law" presented in a Civil Rights

DESSERT OPTION #4: Double Chocolate Cake and Ice Cream: Correct/Rebuke and Then Resist/ Stand or Employ the Principle of Diametric Opposition

Discrimination case, have been "framed" by each opponent.

One of the first things you learn as a student in law school is how to recognize and then how to argue, both sides to every case. It's truly an art form; a person can spend hours and hours just trying to grasp and employ this technique.

Acquiring this skill can be very difficult for a person who only sees in "black and white"; meaning the right side vs. the wrong side.

This was a very difficult concept for me to grasp in the beginning of law school, because at first I was only able to see one side of every case, which would then become *my side* ... the "right" side of course.

However, when you can only see one side or viewpoint of a case, then that makes you a very inept lawyer. That limited perspective causes you to be unable to anticipate your opponent's best moves, defenses and/or arguments; those

DESSERT OPTION #4: Double Chocolate Cake and Ice Cream: Correct/Rebuke <u>and</u> Then Resist/ Stand or Employ the Principle of Diametric Opposition

that they will undoubtedly try to use against you in a court of law.

Therefore, in order to win any case, not only must you be able to see, understand and articulate your best arguments; but you'll need to know, understand and be able to articulate <u>and</u> *defend against* your opponent's best arguments as well.

It is your job as a good lawyer to undermine and/or minimize the effect and affect of your opponent's best legal arguments so that ultimately … you will win the case.

Oh yes! I'm not bashful about saying so: *"It's all about winning!"* -- especially in our context.

Now that you've got the general idea, we will need to modify the term "framing the issue of law" to suit our purposes, so what we'll call it is:

"Re-Framing the Control Freak Issue".

DESSERT OPTION #4: Double Chocolate Cake and Ice Cream: Correct/Rebuke and Then Resist/ Stand or Employ the Principle of Diametric Opposition

The "Control Freak Issue" is obviously whatever the controlling person is trying to get you to do. The term "Re-Framing" means: to re-describe from a different perspective, or to re-label.[97]

In a nutshell, "Reframing the Control Freak Issue" is the ability to holdfast to a perspective, *different than* that of the opposition (or person trying to control you); and then, both respond and take action based on *your own "re-framed" perspective*, not the perspective presented by the spirit of divination.

Your ability to "Reframe the Control Freak Issue" is therefore key to your successful rebuke/correction of the spirit of divination working in the lives of other people who are trying to control your behavior. So when our opponent comes to us with their argument, perspective, or position on any given "Control Freak issue", we then take their argument, perspective, or position as stated, and "re-frame"

---

[97] Wiktionary

DESSERT OPTION #4: Double Chocolate Cake and Ice Cream: Correct/Rebuke and Then Resist/ Stand or Employ the Principle of Diametric Opposition

it into our own argument, perspective or position, in order that our side wins the case!

Both sides are arguing the same case, but they're going at it with two diametrically opposed positions (sound familiar?)

Let's first go through a little re-framing practice in our Civil Rights Discrimination case, just to make sure you've got the idea. When the case goes up on appeal, it will be the same case; but each side will "frame" the issue of law to be decided by the Appellate Court differently, so that their side wins.

Here are the facts: An African American woman with four children, who has had some difficulties getting to work because of lack of reliable transportation, was fired from her job. The firing employer is claiming "good cause" for the firing (which is legal); on the other hand, the woman is claiming racial discrimination for the firing (which obviously, is not legal).

DESSERT OPTION #4: Double Chocolate Cake and Ice Cream; Correct/Rebuke <u>and</u> Then Resist/ Stand or Employ the Principle of Diametric Opposition

Each side files their legal briefs with the Appellate Court "framing the issue of law" from their own perspective in order to win the case. Remember, it's all about winning!

The Employer's legal brief frames the issue of law to be decided by the Court as this:

ISSUE: **SHOULD AN EMPLOYER BE FORCED, BY LAW, TO KEEP EMPLOYEES WHO ARE CONTINUALLY TARDY TO WORK?**

The obvious answer to the legal issue, as framed is: "No".

Who in their right mind would <u>not</u> say *"No, of course not"* to that inquiry? No employer should be forced to keep employees who are always late to work on payroll, especially when they can hire other people who will come to work on time.

DESSERT OPTION #4: Double Chocolate Cake and Ice Cream: Correct/Rebuke and Then Resist/ Stand or Employ the Principle of Diametric Opposition

So as you sit there right now, you're no doubt thinking, "I already know who should win this case; the Employer should, of course."

But before you go too far and pick a side, first take a look at the way the opponent has "framed the legal issue" *and then* decide the case ... *your honor.*

The woman's attorney files her legal brief and frames the issue of law to be decided like this:

ISSUE: **SHOULD A MOTHER OF FOUR BE TERMINATED FROM HER JOB WHEN SHE RUNS LATE, JUST BECAUSE SHE IS BLACK?**

The obvious answer to the legal issue, as framed, is again: "No."

Who in their right mind would <u>not</u> say *"No, of course not"* to that inquiry? Since all employees run late to work, from

DESSERT OPTION #4: Double Chocolate Cake and Ice Cream: Correct/Rebuke <u>and</u> Then Resist/ Stand or Employ the Principle of Diametric Opposition

time to time, it would be unfair to just fire the African American employees who do so; and not the Caucasian, Hispanic, or Asian employees as well.

How do you explain it?

It's the same case up on Appeal, but presented with two different perspectives when "framing the issue of law" and presented to the Appellate Court for a ruling. That's what they teach you in law school.

The "right" answer is obvious…

BUT for *both* positions!

Wow!

Now, take a look at this: There are several occasions when the spirit of divination tried working in and through Jesus' interpersonal relationships with others, to try and control

DESSERT OPTION #4: Double Chocolate Cake and Ice Cream: Correct/Rebuke and Then Resist/ Stand or Employ the Principle of Diametric Opposition

His behavior, especially by using the religious leaders. They always had only a one-sided perspective, their side.

Watch!

Take a look at some of those instances and observe Jesus Himself, the One whose example can take any law practice straight to the top, serving up Dessert Option #4 to the Control Freaks in His life.

Watch carefully how He **"Reframes"** the "Control Freak issue" to the opposition, much like the lawyers in our Civil Rights case framed opposing issues of law. Notice also, how Jesus always maintained control over each situation He faced, as well as Himself. Make sure to attentively study how He corrected and rebuked the controlling comments of others because at some point in the near future, you will be required to do the same.

In Matthew 12:1-15, it says: *"At that time Jesus went through the grainfields on the Sabbath. And His disciples*

DESSERT OPTION #4: Double Chocolate Cake and Ice Cream: Correct/Rebuke and Then Resist/ Stand or Employ the Principle of Diametric Opposition

were hungry, and began to pluck heads of grain and to eat. And when **the Pharisees saw it, they said to Him, "Look, Your disciples are doing what is not lawful to do on the Sabbath***!"* But He said to them, *"Have you not read what David did when he was hungry, he and those who were with him: how he entered the house of God and ate the showbread which was not lawful for him to eat, nor for those who were with him, but only for the priests? Or have you not read in the law that on the Sabbath the priests in the temple profane the Sabbath, and are blameless? Yet I say to you that in this place there is One greater than the temple. But if you had known what this means, 'I desire mercy and not sacrifice,' you would not have condemned the guiltless. <u>For the Son of Man is Lord even of the Sabbath.</u>"* Now when He had departed from there, He went into their synagogue. And behold, there was a man who had a withered hand. And they asked Him, saying, *"Is it lawful to heal on the Sabbath?"*--that they might accuse Him. Then He said to them, *"What man is there among you who has one sheep, and if it falls into a pit on the Sabbath, will not lay hold of it and lift it out? Of how much more value*

DESSERT OPTION #4: Double Chocolate Cake and Ice Cream; Correct/Rebuke and Then Resist/ Stand or Employ the Principle of Diametric Opposition

then is a man than a sheep? <u>Therefore it is lawful to do good on the Sabbath</u>." Then He said to the man, "Stretch out your hand." And he stretched it out, and it was restored as whole as the other. Then the Pharisees went out and plotted against Him, how they might destroy Him. But when Jesus knew it, He withdrew from there…" (KJV).

Here we see two instances where the religious leaders were trying to control the behavior of Jesus and/or His disciples. The first instance was when the Pharisees said: *"It is not lawful to pick the corn and eat on the Sabbath"*.

By making that condemning comment about the law, they were trying to *control* the behavior of the disciples so they would stop picking and eating the corn; and they were trying to get Jesus to bring it to a stop. They were trying to make them all *feel* guilty about violating the law (affect), in order to get them to stop eating the corn (the effect).

Affect drives effect, remember?

DESSERT OPTION #4: Double Chocolate Cake and Ice Cream: Correct/Rebuke <u>and</u> Then Resist/ Stand or Employ the Principle of Diametric Opposition

In response, Jesus reframed the issue, using several scriptural references to rebuke and correct; and then He conveyed the message: When you're hungry, it is not unlawful to go ahead and eat. It's happened before, it's now happened again, so you might as well get over it.[98]

Jesus didn't tell His disciples to comply or to stop eating, He didn't sin, and after the rebuke, they all went on their way, merrily picking and eating corn; at least until arriving at the synagogue, where the next Control Freak issue arose.

In the second instance, they wanted to control Jesus' behavior by trying to get Him to refuse to heal the man with the withered hand, out of fear of breaking the law of the Sabbath right there in front of everybody. That controlling spirit did not want Jesus to demonstrate the healing power of God. They expected Jesus would respond in agreement with their perspective of the "case". But of course-- He didn't.

---

[98] The Janetized Condensed and Consolidated Translation.

DESSERT OPTION #4: Double Chocolate Cake and Ice Cream: Correct/Rebuke and Then Resist/ Stand or Employ the Principle of Diametric Opposition

Notice that instead of entering into a discussion or argument based on how the Pharisees framed the issue, Jesus re-framed the control issue *after* healing the withered hand and said: *"It is lawful to do good on the Sabbath."*

The issue was still the Sabbath, but Jesus reframed the issue by changing the "not doing wrong on the Sabbath" "Control Freak" perspective of the Pharisees; to His own, proper perspective of "doing right on the Sabbath".

No one dared contend with a statement like that! Jesus "reframed" both of these issues and presented them back in a form that only a fool would ever try to argue against!

Wow! Ain't He cool? I suspect you already knew, of course, that He *is* our Advocate.[99]

Next, let's take a look at His **"Reframing"** expertise, as it

---

[99] "Advocate" means one who pleads another's cause before a judge, a pleader, or counsel for defense..." (Ref. 1 Jn 2:1, Strong's #3875, transliterated "Parakletos").

DESSERT OPTION #4: Double Chocolate Cake and Ice Cream; Correct/Rebuke and Then Resist/ Stand or Employ the Principle of Diametric Opposition

relates to the story of the woman caught in adultery found in John 8:2-12:

"Now early in the morning He came again into the temple, and all the people came to Him; and He sat down and taught them. Then the scribes and Pharisees brought to Him a woman caught in adultery. And when they had set her in the midst, they said to Him, "Teacher, this woman was caught in adultery, in the very act. Now Moses, in the law, commanded us that such should be stoned. But what do You say?" This they said, testing Him, that they might have something of which to accuse Him. But Jesus stooped down and wrote on the ground with His finger, as though He did not hear. So when they continued asking Him, He raised Himself up and said to them, "He who is without sin among you, let him throw a stone at her first." And again He stooped down and wrote on the ground. Then those who heard it, being convicted by their conscience, went out one by one, beginning with the oldest even to the last. And Jesus was left alone, and the woman standing in the midst. When Jesus had raised Himself up

DESSERT OPTION #4: Double Chocolate Cake and Ice Cream: Correct/Rebuke _and_ Then Resist/ Stand or Employ the Principle of Diametric Opposition

and saw no one but the woman, He said to her, "Woman, where are those accusers of yours? Has no one condemned you?" She said, "No one, Lord." And Jesus said to her, "Neither do I condemn you; go and sin no more." Then Jesus spoke to them again, saying, "I am the light of the world. He who follows Me shall not walk in darkness, but have the light of life" (KJV).

The religious leaders were trying to _control_ Jesus by presenting Him with this, "adultery case" to see how He'd litigate the matter. By the religious leaders confirming their eyewitness testimony of her "guilt" (having been caught in "the very act"); and by stating what the punishment according to the law was supposed to be; they were trying to incite Jesus (affect) in order to control His behavior (effect), by compelling Him to both declare her "guilty", and then rally the troops to start throwing stones at her.

It's unfortunate, sometimes, that the Bible doesn't have sound effects, don't you think? Just imagine how that Pharisee must have sounded with his condescending tone

DESSERT OPTION #4: Double Chocolate Cake and Ice Cream: Correct/Rebuke <u>and</u> Then Resist/ Stand or Employ the Principle of Diametric Opposition

of voice, his inflections and the like ... Yuck! They all *so* wanted to control Jesus' behavior, but our Advocate?

Nah, He didn't even flinch.

Understand that they were correct, however, that under the law she should have been stoned. Leviticus 20:10 says, *"The man who commits adultery with another man's wife, he who commits adultery with his neighbor's wife, the adulterer and the adulteress, shall surely be put to death"* (KJV).

They brought this "adultery case" before Jesus because they were trying to *control* His behavior, wanting Him to be "the heavy". Look, if it wasn't about that, why didn't they just implement their law themselves, right there on the spot? Why did they bother bringing "the case" to Him? Why did they even bother asking for His *legal opinion?*

DESSERT OPTION #4: Double Chocolate Cake and Ice Cream; Correct/Rebuke and Then Resist/ Stand or Employ the Principle of Diametric Opposition

Answer: They were *trying to control His behavior*, hoping to get Him to do all the "dirty work" by heading up the stoning of the woman caught in adultery.

Yet, even this public pressure did not control Jesus. He responded instead by reframing the issue and saying, *"He who is without sin cast the first stone."*

The facts are the same. We're still talking about the same issue of "stoning", for the same sin of "committing adultery", with the same people involved, and with the same law that applied; but Jesus' perspective on this issue was markedly different than that of the religious leaders who brought her to Him.

Do you see it?

We see Jesus reframe the issue, in what would otherwise have been seen as a cut-and-dried case; a very black and white situation. However, His reframing finesse and His

DESSERT OPTION #4: Double Chocolate Cake and Ice Cream; Correct/Rebuke and Then Resist/ Stand or Employ the Principle of Diametric Opposition

accompanying conduct, forced a different perspective to be adopted by all the people, whether they liked it or not.

The spirit of control would have liked nothing better than to have that woman be stoned to death in a state of unrepented sin; but because of Jesus' wisdom and re-framing finesse "it" did not win out.

However, there are other cases in the Bible, when unfortunately, "it" did:

In Numbers Chapter 13, the Bible recounts the best example of the spirit of divination successfully thwarting the plan of God for the lives of His people. Remember, Moses sends out the twelve spies to search out the Promised Land before going in. There were two opposing reports delivered after the journey; the "evil report" delivered by the ten spies; and the "good report" delivered by Joshua and Caleb.

DESSERT OPTION #4: Double Chocolate Cake and Ice Cream; Correct/Rebuke and Then Resist/ Stand or Employ the Principle of Diametric Opposition

God had already given the directive and told them that the Promised Land was theirs to possess (Lev 20:24, Deut 1:21). So we know which side of the issue the Spirit of God landed on.

Now think about it, when it came to the evil report given to the people, *"We be not able to go up"..."We saw the giants...and we were in our own sight as grasshoppers, and so were we in their sight",* the Bible says that Caleb had to *"hush"* the people because they were all in such a frenzy (affect) after hearing the "evil report" (Nu 13:31 & 33, KJV).

The "evil report" was being used to try to control the destiny of the children of Israel, in a manner contrary to the destiny that God had already planned. The "evil report" was specifically intended to keep them out of the Promised Land; and for that entire generation who came into agreement with the "spirit of divination" -- it worked! They all died out and never made it to the place God had prepared for them (effect) (Nu 14:28-35).

DESSERT OPTION #4: Double Chocolate Cake and Ice Cream: Correct/Rebuke <u>and</u> Then Resist/ Stand or Employ the Principle of Diametric Opposition

Wow!

Unless we are trained to do otherwise, we too normally just accept the issue as it is presented to us. We say, "Ok yeah, that's right ... I see how upset you are; you must be right." We then think we should think, feel and act just like that person and be upset too.

No! *Absolutely not.* Unlike the majority of the children of Israel, we must never come into agreement with the spirit of divination by responding "In-Kind", or we too may lose out on all that the Lord has for us.

Instead, we need to learn to flip the script and Reframe the issue; never buy into the attitude or emotion as it is presented; and never respond "In-Kind" to the Control Freak you're up against.

For those select few that fought against the "evil report" delivered by the spirit of divination and refused to be controlled and instead, confirmed the "good report" saying,

DESSERT OPTION #4: Double Chocolate Cake and Ice Cream: Correct/Rebuke and Then Resist/ Stand or Employ the Principle of Diametric Opposition

"*Let us go up at once, and possess it; for we are well able to overcome...*" (Nu 13:30, KJV) eventually, they made it in.

"Re-framing the Control Freak issue" is a matter of having a different victorious faith-filled perspective when faced with the comments of negative controlling people. It is the key to assuring that your argument wins out every single time and as a result, that the "jugular" is taken out every single time as well!

Here are some additional summarized examples of people trying, but failing, to control Jesus' behavior:

Jesus healed a man with palsy; afterwards, they wanted Him to feel condemned for violating the Sabbath (Matt 9:3-6).

In an attempt to condemn His choice of dinner company, Jesus was criticized for eating with publicans and sinners; but He enjoyed His meal and finished it unaffected (Matt 9:1-13 & Lu 15:1-2).

DESSERT OPTION #4: Double Chocolate Cake and Ice Cream; Correct/Rebuke and Then Resist/Stand or Employ the Principle of Diametric Opposition

Jesus rebuked the criticism received about His disciples' failure to fast and/or wash their hands, and they all carried on as usual (Matt 9:14-17 & Matt 15:1-9).

They tried "laughing Him to scorn" in an attempt to control or thwart His raising of Jairus' daughter from the dead; but Jesus "put them out" and healed her as God had planned (Matt 9:18-25 & Lu 8:49-54).

John the Baptist even tried to control Jesus, by sending word to question if He was really the Messiah (even after being an eye witness to God the Father's confirmation of that fact during Jesus' baptism). John was trying to control Jesus or get Him to *do something* to get him out of prison. Jesus gave correction by commenting on the blessing of not being "offended" and did not comply with John's request to save him from what ultimately was his beheading (Matt 11:2-6).

The religious leaders attributed the marvelous healing works of Jesus, to Beelzebub (the devil); and then asked

DESSERT OPTION #4: Double Chocolate Cake and Ice Cream; Correct/Rebuke and Then Resist/ Stand or Employ the Principle of Diametric Opposition

for their own "sign" in order to force Him, at their command, to prove to them who He was. Jesus rebuked them and refused to give them a sign (Matt 12:24-45 & Matt 16:1-4).

The mother of the "sons of thunder" tried to secure both James and John, a place of authority in Jesus' Kingdom. Jesus rebuked, corrected and refused to comply with mommy's aspiration for her two sons (Matt 20:20-28).

Jesus was questioned about His "authority" in an attempt to control His conduct of performing healings, signs and wonders. If He could not prove His authority, impliedly, His ministry would have to come to a stop. Jesus reframed the issue, delivered a rebuke and continued going about His Father's business (Matt 21:23-27).

When the people called Him "Hosanna" and worshipped Him the chief priests and scribes, in their hot displeasure and in an attempt to get Jesus to tell them to stop, said, *"Do you hear what they are saying?"* He reframed the issue, by essentially stating it was a "perfect" fit for the

DESSERT OPTION #4: Double Chocolate Cake and Ice Cream; Correct/Rebuke and Then Resist/ Stand or Employ the Principle of Diametric Opposition

occasion and as such rebuked them and carried on with the processional (Matt 21:15-16).

Jesus was asked by a man to tell his brother to divide their family inheritance with him. Jesus rebuked/corrected and did not comply with the request (Lu 12:13-21).

Martha was trying to get Jesus to help her control the alleged misbehavior of her sister Mary, who was worshipping at Jesus' feet, instead of helping her with food preparation, by saying *"Don't you care that my sister has left me to serve alone?"* Jesus corrected her and did the opposite of what Martha wanted, by affirming Mary's conduct (Lu 10:38-42).

In John 11, Martha tried to make Jesus feel guilty and condemned for the death of her brother Lazarus when she said, *"If you would have only been here my brother would not have died"* (v. 21, KJV); and Mary did the same (v. 32).

DESSERT OPTION #4: Double Chocolate Cake and Ice Cream: Correct/Rebuke and Then Resist/ Stand or Employ the Principle of Diametric Opposition

Additionally, after Jesus said "*roll away the stone*", Martha tried to dissuade Jesus from raising Lazarus from the dead with her negative discouraging comment that, "*he has been dead four days, by this time he stinketh*" (v.39, KJV); Jesus corrected her (v. 40); and carried on with the plan that God had to be glorified.

When Jesus sought to demonstrate servanthood by washing the feet of the disciples, Peter tried to dissuade His conduct. Jesus corrected Peter and continued on with His illustrated sermon (Jn 13:4-9).

When the lawyer (who was no doubt Jewish) tried to get Jesus to confirm that he'd be making it to heaven, Jesus corrected him with the story of the good Samaritan; which would have been considered a very offensive rebuke to any Jew, especially a lawyer (Lu 10:25-37).

When a Pharisee threatened Jesus that He needed to get out of town because King Herod was going to kill Him, Jesus refused to comply. In response to the threat, He

DESSERT OPTION #4: Double Chocolate Cake and Ice Cream: Correct/Rebuke and Then Resist/ Stand or Employ the Principle of Diametric Opposition

called Herod a "fox" and said that He was going to continue with the miracles and attend to the prophets (Lu 13:31-35).

If we were all sitting as a jury in these cases, we would all have to unanimously agree that Jesus was absolutely brilliant at **"reframing the issues"** presented by the spirit of control. In fact, He was so proficient that He made those Pharisees seeking to "control" Him by trying to "catch Him in His words" (Mk 12:13); look and no doubt feel, like total imbeciles by the end of each interaction that took place.

He truly is our Wonderful "Counsellor" (Is 9:6, KJV).

When you get a chance, start reading the gospels with the spirit of divination in mind. There are an unlimited number of examples where you'll now see how time and time again Jesus **"Re-framed the Control Freak issue"** and gained or maintained control over *"being about His Father's business"*.

DESSERT OPTION #4: Double Chocolate Cake and Ice Cream: Correct/Rebuke and Then Resist/ Stand or Employ the Principle of Diametric Opposition

For our purposes, rather than allowing other people to take you off track and get you caught up in a web of bickering and arguing, you too must start planning on doing the same.

Also, take the time at some point, to go back and review all of those examples above and ask yourself: "What would have happened if ... the spirit of control would have succeed in those instances?" Or, "What would not have happened if ... the spirit of control would have succeed in those instances?"

Wow! Think about it. Some people wouldn't have gotten healed, others wouldn't have been fed, and still others would have remained dead.

Let's move on to some examples where the disciples themselves, had learned to re-frame the Control Freak issue:

DESSERT OPTION #4: Double Chocolate Cake and Ice Cream: Correct/Rebuke and Then Resist/ Stand or Employ the Principle of Diametric Opposition

After the time of tarrying and then receiving the gift of the Holy Spirit, there were people in the crowd "mocking" their speaking in tongues. If the mockers had been allowed to control the situation with their words, this could have stopped the power of God working in the lives of the others. Peter serves Dessert Option #4, **"Corrects and Rebukes"** and as a result three thousand get saved (Acts 2:13-41).

After healing the lame man (Acts 3), Peter and John were taken before the high priest and questioned as to, *"what power, or by what name, have you done this?"* (Acts 4:7). After some explanation from Peter, they were "*commanded not to speak nor teach in the name of Jesus"* (Acts 4:18); and later, they were *"further threatened"* again (Acts 4:21).

Ha! The apostles refused to be controlled by these demands or threats and moved forward carrying on the Lord's agenda with even more boldness (Acts 4:29-32).

Later, when the apostles were taken into custody and brought before the high priest, he said, *"Did not we*

DESSERT OPTION #4: Double Chocolate Cake and Ice Cream: Correct/Rebuke <u>and</u> Then Resist/ Stand or Employ the Principle of Diametric Opposition

straightly command you that you should not teach in His name?" Peter and the others rebuked this attempt to *control* their conduct by saying, *"We ought to obey God rather than men"* (Acts 5:28-29). Even after being severely beaten, they adamantly refused to be controlled and *"ceased not to teach and preach Jesus Christ"* (Acts 5:40-42, KJV).

After the people saw the miracle of Paul healing the impotent man by calling upon him to rise to his feet, they exclaimed, *"The gods are come down to us in the likeness of men"* and they started to worship Paul and Barnabus. In response, the duo would not be controlled into receiving worship from man and they rent their clothes. They then rebuked and corrected them all, putting an abrupt stop to the sacrifice they had intended to offer them (Acts 14:8-18).

Since this is our richest dessert, once you become proficient and get really good at serving Dessert Option #4, all of the other dessert options will become, shall I say ...
a piece of cake ... for you to serve at any given time.

DESSERT OPTION #4: Double Chocolate Cake and Ice Cream: Correct/Rebuke and Then Resist/ Stand or Employ the Principle of Diametric Opposition

Therefore, I have devoted a whole chapter to some real life examples of "Jugular Extraction", including a few with more practice on re-framing the issue.   But before we get to those examples, you must first learn how to handle your last crucial piece of artillery.

This is a real weapon of war.

This what you'll use whenever it's necessary to resort to "the big guns".

This weapon is something you'll need to be ready to pull out of your arsenal, though probably not everyday, but certainly at one time or another, I promise.

This piece of artillery needs to be ready to fire at any time, especially when you're forced to serve double chocolate cake ("Correct/Rebuke") to the spirit of divination upon encountering "it"-- *operating in overdrive.*

This weapon is called, "Escalated Rebuke".

DESSERT OPTION #4: *Double Chocolate Cake and Ice Cream: Correct/Rebuke <u>and</u> Then Resist/ Stand or Employ the Principle of Diametric Opposition*

CHAPTER 36: Escalated Rebuke

These days, there are some people out there who just don't know how to take *"No"* for an answer. Nor are they sufficiently competent to understand even the simplest sentence structures such as, *"Leave me alone."* No matter how many different times and in how many different ways this message is politely conveyed, they still *never get it.*

If ... no, strike that-- *when* you run into a Control Freak Extraordinaire,[100] there will be times when your response to the spirit of divination must increase in intensity in order to effectively extract the jugular.

This is what I call "Escalated Rebuke". Dependent upon the level of control the spirit of divination is using in an attempt to control your behavior, many times it will be

---

[100] Again, a "Control Freak Extraordinaire" functions at the highest level of depravity of all the Control Freak species.

Escalated Rebuke

necessary for your level of rebuke to escalate in order to stand your ground and/or take "it" out.

In other words, you've already employed a series of "Rehearsed Responses", none of which seemed to work. You have not responded "In-Kind". You haven't sinned, though you've increased your tone of voice and looked them straight in the eye when redelivering your message of eradication. You've been "Checking-In" and asking for His wisdom the whole time and you sense that singing a song just wouldn't suit this circumstance.

In other words, you've employed every piece of artillery you know of, but "it" is still pumping. Worse, the spirit of divination hasn't backed down one bit; and in fact, "it" seems to be getting worse.

In these instances, the very last thing you want to do, is pick up your marbles and go home! Oh no! The reason "it" is getting worse is because "it" senses you are in the throes of escaping "its" clutches. Just because the heat has been turned up, that doesn't mean you can quit now and give back the territory you've already gained. In these instances you must employ your "Escalated Rebuke" artillery.

Escalated Rebuke

To get a better understanding of what I mean by "Escalated Rebuke" let's start by first looking at some Biblical examples of the same:

Jesus was criticized after loosing the woman from her infirmity, because He healed on the Sabbath. Jesus used *escalated rebuke* and called His critics all a bunch of "hypocrites" (Lu 13:11-16).

As you well know, being called a "hypocrite" at any given point in the history of mankind, is a "put down". You too may have to employ similar language, tone and force with your words in order to deal with the spirit of divination.

In another "Escalated Rebuke" situation, the Pharisees tried to embarrass Jesus by implying that He was an illegitimate child, born out of fornication. Jesus responded by telling them that their father was *"the father of lies"* and that they were all *"children of the devil"* (Jn 8:13-44).

That's pretty serious talk to be saying to the "religious leaders" of that day. If you don't think so, why don't you try saying the exact same thing to your pastor this Sunday and see how it goes over with him.

Escalated Rebuke

How about this interaction between Jesus and Peter:

"Then He commanded His disciples that they should tell no one that He was Jesus the Christ. From that time Jesus began to show to His disciples that He must go to Jerusalem, and suffer many things from the elders and chief priests and scribes, and be killed, and be raised the third day. Then Peter took Him aside and began to rebuke Him, saying, "Far be it from You, Lord; this shall not happen to You!" But He turned and said to Peter, "Get behind Me, Satan! You are an offense to Me, for you are not mindful of the things of God, but the things of men" (Matt 16:20-23, NKJV).

Here is Jesus, forewarning His disciples about the cross that He would endure. The spirit of divination influences Peter to tempt Jesus into avoiding the cross, by sympathizing with what Jesus had said He was going to suffer. Peter's statement was clearly intended to convince or dissuade, or *control* Jesus and keep Him from having to suffer at all. The spirit of divination obviously didn't want Jesus dying on the cross for the sins of the world.

Escalated Rebuke

Jesus, instead of thanking Peter for his sympathy and sentiment (like most of us would have done), rebukes Peter, calls him "Satan" and tells Peter he is "offensive" to Him. Jesus' going to the cross in defiance of this directive by Peter, is a perfect Biblical example of employing, "The Principle of Diametric Opposition."

Some teachers hypothesize that Satan himself was right there in some form or another, but the Bible said Jesus *"rebuked Peter"* (Mark 8:33), or *"said to Peter"* (Matt 16:23), *"Get thee behind Me, Satan."*

Remember, it was just a few passages earlier when Peter had received revelation straight from heaven saying, *"Thou art the Christ, the Son of the living God"* (Matt 16:16-17). So here you have Peter, a disciple, an apostle, receiving divine revelation one minute; and then exercising the spirit of control the next. Watch out! This can and will happen in your own "Christian" relationships too.

Remember, the spirit of divination doesn't need Satan to literally be present, in order to do "its" dirty work. So this is yet another illustration of how the spirit of divination can use people in your life, those whom you'd never suspect, to try and keep you from fulfilling the plan of God for your life.

Let's now take "it" to another level—and "let's get physical", by looking at a few rebukes rendered by the hand of God when doing just that:

There is an incident found in the book of Acts, where Paul was "withstood" by a sorcerer Barjesus/Elymas while ministering to the deputy. The spirit of divination was not only corrected with very strong words, but this person through whom "it" was working (Barjesus), was afflicted physically as well:

"Then Saul, who also is called Paul, filled with the Holy Spirit, looked intently at him and said, 'O full of all deceit and all fraud, you son of the devil, you enemy of all righteousness, will you not cease perverting the straight ways of the Lord?"

"And now, indeed, the hand of the Lord is upon you, and you shall be blind, not seeing the sun for a time.' And immediately a dark mist fell on him, and he went around seeking someone to lead him by the hand" (Act 13:9-11,

Escalated Rebuke

KJV).

Wow! That's a pretty serious rebuke, is it not? Paul found himself face to face with the spirit of divination and he had to take the appropriate "escalated" measures to successfully disengage the jugular.

Paul rebuked him by calling him "a child of the devil". Then in the power of the Holy Spirit, he blinded him for trying to thwart the move of God and carried on with his evangelism. The deputy was *astonished and believed* (Acts 13:6-12, KJV).

We shouldn't forget the situation with Ananias and Sapphira, where they were trying to control the other church members' perceptions and opinions of their financial commitment to the cause. In that case, it was the Holy Ghost Who personally stepped in and got physical with both of them (Acts 5:1-11).

Let's also not forget, how Jesus "got physical" Himself:

"It was time for the annual Passover celebration, and Jesus went to Jerusalem. In the Temple area He saw merchants

selling cattle, sheep, and doves for sacrifices; and He saw money changers behind their counters. **Jesus made a whip from some ropes and chased them all out of the Temple**. He drove out the sheep and oxen, **scattered the money changers' coins over the floor, and turned over their tables**. Then, going over to the people who sold doves, He told them, 'Get these things out of here. Don't turn My Father's house into a marketplace!'" (Jn 2:13-16, NLT).

Yep! Nowadays, someone could likely be hit with a civil restraining order for displaying "physical" behavior like that. Nonetheless, you must realize that there will come a point in time when you too must escalate the rebuke delivered to the spirit of divination; and that you must do so in a very serious, strict, and certainly <u>not</u> so playful manner.

It may be necessary to say something very loud and outright impolite just like Jesus or Paul did: *"Hypocrite"* *"You child of the devil"* or *"Get thee behind Me, Satan."* You, however, will more likely use common day vernacular for whatever best suits your particular Control Freak situation. You also may need to "get physical" and throw out the drugs, alcohol, pornography and/or excuse the controlling person from your presence. Look, you're up against an evil spirit, now is <u>not</u> the time to be shy.

So that you can better ascertain the range of its use, let's look at two examples of "Escalated Rebuke", each positioned at opposite ends of the "Escalated Rebuke Spectrum":

First, on the low end, say you have a Bible study that you've invited someone to attend and she asks the question, "How many people are coming?"

You change the subject and don't answer that question because God has told you not to fall into the trap of numbering the people; your directive from the Lord has always been: "*don't focus on numbers (quantity), but on individual growth (quality)."*

She never shows up to the study herself, but the next time you speak to this person on the phone, she again asks, "Well how many people are coming to Saturday nights?" You tell her politely, "I don't count; God doesn't want me doing that."

Escalated Rebuke

Naturally, she thinks there are maybe two people there and though your pride may want to explain that would be an incorrect presumption, you don't explain anything. You're just trying to obey the Lord and so you *really* haven't counted. Therefore, your answer was good enough.

Realize now, if you're the Leader, the spirit of control is trying to use this question for you to ponder whether or not your Bible study is a "success" solely based on numbers. The way the carnal mind thinks is, if the numbers are big-- it is; if the numbers are small-- it isn't. If the study doesn't *look* like a success, "it" is hoping that maybe you'll give up on the calling of God sooner than later.

So you talk to this same person once more (and though you've stopped even inviting her at this point), again it's the same question. This time you say, "I don't know". Then she says, "Oh come on, you've got to know, you can at least take a guess."

In response you say, "Carol, look, the Lord has shown me that it's carnal for me to count numbers of attendees because if the numbers are good, I would have a tendency to take all the credit for myself as the Leader. So again, I'm not counting numbers; I'm looking for solid growth in individual lives. You know, you've asked me this several times before and I've tried to be polite about it, but please don't ask me this same question again."

You just rebuked her, by telling her that the question was "carnal"; but you didn't sin and you obeyed by not allowing yourself to be controlled. If she never "gets it", oh well ... you cannot backslide to-- where God has brought you from, just to please a person posing a seemingly very innocent, albeit carnal, question.

At the other end of the spectrum, say you're a woman, and it's late at night and you're walking through a desolate portion of a very large grocery store, way in the back. Some man approaches you, strikes up an innocent enough conversation and invites you to come with him for coffee.

You politely decline.

The man continues to persist on how great looking you are and tries to coax you into coming with him, *"just around corner"*. You continue to indirectly ward him off.

Escalated Rebuke

He then starts making some fairly strong statements about what he *"can do for you."* You tell him, "No thank you." You move away from him in the opposite direction and continue with your shopping.

He approaches again, commenting on your dress; your heart starts to beat faster ("control" has engaged, you've been "affected"). Now feeling threatened, you have to disrupt the focus of your errand and walk the other way, again.

The man persists and follows you, he's now forced you off your own course (effect) and he now says some crude comment about your body; and you respond, "Get lost ... now!"

He says, "I'm not gonna get lost until I'm done with you!" He then grabs you from behind and tries to pull you into the bathroom area in the back.

This is a Control Freak Extraordinaire situation; this is obviously not the time to be concerned about "Christian etiquette". You yell, scream, call him every name in the book and fight him like the dickens.

"CONTROL FREAK"

Escalated Rebuke

In other words, when the spirit of control comes in like a tank to push you down and roll over you; then you've got to pump up the volume and shut that tank down!

Remember, in order to fight off that controlling spirit you may need to raise your voice (but you're not operating in the flesh out of weakness, nor are you out-of-control). Rather, you are intentionally raising your voice to stop that controlling spirit, from bulldozing you over and getting the edge.

Additionally, when you employ "Escalated Rebuke" you should expect to fire off rather curt, or semi-sarcastic remarks, especially when "it" continues to push and push "its" agenda. In no case, however, will it be necessary for you to sin.

Realize that as you refuse to allow others to *control* you, this will cause them to get *very angry* with you (which we already know is just another Control Freak tactic they're using to try to get you back under "its" control). This is when you'll need a list of "generic" "Rehearsed Responses" formulated at varying levels of severity, ready to fire off at any given time.

Escalated Rebuke

We will now go through a few "Escalated Rebuke" examples that have, very roughly, been placed in the order of higher and higher levels of escalation as we move towards the end of the list.

Here they go:

"Fascinating conversation dear, but I've got to go to the restroom" (and then never come back). [It's a modified Joseph escape.]

"I appreciate the input, but I don't completely agree with it."

"Unfortunately, I just can't do *everything* that *everyone* wants me to do."

"I know that's what you'd want me to do, but I won't be taking that action or handling it that way."

"It's obvious what you *want* me to do from the pressure you're attempting to exert on me; but it's not going to happen, so why don't you just change the subject?"

Escalated Rebuke

"Now *you know* I stopped allowing you to make me feel _____ (guilty, angry, hurt, stupid, scared, threatened; you fill in the blank); a long time ago *dear,* remember?"

"I fulfill my God given responsibilities first; and my man-driven responsibilities, later ... that is, *if ...* I have time."

"I'm pretty sure the answer, *'No'* sounds the same in just about every language; so what do you think it's going to take to get *you,* to better understand the word?"

"You're clearly disappointed by my decision; you know, I hate *to see you* that way."

"I'm not going to answer this question again; whatever you don't like about what I'm doing, please just take it up with the Lord directly. You *do* have a relationship with Him ... *don't you?"*

"Honey, I hate to see when you get angry like that, your face gets *really, really* red; I don't think its good for you."

"Look, if you don't simmer down, you're going to have to increase the dosage on your blood pressure medication."

Escalated Rebuke

"Aaah, once again, you're not happy with me; and once again, I'll just have to do my best to get over it."

"Roger, captain! Communication received; yet not intended to be followed."

"I really hate to see you this way when you get angry, isn't there anything *you* can do about it?"

"I've said this same thing to you several times already; and I'm not sure why you still don't understand. Shall I look for a translator to help with your understanding of my communication? What do ya' need, French or German?

"You're thinking far too highly of yourself if you think *your* opinion, is going to change mine."

"Hey did you ever notice? ... When you're *really mad* like this, you've got ... you know that little blood vessel, right there! Yes, right there on your temple, well it gets all big and it pumps ... come to the mirror, quick, look! You really should see it."

"CONTROL FREAK"

Escalated Rebuke

"I want to thank you for being so disagreeable today, it's made me better appreciate those people in my life who are not."

"I now find it very difficult to care what other people have to say anymore; yourself included."

"Listen, before you go; I want to thank you for being so rude to me today, its definitely made *me*, a better person."

LOL! This is where you get to have all the fun and it works! Yes, you're on the border, these are "Escalated Rebukes", which need to be used judiciously. But these are Control Freak Extraordinaires that you're being forced to deal with!

You've just got to take "it" OUT!

You can't let them roll over you, or they'll come back with more force the next time and consume your life. Believe me, "it" will flee! The spirit of divination will flee! It's amazing how "it" will flee; "it" has to because "it" has no authority over you!

Escalated Rebuke

After these kinds of interactions end, sure, you're heart will be pounding a little faster than usual, but you will be absolutely cracking up![101]

Now, in order to increase your "double chocolate cake" dessert service competency we will next provide you with some "Jugular Extraction Practice". These will be "real life" illustrations of exactly how to re-frame various Control Freak issues, to include some instances where the employment of your "Escalated Rebuke" artillery is implemented.

---

[101] "Escalated Rebuke" is not, however, recommended for use with those who are prone to physical violence. By now, volatile, violent Control Freaks should have already been fully eliminated from your life.

CHAPTER 37:
Jugular Extraction Practice

Now that you've been equipped with your last piece of artillery, "Escalated Rebuke", a little more practice employing various "Jugular Extraction Methods" will help you develop what can truly be considered an "art form".

You will now be presented with various interpersonal interaction examples. Each one is intended to demonstrate a variation of how your new artillery can be employed whenever you're called upon to serve one of our "heavier" dessert combinations.

Understand, however, that there are so many potential interpersonal interactions that you have everyday, that it would be impossible to think of every controlling situation, that every Christian has ever faced, and then put them all in this one volume or any number of books or volumes. [102]

It's something similar to what was said about all the works Jesus did here on earth, *"Were every one of them to be written, I suppose that the world itself could not contain the books that would be written"* (Jn 21:25, ESV).

As review, here is a summary of your four dessert options:

DESSERT OPTION #1: Whipped Cream and Fresh Berries; SAY NOTHING; <u>AND</u> THEN SUBMIT OR COMPLY;

DESSERT OPTION #2: Whipped cream on Ice Cream; SAY NOTHING; <u>AND</u> THEN RESIST/STAND OR EMPLOY THE PRINCIPLE OF DIAMETRIC OPPOSITION;

DESSERT OPTION #3: Double Chocolate Cake and Fresh Berries; CORRECT/REBUKE; <u>AND</u> THEN SUBMIT OR COMPLY; and

DESSERT OPTION #4: Double Chocolate Cake and Ice Cream; CORRECT/REBUKE; <u>AND</u> THEN RESIST/STAND OR EMPLOY THE PRINCIPLE OF DIAMETRIC OPPOSITION.

---

[102] The sequel: "CONTROL FREAK" (Trial Practice) is currently in the works, we're compiling more examples for your learning and application pleasure.

Jugular Extraction Practice

Remember, taking out the jugular is not a one-time event; it's like ridding an insect infestation with something sweet and afterwards, staying on constant "alert" so that you're never re-infested. So we serve "dessert" to the evil spirit because as Christians, we are to overcome evil with good (Ro 12:21).

Got it?

Also, remember that "Jugular Extraction Methods" are employed only when you're called upon to serve up our two "heavier" dessert combinations: Dessert Option #3 Double Chocolate Cake and Berries (Correct/Rebuke and then Submit or Comply); and Dessert Option #4 Double Chocolate Cake and Ice Cream (Correct/Rebuke and then Resist/Stand, or Employ the Principle of Diametric Opposition); because in both instances *you are going to "say" something* to correct/rebuke the spirit of divination.

On the other hand, you will never use these kinds of examples below, when serving up Dessert Options #1 and #2, because neither of those combinations requires a rebuke/correct response; rather, you will simply, "Say Nothing".

Jugular Extraction Practice

The examples below can be used whenever you are called on to serve "double chocolate cake" and "rebuke/correct" the spirit of divination. You will see both "on point" "Rehearsed Responses" that "Turn the Tables" and/or "Re-Frame" the "Control Freak issue" and when called for, you will also see examples of "Escalated Rebuke".

A new feature that has been provided in some of the examples below is what I call a: "Control Freak Translation". This is when I take and interpret the "chink in your armor" (CIYA); and then translate how the "spirit of divination" causes the feelings (affect) and actions (effect) of an individual, to be *controlled* by others. "Control Freak Translations" will be provided in order to make sure that everyone stays on board with our "Jugular Extraction Practice Session".

At the conclusion of this chapter, you will then be expected to take all of the principles you've learned in this text; all of the examples you've been provided in this text; every piece of artillery you've been given in this text; and then generalize and apply the whole assortment to suit each "Control Freak" encounter that "you" face in the future.

"CONTROL FREAK"

Jugular Extraction Practice

Remember, from now on, you must always be functioning on "high alert" for whenever a Control Freak steps into the vicinity. So depending on the circumstances, there may be times when you're put in a position to come up with a jugular extraction response rather quickly, without any rehearsal time whatsoever. That's why our prior list of generic responses needs to be memorized, so you'll have them prepared and ready to fire at any given opportunity.

Here we go:

Your mother-in-law makes a negative comment that your dress color doesn't look good with your skin color.

You may first respond, "You know Mom, this is actually one of the hottest spring colors this year."

If that doesn't put an end to the conversation and she says, *"But dear, you look so flushed out."*

You may then respond, "Instead of being stuck in a rut wearing the same old black or blue all the time, I've actually been having a lot of fun exploring other possibilities mom."

If she persists (<u>Control Freak Translation</u>: she's got another dress in mind for you to wear) and says, *"Well honey it just doesn't look good on you."*

You then say, "Gosh mom ... <u>I</u> don't think so. I absolutely love this dress on me, it makes me feel sooo special." You then give her a kiss on the cheek and walk out the door; and, with a strut!

You corrected, you did not comply with her request; there was no sin; but you know you've got a grin. Dessert Combination #4, double chocolate cake and ice cream, has been successfully served.

Some volunteer at church sees you cleaning the storeroom and says, "I can't believe they make *you* do this, don't they have a cleaning service?"

<u>Control Freak Translation</u>: Instead of agreeing with his/her commiseration and feeling slighted by church leadership (affect); and likely deciding not to serve anymore in the future (effect); and while knowing the Lord only has you in training for a season, you say, "Actually I like doing anything for the Lord; it's all good enough for me."

Correction was made, you didn't sin; the conversation comes quickly to an end. Dessert Combination #4 has been successfully served, yet again.

Your wife wants you to get another job to cover paying for her inability to control herself at Nordstrom's. Instead of saying nothing and letting "it" get you angry and holding a grudge you say, "Dear, the next time I get another credit card bill like this, it's time for you to go work for that store, so at least you can get a discount."

Now that's a way of making a correction, without ruining marital relations. You did not sin; you made a correction, you submitted or complied with the situation by paying the bill. Dessert Combination #3, double chocolate cake and fresh berries, has been successfully served.

Someone comes storming into your office furious about the way the boss just spoke to him, and he wants to spew the whole interaction out right on *your* desk. He's done this before and you know you'll be there for an hour or more.

So in response you say, "Not today George, I've got a report due. Why don't you see if you can go blow off some steam at the gym during your lunch break?"

No sin, no compliance, and yet, no control has been exercised over "you" or your time either. Dessert Combination #4 has been successfully served.

There is a spousal support issue being litigated in a divorce matter. The ex-to-be-husband, tells the wife that she's to blame for his recent irregular heart palpitations and that she's putting his very life at risk, "just for money".

Control Freak Translation: Husband is trying to use a guilt complex to control wife into dropping her spousal support claim against him.

Wife first says in response, "If you weren't hiding something about your income, *dear*, you wouldn't be so distressed and your heart would be fine."

The husband responds in anger, "You don't know what you're putting me through. If I die, you'll get nothing!"

Jugular Extraction Practice

In response the wife says, "Oh dear, if I'd only had that kind of influence over you when we were married, we may have never ended up in divorce court in the first place."

Dessert Option #4 served: Wife corrects with an "on point" statement that directly addresses the issue. Namely, she corrects him about how foolish it is for him to think that *she* has so much control over *his very being,* that she could ever cause him to have a heart attack.

The wife also, does <u>not</u> get sidetracked into argument mode, by saying anything about how the law requires him to pay spousal support; or how he makes over three times more than she does, etc. The wife does not comply with dismissing her support claim against the husband and she also does not sin in the process. Double chocolate cake and ice cream has been successfully served to the ex-to-be.

Reversed trend: **Where the husband wants spousal support from his ex-wife-to-be,** so he decides to try and extort money out of her by making a settlement demand. He shows up at her office unexpectedly and drops a three-inch folder of defamatory material about her on the desk, threatening to disseminate the information throughout the land; to her friends, family and business associates, if he is not given the settlement amount he's demanding.

The wife knows that once you give in to an extortioner you will never be free, never! So for the wife, there is no dilly-dallying around with this one, she accelerates straight into the "Escalated Rebuke" phase of this conversation and immediately employs the "Principle of Diametric Opposition."

In response the wife actually "invites" her enemy to just *try* to take her out and says: "Bring it on!" "Give it your best shot!" "Form your weapon boy and *try* all you want. The lower you *try* to pull me down, the higher I'm assuredly going up."

She then promptly dismisses him from her presence and out of her office and then goes on about her day, casting down every imagination that would try to take her back to re-living the threatening incident.

You've got to have that kind of mentality! Remember, it's the spirit of control trying to work against you, so God is clearly on your side; so at the end of the day, everything you say in opposition will come to pass.

Does the defamatory material about the wife, ever get disseminated to others by the husband? Yes, of course it does! But as is obvious in this case by the wife's response, her CIYA is long gone. So she could really *care less.*

Dessert Option #4, at a high rather abrupt level, using "Escalated Rebuke" along with "The Principle of Diametric Opposition", has just been served. Mmmmmm ... yummy!

You've determined that you're going back to the gym to start a regular workout routine after years of being a couch potato. You used to think you were at least a little bit "buff", but once you get to the gym and see the rest of the guys pumping iron you start to feel a bit intimidated (affect). It even seems as if *they all know each other*, because when you first walked in, they all stared you down, practically in unison.

Since the gym was so crowded at that time of day, it forced you to have break-in with some of the other guys to do your sets, just in order to get your workout done. Because you were too embarrassed to lower the weight, you began to lift a much higher, heavier weight than you should have (effect); just in order to show them that "looks can be deceiving" and that you're not really the "pansy" that they all first suspected.

As a result, after your first workout, you are both injured and sore and you can't go back to the gym for two or more weeks.

Control Freak Translation: The CIYA had yet to be shored up. You are still so concerned about what others think of you, that you hurt yourself at the gym; and as a result, "it" was able to destroy your motivation to keep working towards your fitness goals.

After having learned the "hard way" (ouch!) and spending some more time with the Lord working on the "chink in your armor" (CIYA), you decide to give it another try and go back to the gym.

But this time, you've got some "Rehearsed Responses" under your weight belt, along with the express intention of serving up some double chocolate cake and ice cream; and ruining the "protein diets" of every brute you encounter if necessary.

It's now time for you to break-in and do the bench press. The guy that you're breaking-in with snidely remarks, "Do you *have to* lower the weight?"

You say with a chuckle, "It's either that, or I end up as buff as you are!" Without even pausing for a response, you then take off the extra weight to suit your fancy and do your set.

You corrected and you "resisted" the temptation to be controlled into lifting a heavier weight than would have been good for you this time. You didn't sin and you didn't cause any kind of animosity with the junior Mr. America, who later ends up becoming your new work out partner.

Situations where "Christians" come to you with gossip about others, or are trying to elicit gossip from you about others, can control "you" and your behavior.

Control Freak Translation: the Control Freak issue is when the gossiping comment is dropped, the door is opened for you to jump on board and provide confirmation with some negative comment of your own about that person too. Not only do you not want to gossip because it is sin; but every time you get told this kind of information, it pollutes your mind, it captivates your thoughts, it controls your emotions or your feelings about the person being gossiped about (affect); and it usually causes you to treat the person gossiped about differently than you would have otherwise (effect).

So instead of engaging in, or even commenting on the substantive content of the gossip you just heard; you pretend like you didn't even hear the negative comment at all. You act as if you'd been "checked out" in la la land the whole time.

Then, instead of confirming their derogatory comments, you say something very nice and/or complimentary about that *very same person* whom they were hoping to get you to gossip about. You try something like: "Have you ever heard him preach?" "Have you ever heard how great that girl sings?" "Have you ever seen how immaculate she keeps her house?" "Have you seen him lately? He got a new sports car, I think he's doing great in his new business!" and then just move on.

Yes, that'll be the end of that!

Of course you might lose a "friend" – a *gossiping* friend. But don't think for a minute that a gossiping friend won't gossip against *you* too, when the opportunity presents itself. In fact, the minute you do something like this, he or she has already gone on a gossiping rampage, but this time it is all about you! Yet again, the CIYA is gone, so you could absolutely *care less.*

You didn't allow the spirit of divination to *control* you into sinning by participating in the gossip; and you didn't sin in the process of rebuking/correcting "it" either. This totally sinless rebuke will shut that controlling spirit right down; and who knows, maybe the gossip will receive correction from the Holy Spirit at the same time.

Yet, another victory!

Your next-door neighbor, a bit of a car buff, just bought an old antique Ferrari. He's not saved; he's not really

Jugular Extraction Practice

even a friend of yours; and to be quite honest he's always been a materialistic show-off, which has made you a bit repelled by his personality. Nonetheless, as an Ambassador of Christ, you have always continued to be a "good neighbor".

He pulls up while you're working in the front yard and even though you waved "Hi", he just can't keep himself from bragging about his new ride. Without looking over, you can hear that the roar of the engine has ceased (but not before he unnecessarily revved it just one last time); and now, step step step ... here he comes, walking up your driveway.

While pretending like you don't realize he's coming, you're now desperately praying, "Oh Lord, *now* what do I say? I don't want to confirm that having his affections set on the things of the earth is right, but at the same time I don't want to seem jealous because I still drive my old beat-up truck."

The neighbor exclaims, "Hey, George! What do you think of that?" (As he proudly looks back to his new car.) "What a beauty, isn't she? And fast ... oh my... is she fast! You wouldn't believe how she takes the corners. And *boy,* hubba hubba, I'm telling you, you should see how the

"CONTROL FREAK"

Jugular Extraction Practice

ladies look at me when I'm cruzin' down the boulevard!"

You reply, "My yes, Henry, it's a beautiful car. How exciting for you." [All the while thinking to yourself, there's nothing else for heathens to be excited about, so I really haven't been insincere with that comment.]

Henry then, in demonstration of his usual lack of couth, responds, "Don't *you* wish you had one of these jewels to replace that old clunker of yours?"

Slam! Henry couldn't have just accepted the positive acknowledgement and gone back to polishing his chrome rims, could he? No, he just *had* to rub George's nose right into it, didn't he? Yes.

Control Freak Translation: If George doesn't respond correctly to this temptation, he will be angry for another month (affect) because of Henry's materialistically-based pride; and that will not only cause George to resent and begrudge his neighbor (or sin), it may also cause George to act like a bad witness towards Henry in the future (effect).

Jugular Extraction Practice

So understand that this is an exceptionally high-risk temptation facing George right now, especially given the fact that like many men, he could easily fall into the temptation of being covetous over his neighbor's new "toy".

Knowing the risks involved and trying to escape out of this conversation as soon as he possibly can, George then escalates his rebuke a tad and in response to the fiery "old clunker" dart he says, "Well Henry, I'm just not sure that's the way the Lord would have me spend my money."

But what if that doesn't take care of Henry?

What if Henry says something smart back in response like, "Guess your God isn't any fun, is He?"

Wow! Now what do you say ... *George?*

At that point George could respond with, "Oh on the contrary Henry, you just don't know the Creator of the Universe; if you did, you'd find out that there's so much more to life than even your 1972 mint condition red Dino!"[103]

End of conversation.

Henry likely walks away knowing that somehow, he's just lost some leverage, but because it was a sinless rebuke, he's not exactly sure how. He then starts wondering if it had anything to do with this "Creator of the Universe" remark George made. Or, Henry tries to ignore the comment entirely and keeps on talking about his new car.

In either case, it doesn't matter to George, he's not mad; he made the correction; he stood up for the fact there is more to life than just "toys" and he didn't fall into sin.

This is an example of the "Resist/Stand" component of Dessert Option #4. George had to say something to rebuke/correct. Since there was nothing for him to do the opposite about, he made a few statements of correction sufficient to "resist" falling into temptation, while at the same time "standing" his ground as to his Kingdom worldview.

---

[103] Dino Ferrari, that is.

Jugular Extraction Practice

When dealing with murmuring and complaining people on the job, they may ask you: "Can you believe what this company is doing to us by changing our health insurance?" You can "reframe" the issue, by saying something like: "It's better than socialized medical care, so I'm very grateful. Besides, I don't plan on getting sick anyway in Jesus' name!" And then change the subject by commenting on the interior of the workplace, like: "The new bathroom fixtures are sure nice, aren't they?"

No control, no sin, victory again when serving Dessert Option #4.

Say a husband is mad because his wife forgot to pick up a homeowner's magazine he wanted to peruse for a potential purchase. His wife is a full-on "multitasker" personality, but she just didn't get this one thing done today. Instead of the wife getting upset and having the usual "knock down, drag out fight" about the husband not appreciating all the things she actually did accomplish for him that day; she "re-frames" all of the events of the day, employing some lawyering skills that even she didn't realize she had, and puts forth her best "case" by saying

Jugular Extraction Practice

something like this:

"Honey, I went to work to earn money today to help pay off the golf clubs I bought you for your birthday; I cleaned your breakfast dishes; dropped off your pants at the cleaners; picked-up that dessert you like so much, so that you could have it with your favorite roast beef dinner tonight; I paid the light bill like you asked; and I swept out your tool shed ... I mean the long and short of it lovie-dovie, is that I've been too busy trying to make you happy all day today to get that one little itsy bitsy thing done, but I promise I'll do it tomorrow ... You *do* still love me anyways, don't you?" (As she throws her arms around him, kisses him on the cheek and smiles, all the while looking intently and lovingly into his eyes for confirmation).

Talk about reframing the issue! Now, what's he gonna say?

That's a perfect example of service of Dessert Option #3 (Correct/Rebuke and then Submit or Comply), while "re-framing" the issue. The wife provides a laundry list of considerate things she's done to make her husband's life far more enjoyable. Once re-framing the perspective (or issue) in a way that causes the husband to look at the "big picture", it now appears that it would be totally foolish for him to get angry or hold a grudge over this one minor point. The wife has made the correction, but she intends to submit or comply by picking up the magazine for her husband the next day.

Your ex spouse insists on trying to control what you do with the children *during your custody time*, even years after your divorce has been final. Your Ex asks you several detailed questions meant to control both you and the children's behavior in his/her absence.

Control Freak Translation: first, you should *never answer to the interrogation*, because that is the spirit of divination trying to "affect" you by getting, regaining, or retaining emotional control over "you". Instead, you must turn the tables, re-frame the issue and maintain your side of the "case" or perspective while rebuking "it" with finesse.

In this case, the parent decides to repeat a "Rehearsed Response" used to "Turn the Tables" by "Reframing" the "Control Freak" issue. This same substantive response is then conveyed over and over again, to the point of being effectively used in an abbreviated form.

Here's how that works in this situation:

Your first response is, "Now remember the Court orders dear; when the children are with me, I'm the boss; when they're with you, you're the boss. So on Saturday they'll be with me; and on Sunday they'll be with you-- so let's all just act accordingly."

The rebuke is in and yet, no sin.

No matter what is said in response by the Ex, you stay "on point" and say the exact same thing; remembering to beware of getting caught up in the usual argumentative quagmire.

Should he or she persist, your next response is slightly escalated and you say; "Now dear, you realize you lost the right to place me on the witness stand when we divorced right?"

Jugular Extraction Practice

After you use that exact same response to *whatever is said* a few more times, the next time the Ex seeks to interrogate you, now you only have to say, "I'm off the stand, dear" "Dear, I'm off the stand".

Then if he or she tries interrogating you right in front of the children or others in an attempt to control you more easily (expecting you won't dare make "a scene" in front of others), now you only have to say: "Honey, *the stand, remember?*"

If he or she continues on trying to control you in a "public" situation, now you simply say, "Remember the stand, dear" "This witness has been dismissed three years ago" and then leave the interaction and go about your business, not responding any further.

When making these kinds of corrective statements, you're not angry, you're not mad; you're just saying them as a matter of fact. Most importantly, you're not sinning!

This same double chocolate cake and ice cream dessert combination has been served so many times in the past, it's now ready to be dished out, at anytime, in abbreviated fashion.

Say a woman at work is a bit too "friendly" for your taste. She's always "coming on" to you, batting her eyelashes and exaggerating every move, like some "femme fatale". Though you're not married, you're still not interested.

Yet, she seems to always have something to do in your workstation area. It appears as if she continues to walk by you just hoping you'll notice her, what she's wearing; say "hi" to her, or otherwise engage her in a longer, more personal conversation.

She has even asked you out after work a few times before, and you've politely declined each time. She's also asked if she could bake you some chocolate chip cookies (after somehow finding out how much you like them.) To that offer, you politely said, "No, thank you" and commented about how you're, "trying to get in shape."

Control Freak Translation: at this point she is negatively influencing your work productivity by consuming your thought life. Instead of just coming into work to do your job, you are now burdened with trying to avoid yet another interaction with her, like the plague.

It's even gotten to the point where you're actually thinking more about *her* while on the job, than your own work duties: what she's doing now, when she'll be coming back around, what she'll say to you next, what she just said or did, what she's trying to get you to do, or how she grosses you out, etc. Indeed, the minute you clock-in at your place of employment, you start "Control-Freaking Out!"

You cannot live the rest of your work life like this! Not only is she making a total embarrassment out of herself; but since you're absolutely never going to be interested in her in that way, *ever* ... something just needs to be done.

So you "Check-In" with the Lord and inquire, "Lord do you see "it"? You know her heart better than I do, but this is ridiculous, it's got to stop. I can't concentrate, I'm feeling watched all the time ... stalked even. So what do You want me to do?"

Jugular Extraction Practice

Since you're never going to comply with her desire to date, it's obvious that *she's* actually going to be the one receiving some baked goods from you. Due to her persistence, you're now forced to serve her *double chocolate cake* and ice cream (Dessert Option # 4).

So you ask the Lord to give you some "Rehearsed Responses" for the next time she comes around trying to strike up a conversation, while flaunting herself in your face.

Like clockwork, she shows up again just before lunchtime and she comes near your workspace once again pretending like she has something legitimate to do. She then asks you what you're doing for lunch. However, this time, instead of being polite and spending any time answering her usual interrogating questions about tacos and salsa, you say, "Sorry, Claire, no time to chit-chat right now."

You've *never* said anything like that to her before, so she's a bit taken back; and she demurely responds, "Oh, ok." It actually appears for a moment that she's turning around to leave without further incident; but no, she then looks back and says, *"I'll catch you later then."*

Control Freak Translation: Now, if you fail to respond to that last statement of Claire's, "I'll catch you later then" -- you have not extracted the jugular. You've only left "it" "dangling" if you would, but still pumping.

You need to take it OUT! The door has just been reopened for you to complete the extraction process. If you don't fire another *escalated* "Rehearsed Response" she'll be back around in an hour or so asking another dumb question, just to get your attention.

So you respond, "I don't think so Claire; look, you're a very nice girl and I know you're interested in me, but I'm not available."

Notice: you've stayed "on point". You didn't get entangled providing information as to *why* you're not available, like: *"I have a girlfriend"*. Nor, did you explain to Claire exactly *why* you're not interested in her, per se, like: *"You're a 'stalker'"*, *"You scare me"*, or, *"You're just too 'desperate' to ever become my 'housewife'"*.

Jugular Extraction Practice

Are you getting the idea?

You'll see over time that this actually gets to be a whole lot of good clean fun! Just you and the Lord coming up with all these great sinless statements to employ against the spirit of divination, over and over and over; taking "the jugular" O-U-T time and time again, one right after the other! Each time you get the victory, you'll be fully empowered to gain even more Promised Land territory for your life in the future!

When you get freed from that oppressive *feeling* brought on by the spirit of divination, you will have so much joy and be so empowered that you won't believe it's your own life you're living. You won't even believe how far He's brought "you", in such a short time.

In closing, let me explain how this progression in your own life will be experienced.

Jugular Extraction Practice

"CONTROL FREAK"

CHAPTER 38: Closing Arguments

"Brethren, I count not myself to have apprehended: but this one thing I do, forgetting those things which are behind, and reaching forth unto those things which are before, I **press toward the mark for the prize of the high calling of God in Christ Jesus**" (Phil 3:13-14, KJV).

I've learned that once I understand what I'm shooting for, or what "the victory" *is supposed* to look like ... *lived out,* I can usually get there much faster. That's what I mean when I use the term "the mark" in this context.

You are about to enter a new battlefield, one in which you have little or no experience. So in the beginning, you should expect that there is going to be a "learning curve" as you gain entrance to this new territory.

Closing Arguments

When you first start firing your weaponry, expect there to be a little bit of "hit or miss" as you're getting used to handling it in different battlefields. You'll win a few with this Rehearsed Response; and you'll lose a few with that one. You'll try this piece of artillery, then that one. This one will work with that person, that one won't.

So at first you've got to learn to just "roll with the punches" learning everything you can from each interaction. Realize that through that learning process, you're refining your "Jugular Eradication Methodology" as a craft. There is no cookie cutter formula that you can use on every person in every situation. If that were the case, you wouldn't need Him. God wants you to depend on Him, not on man, or some scientific formula for spiritual success.

You'll always need to keep your artillery clean and sharp, ready for use at any time, in any situation, with any number of people in one sequence. After each interaction the Lord will be faithful to show you something else, something new, something you shouldn't have said *that way*, or something you should have done *this way*. Or, how if you had a different approach, with a different attitude, or a different

Closing Arguments

tone of voice, at a different time of day, your method would have worked much better.

There will be times when you feel like a total failure and there will be others, when you feel like you've trampled "it" under foot. Even then, if you don't monitor yourself carefully, by the time the next Control Freak interaction comes, you'll feel like you lost ground ... *again.* Throughout this process, you must realize that as long as you're continuing to press forward, getting back up and trying again, that you're always progressing.

Until one day, you'll realize that this new craft has become so refined in your life that you yourself, have been "transformed" into a "Jugular Eradication Specialist".

Wow! Imagine that.

Below is a rough outline of the stages of progression to that end of pressing towards "the mark" of becoming totally and completely, "Control Freak Free".

You may currently fall into any one of the stages below, but as you begin to employ your artillery to eliminate the spirit of divination from your life, you will continue your progression towards "the mark", no matter where you started off.

In the beginning, before ever reading this text, you did pretty much anything and everything to please the people in your life, even if it was compromise and even if it wasn't in your best interest. You just didn't want to "rock the boat", especially with the people you love (or with whom you had an "emotional link").

As a result, your quality of life was never *really good*. Yes, there were some short-lived enjoyable times, but they always somehow ended up in emotional upheaval (affect). Once in that condition, you would always sin in some way or another (effect). You responded to those *controlling* people in your life by yelling, screaming, wailing, cussing, throwing things, slamming doors and drawers and/or becoming hateful, resentful, begrudging and embittered against them.

As that *control* over your life escalated, you felt worse and worse about yourself because you knew you were living in sin. This caused you to have less and less hope that your life would ever change for the better. You, therefore, were at risk of becoming depressed, lifeless; and in that condition, definitely, useless for the Kingdom.

After gaining an understanding of the principles in this text, you now realize that these people in your life had become your idols; and that the *control* they've been exercising over your life for years now, has sucked you dry. In fact, you're so used to having your conduct controlled by the desires of others, that you're not sure what you'd even do with yourself if you really ever did "break free".

You're still not sure who you really are, what you really like to do, or what you really want to do, even for the Lord. Quite frankly, you're a bit intimidated by the possibilities. So you're even more afraid than ever to carry out what you now know, needs to be done.

You don't think you can come up with even one "Rehearsed Response", and if you were ever called upon to implement it? Ha! You're absolutely terrified to think of how that controlling person in your life would respond. Yet you now know that you don't have a choice; this must be done, otherwise, your entire life will end up being fruitless and meaningless.

So you ask the Lord for His wisdom and empowerment and you sit down and start to at least *try* to prepare for your next Control Freak encounter. Lo and behold, the Holy Spirit comes through and starts giving you things to write down about the people you know who are always trying to control you, as well as the things they always do or say in order to do so.

You pray for wisdom and then a few *potential* "Rehearsed Responses" where you've "reframed" what you anticipate from others in the future, actually come to mind. You practice and rework your wording, you practice and rework your tone, you practice and rework your inflection, you practice and rework your potential timing and you practice and rework your delivery.

You're then reminded, that you'll need the Holy Spirit to provide you the power to exercise "self control" at maximum levels once you're ready to fire these off; so you now find yourself down on your knees, asking for His help.

Closing Arguments

All of a sudden, you seem to be getting just a little bit excited about your new potential. Soon you think you've got a pretty good grasp on a few specific "Rehearsed Responses" and you've taken some of the generic responses provided in this text and modified them to better suit your personality; and you've put them all together in your arsenal. So you *feel* like you're just about as prepared as you can be; at least, you *think*.

You then encounter your next Control Freak situation, but this time, unlike the others, you can see "it" coming from a mile away. It's *so obvious* when "it" shows up now, you wonder to yourself why on earth you never noticed "it" like this before?

The spirit of divination then makes a move and ... *swoosh!*

Oh no! Your head was in the clouds, that one blew right by you! Though you *thought* you had some artillery prepared, you totally missed your opportunity to confront "it" because you were still thinking about why you'd never seen "it" so clearly before. Then, before you knew it, the contact was over and you were left standing there dazed; you just can't believe how that interaction transpired so quickly.

Closing Arguments

You then talk to the Lord about what just happened. "Lord what should I have said? What should I have done? Wow! Lord, now I hate when that happens, I hate being controlled by evil, Lord please don't let it happen again."

You now better realize what *"gird up the loins of your mind"*, really means (1 Pe 1:13, KJV). So you become more mentally alert knowing that when the opportunity arises to "take it out" you must act right then! There'll be no more lackadaisical existence for you; you've got to be functioning on "high alert" at all times. You've determined that you will not be caught napping and miss the next opportunity that you have to take "it" out.

"It" then comes back, in another form and fashion, by use of another unwitting individual. This time you did say something, it wasn't a "Rehearsed Response" (you didn't think of one for this person/situation); but *at least you said something* this time and the pitch didn't blow right by you!

Unfortunately, this person was able to make you emotionally upset and cause you to become angry and cry after the interaction.

Closing Arguments

You think to yourself, *"How did that happen?"*

Oh geeze! You forgot to "Check-In" with the Lord to ask Him for direction. Was that a battle He wanted you to fight, or should you have simply submitted? You must have served the wrong dessert combination. Was your attitude wrong? You say, "Lord, how can I tap into more 'self control' so I don't end up becoming an emotional wreck next time?"

You're agitated, all you know is that you can't get what they said out of your mind; you can't stop the instant replay of the interaction. Yes, "it" got to you and you're now "Control-Freaking Out" about the entire interaction, plus you sinned.

Bummer!

You go back to the Lord and ask Him to show you what you *could have done differently*, what "Rehearsed Response" you *could have* said or how you *could have* better "Reframed" what they said; what Dessert Option you *should have* served; and when you *should have* left the interaction in order to avoid the *control* they just exercised over your life, by eliciting an emotional response out of you.

He faithfully delivers the information you need and you adjust your weaponry for the next time. During this conversation with the Lord, you also again ask Him to do something about ridding this person and/or these *controlling* people from your life.

Yet, instead of the comfort you're expecting in response, this time the Holy Spirit sternly corrects you. It's actually "you" He wants *you* to do something about, not them.

One lady, while describing her experience at this stage, said the Lord responded, "Well when *are you* going to do something about you?"

Though hard, you receive the correction and go back to cleaning and polishing your artillery. This "Jugular Extraction Practice" is a little harder than you thought it would be; you actually have to "think" and "work" and "plan" your new life of victory.

Closing Arguments

You now realize that you must indeed put forth a lot of effort and always be "on guard" in order to improve your "quality of life". This victory is not going to be served to you on a silver platter as you had hoped; it must be battled for and taken by force; blood; sweat; and yet, with as few tears as possible.

The next Control Freak situation arises, this time you remember to "Check-In" with the Lord, but He tells you to serve whipped cream with fresh berries, so there was no "rebuke/correction needed. But at least you remembered to "Check-In" and at least you heard His directive. So you're feeling pretty good about it.

As time passes and you continue your pursuit towards "the mark" you begin to experience one Control Freak situation after another, day after day, always learning something new. You improve and refine, buff and polish, and purify this ongoing process in your life. You win a few and lose a few, but you keep on refining. You "reframe" what they said the last time, while preparing your next set of "Rehearsed Responses".

Closing Arguments

During each interaction, you're learning not to miss using even one piece of your artillery. Though you still fumble around a bit, at least you're remembering what weaponry you have on hand and ready for use when appropriate. As to those victories you do experience, afterwards, the Lord is also showing you how you still could have done an even better job.

During your next Control Freak encounter, the interaction escalates and after "Checking-In" you're called upon to serve the "heavier", Dessert Option #3. You must correct/rebuke *before* you submit/comply. So what you did was "Confront with Authority" but what you forgot was, you were supposed to *"Expect Attitude"*.

You hadn't prepared for that ... so "it" caught you off guard, *again*. The spirit of divination came in with a greater controlling force; you were unprepared, so you fell. You feel like you lost all the ground you thought you had, because you sinned by hysterically yelling back at the person.

You can't even believe you sinned, *again*, in this same type of situation. You know better! You're like, "Lord I cannot believe I fell for that!" So you ended up complying with their demand like you were going to do all along, but you sinned; so you did <u>not</u> get the victory.

You go to the Lord again; He gives you another way of dealing with that same situation, with that same person; but this time, you'll be prepared for their same rebellious "attitude". You then pack that bit of wisdom away with your weaponry for future use.

After more time laboring and practicing, all of a sudden one day you look back and realize that your defeats have started to become very few and far between. In fact, for every defeat, there are several more victories that you can recall.

Your next encounter is with a Control Freak Extraordinaire whom the Lord wants sternly corrected. Since this has been an ongoing troubled relationship for you, you've already got a "Rehearsed Response" or two, specially prepared and ready to aim and fire, whenever the Commander so directs.

Closing Arguments

You "Check-In" and just as you expected, you're serving Dessert Option #4. You remember what to say and how to say it; you wait for the right timing, He then says, "Now", you fire and ...

Bam!

You hit! *Nice* shot.

They're taken back by what you just said. With bewilderment in their eyes, they just look at you in wonder and say nothing. They say, absolutely nothing, at all.

"It", has been wounded.

You can tell they can't believe *what you just said*; and since it was a "sinless" remark, now they're really baffled. They say nothing to you in response and you politely excuse yourself from the interaction, knowing that the sooner you get alone, the sooner you can yell "Hallelujah!"

You did it! You "Checked-In", you fired a "Rehearsed Response", you exercised "self control" (maintaining your emotional composure); you "Confronted with Authority" (with the boldness necessary to eradicate the jugular); and yet, you didn't sin <u>and</u> you most certainly did not comply with "its" demand ... Wow! That felt good; that felt really, really good.

This is your first complete victory! This has never happened to you before; so you want to throw a party because this interaction was with one of the worst Control Freaks you've ever known. You feel empowered, because you took "it" out-- without-- sinning. You're free! Full of joy and excitement as you exclaim, "This is actually getting to be kinda fun now!"

Continuing in your pursuit upward, you're not mad at the Control Freaks in your life anymore. Nor, are you mad at their emotional abuse tactics, or when they try to verbally rip you to shreds, or even when they give you the "silent treatment". Whereas before these things would have thrown you into a panic and you would always act "In-Kind", it just doesn't phase you like that anymore. Sure you notice it. Sure you talk to the Lord about it and of course He notices it; but you're no longer *controlled* by it.

"You" are breaking free!

Closing Arguments

As a result, your lifestyle has changed a bit; you are now freed up to go back to doing things you used to enjoy doing with the Lord. Those fun things that the demands of controlling people had previously choked out of your life, you now have the time to bring back into your life.

You've gone back to spending quality time with Him each morning, going to more than just the usual church services, going back to school, spending time leisure reading, starting up music classes, going to the library, working out and getting back into shape, putting a healthy diet together, painting, improving the house, playing pool, hunting, decorating and planting in the garden.

Best of all, you now have time to stop and help meet the needs of other people, *voluntarily.* Imagine that? What was once "sucked dry" by the spirit of control is now slowly but surely being restored and replenished by the Holy Spirit. You can tell because you're serving others both in the church and in the streets. You're sincerely praying with people, you're back to spending quality time with people. You now genuinely "care" about and for other people; and though you're now expending far more energy than you have in years, *you're not tired!* Wow! That unfeigned love

Closing Arguments

is back! It's the Lord working in and through your life! He's back!

Most importantly, you actually feel good about it! You don't feel guilty, or worried about what someone thinks of you, or who is mad about how you're spending your time, or money. You're so connected with the Lord, you now only care about staying close to Him and obeying His directives.

If you're honest, from time to time, you still don't feel totally free from those controlling people with whom you've had an "emotional link" in the past. You catch yourself reminiscing and thinking about them and the last Control Freak encounter you had with them. Though you took "it" out, you wonder if you were too harsh?

"No", you remind yourself; you can never be too harsh with the spirit of divination. Your jugular extraction success will only make that relationship better, because you're eliminating any ongoing dysfunction. So you fight the good fight of faith in your heart/mind and *cast down the control your own thoughts* have given place to, and soon enough, you're feeling free again.[104]

With a few more victories, on varying levels and in varying situations under your belt, you start feeling empowered, and that, on a regular basis. You're starting to realize these interpersonal relationships that you were so worried about all your life, really never had the value and/or meaning you once thought they did, especially in light of "the big picture" of your God-given destiny.

At the next level, you are now able to totally dispense with the misbehavior of the Control Freaks you encounter. "It" neither effects, nor affects, you anymore; "it" has been reduced to only something you have to deal with everyday, like brushing your teeth. You no longer feel any pressure to converse or engage in an argument with "Control Freaks" in an attempt to try and get them to see your point of view. You observe "it" carrying on with "its" evil purpose by tripping up everyone else you come across. Though

---

[104] *Casting down imaginations,* and every high thing that exalteth itself against the knowledge of God, and bringing into captivity every thought to the obedience of Christ (2 Cor 10:5, KJV).

Closing Arguments

you can now see how "it" so easily controls others, you rejoice in the fact that "it" sure can't control "you" *anymore*.

The closer you get to totally breaking free, the better you become at serving the "heaviest dessert" combination #4; and employing the Principle of Diametric Opposition-- right to "its" face!

While you'll never lose the physiological aspect of the battle (your heart races, your adrenalin flows, etc.), in a weird kind of way, you're totally under control, exercising Holy Spirit empowered "self-control". You notice that you now only raise your voice, intentionally, when you need to, not because you're "in the flesh" and have no control over yourself, but only in order to force "it" to back down.

Mistreatment no longer hurts you; instead, you go about your business as a productive, responsible person on the outside; though at times, you may still feel a little "bugged" at the conclusion of a select few interactions on the inside. Whenever that happens, you *captivate those thoughts, cast them down in an instant*; and you tell yourself, *"I've been trained for this!"*

Closing Arguments

You do the exact opposite of what "it" wants you to do (which is think about "it" over and over); and you walk away from the interaction unscathed; thanking the Lord for the victory of being able to fully eliminate any aftermath of the battle, from your heart and mind.

Without a doubt, you're starting to gain some momentum. What at first seemed like a lot to do, is now starting to become ingrained into your personality ... like second nature. You begin ripping out one jugular after another; in this situation, with someone you hardly know, in that situation with one of your closest loved ones. All the while you're not upset, you're not in sin, but boy! Your level of joy is sure on the rise.

It's almost as if you don't even have a dog in the fight. You've so given this over to Him, you really don't care what Dessert Option you're told to serve anymore. You're told by Him to "fire" in one situation and told by Him to "stand down" in the next. Anything is fine with you at this point. "Lord, just tell me what to do", cause, "It's all good!" you say.

"CONTROL FREAK"

Closing Arguments

You've noticed that even the most *controlling* people in your life, are beginning to "back off". In fact, those with whom you've already had several eradication interactions, at this point, are either long gone or have given up even trying to control you anymore. They're all perplexed and still not quite sure what to think of the "new" you.

So they begin to ask you questions about what you've been doing with yourself, where you've been going to church, who you've been spending time with; and they make comments about how "business must be good", you seem so "peaceful" and "content". "You're looking so young and well rested."

You next learn how to take your focus off of people and what they're doing to you; and you turn your focus into an inquiry about how *you are doing with Him*. Your entire focus in life ... has moved from *them* ... to *Him*.

Hallelujah, it's no longer all about them! It's no longer about them; very simply, because no matter how hard they try, they can't *control* you anymore.

Closing Arguments

Your conversation with the Lord goes <u>From</u>: "Did you see what he/she did to me this time, Lord? Did you see how they mistreated me?" <u>To</u>: "How am I doing with you today Lord? Or, better yet, "How are *You* doing today, Lord? Universe running ok?"

Instead of getting yourself in a panic about the continued Control Freak mistreatment from other people, you go about your business unaffected emotionally. This time "its" silly little attempt to upset you, didn't ruin your day; no, not one bit.

While Control Freaks, in various forms and fashion, are still attempting to throw you off course, you've now undisputedly, got the edge. As you continue to work with the Holy Spirit and seek the wisdom of God, you will see a progression in your life towards being less and less controlled by the spirit of divination; and becoming more and more led by the Holy Spirit, in every single situation you face.

But BEWARE! Don't let your guard down and fall back into being controlled by your ongoing relationships! This is a

"CONTROL FREAK"

discipline, a life long discipline that you must employ in order to make it to God's Plan and destiny for your life.

Then one day, down the road of life, you will have become so familiar with your artillery, that at some level, you won't even need to talk to the Lord anymore about the "obvious". The Lord already knows, and you've become so close, you no longer want to bore Him with the details if you don't have to.

Your weaponry has now become so vast and its use has become second nature to you, so all you need to know from Him is what Dessert Combination He wants you to serve. You don't even have to work on any "Rehearsed Responses" or "reframing" the issue anymore, the Lord just gives you something "fresh baked" to serve for dessert with each and every new Control Freak encounter you face.

After doing your part, you may think about it again, but only for refinement purposes; you're never *controlled* by "it" again. "It" is simply not permitted to do that anymore. In fact, many times you quickly forget about the last Control Freak interaction you just had and the fact that *yet another* jugular had just been extracted; and even the victory you just experienced. You don't need to throw a party anymore, because now, this is just *"how you roll".*

Your "quality of life" has gone up higher and higher, it's practically entering into the stratosphere, with each successful Control Freak interaction you face. As a result, you don't really need to relish in every victory like you did in the beginning. This has now become a "way of life"-- it's the new "you".

Almost immediately after you serve dessert and eradicate yet another Control Freak situation, you and the Lord go straight back to talking about His plans for your life. Oh yes, now that "you" are finally free, you're also finally catching the vision that the Lord has big plans for your life!

You must realize that it's really not that the Lord's plan for your life ever got any bigger. They were "before ordained" so *they* never changed (Eph 2:10, KJV).[105]

---

[105] *"For we are His workmanship, created in Christ Jesus unto good works, which God hath **before ordained** that we should walk in them."* Strong's #4282, transliterated "Proetoimazo"; to prepare before, to make ready beforehand.

Closing Arguments

It's just that "you" are the one who is now finally beginning to realize how big His plans for your life have *always been.* You're the one that changed. Now that "you" are free from the *spirit of control* and all that "Black Noise"; now that you can clearly hear His voice and receive His revelation; now that you're free to take His direction and fulfill the assignments He gives you each day; it is now "you" that is *finally coming on board* and starting to get an initial glimpse of the "big plans" He has for your life!

In fact, they're so big, the two of you just can't stop talking about them. Either you're talking or doing, waiting, or praying, reading or watching. You receive one directive after another from Him and you're moving forward carrying out only His assignments and directives for your life.

Your life is so different since you're now totally free. His plans for your life and how He's directing you to fulfill them, ends up being *the only thing you really ever want to talk about anymore;* whether with Him, or anyone else for that matter. You don't even waste one minute talking to others about the people through whom the spirit of divination just tried to trip you up or lock you down; unless, of course you're providing further directives to those who are working "Extraction Clean-Up Detail".[106]

You'll know you hit "the mark" when you are no longer intimidated by the usual Control Freak tactics of others; you no longer become fearful or emotionally upset by these encounters (affect); and of course, you no longer sin in response to them either (effect).

Since there is no more baggage to carry around with "you" in your heart/mind because you will no longer allow it; you're now experiencing real joy, living day-by-day with the freedom of doing what God wants you to do with your life. Your life now has much more value and meaning because you're now focused on the far more important things that you're doing for the Kingdom.

"The mark" is that condition or state of perpetual victory that you're ultimately aiming to achieve by employing everything you've learned in this text. "The mark" is that "quality of life" that is inundated with one victory after

---

[106] "Extraction Clean-Up Detail" is when you are forced to make others aware of the boundary lines you've drawn for your life, as it relates to one or more of the Control Freaks that you've eradicated from your life.

another: victory over your thoughts and emotions (affect); victory over your words and actions (effect); victory over the CIYA; victory over being controlled by the demands, expectations or ultimatums of other people; and victory in becoming so close to the Lord (through the need for His wisdom and guidance to take "it" out), that when He speaks or directs, you hear Him clearly and immediately obey. All that "Black Noise" you used to experience, has now gone a on permanent hiatus.

In sum, it looks like this:

1. Having the ability to see the *spirit of divination* enter a room and start "its" wily work;
2. Having a close enough relationship with the Lord, that without a word, you and He, *just nod;*
3. Having an alert mind, which is already processing all of the necessary inquiries: Checking-in and receiving the directive from Him on which Dessert Combination to serve; asking for wisdom, Rehearsed Responses, or special "on point" words for if and when you're called to rebuke or correct;

4. Having the ability to demonstrate "self-control", in conjunction with the power and authority to serve any one of the four Dessert Combinations as directed by the Holy Spirit; and finally,

5. Once you receive your directive, you employ your artillery and you take the jugular O-U-T! You kick the spirit of control straight to the curb, and without missing a beat, you walk on to the destiny God has for your life-- all, *without* sinning.

As you flip these Control Freak situations around in your life; as you implement your artillery; and as you serve the appropriate Dessert Option to that controlling spirit, what the adversary was trying to use to bring you down, will actually make you stronger, and bring you up higher than ever before!

Now, isn't *that* cool? The greatest thing about this battle is that the Lord will actually take those same "wiles" that the spirit of divination was trying to use to throw you off track; and then with the use of your new weaponry, He will strengthen and train you up to be the one to bring about "its" ultimate defeat.

Closing Arguments

By daring to come into your presence, the spirit of divination is now giving *you* the opportunity to destroy "its"-self! When you turn this around like you've now been trained, "its" workings in your life will end up amounting to one suicide mission after another, *for* the enemy!

You will have a blast, extracting jugular after jugular with the Lord! I promise it will be so worth it. Not only will you have a great ongoing, intimate, life changing experience in your relationship with your Lord and Savior; but you will marvel at how you're becoming more and more transformed into *"His image"* (Ro 8:29, KJV).

"For I reckon that the sufferings of this present time are not worthy to be compared with **the glory which shall be revealed in us**" (Ro 8:18, KJV).

You'll always be improving on this art form, but you'll know you've hit very close to "the mark" and that you're in "that place" of untainted, uninhibited communication with our Lord when circumstances and people, though they still try, are no longer able to *control* "you" or your life anymore, *ever*.

Closing Arguments

Yes I mean *ever*. Just imagine that! If you can see it, you can get there too.

As a result, you hear His every directive clearly and you carry them out without delay. Since it's now so easy to spot whenever "it" is trying to inhibit you, whenever that happens, you pull out your artillery promptly, you make your move proficiently, and you take it OUT permanently!

Yes, *every* time, just like a sharpshooter.

Then proceeding forth, totally unscathed, you forget about "it" and the most recent encounter, and you carry on with life as usual, right where you left off: "Sorry for the interruption Lord, what was that You were saying?"

As you walk with Him in this way, you will see things start to move in your life on a supernatural level because there is no more interference, or "Black Noise" permitted. As a result, you are now progressing towards the direction of your destiny far, far more quickly.

Here's an example of one Control Freak incident where the sum of this text got me where He wanted me to be, much faster than I would have otherwise, had I allowed myself to be controlled:

One day, just before signing another lease in an apartment complex, I saw a sign where a house was for rent in an area that I had always wanted to live. Despite my recent financial storm I was given that rental, place #1 to lease for one year; which in and of itself, was really, supernatural.

About six months later, without asking, I was given an opportunity by another owner to move into place #2, which had a much better location in that same community. This owner, himself, had lived there years earlier and had done some phenomenal things for the Kingdom of God. Prior to that offer to move into place #2, the Lord had started stirring up my desire to move and had actually shown me that He wanted me to move, *before* I ever got the offer to do so. So once the offer for place #2 was made, I knew I was on my way out! Supernatural.

However, I didn't want to wait for the remaining six-months on my lease because based on several scriptural references that I had been getting, I had the spiritual impression that place #2 was going to be "the place" where the Lord was going to turn my world around, after having weathered very torrential storms for over the past three years.

As a result, I just knew in my spirit that I had to get to "that place", physically, just as soon as I could. Unfortunately, I didn't think I could make the move right away because I was stuck in a lease with place #1 for six more months.

What's worse, was that under the lease with my present landlord in place #1, my rent was due to increase the next month. So I sent my landlord an email saying that since my rent was going up, I wanted some of the things that had not been working in the house to be repaired. Without me asking if I could be released from the lease early, the landlord *then offered* that I could move out as soon as I wanted to, if I helped her to find another renter. Supernatural? Yes, but don't think she was all that magnanimous. She was going to charge the next renter more than I was paying.

So the door to my better location place #2 opened sooner than expected and *without my even asking.* I immediately started putting up the landlord's "For Rent" signs and there were quite a few people who came through to look at place #1 while I was still living there.

However, it seemed like every time someone was interested, the landlord would find some reason to either deny him/her, or delay the process for so long that they would get frustrated and just say, "Forget it!"

After she basically blew up the deal with at least two decent potential renters, I was like, "*Lord,* this lady is keeping me here in bondage!" (By that time I was chomping at the bit to get out of there for several other creepy reasons, that I won't waste any time "Control Freaking" you out about.)

The point was, that I knew the Lord wanted me at that *other place.* I thought that once I got there *physically,* my whole world *circumstantially,* was going to turn around for the better.

When yet another potential tenant was at first approved, to the extent that the landlord set a "move out" date for me; and then a few days later, called me back having changed her mind again saying that I couldn't move out; I then said to myself, "Wait a minute. Now, wait just a minute!" "Lord, what's up with this?"

I felt the Spirit of God say to my heart, *"How long are you going to let her keep you out of the Promised Land?"*

BAM! It was a Control Freak issue!

Wow! Even though this landlord *said* I could move-- at the same time, she was still holding me back.

I then remembered how it was just like that with Pharaoh, who on a few occasions *said* the children of Israel could leave; but later changed his mind and retracted his permission. When you think about it, Pharaoh's fickle conduct is what actually got him drowned in the Red Sea. If he hadn't changed his mind and chased after the children of Israel, he wouldn't have died that kind of gruesome (albeit awesome) death.

This is a real life example of how people can try to hold you in a place, that God wants you to move from. If you don't do your part to get out of there and refuse to tolerate being governed by the *control* that others want to exert over your life, you could miss what God has for you.

Once I realized that the landlord was being used to try to *control* my life and hinder my move to "the place" God wanted me to abide with Him; I immediately employed the Principle of Diametric Opposition and told the landlord I was moving out on the date she had already agreed to. Period.

Now, pronounce the CIYA with me like this: "CI-YA" or, "See-ya!" Yep, that's exactly what you're going to learn to say to "it" from now on. Instead of complying with what the spirit of control would have you to do, which is in opposition to what the Holy Spirit would have you to do; from now on, you're just going to say, "See-ya!" And so I did.

My spiritual impression was absolutely correct. Ever since I made the move, everything has turned around in my life. Unbelievable opportunities and experiences take place on a daily basis. I've never been happier or freer, emotionally, mentally and spiritually.

"That place" is where this text was written.

Closing Arguments

*"The LORD your God will choose **a place** out of all your tribes to live and put His name. Go there and worship Him ... There, in the presence of the LORD your God, you and your families will eat and enjoy everything you've worked for, because the LORD your God has blessed you"* (Deut 12:5 & 7, GWT).

As you walk with Him "Control Freak Free" you too will get to every "place" of destiny and blessing that the Lord has for you in this lifetime. Once you get there, you will defend, protect and safeguard your new "quality of life" in the Promised Land, like nothing else you've ever possessed.

Let it be said of everyone who reads this text, "When *the Lord* speaks, we listen!" Anyone else? Well, you've got a 50/50 chance.

You've now got your artillery and your assignment soldier. Make our Daddy proud!

(The End)

An Invitation

To all Teachers of the Word of God, especially those favorably referred to in the OPENING ARGUMENT of this text, to whom I give honor; should you decide to teach these concepts in the future, it would be a blessing if you would consider sharing your teaching series with me. I so look forward to listening to how the Lord uses your knowledge of the Word, unique gifts and anointing, as well as *your* personality and delivery, to convey this *message of jugular eradication.*

For those of you who would like to share your own testimony about how you became victorious by employing the principles and artillery found in this text and/or to contribute some of your own personalized "on point" "Rehearsed Responses" for our upcoming sequel, please send your inquiries, comments, and/or testimonies to:

ControlFreakFree@aol.com

Your contribution will automatically be considered for inclusion in our upcoming sequel entitled:

"CONTROL-FREAK-FREE" (Trial Practice)

If you would like to host a "**Control-Freak-Free Training Conference**" in your area, please go www.JanetCarter.org or send an email to ControlFreakFree@aol.com.

"CONTROL FREAK"

An Invitation

"CONTROL FREAK"